M000159581

INCLUSION, PLAY AND EMPATHY

The Busker's Guide to Participation, Second Edition
Philip Waters
Illustrated by Chris Bennett
ISBN 978 1 78592 023 3
eISBN 978 1 78450 269 0
Part of the Busker's Guides series

The Busker's Guide to Risk, Second Edition
Shelly Newstead
Illustrated by Chris Bennett
ISBN 978 1 84905 682 3
eISBN 978 1 78450 191 4
Part of the Busker's Guides series

How to Be a Great Leader in Early Years
Jennie Johnson
ISBN 978 1 84905 674 8
eISBN 978 1 78450 180 8

The Teacher's Introduction to Attachment
Practical Essentials for Teachers, Carers and School Support Staff
Nicola Marshall
Foreword by Phil Thomas
ISBN 978 1 84905 550 5
eISBN 978 0 85700 973 9

Play and Art in Child Psychotherapy
An Expressive Arts Therapy Approach
Ellen G. Levine
ISBN 978 1 84905 504 8
eISBN 978 0 85700 919 7

Video Interaction Guidance
A Relationship-Based Intervention to Promote
Attunement, Empathy and Wellbeing
Edited by Hilary Kennedy, Miriam Landor and Liz Todd
ISBN 978 1 84905 180 4
eISBN 978 0 85700 414 7

Play as Therapy
Assessment and Therapeutic Interventions
Edited by Karen Stagnitti and Rodney Cooper
Foreword by Ann Cattanach
ISBN 978 1 84310 637 1
eISBN 978 1 84642 928 6

INCLUSION, PLAY AND EMPATHY

Neuroaffective Development in Children's Groups

Edited by Susan Hart

Foreword by Phyllis Booth

Jessica Kingsley *Publishers*
London and Philadelphia

First published by Hans Reitzels Forlag, Denmark in 2015
English language edition first published in 2017
by Jessica Kingsley Publishers
73 Collier Street
London N1 9BE, UK
and
400 Market Street, Suite 400
Philadelphia, PA 19106, USA

www.jkp.com

Library of Congress Cataloging in Publication Data
A CIP catalog record for this book is available from the Library of Congress

British Library Cataloguing in Publication Data
A CIP catalogue record for this book is available from the British Library

ISBN 978 1 78592 006 6
eISBN 978 1 78450 243 0

Printed and bound in the United States

Contents

Foreword

My Life with Play

Phyllis Booth

'One for the money
Two for the show
Three to get ready, and...'

I'm 3 years old and perched on my father's knees as he lies on the floor holding my hands and smiling up at me as he chants these familiar words. I'm on top of the world. He sees me, he senses my rising excitement and he knows just the moment for the big surprise: *'Four to Go!'* He drops his knees and down I go into his welcoming arms. 'More, more,' I say, and he helps me scramble to the top again. Over and over we repeat the game with its eager anticipation, sudden surprise and final all-encompassing hug.

Another memory: I'm 6 years old and feeling irritable. My mother senses that something is wrong and puts her hand to my forehead. She says, 'Oh, you have a fever!' She puts me to bed and I snuggle into the cool, clean sheets and relax. I am no longer alone with my discomfort. My mother will take care of me. All is well.

These two vivid memories epitomize my generally happy childhood. I did not have a 'perfect' childhood, but I had parents who were the 'ordinary, devoted' parents that Donald Winnicott describes as essential to healthy emotional development (Winnicott, 1984, p.4). What a gift it was to have a playful father, who confidently held me as we reveled in our shared excitement, and a devoted mother, who could always be counted on to nurture and comfort me. Together they created the climate of safety, playful encouragement, and comfort that has stayed with me and supported me over the years.

In this environment of engaging, lively social interaction and nurturing, comforting care, I learned many things about myself and the world I lived in: I am loved and lovable, I can master challenging things, I can share good feelings, I'm in good hands, I can count on others to help me both relish and contain my excitement. From my perch on top of my father's knees and even from my sick bed, the world seemed a safe and good place.

In my many years of playing with children, I have always had these early experiences somewhere in my mind (and body) as a model for how to help children and their parents find a healthy way of being together. This legacy informs my ongoing view of the role of play and empathic responding in the neuroaffective development of children; it is the foundation of my work in Theraplay™ (Booth and Jernberg, 2010; Jernberg, 1979; Jernberg and Booth, 1999).

In this foreword, I would like to give some brief personal background to the development of Theraplay and lend my support to the important work being described in the chapters of this book. There is a strong thread connecting my childhood experience with my ongoing interest in how to create secure and healthy attachment relationships. Having had a good early experience growing up, I turned naturally and with pleasure to working with children: I became a nursery school teacher. In 1949–1950, while at the University of Chicago Nursery School, I had the good fortune to have Ann Jernberg (the creative genius behind the Theraplay approach) as one of my assistant teachers.

In 1965, when Head Start – a US government-funded preschool program for disadvantaged 3- and 4-year-olds – was created, Jernberg was awarded the contract to provide psychological services to all the Head Start programs in Chicago. She recruited me to join her team of Mental Health consultants. We identified many children who needed help but soon found that there was no help available at existing mental health clinics – waiting lists were long, treatment was expensive, and families found it very difficult to get their children to the rare treatment center that had an opening.

Jernberg came up with a simple solution to the problem: we would recruit and train lively young people to go into the schools and play with the children who needed help. We asked them to engage each child assigned to them in the same way parents interact with their young children: sensitively, spontaneously, face to face, with no need for toys, simply inviting the child to join them in joyful, interactive play. In weekly supervisory sessions we helped these young mental health workers reflect on their own and the child's experience in order to be more attuned to each child's needs. Together we created new activities that we could use to engage and delight the children as well as to calm and comfort them.

We found that our play made a great difference. Soon, unhappy, withdrawn children became livelier, more outgoing and responsive; angry, aggressive, acting-out children settled down and began to interact appropriately with others. It was obvious that these children felt much better about themselves and were ready to engage with classmates and teachers in a comfortable friendly way. They became lively, alert youngsters who, when we visited a few of them three years later, were thriving (Jernberg, Hurst and Lyman, 1969, 1975). During the process of editing our first film, *Here I Am*, the filmmaker suggested the name 'Theraplay' to distinguish our hands-on playful approach from the more traditional play therapy of the time.

In 1969–70, just as our program got under way, I spent a year studying at the Tavistock Clinic in London. Once a week I heard John Bowlby describe his new theory about the role of attachment in healthy development, watched James and Joyce Robertson's films documenting the devastating effects on young children of long separations from their parents, and attended case conferences led by Donald Winnicott. Looking back, I see that I was at the beginning of a groundswell of interest in the power of early attachment relationships – what actually goes on between parents and their children – to create or disrupt long term social-emotional development.

Since Bowlby and Winnicott have had such a profound influence on my thinking about my work with children, I want to briefly give my personal impressions of the two men. Bowlby, to my American eyes, was an upright, proper, and somewhat austere man. I did not warm to him, but I respected his intellect and the creativity with which he combined insights from his own object relations approach to psychoanalytic theory with Konrad Lorenz's new ethological studies of bonding in young animals. Later I learned from his very warm and personable son that his father had not had a close relationship with his own mother but rather with a nanny who disappeared from his life when he was still quite young. Perhaps losing his beloved nanny created a need to explore the importance of attachment relationships and what he describes as the 'pathogenic potential of loss' (Bowlby, 1969, p.xvii).

I experienced Winnicott as a warm, gentle man with a delightful twinkle in his eye. As a pediatrician he had gained an intimate knowledge of the nature and importance of the mother–child relationship. His famous statement 'There is no such thing as a baby... [there is only] a nursing couple... Without a good-enough technique of nursing care, the new human being has no chance whatever' (Winnicott, 1958, p.99) is a testament to how highly he valued the devoted, life-supporting role of the 'ordinary devoted mother'. He extended his faith in the healing power of relationships to the therapist–patient relationship as well. In a lecture to a group of young psychoanalysts-in-training, which I attended, he urged them to rely on the relationship between themselves and their clients and not to rush into making clever interpretations.

When I returned to Chicago and to the Head Start program, I found myself making use of Bowlby's and Winnicott's ideas to explain our success with the children. I remember saying to Ann Jernberg, 'We are providing the children with the kind of "holding environment" that Winnicott says is a crucial quality of a healthy relationship between a mother and her baby.' Devoted mothers create an atmosphere of safety, focus exclusively on the baby, respond empathically to the baby's needs, and when the baby is ready, engage her in playful interaction. This is exactly what we were trying to create for our Head Start children.

When we used healthy parenting as our model, we were behaving in what Bowlby calls a 'mothering way', which he describes as 'engaging in lively social interaction with...[her child], and responding readily to his signals and approaches' (Bowlby, 1969, p.306). In a later statement about the clinical application of attachment theory he says, 'The pattern of interaction adopted by the mother of a secure infant provides an excellent model for the pattern of therapeutic intervention...' (Bowlby, 1988, p.126).

As the Head Start children got better, it became clear that, in Bowlby's terms, we had helped them gain a more positive internal working model. Their negative views of themselves and their fears that they couldn't count on a caring response from adults no longer held them hostage. The faces and actions of our cheerful, engaging, and caring young mental health workers had reflected a much more positive view of each child as well as of what each could expect from others. The dyadic experience of feeling safe, being sensitively responded to, validated, and enjoyed, had created a new and more hopeful internal working model for each child.

Play is at the core of Winnicott's theory: the responsive, attuned play of a mother with her baby, as well as the creative play of ideas between patient and therapist. He says:

> *Psychotherapy is done in the overlap of the two play areas, that of the patient and that of the therapist.* If the therapist cannot play then he is not suitable for the work. If the patient cannot play, then something needs to be done to enable the patient to become able to play… The reason why playing is essential is that it is in playing that the patient is being creative. (Winnicott, 1971, p.54)

The practice in his generation of psychoanalysts was to listen quietly, often sitting out of the patient's view, leaving the client free to talk freely about whatever was on his mind. As the issues became clear, the analyst would make wise interpretations. It is clear from Winnicott's writings that he did not adhere strictly to this practice; valuing, as he did, the lively play between therapist and patient, he often engaged with them in more active ways. He created a game that he called 'The Squiggle Game': with a pencil, he would make a rapid mark on the paper and invite the patient to add his own squiggle. These spontaneous gestures came together to create an important shared meaning. In one of his case studies of work with a child, he describes a lovely moment in which he initiates playful interaction: anticipating the arrival of a shy child, he put a small teddy bear in his pocket and had the teddy invite the child to play with him.

In the many years since my initial introduction to Bowlby and Winnicott, a great deal of research into the nature of early dyadic experiences, including their effect on the developing brain, has expanded my view of the crucial elements that foster neuroaffective development. It is now clear that playful, reflective, responsive, co-regulating interaction between parents and their young children is essential to the development of the later capacity for self-regulation.

While the early parent–child relationship is crucial to providing the foundation for healthy social-emotional development, it is important to continue to support this process as the child grows older.

When children go to school, they are faced with the challenge of learning new cognitive skills, but equally important is the challenge of learning new ways of interacting with a wider group of peers and adults.

The chapters in this book invite us to look at the many creative ways that the authors have found to extend the qualities and benefits of early playful, attuned dyadic relationships to working with older children in groups. Group experiences contribute to and support the growing capacity to interact with others in healthy, life-affirming ways.

References

Booth, P. B. and Jernberg, A. M. (2010) *Theraplay: Helping Parents and Children Build Better Relationships through Attachment-Based Play*. San Francisco, CA: Jossey-Bass.

Bowlby, J. (1969) *Attachment and Loss: Volume I Attachment*. London: Hogarth Press.

Bowlby, J. (1988) *A Secure Base: Parent–Child Attachment and Healthy Human Development*. New York, NY: Basic Books.

Jernberg, A. M. (1979) *Theraplay: A New Treatment Using Structured Play For Problem Children and Their Families*. San Francisco, CA: Jossey-Bass.

Jernberg, A. M. and Booth, P. B. (1999) *Theraplay: Helping Parents and Children Build Better Relationships through Attachment-Based Play* (2nd edn). San Francisco, CA: Jossey-Bass.

Jernberg, A. M., Hurst, T. and Lyman, C. (1969) *Here I Am*. 16 mm film. Evanston, IL: The Theraplay Institute.

Jernberg, A. M., Hurst, T. and Lyman, C. (1975) *There He Goes*. 16 mm film. Evanston, IL: The Theraplay Institute.

Winnicott, D. W. (1958) *Collected Papers: Through Pediatrics to Psychoanalysis*. London: Hogarth Press.

Winnicott, D. W. (1971) *Playing and Reality*. London: Tavistock Publications.

Winnicott, D. W. (1984) *Babies and Their Mothers*. New York, NY: Addison-Wesley Publishing.

Introduction

Susan Hart

In 1994, Salamanca in Spain was the venue for the World Conference on Special Needs Education. The conference was organized by the Spanish government in cooperation with UNESCO and welcomed about 300 delegates from 92 countries and 25 international organizations. The conference adopted an official statement acknowledging the right of all children to attain and maintain an acceptable level of learning and calling for education systems and learning processes to accommodate the major differences in children's needs and conditions. Children with special needs were to have access to regular schools, which should be able to accommodate their needs by applying educational approaches centred on the individual child (The Salamanca Statement, 1994). The Salamanca statement introduced the ideological call for inclusion in the regular education system. The question now is what it takes for the individual teachers to be able to translate this grand vision into everyday practice. The coming years will show whether our education systems will be able to rise to the challenge, and whether individual teachers are going to receive sufficient support in their role as 'caravan leaders' for their class. This includes opportunities for them to improve their knowledge both of theory and of practice as well as opportunities for personal development and growth. The focus of this book is how individual teachers can improve their interpersonal skills to be able to meet all their students' growth and development needs, and how they can embrace an educational approach that balances the children's individual needs with the need to create a safe group environment.

Today's society places a high priority on children's learning, especially with regard to literacy, maths, foreign languages, and so on – cognitive competences that we need to compete in the global marketplace. With the current emphasis on individual learning in educational research, the overall result is a clear focus on the development of individual cognitive competences. Inclusion policies imply a different, perhaps less acknowledged point: that human development has not been driven exclusively by scientific (i.e. cognitive) accomplishments but has relied equally on our ability to engage in complex communities, where empathy, cooperation and cohesion are paramount requirements. The high IQ of our species notwithstanding, we would not have gone far had we not also developed a personality capable of directing our development as a species towards a common, humanitarian goal. Intelligence without emotions and a sense of mutual responsibility for other humans can be extremely destructive!

The question, then, is what invisible competences we need to develop to be able to cooperate, be creative together and foster compassion and empathy. We are well aware that cognitive skills need to be strengthened through studying and training, but what about the children who have failed to develop the basic skills required to develop healthy emotional and social capacities? What about the children who are unable to manage difficult emotions without assistance? What about the children who feel inadequate and lack self-esteem, and who are therefore trapped in conduct disorders or withdraw from interactions with others?

Since the 1990s, we have seen a growing number of children undergo assessment and receive psychiatric diagnoses, and we have seen how difficult it is to offer these children any help besides symptom reduction, often in the form of medication. Since the late 1990s, we have also seen the stigmatization associated with special needs schools and classes. For inclusion to be a successful long-term strategy, the principles of inclusion need to be translated into practice with humility and respect for the added demands on teachers, who are not only tasked with developing the children's intellectual resources but also need to engage on a much more personal level.

Like the development of cognitive and motor skills, the development of emotional and social capacities involves learning processes that are driven by stimulation. The main difference between stimulating cognitive and motor functions versus emotional functions is that the medium of emotional stimulation is interpersonal interactions, initially with the closest caregivers. Later in life, the child receives this essential interpersonal stimulation in interactions with other authority figures and with peers. Therefore, the ability of preschool and school teachers to engage in interactions with the individual students and facilitate appropriate group processes is crucial for facilitating individual development as well as a sound balance between individual and group needs.

Although we have come a long way since the days of René Descartes, our society still tends towards a dualist mindset, where reason and emotions are treated as separate entities, and our emotional development is expected to take care of itself. As a consequence, emotional imbalances and psychological difficulties are not addressed until they become so troublesome that they are categorized as pathological and the person is fitted with a psychiatric diagnosis. The general tendency to ignore the development of emotional competences also implies a general lack of interest in the link between the development of emotions and personality and the development of social skills. Initially, these capacities all develop in asymmetric relationships, most prominently in the parent–child dyad. Later, they develop in complex groups with a well-defined 'caravan leader', for example a preschool or school teacher; and eventually they unfold in larger social communities. We acquire, develop and train these capacities – not least our emotional capacities – in contexts where the asymmetry may be more or less well defined, and where we take turns seizing the initiative and responsibility.

In evolutionary terms, even reptiles establish hierarchies when they interact, and mammals engage in a constant exchange to negotiate and define their place in hierarchical structures. A common topic of debate today is the schism between individual versus collective needs – for example, the extent to which preschools and schools should require individual children to adapt to the group versus requiring the group to accommodate individual students by providing maximum space for autonomy and self-expression. As Director of Studies Elsebeth Jensen, PhD, and Professor Svend Brinkmann (2012) point out, this distinction makes it easy to forget that an individual can only be an individual when communities allow individuality to flourish. Without the social communities constituted by families, preschools and schools, we could never learn to become individuals. As humans, we are not born with a fully developed capacity for making choices and taking responsibility. We are born to interact and develop our emotional and social capacities through relationships with others. In other words, we develop our personality in the framework of social communities, and the quality of these communities determines how we individuate and how we integrate into social and cultural communities. As noted by Jensen and Brinkmann (2012), instead of looking at inclusion in terms of individual factors, capacities and intelligence, we should approach inclusion from a group perspective, focusing on providing stable and predictable everyday routines, consistent partners over time and creative educational approaches and activities that foster solidarity and innovation.

Most children are aware that they attend school not only to acquire specific skills but also in order to develop a social life. In school, the child's most stable network is usually the classroom group, which is often described either as 'bad', because the students bully each other, underachieve, go through repeated changes in the teaching staff, etc., or as 'good' because the class has a good social climate and the students attain their learning goals. Naturally, some classes tend to get along better than others from the outset, but most groups of children or adults will undergo a certain development process to build group cohesion (Jensen and Brinkmann, 2012). That requires a 'caravan leader' who deliberately seeks and knows how to build inclusive communities. Another key condition is good teacher–parent relations, where the teachers meet the parents at eye-level, in emotional as well as social terms, with an approach that engages them as partners in a collaborative effort.

Emotional competences and self-regulation strategies develop through our interactions with others, not through cognitive learning. When a child has failed to develop adequate strategies for engaging successfully with his or her peers, the adults around the child need to be able to see what sort of support the child requires, and in what situations. To a wide extent, human learning is initially based on rhythm and sensorimotor training (Trevarthen, 1993), and play is crucial in the development of our personality as well as our emotional and social capacities, in part by influencing our mutual synchronization. These capacities underlie our ability to engage in advanced roleplay as well as our later ability to engage in creative and innovative collaboration at work. Play is important for all mammals; and as Jaak Panksepp (Panksepp and Biven, 2012) has demonstrated, play activity increases the more intelligent a mammal is. Donald Winnicott (1971) also emphasized the role of play, and Peter Fonagy (Fonagy *et al.*, 2002) highlights the importance of play for the development of a mentalizing capacity.

All children develop within the framework of their relationships, and good relationships are an important foundation for the child's development of a self-regulation capacity. For a variety of reasons, innate and/or environmental, some children fail to develop the necessary coping strategies to engage in successful interactions with others. As pointed out by Boel *et al.* (2013), when the relationship between a professional (e.g. a teacher or a therapist) and a child is troubled, the reason is often that the adult feels powerless to make the child follow instructions. Feeling powerless, the adult often resorts to blaming the child for inappropriate behaviour or lack of cooperation. This disrupts the good, supportive relationship, and the child is required to perform in a way that is essentially beyond his or her capability.

Successful inclusion in the regular school system requires cross-disciplinary knowledge about children's personality development, on a theoretical as well as a methodological level. Therefore, many psychologists and teachers focus on finding ways of systematically fostering empathy and cohesion in groups of children. To be able to achieve this, the teachers have to develop their own agency (e.g. through opportunities for personality development). An important consideration is how political decision-makers and school administrators can provide conditions that facilitate these efforts.

By now, we have accumulated considerable knowledge about what it takes to help vulnerable children engage in communities, and many competent teachers, psychotherapists and others have made a personal contribution by supporting traumatized children in disaster areas. If we want to pursue inclusion in a way that promotes healthy development, we need to learn from these experiences and strive to apply the insights in our work with children in the regular school system. This includes children with special needs, ranging from innate vulnerabilities, such as autism or sensorimotor difficulties, to severe attachment disorders and psychological trauma. We need to bring together the available expertise about how children form meaningful communities that embrace as many children as possible, and where all children are *seen* in the sense that their competences are recognized, while they are offered protection in the areas where they are vulnerable. Another important task is finding ways to help thriving children with many resources develop the necessary empathy to embrace their weaker peers. This will serve the larger goal of creating a more equitable and socially sustainable society. Clearly, parental involvement plays a key role in this regard, but older children also need to develop their interpersonal competences in relation to their peers. There are no low-cost solutions, but by investing the necessary resources, we can create the necessary conditions for children to develop prosocial communities. This does not mean that preschool and school teachers should act as psychotherapists and engage in group therapy processes. However, school and preschool professionals should draw inspiration from approaches based on psychotherapy or environmental therapy, which have been tested efforts aimed at the most vulnerable children. In other words, they should absorb and incorporate inspiration from professionals who know how to make children feel safe and open to learning communities.

The authors of this book focus on establishing emotionally supportive group settings for 4–12-year-old children with the aim of supporting the children's development by providing a structured, safe and predictable environment where the children can develop mutual attachment bonds. To bring together some of the creative minds in this area, I have contacted preschool and school teachers, psychologists, music therapists, occupational therapists and psychotherapists who have inspired my own work for years and who have made a special contribution by fostering supportive interactions with children in groups. All these professionals, from all over the world, have taken creative steps to facilitate group development processes, enabling the children in their care to engage in close relationships with others, develop self-regulation and thus foster personalities with strong mentalizing capacities. These capacities are, ultimately, a prerequisite for the children's eventual ability to pass the gift of secure attachments on to the next generation: their own future children.

It is a great pleasure for me to present this book, which will hopefully inspire early childhood educators, teachers and others working with children across preschool and school settings. It is essential that we continue to improve our ability to work with groups of children in a way that makes a positive difference. This effort should be guided by our knowledge that adults who show appropriate authority, engagement and creativity can create the sense of security needed to give children the courage and hope they need to be able to undergo a transformation process and develop their emotional, personal and social potential.

An overview of the book

The first chapter is written by the two legendary pioneers Colwyn Trevarthen and Jaak Panksepp. A few years ago, I had the pleasure of meeting Jaak Panksepp when he visited the Danish city of Aarhus to speak about his exciting research aimed at mapping the primary emotional circuits in humans. This research was based on studies of the play behaviour of rats and their far more primitive, but therefore also far more accessible nervous system. About a year later, I had the honour of meeting Colwyn Trevarthen on a visit to Denmark, where we engaged in an hour-long conversation about his research. In my view, Trevarthen's work has been just as seminal as Daniel Stern's in shaping our understanding of the human need for close relationships based on micro-synchronized interactions. The two in fact began their research projects around the same time but on two different continents – Stern in the United States, and Trevarthen in Scotland.

In Chapter 1, Trevarthen and Panksepp offer their theoretical insights into the crucial importance of playful interactions for our emotional development and attachment-building. Both Trevarthen and Panksepp have had long and distinguished research careers. A few years ago, they began to combine their thinking and bodies of work in writing, and they kindly accepted my invitation to write a chapter for this book on research-based knowledge about the importance of musicality and play, also in relation to children's groups. Their chapter describes how humans grasp meaning by acting in synchronicity and compassion with others' emotions in brief, present moments. As humans, we project our feelings into the world to render the world meaningful by means of mutual acts and the communities this cooperation gives rise to. The well-being both of teachers and of students depends on mutual sympathy, playful experimentation and the joy of shared meaning-making. In order to build resilience, children need to generate joy through the engagements they create in order to fill out lived moments. Educational practices that acknowledge children as active knowledge-seekers will promote settings that encourage and reward individual exploration, offer optimal conditions for joy-filled social activities and promote learning.

In Chapter 2, I present the neuroaffective view of sympathy, empathy and mentalization as competences that develop on the basis of thousands of everyday subtle and mutual synchronizations. These synchronizations take place, for example, in the context of playful, creative interactions, where the child's personality and interpersonal competences can unfold. The chapter describes how emotional learning occurs in the child's zone of proximal development and explains the child's need to relate to an adult who takes responsibility for the synchronization. Once the child has developed an attachment to an empathic and caring adult, the child will have the opportunity to develop the self-regulation strategies necessary for engaging in adaptive interactions with others. This is, in turn, a condition for developing self-esteem and, ultimately, developing a mentalizing capacity. Inspired by the American neurophysiologist Paul MacLean's model of the triune brain, the chapter reviews the hierarchical development of our emotional capacities. In this hierarchical progression, sensory- and arousal-regulating competences need to be in place before affect-regulation and empathy skills, which in turn need to develop before the mentalization capacity can unfold. For normal, healthy development, children need to sense a connection with another who conveys 1) 'I want to be with you', and who is able to contain the child's emotions, thus conveying 2) 'I sense how you feel', and who engages in a shared understanding of what is happening, conveying 3) 'I can help you shape a meaningful narrative about what is happening'. Each of these aspects activates a different hierarchical level in the human brain and unfolds at a specific developmental stage.

In Chapter 3, I focus on the importance of play for the child's development of sympathy and empathy, in part because it allows the child to engage in synchronized experiences with others. The chapter describes how play prepares the child to adapt to his or her environment, come up with new ideas and soothe stressful states, in part because play encourages new social relationships. Children spend much of their time playing, and since they spend most of their early years in the company of their primary caregivers, these relationships form the foundation of play. In order to develop self-esteem, feelings of competence and self-agency, the child needs to be exposed to manageable challenges. In play, children have fun and develop their creative capacity and cooperation skills, but play is also an important arena for learning to cope with anxiety or impulses that provoke anxiety if the child is unable to manage them. In the macro- and micro-regulation processes of play, children learn to master these competences. Macro-rhythms are regulated through the creation of structure, frameworks and predictability, while micro-rhythms pertain to tiny, almost invisible synchronizations. For good macro- and micro-regulation in a group of children, this 'children's caravan' needs a good 'caravan leader'. Like parents, preschool and school teachers should offer predictability, security, structure and regulation. Stable social hierarchies are an important feature of social groups, because they frame our ways of being together, and both friendship and status are important motivating factors in human communities, families and working relationships. The chapter describes how conflict resolution is part of our social culture, and how each group seeks its own balance between competition and cooperation.

In the following chapters, ten different authors describe specific ways of working with groups of 4–12-year-old children to promote emotional development and maturity by facilitating creative, synchronized interactions in a structured, safe and predictable setting. These descriptions and discussions are illustrated with case studies. Human synchronization is based on rhythm and rhythmic sensorimotor experiences, and Chapter 4 offers a fascinating look at how sensory integration training in children's groups can be understood in a neuroaffective framework. The chapter is written by the neuroaffective psychotherapist Marianne Bentzen, my long-standing partner in the development of neuroaffective psychotherapy, and occupational therapist Christine Lakoseljac-Andreasen. They offer insight into ways of promoting the development of a self-regulation capacity and empathy in children's groups, and how personal and social maturation is fuelled by mutual attunement, pleasure and satisfaction, typically in interactions based on joy-filled emotional contagion. Teaching methods, whether they are focused on sensorimotor skills or literacy, form a framework or 'macrostructure' for interactions that are appropriate for the children's competence level. In this macrostructure, everyone knows exactly what to do when they are together, which provides optimum conditions for cooperation. The quality of this cooperation derives initially from the gaze contact, use of voice, facial expressions and body posture that the adult 'caravan leader' uses to convey the macrostructure; it continues in the countless tiny interactions among the children and between the children and the adult. This synchronized attunement is the core of the joy and infectious engagement that characterizes motivating learning processes.

Some years ago I encountered a method for working with children's emotional and social development developed by therapists who had seen how verbal dialogues are often an inadequate way to reach emotionally vulnerable children and make a real difference. The method was Theraplay™, which had its beginnings in Chicago in the 1960s, where the psychologist Ann Jernberg and her team were tasked with identifying children in need of counselling in an inner-city school in Chicago and refer them for treatment. The psychologist Phyllis Booth, who wrote the Foreword to this book, was involved in this pioneer effort. She was profoundly inspired by what she had learned from John Bowlby and Donald Winnicott in England. The team realized that the existing services were inadequate, and that they needed to establish their own service based on an approach that was easy to grasp and practise for relatively inexperienced mental health professionals. To Phyllis Booth and her team, it seemed an obvious choice to base this approach on the playful interaction patterns that come naturally to adults who like children and who enjoy spending time with them. This led to the development of Theraplay, an approach based on positive parent–child interactions and inspired by John Bowlby, who emphasized active engagement and close interactions between child and teacher with direct body and eye contact and a focus on what is happening in the here-and-now rather than in the imagination. Later, the Theraplay Institute in Chicago developed Theraplay with children's groups, the so-called 'Sunshine Circles'. When I asked Phyllis Booth who she would recommend to write the chapter on Theraplay for this book, she immediately suggested that I contact Phyllis Rubin and Marlo Winstead, who for several years have been involved in developing the Theraplay concept for children's groups.

Chapter 5 describes Group Theraplay, an experiential and relational approach that revolves around interpersonal interactions and the sense of joy that may emerge among friends in shared and joy-filled present moments. Theraplay is framed by five dimensions: structure, engagement, nurture, challenge and playfulness. In Group Theraplay, these dimensions are translated into three explicit and one implicit rule. The explicit rules are *No Hurts, Stick Together* and *Have Fun*. The implicit rule is *The Adult is in Charge*. By following and enforcing these rules, the group leader creates a safe, accepting and emotionally connected experience.

The Department of Communication and Psychology at Aalborg University offers a degree in music therapy. It is the only place in Denmark that gives methodological and scientific recognition to the importance of the profound transformation processes that are generated when we experience, feel and develop rhythms, prosody and tonality, and which promote and strengthen human communities. It is also the only place in Denmark where psychotherapy is recognized at a university level and made the object of scientific, evidence-based studies. It was therefore a natural choice for me to invite two therapists with PhD degrees in music therapy who specialize in music, relationships and children – Ulla Holck and Stine Lindahl Jacobsen – to write a chapter for the book, focusing on music therapy with children's groups. Fortunately, they accepted my invitation, and in Chapter 6 they describe the rare capacity of music to affect us all – the capacity of pulse and rhythm to induce movement and the capacity of notes and harmonies to evoke and express emotions. They describe how musical interplay can create communities across language differences and other boundaries and capture a child's immediate attention. In the chapter, they present six case stories about the capacity of shared music-making to promote attention, concentration, emotional bonding and social skills in groups. In the final case story, they discuss its capacity to improve the quality of parent–child interactions. Their point is that music offers a way to relate to children that offers a strong foundation for promoting adaptive group dynamics. They also argue that if music-making is done in a way that is fun for the children, the interaction will inevitably lead to mutual attunement.

I wanted to include a chapter by a psychologist who had in-depth and first-hand knowledge of everyday life in schools and who also had experience working in a school setting with children who have severe attachment-related trauma or secondary traumatization. I had met psychologist Dorothea Rahm on a training course that Marianne Bentzen and I held in Dusseldorf, Germany. I knew that she had completed American trauma therapist and founder of Somatic Experiencing Peter Levine's training course in Somatic Experiencing, and that she was passionate about helping children who were struggling in school. In Chapter 7, Rahm reviews a case study from a group process with children who had severe psychosocial dysfunctions and were deemed to be beyond therapeutic reach. Most of the children came from immigrant families. She describes how the group process was driven by the question of whether it is possible to do something for children who seem doomed to fail in the school system, often because their parents are not seen to be 'good enough', both because of their personal traumas and because of their inadequate grasp of the local language and culture. As the chapter unfolds, we see that there is indeed hope for these children, provided we devote the necessary time and resources to put together a team of dedicated and committed teachers. It is possible to help these children, who have spent most of their lives living under highly difficult and stressful circumstances, and who need a specialized effort to achieve a positive change. With Rahm as our travel guide, we learn what it can be like to work with a group of children facing profound challenges.

When I did a series of master classes about attachment and traumas together with Peter Levine in Copenhagen and Zurich, he gave me some films that had inspired his own work over the years. Among these films, one in particular caught my interest. Levine had invited Eldbjørg Wedaa, a music and drama teacher in Bergen, Norway, who is trained in Somatic Experiencing, to New York to work with a group of vulnerable children, all of whom faced social and emotional difficulties. Decades ago, Wedaa had established her own music and drama school, Pinocchio, in Bergen. When I visited Bergen in connection with my work, I went to see her because it was clear to me that her work with children's groups was really guided by a neuroaffective developmental perspective, although she had never encountered this formal framework. In Chapter 8, she describes how she helps children experience all the things that play has to offer as a means of providing them with experiences of safety and joy. Her goal has always been for the 'Pinocchio children' to know that they possess a creative force, which they can continue to develop and draw on as a life-long resource, regardless of what sort of future they build. Wedaa's work revolves around letting the children unfold their creative force through play, music, imagination, images and emotions, expanding their experiences with themselves and their world. To shoulder the responsibility of guiding and facilitating this growth, the teacher needs to know and understand the stages in children's development and continuously stimulate the child to take on new areas of development. Wedaa describes how she uses drama, theatre, music and movement to support the children's ability to cooperate and thus promote their individual growth in a group setting. The children develop their expressive repertoire in a process framed by music, drama and play. Thus, in a setting characterized by empathy, compassion and expression, they build confidence and come to view their own contributions as valuable.

I met Pat Ogden when we were both keynote speakers at the recurring Theraplay™ conference in Chicago. She is the founder and education director of the Sensorimotor Psychotherapy Institute in Colorado and began her work with children in the 1960s as a primary school teacher in a low-income urban area. She gradually developed an interest in the impact of stressful and traumatic experiences on the body and in addressing mental stress and traumas by working with the body. For several years she has worked with Bonnie Goldstein, who aims to help children and young people deal with relational challenges or support children's healing processes after traumas, grief and loss. Today, Goldstein is part of a team of trainers in Sensorimotor Psychotherapy working with Pat Ogden to adapt the treatment model to children.

In Chapter 9, Ogden and Goldstein describe how the development, vitality and well-being of any child are affected by the combined effects of helpful and harmful experiences in the home, in peer interactions and in school. The personal meaning children derive from these experiences is not only expressed in words but also in physical behaviour. Even very young children express the meaning of their interactions with others in physical acts and, in particular, in the implicit organization of their body posture and action sequences. When certain acts consistently fail to elicit the desired response from important people in the child's life, the child eventually gives up these acts or behaviours. The child's patterns of physical tension, movement, gestures, body posture, physiological arousal, gait and other action sequences form a body language that tells a story. Reviewing a specific case, Ogden and Goldstein describe how verbal and somatic interventions can help children address unconscious patterns directly.

The Brazilian therapist Alé Duarte works all over the world to provide group therapy to children who have been exposed to shocking and traumatic experiences. He works in close collaboration with agencies, hospitals and other multi-disciplinary institutions working with survivors, and he has provided support for professionals in crises and disasters, including the Indian Ocean tsunami in 2005, the earthquake in China in 2008 and the earthquake and tsunami in Japan in 2011. In 2014, he worked with teachers and children in a Syrian refugee camp. In his home city of Rio de Janeiro, he has worked with parents of high-school shooting victims. Based on this extensive experience he has developed a training programme for disasters and critical situations. Like Wedaa and Rahm, Duarte is trained in Somatic Experiencing, and he often visits Denmark to give courses on his method for working with groups of children who have undergone traumatic experiences. In Chapter 10, he describes how a sense of safety is the foundation for self-regulation and homoeostasis. When children feel safe in the company of an adult, their arousal level is reduced, their inner sense of anxiety and discomfort is diminished, and they begin to express their needs and are quick use the re-establishment of physical safety to create opportunities for self-healing. To promote self-regulation, group leaders need to provide a tangible sense of safety by means of their physical presence, tone of voice, attuned gestures, coherence of inner states and external expressions/acts, clear instructions and eye contact, and by clearly appreciating and acknowledging each individual child in the group. In Duarte's approach, the group leader's grounding, orientation and inner sensations act as crucial sources of safety for the children. Instead of insisting on structure, the group leaders strive to move the group towards ever-greater levels of synthesis. Using the potentials of play, they give the children opportunities to re-enact elements of traumatic experiences in a safe environment in order to promote their natural self-regulation process.

NASSA stands for NeuroAffective Structured Social Activity, a developmental play-based group approach for 3–12-year-old children that aims to rebuild and enhance the children's social, emotional and personality resources by means of structured play. The development of NASSA began in 2010, when Varde Municipality and the Department for Survivors of Trauma and Torture under the psychiatric services in the Region of Southern Denmark engaged in a partnership to develop a method to prevent traumatization in children in families with a history of trauma. A report on social inequality from the Danish Health Authority emphasized that preschools and schools can have a significant positive impact on children's development; to some extent, the right educational setting may compensate for inadequate stimulation in the home. Social and family services in Varde Municipality had seen how some of these problems were manifest in children living in families with a history of trauma. The partnership led to a three-year project aimed at developing a method to rebuild children's psychosocial resources by means of structured play. The development project was co-funded by the Danish Health Authority and the two project partners. When the development section of the Department for Survivors of Trauma and Torture in the Region of Southern Denmark was closed, NASSA could not be continued in this setting. When NASSA's developers contacted me, I agreed to take over the NASSA programme and have since reshaped it as a developmental programme based on the theory of neuroaffective developmental psychology.

The purpose of NASSA is to develop and strengthen children's psychosocial resources in structured play processes that provide opportunities for enhancing relational resources and self-insight and developing greater resilience to psychological stressors. In Chapter 11 the reshaped version of NASSA is described. It is highlighted that the pedagogues and teachers in charge of the groups are not supposed to be or act as psychotherapists. However, they should be able to embrace and implement a developmentally oriented programme that revolves around the developmental principles of play to facilitate children's capacity for affect regulation, emotional attunement with others, developing mentalization and engaging in social relations. NASSA draws inspiration from approaches around the world that draw on the fundamental role of play in human life. NASSA is a structured developmental programme, not a manual-based approach. This means that the progression of the programme is guided by the actual emotional and social development level of the children in the group, and selected sessions may be repeated if the group as a whole is not ready to proceed to the next level. The programme consists of four levels with a total of 18 steps. Thus, if a NASSA trainer finds that the group needs to repeat a step once or even several times, that option is incorporated into the programme. The trainer in charge of implementing the NASSA programme has to complete a relatively brief training process, which involves trying all the activities first-hand.

For many years, psychologist Helle Jensen has provided supervision to professionals who work with vulnerable children. In her assessment, a common feature in these children is inadequate or deficient self contact. Unfortunately, in many cases, this has caused the teachers who are supposed to help the child re-connect with him/herself to lose touch with their own feelings, acting in despair rather than engaging with authenticity and empathy. After completing a continuing course in family therapy and relational skills headed by Jesper Juul at the Kempler Institute, Jensen began to teach relational skills and family therapy to professionals. In the mid-1990s, challenges in her personal life inspired her to learn some of the meditation techniques that people have used for millennia – to enhance their empathy, mindfulness and focused awareness – at Vaekstcenteret (Centre for Growth). She found the techniques tremendously helpful in re-connecting with herself and learning to maintain her balance, even in difficult situations, and thought that they might benefit others in a similar way.

In order to explore whether children, including vulnerable children, might profit from connecting with their inner resources, Jensen co-founded the Society for the Promotion of Life Wisdom in Children with a group of like-minded colleagues. The group has focused mainly on children's groups in regular school and preschool classes and on determining what it takes to create a good learning and development environment. These insights are the focus of Jensen's contribution in Chapter 12. Here, she describes how studies have found that empathy, relational competences and mutual interest and respect create the optimal setting for learning and development, regardless of the subject area. Because so many children today are diagnosed with attention deficit disorders, she has focused on identifying ways to help the individual child achieve improved mindfulness and focused awareness. In this chapter, Jensen describes the development of these competences through the 'Pentagon' of heart, mind, body, breathing and creativity. Part of the training consists in developing the relational capacity of the professionals working with these children, because they need it to ensure the children's social and emotional development. She describes exercises based on competences that we all possess from birth, and which she believes everyone can unfold and benefit from to stimulate the innate competences we need to provide the necessary space and attention for body sensations, feeling from the heart, breathing deeply and mindfully, allowing the unhindered flow of spontaneous creativity and being mindfully present in the moment.

I met the London-based child psychiatrist Eia Asen in connection with a two-day conference that I planned together with Marianne

Bentzen as part of our work on the book *Through Windows of Opportunity: A Neuroaffective Approach to Child Psychotherapy* (Hart and Bentzen, 2015). In addition to his own therapeutic work with children, Asen is dedicated to finding ways to support parents and help them in turn support their children. Over the years, he has engaged in a creative effort to develop and refine his own approach in a systemic and mentalization-based framework, including his multi-family school, where families inspire and learn from each other. In recent years, he has intensified his collaboration with the English psychologist Peter Fonagy, who originated the mentalization-based approach, and today, Fonagy and Asen work together at the Anna Freud Centre in London. It therefore seemed a natural choice for me to ask Eia Asen whether someone from his staff would write Chapter 13 about this parent-focused approach. He recommended Serena Potter, who has taught at a 'Froebel School', which put a priority on developing the students' empathy and emotional intelligence. In this chapter, Potter describes the focus of the multi-family model, which is that children thrive when parents and teachers work together and pull in the same direction. In the multi-family school setting, children and adults take part in a shared workshop led by family therapists/teachers aimed at enhancing the individual family members' affect regulation and strengthening their attachment relationships. Even if the model requires certain language and reflection skills, the action-based approach gives all participants a chance to bring into play personal resources that are not necessarily language-based. Many of the families who are referred to the multi-family classes today have already been in touch with a wide range of professionals and counselling services; they struggle with long-term and ingrained difficulties and may have seen little change for the better in this process. Therefore, the school makes a deliberate effort to secure referrals at an earlier stage. An intensive version, the Family Education Centre, was established in the 1980s and arose from The 'Family Day Unit', where up to eight families take part in daily sessions over a period of several months. The core element in the model is the notion of families helping families. In this final chapter, Potter describes how the multi-family context makes it possible to challenge recurring problematic behavioural and interaction patterns and bring new ideas and perspectives into play. The approach of bringing children and parents together across family units in a common activity makes room for new and different interactions, which in turn makes it possible to see oneself in a different light.

References

Boel, K., Clasen, S., Jørgensen, J. K. and Westenholz, P. (2013) *Inklusion i Folkeskolen.* Copenhagen: Dansk psykologisk Forlag.

Fonagy, P., Gergely, E., Jurist, L. and Target, M. (2002) *Affect Regulation, Mentalization and the Development of the Self.* New York, NY: Other G. Press.

Hart, S. and Bentzen, M. (2015) *Through Windows of Opportunity: A Neuroaffective Approach to Child Psychotherapy.* London: Karnac Books.

Jensen, E. and Brinkmann, S. (2012) 'Fællesskab er en udfordring for alle.' *Dagbladet Information,* 6 February.

Panksepp, J. and Biven, L. (2012) *The Archaeology of Mind: Neuroevolutionary Origins of Human Emotions.* New York, NY: W. W. Norton.

The Salamanca Statement (1994) *The Salamanca Statement and Framework for Action on Special Needs Education.* World Conference on Special Needs Education, Salamanca, Spain, UNESCO. Available at www.unesco.org/education/pdf/SALAMA_E.PDF, accessed on 19 June 2016.

Trevarthen, C. (1993) 'The Self Born in Intersubjectivity: The Psychology of an Infant Communicating.' In U. Neisser (ed.) *The Perceived Self: Ecological and Interpersonal Sources of Self Knowledge.* New York, NY: Cambridge University Press.

Winnicott, D. W. (1971) *Playing and Reality.* London: Penguin.

1

In Tune with Feeling

Musical Play with Emotions of Creativity, Inspiring Neuroaffective Development and Self-Confidence for Learning in Company

Colwyn Trevarthen and Jaak Panksepp

> *We believe that the evolutionary roots of musicality must lie in the repetitive rhythms and emotions at the source of moving. Especially important are the emotional sounds by which birds and mammals communicate. We mammals are social creatures who depend critically on resonance with the inner purposes and concerns of others.*
>
> *(Panksepp and Trevarthen, 2009, p.108)*

Emotions as stories in company with the time of movement

In their lifetime a person grasps knowledge of the world using the expressive wisdom of the human body in movement, gaining common sense by acting in synchrony and sympathy with feelings and beliefs expressed by the movements of companions (Trevarthen, 2012). This emotional awareness relies on tones and surges of feeling we all experience within ourselves and between us, and on a sense of times in movement generated within every brain – in the rhythms of the 'present moment', through the melodic phrases of narrative, and with lasting memories of other days. There is a give and take between imagination and memory, both of which are carried forward by the will of motor intelligence and the emotional dynamics of an imaginative actor seeking company in art of story-telling. The philosopher Susan Langer famously recognized, in *Philosophy in a New Key: A Study in the Symbolism of Reason, Rite, and Art*, that the vitality of 'inner life' has the story-telling forms of music (Langer, 1942, p.228).

This is the 'human nature of culture', a process of experience with feelings shared by purposeful, imaginative and concurrently expressive brains and bodies, in individuals who communicate thoughts and emotions richly, even when they do not speak to each other (Bruner, 1990; Trevarthen, Gratier and Osborne, 2014). They transmit habits of a self-with-other awareness, gaining skill in the practical use of objects and becoming informed by conventions that record experience from past generations. And all aesthetic and moral appreciation of what is known and what can be done in cooperation comes from the social emotions of innate human vitality projected from past experiences to future expectations. Any object the mind takes up, identifies and transforms, any place it explores and to which it must become adapted, any code of social conduct invented philosophically and recorded in a non-living product, must be appreciated with this intrinsic vitality to have any effect in the world. Our feelings are projected into our world and shared to make what we encounter meaningful, in an ecology of action in company with intimate relations at the centre (Bronfenbrenner, 1979). The physiologist Charles Sherrington in *The Integrative Action of the Nervous System* (1906) called the mental grasping of information from the 'distance receptors' (especially vision and hearing) 'projicience', and said that anything that is grasped perceptually and attributed form and place and meaning must be brought to the body for 'affective appraisal'. He further stated: 'We know that in ourselves sensations initiated through these receptors are forthwith 'projected' into the material world outside the 'material me' (Sherrington, 1906, p.324).

It follows from the creativity of awareness that all types of learning aimed at enriching children's natural abilities must be 'taken up' by the child's imagination and feelings. In practice, what Alfred North Whitehead (1929) called the 'zest for learning' and the pleasure of sharing discovery in a creative ecology of relations implies that the discovery of new knowledge is driven by the inherent curiosity of acting in ways that are perceived as meaningful by others. It is not just passive importation of facts defined according to the presumed needs of a productive economy or the sometimes sterile needs of a well-rounded formal education. The well-being of teachers and learners themselves depends upon mutual affection, playful experimentation and the joy of consent in the making of meaning, which Margaret Donaldson (1978) identified as 'human sense'. Ancient knowledge and new ways of art and industry are passed on as 'common sense' (Donaldson, 1992). They are created with love of company and with care for fear of opposition and exclusion. These are emotions that give the mind its energy and values from the first movements and moments of life. They become of great importance in any therapy to help overcome the paralysis, fear and confusion of one who has been traumatized and shamed by misfortune, neglect or cruelty (Schore, 2012).

To restore resilience, one must restore *joie de vivre*. And as we will see, there is no better vehicle for that than natural play – the engagement that children themselves devise to pass the living moment (Trevarthen, 2013; Trevarthen and Delafield-Butt 2013a; Trevarthen and Delafield-Butt, 2013b). This has become much undervalued in modern educational schemes, and we take away the fundamental sources of social joy at our cultural peril (Narvaez *et al.*, 2013; Panksepp, 2007a, 2007b, 2008). Unfortunately, as Whitehead (1925) warned in his writings on education for precision in science and mathematics, attention to the material properties of objects and a focus on efficiency of work, and texts and routines to formulate how to transform materials into efficient technical products can imprison the spirit of discovery with 'rules' and 'facts', making it harder for full meaning and values of human curiosity in activity to be appreciated and passed on. Discipline is necessary for acquiring skills of action and thought (Donaldson, 1992), but the child at school may be misled into believing that all knowledge comes from a truth that carries none of the values of human interaction – that lacks its sense of time and its beauty and justice. The same feelings should be activated in psychiatry, since limiting attention to diagnosed faults in organic processes can only give partial and temporary help. To appreciate the aesthetic and moral values, we need to pay attention to the universal principles that motivate animal life in animal minds and bodies, and how habits that grow in individuals are formed to be cooperative in a community.

We communicate our interests and emotions, whether we intend to or not, and they accompany all we try to do. Educational practices – especially in the early grades – that do not respect such fundamental principles of life, such as the urge of children to seek information on their own and to play, do inadequate service for the deeply ingrained social and intellectual growth of our children. Educational practices that recognize that all young children are seekers of knowledge will cultivate environments in which individual exploration is encouraged and rewarded, with abundant opportunities for social joy and encouragement for learning. Surprisingly, modern computers have increased such opportunities for everyone, to the point where internet searching can become obsessive and addictive. This is one of the shortcomings of the primary-process SEEKING emotional system – shared with all the other mammals – that encourages all of us to engage enthusiastically with the world.

By persistent attention to animal lives recorded in his notes about their diversity, Charles Darwin (Darwin, 1872) proved the value of emotions in the generation of adaptive habits from innate powers of active body forms and their senses. By reflecting on his own secure childhood and through loving attention, with the valued advice of his wife Emma, to the human nature of his own children (Darwin, 1877), he strengthened the foundations of the sciences of health, of psychology and of social policy, making it possible for the organic roots of all human intelligence to be appreciated, and not denigrated as primitive, uncultivated and irrational.

Modern psychology and educational theory tend to wander away from this enlightenment concerning the primary forces of human nature and instead place importance on the measurement and treatment of disorders and the enhancement of productivity by focusing attention on matter, facts and the provision of information. Overzealous use of assessment and intervention or training can stifle children's natural agency and their desire to act together with other children, regardless of age, to make use of the artful discoveries that arise through play.

It is becoming clear that our own playful urges come from the same ancestral sources as the ludic activities of other mammals (Panksepp, 1998; Panksepp and Biven, 2012). The ancient mammalian PLAY system still brings us abundant social joy. One of the developments that set us apart is the massive mushrooming of our neocortex, permitted in part by the discovery of cooking, which relaxed the pressures on the massively thick cranial plates and robust masseter muscles of plant-chewing apes, permitting space for human-trajectory brains to grow beyond the bounds of common sense. In the current era of enthusiasm for evolutionary psychology, where speculations have multiplied way beyond what neuroscientific evidence can support, it is not yet recognized that the human neocortex is probably born closer to a *tabula rasa* than the beehive of evolutionarily specialized modules in the deeper-seated and older sections of our nervous system (Panksepp and Panksepp, 2000). It is well known that even the visual cortex derives its ability for acute vision though life experiences rather than genetic specialization, and indeed, probably all cortical tissues are born with the potential capacity for vision, as long as they receive visual input from the subcortical, genetically designated visual pathway (Sur and Rubinstein, 2005). Scientifically demonstrated evolutionary specialized abilities in the neocortex remain largely undemonstrated and are probably quite modest. At birth the repetitive columnar organization of the neocortex resembles *random access memory* space more than evolutionarily specialized modules and is closer to an empty slate upon which our senses and our ancient subcortical systems, including basic values coded as affects, engrave knowledge, ideas and cultural values, which are then passed down from one generation to another through learning. If these cultural resources are not imbued with social joy at the outset, it is hard to restore such gifts of nature, especially in an environment characterized by disequilibrium. A fact that has emerged from our understanding of the neurobiology of animal play is that the executive circuits for social joy are situated below the neocortex, and that the whole neocortex is massively activated by play at both neuronal and genetic levels (Burgdorf, Panksepp and Moskal, 2011; Panksepp *et al.*, 2014). In other words, early play helps to programme our intellectual abilities and sensitivities, and it is much underutilized in early educational systems around the world, to the detriment of children and potentially cultural evolution. Our understanding of play-induced genetic changes in the neocortex of laboratory rats has now yielded a novel anti-depressant concept, resulting in a medicine that is designed to fight depression by facilitating the capacity for social joy within the brain (Burgdorf *et al.*, 2011). This new medicine, GLYX-13, currently being tested on humans, has a wonderful ability to facilitate learning as well. We can anticipate that it will facilitate positive affect and resilience in the brain, enhanced markedly by supportive and stimulating environments in the company of creative others.

Social joy in the midst of play is punctuated by laughter in both juvenile rats (Panksepp, 2007b; Panksepp and Burgdorf, 2000) and humans (Figure 1.1). One of the great tragedies of childhood urges to play is that they are less and less satisfied in our modern culture. The spaces and opportunities for children to play have diminished severely in post-modern cultures, where children's lives are increasingly regimented for academic achievements, often of the kind that their minds do not desire. But the desire for play is a regulated process. The longer children have gone without play, the more they want to play, just like other young animals (Panksepp and Beatty, 1980). In environments where play is discouraged, or those filled with tedium (e.g. many of our classrooms), the play urge is bound to seep through and yield disruptive behaviours, which may be diagnosed as attention deficit hyperactivity disorder (ADHD), leading in some cultures to prescriptions of psychostimulants that are robust inhibitors of play (Panksepp, 2007a, 2008). These lessons are also receiving increasing attention in human studies.

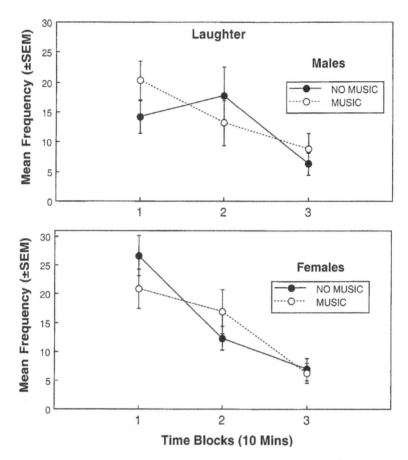

Figure 1.1: *Laughter of 20 boys and 20 girls aged 3–6 years who knew each other, filmed unobtrusively in same-age and same-sex pairs as they played at home or in a school room cleared of toys*

The figure shows that laughter reliably declined from the beginning to the end of the play session, as is the case for 50 kHz 'laughter'-type chirping in rats during a half-hour play session. At times, lively, happy songs were played to test the effect of music. Data points represent the mean number of laughter bouts within five-minute intervals; vertical lines indicate standard error of measurement. There were no overall significant differences between males and females, although the two-way interaction between time and gender was significant ($p<.05$), as was the three-way interaction among time, music and gender ($p<.05$). (Data adapted from Scott and Panksepp, 2003.)

Why we need to play and the freedom to create in company

The anthropologist Victor Turner studied meaning-making in African cultures, and in a book entitled *From Ritual to Theatre: The Human Seriousness of Play* he presented his concept of 'sociodrama' as a creative 'ethnography' of process that shared the experience of celebrations and imaginative projects in which 'something new may be generated. The performance transforms itself...the "flow" of action and interaction...may conduce to hitherto unprecedented insights and even generate new symbols and meanings' (Turner, 1982, p.79). He commented that 'Cartesian dualism has insisted on separating subject from object, us from them... The deep bonds between body and mentality, unconscious and conscious thinking...have been treated without respect' (Turner, 1982, p.100).

Time and time again, ambitious leaders, in their efforts to regulate society, have created rules and regulations and imposed laws for cultivating health and education. Since the days of Plato and Aristotle, they have insisted on the need to regulate and restrict play, to impose discipline, structure and definition or prescription to learning. The contributors to this book, all working with vulnerable children, seek to create a vital balance that recognizes and values the child's own initiatives to regulate his or her emotions in movements that also promote well-being and cooperation in companionship (Trevarthen, 2001a).

With evidence from the psychobiology of emotions and the natural science of learning we support the importance of working with children in creative relationships to help their well-being. The making of human sense begins with play through sympathetic relationships in early childhood (Trevarthen and Aitken, 2001). Small communities of learners, admitting all ages, become inventors of new and valued meanings that are stored as important memories. Human memory is generated through motor activity in a mobile body with many forms of expression that are sensed through the vitality that this creates and are developed in sympathetic sharing.

How the brain gives life to the body in moving and communicating feeling

People of all ages and in every community share the pleasures and pains of body movement. Their powers of relating are strongest at the beginning of life, in childhood and adolescence, and also in old age, when the capacities of body and mind are changing more quickly, and when learning about and 'making' the world are not the primary preoccupations. The brain moves the body with rhythm as it feels, and it is from the start concerned with the vitality of the body. Later, higher and higher variations of emotions arise to express this vitality. Before birth, the body shares its building of autonomic regulations of inner well-being with the mother, including her states of motivation and emotion. We have defined this shared autonomic regulation as 'amphoteronomic', meaning self-regulation in partnership (Trevarthen *et al.*, 2006) (Figure 1.2).

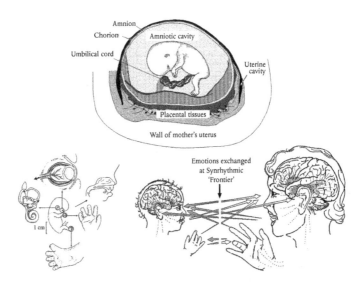

Figure 1.2: *First intimacy of life and development of the organs of conversation, for sharing states of mind (Trevarthen et al., 2006)*

Above: Early foetus showing the attachment between the mother's tissues and those of the foetus via the placenta. The placenta constitutes a complex frontier for the amphoteronomic regulation of the vital states of both foetus and mother.

Below left: An 8-week foetus has the special human organs of sight and hearing, oral organs for speaking, and hands and feet for gesturing, all of which move to express interests, intentions and feelings to other people, who may sense their expressions.

Below right: A young infant shares a protoconversation, exchanging interest and emotions with the mother. Each watches the eyes, face, mouth and hands and listens to the voice of the other through the synrhythmic communication of interest and affections.

During the first year after birth, the child's separate body takes over the task of mediating with a mother's intimate care through expressive vital rhythms that express emotion with hands, eyes, face and voice (Trevarthen and Aitken, 2001). This shared life with more body movement and mutual sympathy, expressed through motives and feelings, we call 'synrhythmic'. At every new stage of development, with every gain in mobility and social sensibility, there is an increase in emotional activity, including joyful as well as fearful or defensive emotions (Trevarthen, 2001b). The right half of the forebrain, which elaborates feelings to sustain well-being, grows most in the first three years. Between 3 and 8 years, there is a substantial gain in a sensorimotor intelligence where the child engages more with the world and talks about it – abilities that require the special talents of the left half of the brain. Then the right hemisphere becomes more active again as new relationships and new challenges to social learning emerge in adolescence. We have learned much about the neurochemistries of systems that guide this development of awareness, feelings and affections from organs deep in the brain through studies of animals that have less ambitious social ecologies (Panksepp, 1998; Panksepp and Biven, 2012).

The laughter of young rats in rough-and-tumble play (noted above), the contented purr of a kitten by the fire, the cry of loneliness of a puppy or chicken that has lost its mother, the yelps of joy in play or barks and growls of conflict of dogs on the beach, the honks of geese flying inland to rest, the songs of a nightingale – all are sounds that express vitality for sharing in a community of relationships more or less intimate and secure. They are the ancestors of song and music, which evolved and allowed humans to share more imaginative and more intricately contrived passions of life within the conventions of culture.

The neuroscience of moving in time, pioneered by Sherrington (1906), von Holst (von Holst and Mittelstaedt, 1950), Lashley (1951) and Sperry (1952), is intricately linked to the evolutionary neuroscience of emotional well-being and its expression for social cooperation (Burgdorf and Panksepp, 2006; Sheldon, Kashdan and Steger, 2011). This neuroscience has, in return, been enriched by research into the life of infants and how it is sustained by the intimate affections displayed in parental care. The cerebral hemispheres of an infant adapt in different, complementary emotional ways to develop intelligent awareness and memory of what the objective world affords and its benefits and dangers. The infant brain is primarily concerned with the receptive and expressive functions that arise through the intimate affective attachment, body to body, animated by love or, on occasions more sadly, by fear or hate (for many relevant reviews, see Narvaez *et al.*, 2013).

All these topics can contribute to a theory of the capacity of more play, loving and physical care to support vulnerable young people, especially those who have been deprived of the secure intimacy of parental care or who are fearful in their relations with the world and excluded from the joy of being part of a group. Play requires the enjoyment of companionship in imagination and creativity of movement. We are born with a moving body, ready to share its rhythms and melodies of joy or anguish. Our vitality is by nature that of a dancer or musician, and this intelligence in movement gives us signals to be shared. The dancing motions of many bodies in motion create shared projects that may bring well-being to a group, not just to ourselves or to those few with whom we live in the intimacy of attachment but also in larger communities. When we are troubled, others can share their will to live and give us confidence through their way of being with others.

Our brains develop through regulations of vitality that are displayed for cooperation in step with other brains in other bodies, measuring pleasure and displeasure in complementary, sympathetic ways within affectionate attachments. We share this biological capacity for moving with feelings with other animals. Scientists have uncovered the principles of shared vitality by careful research that reveals the neurochemistry of emotions and relates it to the impulses that coordinate the actions of hosts of muscles, connecting activity in different parts and giving the body a single agency or self that acts with power and grace. All this happens when groups of children play with their imaginations and act with synchronized movements.

The communicative musicality of infants and young children, and its affecting stories

The proof we now have that an infant is a musical being should not surprise us. There is no way of moving a human body with efficient and healthy purpose except with graceful rhythm of biological clocks regulated by the feelings of inner vitality and its hopes and fears (Osborne, 2009a; Trevarthen, 2009a, 2016). This is the essence of poetry, dance and music, which all human communities create and share with delight from childhood – Victor Turner's 'human seriousness of play' (Turner, 1982). The Scottish moral philosopher Adam Smith (1723–1790), who took a side interest in economics, was fond of music, of which he said:

> After the pleasures which arise from gratification of the bodily appetites, there seems to be none more natural to man than Music and Dancing. In the progress of art and improvement they are, perhaps, the first and earliest pleasures of his own invention. (Smith, 1777)

Smith's theological friend Thomas Reid said:

> It is by natural signs chiefly that we give force and energy to language... Thus writing is less expressive than reading, and reading less expressive than speaking without book; speaking without the proper and natural modulations, force, and variations of the voice, is a frigid and dead language...; it is still more expressive when we add the language of the eyes and features; and is then only in its perfect and natural state, and attended with its proper energy when to all these we superadd the force of action. (Reid, 1764)

Nevertheless, 350 years later we still have elaborate and influential theories of the human mind and its brain processes that choose to disregard the powers of movement and time (Goodrich, 2010), without which there can be no music and no language (Trevarthen and Delafield-Butt, 2013b). Many psychotherapeutic traditions exclusively hold that only the verbal or narrative content has the capacity to alleviate mental suffering. Fortunately, we are in an era where emotions are increasingly being placed at the forefront of productive theories about the best approaches for the treatment of distressed and disordered lives (Ecker, Ticic and Hulley, 2012).

Here, research on the infant's natural communicative talents makes an important contribution. As a young child psychiatrist beginning training as a psychoanalyst, Daniel Stern had observed infantile skills in a study of 'behaviors regulating social contact between a mother and her three-and-a-half-month-old twins' (Stern, 1971). He used micro-analysis of film, which had been developed in the preceding decade, as a method to reveal the natural rhythms of expression that

Reid had called 'natural language' (Birdwhistell, 1970; Condon and Ogston, 1966; Jaffe and Feldstein, 1970).

With a group of colleagues at Columbia University, Stern applied the new awareness of how human vitality is shared with 'affect attunement' to shape a new and richer understanding of psychotherapy (Beebe, Stern and Jaffe, 1979; Stern et al., 1985). He identified the importance of 'the present moment' in the everyday life of relationship in movement as well as in therapy (Stern, 2004). In 1985 he published his seminal classic *The Interpersonal World of the Infant*, intended to apply the new psychology of infancy to transform psychoanalytic theory and its application. In the introduction to the second edition of this book he acknowledged its enthusiastic reception by therapists who use non-verbal communication, such as dance and music (Stern, 2000, p.xv).

With an intense interest in the arts, especially dance and choreography, and after 40 years' experience expanding his awareness of the innate capacities of infants and their mothers for being in affective connection, Stern, in his latest book, *Forms of Vitality: Exploring Dynamic Experience in Psychology, the Arts, Psychotherapy and Development*, defined a science of 'vitality dynamics' (Stern, 2010, pp.29, 46). Drawing on information from research on movements of foetuses, infants and their mothers and relating these to the principles studied by performing artists, this concept of life in movement enriches our understanding of the nature of well-being and learning for human beings of all ages and of the appreciation of music as natural communication. All our arts and sciences, our literature and even much of technology grow from the expressive impulses of infancy: the pulse, quality and narrative of gestural and vocal story-making in good company.

Toddlers enjoy exploring new and exciting powers of whole-body movement: jumping, running, dancing, singing and talking enthusiastically with playmates of all ages in a familiar community (Custodero, 2007) (see Figure 1.3). They create in their play a 'children's musical culture' full of audacious experiments in sound (Bjørkvold, 1992, p.22); they are 'linguistic geniuses' (Chukovsky, 1968, p.4).

Figure 1.3: Ana Almeida in the Institute for Music and Human
Social Development (IMHSD), Edinburgh University, records how
4- and 5-year-old children move their bodies when they hear music

Each child was invited to move within a square while musical rhythms were played for them. They were told, 'When you hear the music you move as you wish and when the music stops you freeze like a statue.' These three children move with their whole body, running, jumping and arresting their movements, making eloquent gestures with their hands, translating the rhythmic patterns and moods. Their faces glow with delight. The children create a variety of performances, responding to the beat and changes of tempo, each child expressing an individual repertoire of movements.

Young children respond enthusiastically to encouragement to engage in creations of body movement and to the sounds of song and music. They move in felt immediacy with the human-made sounds, using their whole bodies skilfully. They are capable of making creative productions that combine all the arts (Figures 1.4 and 1.5).

In a project run by Robin Duckett of the Sightlines Initiative in Newcastle-upon-Tyne, UK, two musicians worked with the school staff in Trimdon Grange Infant and Nursery School, Trimdon, County Durham. Between March and July 2010 they worked with eight 5-year-old girls who were good friends, recording their expression in music and dance with the aim of encouraging their educators to value the children's creative music-making. The girls decided to make a new version of 'Sleeping Beauty', called 'Awakening Beauty', the story of a princess who danced with good fairies, was put to sleep by wicked fairies and then was eventually rescued by a prince. They composed the story with ballet-style choreography and developed their own moves and music. They were asked to talk about their feelings and to represent these feelings in movements and drawings. They were offered instruments with different tones, including drums and stringed and wind instruments, to 'play' the full range of their feelings. The good fairies danced gracefully to the 'happy' plucked string melodies. Then angry music was played on drums, while one of the girls acted as the energetic, dancing leader of the musicians, using her whole body. She became 'Evil Bird', one of the wicked fairies who put the princess to sleep.

Figure 1.4: *Project run by Sightlines at Trimdon Grange Infant and Nursery School to encourage teachers to value children's creative music-making. In these pictures the girls experiment with the musical instruments and dancing, making their own creative projects, some inspired by well-known stories or the media*

Figure 1.5: *On the day of the performance, the children were extremely excited. The whole school came to watch them, along with their parents and other visitors. Here is shy Sleeping Beauty awakening and her brave prince after the show and the final bow*

The Norwegian musicologist Jon-Roar Bjørkvold (1992) studied the musical games of children in Oslo, Moscow, St. Petersburg and Los Angeles, where educational, cultural, social and political practices are very different. He found that in all three countries, children showed spontaneous musicality, but in Russia and the United States, where formal training in music was given greater value than in Norway, he found reduced spontaneous music-making. He insists, 'It is critically important for children to master spontaneous singing, for it is part of the common code of child culture that gives them a special key to expression and human growth' (Bjørkvold, 1992, p.63). This progressive 'ritualization' of vocal creativity clarifies the adaptive motives for learning to sing and the expression of increasing narrative imagination for sharing ideas in culturally specific ways (Eckerdal and Merker, 2009; Gratier and Trevarthen, 2008). Its natural development parallels the way language is mastered (Chukovsky, 1968).

Supporting the motives of health in companionship with body movement therapy – applying affective neuroscience

Eminent scientists have opposed the repeated reduction of brain function to hypothetical cognitive or input processes in mechanisms for perception and learning. By studying the anatomy and physiology of nerve tissues and their growth, they have established that the brain is shaped primarily for its output in body movement (Bernstein, 1967; Damasio, 1999; Sherrington, 1906; Sperry, 1952). Research is making it ever clearer that our fundamental emotional structures engender dynamic patterned actions as well as motivation and feelings (Panksepp, 1998; Panksepp and Biven, 2012; Trevarthen, 2009b). The function of the brain is to make the body engage the environment by moving its muscles in coherent ways with refined economy of the physical and chemical energies required to sustain mental balance. Good living moves harmoniously with wonderful efficiency and with playful good humour (Trevarthen, 2013). Illness and distress cause weak or impulsive actions that meet the environment erratically and cause inner pathologies and conflict in communication (Trevarthen and Delafield-Butt, 2013a).

The coordination and regulation of movement that enables the body to engage with the world is coupled with the autonomic regulations of visceral functions that sustain all vitality systems. The neurochemistry of autonomic and visceral sensorimotor systems has many functions in the newborn infant. Among other functions, it generates the enteric neuropeptides that regulate our viscera and the emotional systems of our brains. All these structures also link the inner life with actions addressed to the awareness of companions, seeking to use cooperative environmental resources through expressions of emotion that signal intentions and feelings to others, and that imitate their feelings (Kugiumutzakis and Trevarthen, 2015), enabling affectionate cooperation (Figure 1.6). Every gesture, look or cry telling others how we feel or what we intend to do employs organs that were evolutionarily built within our human bodies and animated by our ancient, subcortical animal brains before we greet our mother's indulgent gaze and recognize her voice as the one we heard before birth (Porges, 2013).

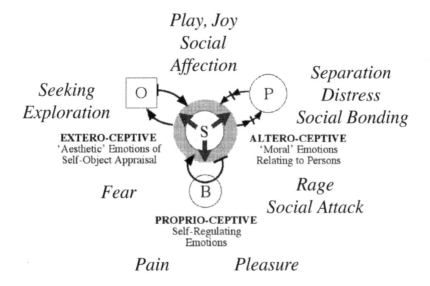

Figure 1.6: *The map of emotions in the regulation of sensorimotor engagements and purposeful acts of the Self (S) with the Body (B), with Objects (O) and with Persons (P)*
(Panksepp, 1998; Panksepp and Trevarthen, 2009)

An infant is gifted to share the rhythm and emotions of life without words, learning by exploring the sensations of moving (Trevarthen, 2009b). This lets the child gain confidence and engage in intimate relations with playful love from another. It is this relationship that later enables us to offer and receive sympathetic care for pain and fear, for hunger and loneliness. In the same way, we keep company with others to build self-confidence all our lives, moving our bodies with emotional sensitivity as we gain responsibilities in society and pick up the ambitious tasks that characterize our given culture.

Human individuals never lose consensuality, or mutual awareness, in movement and its need for response. These states of motives are active in relationships through all stages of development, from the 'dyadic regulation of psychobiological states' (Tronick, 2005, p.294) to participation in a meaningful culture. A sensitively supportive partner may transform painful psychological conditions, bringing vitality to weakened motives for sharing (Trevarthen et al., 2006). This enables human beings to find enthusiasm together for great and small actions, both inventively and cooperatively (Csikszentmihalyi and Csikszentmihalyi, 1988). William James (1890) drew attention to the creative 'flow' of consciousness that animates practical cooperation, which is the foundation of psychotherapies that aim to foster dialogue in imaginative and playful interactions. This helps to build or rebuild a secure personal identity in a present emotional relationship (Meares, 2005; Ryle and Kerr, 2002; Stern, 2004). In the therapeutic process, 'reconsolidation' occurs in memory processing, because each memory, when retrieved, is re-stored within the brain along with the emotion that arises in the new present moment. This can be systematically applied in therapy to soften painful memories and is becoming a mainstay concept of new psychotherapeutic approaches (Ecker et al., 2012). Thus, our living memories are embedded in affective contexts and can be used in the therapeutic process (Schore, 2012; Trevarthen and Delafield-Butt, 2013a).

The authors of this volume seek to discover creative ways of rebuilding confidence and health in children and young people who feel discouraged and excluded. These creative ways are found in the ability to enjoy moving in concert. They assist children and young people who need partners to develop in playful invention, especially those who have lost trust in themselves and in others, who feel sad and lonely and who need their autonomy boosted (Erikson, 1950). Through play, these children and young people develop capacities for regulating emotions in relationships that animate the development of their minds and the sharing of meaning (Schore, 2001; Siegel, 1999). The use of interventions that focus on body dynamics, including playful interactions, is increasingly recognized as an important but long-neglected aspect of psychotherapy. This therapeutic approach can often yield more rapid progress in adults and children alike than treatment that restricts itself to the cognitive level of interaction (Ogden, Minton and Pain, 2006).

Music therapy

Music is a sensorimotor language that needs no words. Improvised music therapy is a creative partnership that progresses with the sensitive guidance of a skilled musician who has been trained in the responsive performance of movement with feeling. In one-to-one sessions, the aim of the therapist is to strengthen self-confidence and to explore and enable the resolution of feelings that prevent both happiness and achievement. The principles resemble those in jazz improvisation (Duranti and Burrell, 2004; Kühl, 2007; Schögler and Trevarthen, 2007), which is based on reference themes and rules of variation, predictability challenged with chance accidents and discoveries, which 'play' with or 'tease' a partner's anticipation (Ansdell, 1995; Gratier and Trevarthen, 2008). The creativity of music therapy springs from the ongoing negotiation of a sensitive and sympathetic 'contract' between therapist and client in intimate communication (Meares, 2005; Wigram and Elefant, 2009).

An anxious, confused and self-absorbed child can experience confidence and joy in company through self-expression in carefully managed steps with an adult who uses imitation and creative extension within an unfolding predictable structure. This transformative process unfolds in 'playful' dialogues that lead to a fuller participation in a flowing musical collaboration, with mutual affection (Bond, 2009; (Bruscia, 1987; Nordoff and Robbins, 1977/2007; Oldfield, 2006; Osborne, 2009b; Pavlicevic and Ansdell, 2004; Wigram, 2004; Wigram and Elefant, 2009; Wigram, Pedersen and Bonde, 2002; Zeedyk, 2008).

Group music therapy, dance therapy and drama therapy recruit the spirit of collaboration among performers, strengthening different ways of being, different personalities and different talents. Experimental and non-experimental case studies confirm the therapeutic value of improvisational music therapy (Bruscia, 1987; Edgerton, 1994; Nordoff and Robbins, 1977/2007; Oldfield, 2006; Warwick, 1995; Wigram and Elefant, 2009; Wigram and Gold, 2006; Wigram *et al.*,

2002). Stages of the process of music therapy can be measured by detailed analysis of the cooperative music-making by groups in recorded sessions, demonstrating the gain in confidence and shared experience for individuals who have in the past found communication and relationships difficult (Pavlicevic and Ansdell, 2004). There is a strong theoretical foundation for the creative and curative effects of intersubjective 'art' therapies that employ what Stern has called 'vitality dynamics' (Stern 2010, pp.29, 46) in live engagement to encourage communication and cooperation, and to heal disorders of autonomic regulation that harm essential functions of the body. Nigel Osborne, who has helped young people severely traumatized by war for 20 years since his work began in Bosnia-Herzegovina, explains how his work is guided by a 'biopsychosocial paradigm' that seeks to tie physiological, psychological, and social concerns together in a single, integrated model. The model defines a space 'in which practitioners may feel confident in the potential of their work to effect positive change, and where the development of practical methods and methodologies may take place with the general support of current scientific research' (Osborne, 2009b, p.335). He reviews studies of the effects of war experience on hearing, on functions of the heart, on respiration, and on movement, and the beneficial effects of sharing the pleasure of music. Both in adults and in children, the stress caused by violence and trauma is accompanied by a wide range of symptoms. In addition to depression, fear, distracted attention and loss of sensory acuity, which trouble actions and communication, stress is accompanied by autonomic problems, including dysregulation of hormonal and neurotransmitter systems related to stress and relaxation, confused movements and pain. Music can help a child who has been abused deal with both the psychological and physiological symptoms of mental trauma (Robarts, 2009). It is well established that music, besides arousing emotions, can directly modulate brain systems to reduce not only psychological pain but also physical pain (Bernatzky *et al.*, 2011).

In conclusion

As usual, the fruits of neuroscience lag far behind clinical understanding. However, we are finally in an era where the ever-increasing power of neuroscience techniques is able to counter a century-long rigidity of thought fostered by a radically reductionist era of behaviourism that saw no need to consider the emotional qualities of human and animal minds. The great transformation towards a realistic understanding of human and animal minds has finally begun with the recognition that all mammals are 'brothers' and 'sisters' at the evolutionary foundations of the mind, where a variety of ancestral affective processes that govern fundamental life values form a shared mammalian heritage (Panksepp, 1998; Panksepp and Biven, 2012), expressed in part in the rhythms of movements (Trevarthen, 1999, 2009a). The endless neuroscientific details of neurological changes are rightfully of little concern to clinicians, but it is increasingly evident that all effective psychotherapies change the brain. Relevant evidence has been accumulating for 20 years, ever since modern brain imaging techniques allowed us to visualize the faint glimmers of therapeutic changes in the human mind (for summaries, see Cozolino, 2002, 2010). Of course, it should be kept in mind that the interpretation of functional magnetic resonance imaging (fMRI)-based brain imaging remains very controversial in terms of what is actually being measured (Vul et al., 2009, Mather et al., 2013). Although modern neuroscience has had relatively little to offer for the practice of education, psychology and psychotherapy, this will change as we begin to truly fathom how affects are constructed in the brain. There will be new medicines, which do no harm, that will be able to gently facilitate productive movement into the world by strengthening the positive emotions and the associated learning mechanisms that govern who we will become. Such medicines have already been discovered (Burgdorf et al., 2011; Moskal et al., 2011) and are currently being tested, with promising results, in human adults with severe depression. Of course, they will only be needed for those who have congenital brain abnormalities or whose brain functions have been injured by impoverished lives. Before the radical choice of pharmaceutical treatment is considered, however, each child should first be exposed to therapies that enhance the deep creative and restorative powers of human nature.

References

Ansdell, G. (1995) *Music for Life: Aspects of Creative Music Therapy with Adult Clients.* London: Jessica Kingsley Publishers.

Beebe, B., Stern, D. and Jaffe, J. (1979) 'The Kinesic Rhythm of Mother-Infant interactions.' In A. W. Siegman and S. Feldstein (eds) *Of Speech and Time: Temporal Speech Patterns in Interpersonal Contexts.* Hillsdale, NJ: Erlbaum.

Bernatzky, G., Presch, M., Anderson, M. and Panksepp, J. (2011) 'Emotional foundations of music as a non-pharmacological pain management tool in modern medicine.' *Neuroscience and Biobehavioral Reviews 35*, 1989–1999.

Bernstein, N. (1967) *Coordination and Regulation of Movements.* New York, NY: Pergamon.

Birdwhistell, R. (1970) *Kinesics and Context.* Philadelphia, PA: University of Pennsylvania Press.

Bjørkvold, J.-R. (1992) *The Muse Within: Creativity and Communication, Song and Play from Childhood Through Maturity.* New York, NY: HarperCollins.

Bond, K. (2009) 'The Human Nature of Dance: Towards a Theory of Aesthetic Community.' In S. Malloch and C. Trevarthen (eds) *Communicative Musicality: Exploring the Basis of Human Companionship.* Oxford: Oxford University Press.

Bronfenbrenner, U. (1979) *The Ecology of Human Development: Experiments by Nature and Design.* Cambridge, MA: Harvard University Press.

Bruner, J. S. (1990) *Acts of Meaning.* Cambridge, MA: Harvard University Press.

Bruscia, K.E. (1987) *Improvisational Models of Music Therapy.* Springfield, IL: Charles C. Thomas Publications.

Burgdorf, J. and Panksepp, J (2006) 'The neurobiology of positive emotions.' *Neuroscience and Biobehavioral Reviews 30*, 173–187.

Burgdorf, J., Panksepp, J. and Moskal, J. R. (2011) 'Frequency-modulated 50 kHz ultrasonic vocalizations: A tool for uncovering the molecular substrates of positive affect.' *Neuroscience and Biobehavioral Reviews 35*, 1831–1836.

Chukovsky K. (1968) *From Two to Five.* Los Angeles, CA: University of California Press.

Condon, W. S. and Ogston, W. D. (1966) 'Sound film analysis of normal and pathological behavior patterns.' *Journal of Nervous and Mental Diseases 143*(4), 338–457.

Cozolino, L. (2002) *The Neuroscience of Psychotherapy: Building and Rebuilding the Human Brain.* New York, NY: W. W. Norton.

Cozolino, L. (2010) *The Neuroscience of Psychotherapy: Healing the Social Brain* (2nd edn). New York, NY: W. W. Norton.

Csikszentmihalyi, M. and Csikszentmihalyi, I. S. (eds) (1988) *Optimal Experience: Psychological Studies of Flow in Consciousness.* New York, NY: Cambridge University Press.

Custodero, L. A. (2007) 'Origins and expertise in the musical improvisations of adults and children: A phenomenological study of content and process.' *British Journal of Music Education 24*(1), 77–98.

Damasio, A. R. (1999) *The Feeling of What Happens: Body, Emotion and the Making of Consciousness.* London: Heinemann.

Darwin, C. (1872/1998) *The Expression of the Emotions in Man and Animals* (3rd edn). New York, NY: Oxford University Press.

Darwin, C. (1877) 'A biographical sketch of an infant.' *Mind 2*(7), 285–294.

Donaldson, M. (1978) *Children's Minds.* Glasgow: Fontana/Collins.

Donaldson, M. (1992) *Human Minds: An Exploration.* London: Allen Lane/Penguin Books.

Duranti, A. and Burrell, K. (2004) 'Jazz improvisation: A search for hidden harmonies and a unique self.' Ricerche di Psicologia 27(3), 71–101.

Ecker, B., Ticic, R. and Hulley, L. (2012) *Unlocking the Emotional Brain.* New York, NY: Routledge.

Eckerdal, P. and Merker, B. (2009) '"Music" and the "Action Song" in Infant Development: An Interpretation.' In S. Malloch and C. Trevarthen (eds) *Communicative Musicality: Exploring the Basis of Human Companionship.* Oxford: Oxford University Press.

Edgerton, C.L. (1994) 'The effect of improvisational music therapy on the communicative behaviors of autistic children.' *Journal of Music Therapy* 31, 31–62.

Erikson, E. H. (1950) *Childhood and Society*. New York, NY: W. W. Norton.

Goodrich, B. G. (2010) 'We do, therefore we think: Time, motility, and consciousness.' *Reviews in the Neurosciences 21*(5), 331–361.

Gratier, M. and Trevarthen, C. (2008) 'Musical narrative and motives for culture in mother-infant vocal interaction.' *Journal of Consciousness Studies 15*(10–11), 122–158.

Jaffe, J. and Feldstein, S. (1970) *Rhythms of Dialogue*. New York, NY: Academic Press.

James, W. (1890) *The Principles of Psychology*. New York, NY: Henry Holt & Co.

Kugiumutzakis, G. and Trevarthen, C. (2015) 'Neonatal Imitation.' In J.D. Wright (ed.) *International Encyclopedia of the Social & Behavioral Sciences* (2nd edn), Vol 16. Oxford: Elsevier.

Kühl, O. (2007) *Musical Semantics*. Bern: Peter Lang.

Langer, S. K. (1942) *Philosophy in a New Key: A Study in the Symbolism of Reason, Rite, and Art*. Cambridge, MA: Harvard University Press.

Lashley, K. S. (1951) 'The Problems of Serial Order in Behavior.' In L. A. Jeffress (ed.) *Cerebral Mechanisms in Behavior*. New York, NY: Wiley.

Mather, M., Cacioppo, J.T. and Kanwisher, N. (2013) 'Introduction to the Special Section: 20 years of fMRI: What has it done for understanding cognition?' *Perspectives on Psychological Science* 8, 41–43.

Meares, R. (2005) *The Metaphor of Play: Origin and Breakdown of Personal Being*. New York, NY: Routledge.

Meares, R. (2016) *The Poet's Voice in the Making of Mind*. London/New York: Routledge.

Moskal, J. R., Burgdorf, J., Kroes, R. A., Brudzynski, S. M. and Panksepp, J. (2011) 'A novel NMDA receptor glycine-site partial agonist, GLYX-13, has therapeutic potential for the treatment of autism.' *Neuroscience and Biobehavioral Reviews 35*, 1982–1988.

Narvaez, D., Panksepp, J., Schore, A. and Gleason, T. (eds) (2013) *Evolution, Early Experience and Human Development: From Research to Practice and Policy*. New York, NY: Oxford University Press.

Nordoff, P. and Robbins, C. (2007) *Creative Music Therapy: A Guide to Fostering Clinical Musicianship* (revised edn). Gilsum, NH: Barcelona Publishers.

Ogden, P., Minton, K. and Pain, C. (2006) *Trauma and the Body: A Sensorimotor Approach to Psychotherapy*. New York, NY: W. W. Norton.

Oldfield, A. (2006) *Interactive Music Therapy in Child and Family Psychiatry*. London: Jessica Kingsley Publishers.

Osborne, N. (2009a) 'Towards a Chronobiology of Musical Rhythm.' In S. Malloch and C. Trevarthen (eds) *Communicative Musicality: Exploring the Basis of Human Companionship*. Oxford: Oxford University Press.

Osborne, N. (2009b) 'Music for Children in Zones of Conflict and Post-Conflict: A Psychobiological Approach.' In S. Malloch and C. Trevarthen (eds) *Communicative Musicality: Exploring the Basis of Human Companionship*. Oxford: Oxford University Press.

Panksepp, J. (1998) *Affective Neuroscience: The Foundations of Human and Animal Emotions*. New York, NY: Oxford University Press.

Panksepp, J. (2007a) 'Can PLAY diminish ADHD and facilitate the construction of the social brain.' *Journal of the Canadian Academy of Child and Adolescent Psychiatry 10*, 57–66.

Panksepp, J. (2007b) 'Neuroevolutionary sources of laughter and social joy: Modeling primal human laughter in laboratory rats.' *Behavioral Brain Research 182*, 231–244.

Panksepp, J. (2008) 'Play, ADHD and the construction of the social brain: Should the first class each day be recess?' *American Journal of Play 1*, 55–79.

Panksepp, J. and Beatty, W. W. (1980) 'Social deprivation and play in rats.' *Behavioral and Neural Biology 30*, 197–206.

Panksepp, J. and Biven, L. (2012) *Archaeology of Mind: Neuroevolutionary Origins of Human Emotions*. New York, NY: W. W. Norton.

Panksepp, J. and Burgdorf, J. (2000) '50k-Hz chirping (laughter?) in response to conditioned and unconditioned tickle-induced reward in rats: Effects of social housing and genetic variables.' *Behavioral Brain Research 115*, 25–38.

Panksepp, J. and Panksepp, J. B. (2000) 'The seven sins of evolutionary psychology.' *Evolution and Cognition 6*, 108–131.

Panksepp, J. and Trevarthen, C. (2009) 'The Neuroscience of Emotion in Music.' In S. Malloch and C. Trevarthen (eds) *Communicative Musicality: Exploring the Basis of Human Companionship*. Oxford: Oxford University Press.

Panksepp, J., Wright, J. S., Döbrössy, M. D., Schlaepfer, T. E. and Coenen, V. A. (2014) 'Affective neuroscience strategies for understanding and treating depression: From preclinical models to three novel therapeutics.' *Clinical Psychological Science 2*(4), 472–494.

Pavlicevic, M. and Ansdell, G. (2004) *Community Music Therapy*. London: Jessica Kingsley Publishers.

Porges, S. W. (2003) 'The Polyvagal Theory: Phylogenetic contributions to social behavior.' *Physiology and Behavior 79*, 503–13.

Reid, T. (1764) *An Inquiry into the Human Mind on the Principles of Common Sense*. London: A. Millar; Edinburgh: A. Kincaid & J. Bell.

Robarts, J. Z. (2009) 'Supporting the Development of Mindfulness and Meaning: Clinical Pathways in Music Therapy with a Sexually Abused Child.' In S. Malloch and C. Trevarthen (eds) *Communicative Musicality: Exploring the Basis of Human Companionship*. Oxford: Oxford University Press.

Ryle, A. and Kerr, I. B. (2002) *Introducing Cognitive Analytic Therapy: Principles and Practice*. Chichester: John Wiley & Sons.

Schögler, B. and Trevarthen, C. (2007) 'To Sing and Dance Together: From Infants to Jazz.' In S. Bråten (ed.) *On Being Moved: From Mirror Neurons to Empathy*. Philadelphia, PA: John Benjamins.

Schore, A. N. (2001) 'The effects of early relational trauma on right brain development, affect regulation, and infant mental health.' *Infant Mental Health Journal 22*, 201–269.

Schore, A. N. (2012) *The Science of the Art of Psychotherapy*. New York: Norton.

Scott, E. and Panksepp, J. (2003) 'Rough-and-tumble play in human children.' *Aggressive Behavior 29*(6), 539–551.

Sheldon, K. M., Kashdan, T. B., and Steger, M. F. (eds) (2011) *Designing Positive Psychology: Taking Stock and Moving Forward*. New York, NY: Oxford University Press.

Sherrington, C. S. (1906) *The Integrative Action of the Nervous System*. New Haven, CT: Yale University Press.

Siegel, D. J. (1999) *The Developing Mind: How Relationship and the Brain Interact to Shape Who We Are*. New York, NY: Guilford Press.

Smith, A. (1777/1982) 'Of the Nature of that Imitation which takes place in what are called the Imitative Arts.' In W. P. D. Wightman and J. C. Bryce (eds) *Essays on Philosophical Subjects*. Indianapolis, IN: Liberty Fund.

Sperry, R. W. (1952) 'Neurology and the mind-brain problem.' *American Scientist 40,* 291–312.

Stern, D. N. (1971) 'A micro-analysis of mother-infant interaction: Behaviors regulating social contact between a mother and her three-and-a-half-month-old twins.' *Journal of American Academy of Child Psychiatry 10,* 501–517.

Stern, D. N. (2000) *The Interpersonal World of the Infant: A View from Psychoanalysis and Development Psychology* (2nd edn). New York, NY: Basic Books.

Stern, D. N. (2004) *The Present Moment: In Psychotherapy and Everyday Life.* New York, NY: W. W. Norton.

Stern, D. N. (2010) *Forms of Vitality: Exploring Dynamic Experience in Psychology, the Arts, Psychotherapy and Development.* Oxford: Oxford University Press.

Stern, D. N., Hofer, L., Haft, W. and Dore, J. (1985) 'Affect Attunement: The Sharing of Feeling States Between Mother and Infant by Means of Inter-Modal Fluency.' In T. M. Field and N. A. Fox (eds) *Social Perception in Infants.* Norwood, NJ: Ablex.

Sur, M. and Rubinstein, J. L. (2005) 'Patterning and plasticity of the cerebral cortex.' *Science 310,* 805–810.

Trevarthen, C. (1999) 'Musicality and the Intrinsic Motive Pulse: Evidence from Human Psychobiology and Infant Communication.' In *Rhythms, Musical Narrative, and the Origins of Human Communication: Musicae Scientiae,* (Special Issue, 1999–2000). Liège: European Society for the Cognitive Sciences of Music.

Trevarthen, C. (2001a) 'Intrinsic motives for companionship in understanding: Their origin, development and significance for infant mental health.' *Infant Mental Health Journal 22* (1–2) 95–131.

Trevarthen, C. (2001b) 'The Neurobiology of Early Communication: Intersubjective Regulations in Human Brain Development.' In A. F. Kalverboer and A. Gramsbergen (eds) *Handbook on Brain and Behavior in Human Development.* Dordrecht, The Netherlands: Kluwer.

Trevarthen, C. (2009a) 'Human Biochronology: On the Source and Functions of "Musicality".' In R. Haas and V. Brandes (eds) *Music That Works: Contributions of Biology, Neurophysiology, Psychology, Sociology, Medicine and Musicology.* New York, NY: Springer.

Trevarthen, C. (2009b) 'The Functions of Emotion in Infancy: The Regulation and Communication of Rhythm, Sympathy, and Meaning in Human Development.' In D. Fosha, D. J. Siegel, and M. F. Solomon (eds) *The Healing Power of Emotion: Affective Neuroscience, Development, and Clinical Practice.* New York: Norton.

Trevarthen, C. (2012) 'Embodied human intersubjectivity: Imaginative agency, to share meaning.' *Cognitive Semiotics 4*(1), 'The Intersubjectivity of Embodiment', 6–56.

Trevarthen, C. (2013) 'Born for Art, and the Joyful Companionship of Fiction.' In D. Narvaez, J. Panksepp, A. Schore, and T. Gleason (eds) *Evolution, Early Experience and Human Development: From Research to Practice and Policy.* New York: Oxford University Press.

Trevarthen, C. (2016) 'From the Intrinsic Motive Pulse of Infant Actions, to the Life Time of Cultural Meanings.' In B. Mölder, V. Arstila and P. Øhrstrom (eds) *Philosophy and Psychology of Time Springer Studies in Brain and Mind* (vol. 9). Dordrecht: Springer International.

Trevarthen, C. and Aitken, K. J. (2001) 'Infant intersubjectivity: Research, theory, and clinical applications.' Annual Research Review. *The Journal of Child Psychology and Psychiatry and Allied Disciplines 42*(1): 3–48.

Trevarthen, C. and Delafield-Butt, J. (2013a) 'Autism as a Developmental Disorder in Intentional Movement and Affective Engagement. Frontiers in Neuroscience (Integrative Neuroscience), Research Topic 'Autism: The Movement Perspective' hosted by E. B. Torres, R. W. Isenhower, C. Whyatt and A. M. Donnellan. Submitted March 2013.

Trevarthen, C. and Delafield-Butt, J. (2013a) 'Biology of Shared Experience and Language Development: Regulations for the Inter-Subjective Life of Narratives.' In M. Legerstee, D. Haley and M. Bornstein (eds) *The Infant Mind: Origins of the Social Brain.* New York, NY: Guilford Press.

Trevarthen, C., Aitken, K. J., Vandekerckhove, M., Delafield-Butt, J. and Nagy, E. (2006) 'Collaborative Regulations of Vitality in Early Childhood: Stress in Intimate Relationships and Postnatal Psychopathology.' In D. Cicchetti and D. J. Cohen (eds) *Developmental Psychopathology* (2nd edn, vol. 2). Hoboken, NJ: John Wiley & Sons, Inc.

Trevarthen, C., Gratier, M. and Osborne, N. (2014) 'The human nature of culture and education.' *Wiley Interdisciplinary Reviews: Cognitive Science 5,* 173–192. doi: 10.1002/wcs.1276

Tronick, E. Z. (2005) 'Why is Connection with Others so Critical? The Formation of Dyadic States of Consciousness: Coherence Governed Selection and the Co- Creation of Meaning out of Messy Meaning Making.' In J. Nadel and D. Muir (eds) *Emotional Development.* Oxford: Oxford University Press.

Turner, V. W. (1982) *From Ritual to Theatre: The Human Seriousness of Play.* New York, NY: Performing Arts Journal Publications.

von Holst, E., and Mittelstaedt, H. (1950) 'Das Reafferenzprinzip.' *Naturwissenschaften 37,* 256–272.

Vul, E., Harris, C., Winkelman, P. and Pashler, H. (2009) 'Puzzlingly high correlations in fMRI studies of emotion, personality, and social cognition.' *Perspectives on Psychological Science 3,* 274–290.

Warwick, A. (1995) 'Music Therapy in the Education Service: Research with Autistic Children and Their Mothers.' In T. Wigram, B. Saperston and R. West (eds) *The Art and Science of Music Therapy: A Handbook.* London: Harwood Academic.

Whitehead, A. N. (1925) *Science and the Modern World.* New York, NY: Macmillan.

Whitehead, A. N. (1929) *The Aims of Education and Other Essays.* New York, NY: Macmillan.

Wigram, T. (2004) *Improvisation: Methods and Techniques for Music Therapy Clinicians, Educators and Students.* London: Jessica Kingsley Publishers.

Wigram, T. and Elefant, C. (2009) 'Therapeutic Dialogues in Music: Nurturing Musicality of Communication in Children with Autistic Spectrum Disorder and Rett Syndrome.' In S. Malloch and C. Trevarthen (eds) *Communicative Musicality: Exploring the Basis of Human Companionship.* Oxford: Oxford University Press.

Wigram, T. and Gold, C. (2006) 'Music therapy in the assessment and treatment of autistic spectrum disorder: Clinical application and research evidence.' *Child: Care, Health and Development 32*(5), 535–542.

Wigram, T., Pedersen, I. N. and Bonde, L. O. (eds) (2002) *A Comprehensive Guide to Music Therapy: Theory, Clinical Practice, Research and Training.* London: Jessica Kingsley Publishers.

Zeedyk, S. (ed.) (2008) *Promoting Social Interaction for Individuals with Communication Impairments.* London: Jessica Kingsley Publishers.

2

Empathy and Compassion Are Acquired Skills

Susan Hart

We communicate through emotions, whether we intend to or not, and our emotions follow us in everything we do. A school that fails to embrace this fundamental principle of life as a key learning competence may produce academically brilliant students but expect the children's personal, social and empathic learning to emerge automatically as a hidden skill. In children's lives especially, play has a crucial role in the development of the key life skill of interacting with others. At a time when schools place a strong emphasis on inclusion, we need to focus on emotional learning. Instead of focusing exclusively on academic skills, based on individualized learning approaches and a competition for top marks, we also need to embrace *homo ludens*: humans as playful and social beings who seek joy-filled moments with others and take delight in discovering the world together. This need might be expressed in many different ways – for example, we are currently seeing how Facebook can act as a highly addictive social forum. An emotional system that drives us to engage with others is something we take with us from earlier stages in our evolution, and which we share with many other social mammals.

All learning, whether cognitive, motor or emotional, is mediated by neural stimulation. Cognitive learning is mediated by a stimulation of brain areas involved in language learning, maths skills, etc. The facilitation of this type of learning has traditionally been the school teacher's primary classroom task. Motor learning requires us to train motor functions. To learn how to ride a bicycle, for example, we have to get on the bike – we cannot learn cycling from a book. When it comes to emotional learning and development, we have to engage in adaptive relationships with others, and the younger the child is, the more important it is that parents and teachers take charge. Emotional learning, personality development and social learning take place through thousands of subtle daily synchronizations with others. These processes regulate how we relate to others – that is, how we self-regulate and engage in adaptive relationships. For example, when the child engages in synchronized interactions with caregivers via facial expressions, eye contact, prosody, body movements and timing in connection with play and other forms of reciprocal contact, this strengthens the formation of brain synapses during childhood. This sort of synchronization is the medium of human attunement and aids the development of an adaptive personality. Calming children through these attunement processes improves their ability to deal with developmental demands and cognitive processes.

Children's capacity to engage in synchronized experiences with others and the quality of these exchanges depend on the extent to which the child has previously been involved in co-creating these states with others, especially the primary caregivers. The child's ability to engage in social relations is shaped by the mutual regulation that the child experiences and comes to expect. Emotions and personality can only develop in a close relationship with significant others. In this chapter, we look at the basic requirements for building learning spaces for emotional development. Humans are highly advanced, social mammals who establish social hierarchies. The most important hierarchy is the generational hierarchy, and our most important condition for developing cooperative relationships is our capacity to engage in playful, creative relationships with a good balance between cooperation and competition.

Learning in the zone of proximal development

Our genetic potential matures continually throughout life but especially in childhood. It takes a suitable environment to shape, support and optimize these transformation processes, which initially unfold in interactions with the primary caregivers and later with peers and other significant adults. The maturation of the brain's emotion areas determines which interactions the child invites and engages in. The responses that the child receives from other people will shape emerging neural structures, which in turn shape the child's behaviour. All the higher personality functions, including attachment, emotional self-regulation, impulse control and reflection, are acquired through countless social micro-interactions that are gradually internalized and shape the child's intra-psychological habits and structures.

This learning and internalization can only occur on the child's current level of maturity and within the zone of proximal development. Therefore, to understand the process, we need insight into the brain's maturation process and growth spurts. Children who function on a normal or typical level show a good match between their actual (chronological) age and their level of maturity, while children who are genetically vulnerable or who have suffered neglect show a far more complex maturation process. For example, an 8-year-old boy may have an age-appropriate development zone with regard to understanding adults' requests and demands, while his capacity for emotional regulation may be closer to that of a 6-month-old infant. School or preschool teachers therefore have to be able to provide interaction forms that satisfy both the age-appropriate development need and the immature development needs of the children they work with.

To paraphrase Vygotsky's famous concept of the zone of proximal development (Vygotsky, 1978, p.86), parents and teachers create the conditions for the child to learn in his or her zone of proximal development. When the child struggles with an activity, the parents therefore need to offer additional support and lower their demands; and when the child demonstrates that he or she masters the task, the parents should reduce the amount of support and increase the demands in the interaction. Thus, parent–child games unfold as synchronized activities where both parents and children are sensitive to each other's behaviour in order to maintain a playful interaction that fosters mutual engagement. The younger the child is, the more adult support is needed to achieve and maintain the mutual interaction. The parents' synchronization with their child in this asymmetrical relationship is probably what enables the child to achieve a similar synchronization in subsequent interactions with peers. In other words, children learn to play in asymmetrical relationships but practise their play skills in symmetrical relationships (Pellegrini, 2009).

It is helpful for teachers to know what typically developing children are capable of at different ages, emotionally as well as cognitively. For example, a 6-month-old child will have learned how to initiate interactions with his or her mother, and slightly later, will be able to engage in social rules (e.g. in peek-a-boo games). At around 9 months, the child actively takes part in games. Around 1 year of age, the child is able to engage in negotiations about who takes the lead in the game, and who is the follower, and the child is able to move more flexibly between the two positions (Bruner, 1983; Cohen, 2006). At this age, the child is able to apply rules, such as waiting for the count of three, and can take part in simple games that require knowing when to start, stop, take turns, etc. Self-awareness, self-recognition and higher forms of empathy develop around the age of 18–24 months – a capacity that is also found in apes. In order to unfold our capacity for sympathy and empathy, we need to be able to distinguish between our own and others' emotions. Our sense of empathy and morality also develop in interactions with others. The primatologist and ethologist Frans de Waal (2006) describes how the same applies to apes. He tells a story about the chimpanzee, May, who sometimes saves the best branches for herself but gives the rest away, while Georgia keeps everything for herself, which makes her less popular among the other members of her group. If she wants food from another chimpanzee, she has to wait a long time, while May simply has to approach the others in order to be offered food. Both in primate and human communities, generosity pays off, and most reciprocal favours in close relationships occur without much forethought. That is also how we acquire our sense of fairness, which is the basis of revenge but also of justice.

From external control to internal regulation

As described in Chapter 1, our higher personality functions, such as our capacity for attachment, self-regulation, impulse control and reflection, develop and are shaped by countless social micro-interactions that are internalized and become part of the child's intra-psychological habits and structures. These interactions begin just after birth in exchanges with the closest caregivers. Slightly later, the children practise these micro-interactions with peers but still require adult support to provide structure and regulation. As children grow older and become more mature, they get by with less and less adult supervision and intervention.

Because the frontal lobes are the last to develop in the human brain, and because humans have such a long childhood, compared to other species, it takes many years before children are capable of engaging in reciprocal peer relationships without having adults present to handle conflicts. Like cognitive and motor skills learning, emotional learning also involves developmental stages that should be mastered at specific age levels. Learning and internalization can only take place at the child's current level of maturity and in the child's zone of proximal development.

Children's emotional regulation and coping strategies develop in a trusting relationship with a parent or teacher who accepts an asymmetrical responsibility. These subtle, often near-invisible exchanges form the basis of self-regulation and the later developing mentalization capacity. The mentalization capacity has a lengthy development period, and it is only once it has begun to emerge that the child is able to self-regulate on the basis of language, symbolization and interpretation. These subtle regulations shape the child's ability to relate to others in synchronized experiences, and the quality of these exchanges depends on whether the child has previously been involved in co-creating them with others, initially the primary caregivers. Our emotional and relational interactions are shaped by the mutual regulation that we have experienced and come to expect. The countless social micro-interactions and present moments that are part of these interactions form the basis of the child's ability to develop more complex and coherent ways of being with significant others (Hart, 2011, 2012; Hart and Bentzen, 2015).

As the Russian psychologist Lev Vygotsky (1978) pointed out, any function in the child's cultural development is transformed, initially in social processes and later in individual processes – first in interpersonal exchanges and later internally. All higher functions have their origins in real, interpersonal relationships. What was implicitly shared by two individuals in an external interpersonal process becomes an internalized, intrapersonal, psychological skill. The child's capacity for self-regulation fosters confidence and self-worth, which develops from confidence in the caregiver to confidence in oneself *with* the caregiver and, eventually, to confidence in oneself in relationships with others. If the attachment system is not established, the child misses out on the opportunity to develop the regulation mechanisms that are needed to organize mental content. If the child fails to develop an attachment system with his or her primary caregivers, he or she will have a 'second chance' in nursery school, preschool and school, provided these facilities offer adequate resources: teachers who are able to act as good 'caravan leaders' and who have the time and commitment to care for the child.

Play as a context for developing personal maturity

The human nervous system requires stimulation to develop in the person's zone of proximal development (Vygotsky, 1978). For example, the child engages in nonverbal dialogues, called 'protoconversations', from the age of 3–4 months. Later, these protoconversations come to form the 'background music' for the child's communication with others. Already from around 2 years of age, language plays a key role for the child's ability to convey experiences to others. Although children express their emotion and bodily impulses through play and other behaviours, they use language to build dialogues. The better children are at conveying experiences through language, the better are their chances for sharing nuanced experiences and being met with understanding. It is crucial for children to integrate the different levels of mental organization, and if this is not possible in the child–caregiver relationship, one hopes it will be possible in other contexts – for example, in the groups of children that they relate to later in life. This is possible if the child has the experience of being contained, understood and acknowledged. Children need to feel seen, with their experiences, and they need to be able to share these experiences in the framework of attuned interaction experiences and narratives, which are created in early childhood interactions.

Already from the first days of life, the infant has the capacity to attune with another human being. Infants respond to others' emotional states, and just after birth, they are sensitive to emotions in vocal expressions and touch. Infants respond more emotionally to rhythms in human body movements, human sounds and music than to other auditory stimuli. This playful behaviour and the use of the body as an expressive instrument is a precursor of the creative imitation that is so characteristic of slightly older children's play behaviour and their imaginative stories, complete with plots and emotions. This creates the basis of conscious and emotional understanding, which in turn underlies cultural intelligence, including language (Hart 2011, 2013b). As we see in most of the chapters in this book, music, rhythms and play are crucial factors in our personal development.

Research (Cohen, 2006) has found that most children have grasped the 'grammar' of play by around the age of 3 years. At this age, they are able to spot actions that contradict the play narrative and seem incongruous, such as someone pretending that a colander is a shoe. Around the age of 6 years, however, children have a much wider set of strategies for engaging in social pretend play. Until children are around 5 years old, their parents typically control who their playmates are, but after the age of 5, children increasingly select their own playmates (Ladd and Hart, 1992).

Play behaviour follows a certain development path, and it takes a long time before children engage in more sophisticated symbolic play. This can be illustrated, for example, by showing a 3-year-old and a 4-year-old child a sponge that has been painted to look like a rock. When the children are allowed to touch the object, the 4-year-old child would say that it is a sponge, but he or she would know that it still looks like a rock. In other words, 4-year-olds are able to distinguish between what an object looks like, and what it really is. Three-year-olds have yet to develop this ability. What they see is perceived as fact, so when they see an object that looks like a rock, it is a rock. As soon as they discover that it is really a sponge, they will say that it looks like a sponge. The way the object feels creates a new reality for a 3-year-old. Four-year-olds are no longer constrained by their perception of objects but are able to grasp the simultaneous existence of objects on two levels. What they see and what they sense by touch do not necessarily have to coincide. This experiment has parallels to the way children perceive other people and their abilities – occasionally, everyone behaves the way young children do in the sponge experiment, taking the world at face value and expecting others to feel what they feel (Flavell et al., 1992).

All 6-year-olds and about half of all 4-year-olds are able to distinguish between fantasy and reality. Of the 4-year-olds who make mistakes, few do so consistently. Thus, most of these children have no difficulty distinguishing between fantasy and real life. But even if the children do not believe in made-up imaginary stories, they do show signs of being frightened by them. In another experiment, 48 children were shown two boxes and asked to imagine that there was a puppy in one and a monster in the other. They were allowed to look inside both boxes to see that neither box contained a puppy or a monster. Nevertheless, they were very cautious around the box that they had been asked to imagine contained the monster. So even if the children knew the difference between fantasy and real life, they still showed signs of magical thinking and were scared of the 'monster box' (Harris et al., 1991). Several researchers, including Fagen (1981), believe that play gives us a general capacity to adapt to new elements in our surroundings and helps us develop both mental and behavioural agility for problem-solving, adapting to new surroundings and engaging in new relationships. At the age of 4–6 years, children also learn that we do not have to reveal our thoughts and feelings to others, and that we might sometimes say the opposite of what we think and feel, if it helps us fit in better.

Several researchers have described sequences in play development. For example, Howes and Matheson (1992) suggested the following sequence and later developed the Howes Peer Play Scale:

- *Parallel play:* Two children playing alongside each other.

- *Parallel aware play:* Children playing alongside each other and being aware of each other.

- *Simple social play:* The children make simple contact attempts.

- *Complementary and reciprocal play:* Play is still parallel, but there are reciprocal initiatives.

- *Cooperative social pretend play:* Play that makes it possible to engage in mutual pretend play.

- *Complex, social pretend play:* The children are able to use their mentalization capacity in play and are able to use play to overcome difficult earlier experiences.

The triune brain

Paul MacLean (1990) has been a major source of inspiration for the understanding of human development processes and, specifically, for the development of neuroaffective developmental psychology. In the late 1950s, he developed his theory of the triune brain, which divides brain structures into three tiers representing quantum leaps in the evolution of the human brain (see Figure 2.1). Many neuroscientists reject the model as overly simplistic because they see it as undermining the understanding of the brain as a highly integrated entity. Despite the criticism, I choose to use the model as a useful synthesis that may help bring order to the many complicated structures of the brain. For, as Professor of Psychobiology Jaak Panksepp (1998, p.43) writes:

> Although the triune brain concept is largely a didactic simplification from a neuroanatomical point of view, it is an informative perspective. There appear to have been relatively long periods of stability in vertebrate brain evolution, followed by bursts of expansion. The three evolutionary strata of the mammalian brain reflect these progressions.

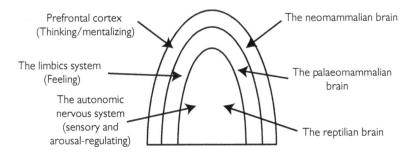

Figure 2.1: *The triune brain*

MacLean (1990, p.12) assigned three different mentalization forms to the three brain structures, labelling the most primitive tier 'protomentation', the middle tier 'emotional mentation' and the top tier 'rational mentation'. More recently, Jaak Panksepp (Panksepp and Biven, 2012) has referred to the three tiers as the 'primary', 'secondary' and 'tertiary' levels. MacLean (1990) referred to the level of protomentatation, or the autonomic, sensory level, as the 'reptilian brain'. Processes in this brain structure are instinctive and enable us to regulate our arousal (energy level) and sense our emotions; and it plays an important role in our ability to maintain attention on whatever holds our interest (Damasio, 1999; Lewis, Amini and Lannon, 2001). MacLean (1990) referred to the area of emotional mentatation as the 'paleomammalian brain' or the 'limbic system'. The limbic system enables us to engage in social interactions and thus to experience emotions such as playfulness or sadness. The area of rational mentatation was labelled as the 'neomammalian brain' in MacLean's (1990) system. This structure includes our frontal lobes, and enables us to process cognitive rationales and to mentalize, strategize and preserve mental images (Hart, 2008). The degree of complexity increases as one moves up in the brain's hierarchical structures, and this maturation sequence defines the child's zone of proximal development and determines which types of interactions will promote maturation.

From the age of 0–3 months, children need to engage in interactions that enable them to experience comfort and discomfort and regulate their arousal (energy level). From the age of 2–3 months until 9–12 months, children learn to distinguish between 'me' and others – based on pleasant as well as unpleasant emotions, they learn that there is a difference between one's own and others' emotions. From around the age of 12 months, children learn to inhibit their impulses in order to do certain things instead of only doing what they feel like doing. From this level, children develop their mentalization capacity in a gradual process that is not fully completed until around the age of 20 years. At the autonomic level, children learn to engage in rhythms and interactions with other people, and during the limbic period they learn to exchange emotions through facial and bodily expressions. Our frontal lobes take longer to develop than any other brain structure, and thus, children are not able to engage in fully competent symbolic play until around the age of 8–10 years.

The emotional levels in the brain are stimulated and develop through interactions with others, and at early development levels, this involves interactions with close adult caregivers. The mental organization at each of the three levels determines the nature of the moments of meeting and the attunement processes in which the children are able to engage. This means that the caregiver has to be able to provide and engage in three primary interaction forms to promote the child's emotional development:

1. *At the autonomic level:* the synchronized 'dance' with the child's sensory impressions.

2. *At the emotional level:* attunement with the child's emotions.

3. *At the mentalizing level:* verbal dialogues with the child.

When the autonomic and limbic areas have matured, children use narrative processes to attempt to make sense of the world and manage their own inner states. Sometimes, the narratives are also used for cognitive self-reflection. The exchange of narratives helps to strengthen and develop the brain's emotion and impulse-inhibiting structures, and through the narrative organization, raw emotions are reshaped into symbols. We use verbal symbols to attribute meaning to our sensory and perceptual experiences. Through self-reflection, we connect emotions with an explicit understanding capable of editing our narratives about who we are and creating mentalized interpersonal connections. This process requires an activation of the autonomic and limbic areas.

Maturation processes in the autonomic sensory brain are promoted by the creation of motor-rhythmic synchronization and variations in arousal, bodily care situations and safe, interesting sensory experiences. This is illustrated, for example, in Chapter 5, in the opening ritual, which involves singing a hello song and thus acknowledging the presence of the participants by mentioning their names in the song while completing the circle; and also in Chapter 6, where the children begin by singing a familiar song together while clapping in time to the chorus, with an after beat, a little rhythm sequence in between the verses, etc., which enhances the children's awareness and sense of their own learning. The same occurs in drumming or clapping songs that provide a common pulse and awareness in the group.

Supporting maturation processes in the limbic emotional brain requires emotional attunement and joy-filled and exciting activities with various types of challenges, the repair of emotional misattunement and support for relevant care and creative cooperation impulses among the children. This is illustrated in Chapter 4, for example, where two boys take turns rolling face down on a skateboard, picking up two puzzle pieces each with every turn. Eventually, they have enough pieces to begin to complete the puzzle in a coordinated effort, and they proudly present the result. There is a similar process in Chapter 5, where a handful of moisturizer is passed around to check just how many times it can go around the circle before it is gone. Once a child has passed on the moisturizer, the child next to him or her checks whether there is any moisturizer left on his or her hand. If there is, the child makes it disappear – for example by gently rubbing it in. Once the handful of moisturizer reaches the teacher, who initially sent it round the circle, the teacher acknowledges that it has been returned, and that there is still plenty left. At the outset, the teacher helps to build up tension by asking the children how many times they think the moisturizer can go round the circle before it is gone.

Adults can promote maturation processes in the prefrontal, thinking brain with language games and stories that the children can embrace and expand on and by supporting the children's mutual regulation of roleplay and turn-taking and their reflections about their own and other children's thoughts and emotions in various situations. This is illustrated in Chapter 7, for example, where a child in close contact with an adult is suddenly able to articulate an understanding of his own situation as the son of mentally rigid and unempathic parents; this helps him achieve a new understanding of his parents. Or in the NASSA programme (see Chapter 11), where the children work with the characteristics of their basic emotions– that is, how they express and sense these emotions – and then connect these emotions with a story. For example, based on a picture of a crying child, they are asked to shape a generalized story about what might have happened to make the child so sad. In the final sessions of the programme, they discuss both the good and the difficult aspects of having relationships with others, including losing, helping and trusting others.

With inspiration from MacLean's (1990) three-tier structure, the following three sections look at the role of the primary level through synchronization and rhythms, the role of the secondary level through the attunement of emotional exchanges and the role of the tertiary level through verbal dialogues.

Synchronization – the rhythms and melody of life

The development of the basic regulation of the autonomic functions helps children regulate and coordinate their arousal level and maintain focus. Children learn this through attuned contacts, and in this process, they acquire strategies for self-soothing and for recovering their equilibrium. They experience feelings of comfort and discomfort through the autonomic nervous system and lay the foundation for experiences and assessments that will later govern their thoughts and behaviour. The earliest and most basic types of stimulation occur through the body, that is, through the bodily reactions initiated by stimuli that influence the autonomic nervous system.

Touch and the development of the kinaesthetic sense are important for the gradual development of a sense of one's own existence and delimitation. Bodily sensations, which the infant probably senses as various forms of inner flow, tension, vitality, etc., and which Daniel Stern (1985, p.54–57) labelled 'vitality affects', enable the infant to perceive sensory wholes and connectedness. The infant's experiential world is coloured by the specific vitality affects that are triggered, and these help the child navigate in the world. Many children's games involve touching, and fortunately, many school and preschool teachers consider it natural to give the child a reassuring pat on the back or, sometimes, to hold the child's hand.

Meltzoff and Moore (1977, 1999) described how children imitate their caregivers' gestures and facial expressions shortly after birth. This capacity for imitation lets the child copy subtle physical reactions as they are reflected in others' facial expressions from moment to moment and attune with them. Newborns and infants imitate body postures, facial expressions and prosody, and via deep-seated regions of the brain, imitation and bodily sensations are connected with others' attuned support. When children synchronize with others through imitation and bodily sensations, they develop a sense of others' emotional states, which is a precursor of empathy. This imitation capacity helps children regulate and find a rhythm in their physiological regulation. The so-called mirror neurons enable us to experience others' actions and emotions simply by observing the action or the emotional state without necessarily imitating it. We experience the other's act as if we were carrying out the same act; we feel the same emotion or are affected in the same way as the other. This inner mirroring makes the interaction interesting and gives rise to curiosity and engagement. The first step in the maturation of the autonomic system is thus the establishment of macro-regulation: the basic rhythms that govern life and interpersonal contact. In group contexts, this involves regular contact routines for how to initiate and end an activity and for the way the teacher frames activities and handles conflicts. Within this clear framework, the next task is to capture the group's attention with an exciting activity and to create sufficient variation in the activity to keep the children's interest or bring them back when they stray. The teacher's vivid facial and bodily expressions and bodily invitations to the children to imitate are important factors in this meeting. This gives the children an opportunity to mirror the important link between 'gut feeling' and facial expression that connects bodily synchronization with emotions. This is often referred to as the nonspecific factors of an intervention, where the teacher's self-agency plays a crucial role.

This autonomic maturation is driven by bodily and perceptual synchronization, which is most easily established in games that involve rhythmic and bodily attunement through all the sensory channels. These games are a more or less specific part of many methods developed for children's groups and they play an especially explicit role in music therapy. This rehearses the children's ability to be calmed down and activated by adult interventions. It is important for the teachers to adapt their invitations and activities in tune with the children's indications of comfort and discomfort in a safe and predictable way, because children, and especially vulnerable children, need a high degree of acknowledgement at this level. The focus at this level is on establishing a predictable framework, rhythmic bodily games and contact rituals (Hart, 2011; Hart and Hvilshøj, 2013). As Trevarthen and Panksepp described in Chapter 1, children possess the wonderful gift of being able to share rhythms and emotions without relying on words. They can learn to explore their sensations by moving and thus gain confidence and knowledge about close relationships in a setting of kind and caring play with others, both in interactions with loving adults and in peer interactions with adult support. This capacity for attachment lets us engage in human fellowship and find pleasure in cooperating with others.

Emotional containment and attunement

The limbic system enables us to express social emotions such as joy, sadness, anger, etc., and to engage in playful social interactions, thus refining our capacity for refined interactions. Humans develop the so-called 'categorical emotions', which are reflected in our facial expressions. The categorical emotions are universal emotional categories. The American psychologist Paul Ekman (2003) operated with seven categories: joy, surprise, sadness, fear, anger, disgust and contempt. These emotional states give rise to action impulses, and the limbic system is therefore also sometimes referred to as the motivation system.

At this level, both children and adults experience many nuanced positive and negative categorical emotions. Thus, the child experiences how emotions can vary, both in intensity and between positive and negative. Similarly, children will vary between taking a healthy, self-centred interest in objects and activities that they find interesting and satisfying, and taking an interest in other people's actions and, eventually, their inner states. Thus, children are able to engage in social interactions by first becoming aware of the other, sharing his or her experiences as if their own experiential perspective were centred in the other. The limbic system lets us distinguish ourselves from others, combining self-awareness with awareness of the other and providing emotional regulation.

To promote limbic maturation, teachers need to use their own emotional sensitivity to make room for ideas and activities to emerge. These initiatives need a safe space to unfold as well as a supportive structure to prevent conflicts and dangerous situations. That is why Group Theraplay™ (see Chapter 5) revolves around three explicit and one implicit rule: 'No Hurts', 'Stick Together', 'Have fun' and (as the implicit rule) 'The Adult is in Charge'. For example, the teacher has to stop the activities before they either lead to conflict or get too boring. Because misattunement and disagreement are also a part of life, however, the teacher should also be able to help the children handle disagreement and emotional conflicts and help them re-attune and re-establish shared play. For example, it can be a big challenge to deal with children who are constantly initiating conflicts. In Chapter 5, this is exemplified by the situation where two children's disturbing behaviour formed an obstacle for the group's goals and prevented the other children from benefiting fully from the group. The group was therefore split into two smaller groups, and the two disruptive children were separated; this made it possible to do something specifically for the two disruptive children as well as for the other children. With adult support and control, the two disruptive children made great progress in the smaller groups, where they participated actively and made positive contributions. After six weeks it was possible to re-establish the big group, and the two children who had previously been disruptive were told how impressed everybody was with their progress, and how much everybody enjoyed playing with them. Subsequently, all the children happily took part in the activities, supporting, encouraging and helping each other. The two children who had previously been disruptive were placed next to the adults so that they could intervene quickly if the children needed special attention and care. One child leaned against the teacher's leg to preserve the close physical contact and thus a sense of safety.

The first step in limbic maturation in a group of children is to develop a variety of emotional expressions in play, initially with an emphasis on positive emotions, such as joy, surprise, curiosity and positive anticipation, and on empathic activities, such as mutual massage or rocking each other gently. Later, the activities come to include the shared playful expression of negative emotions, such as anxiety or anger – for example, in the encounter with a pretend monster. All the methods for children's groups that are described in this book revolve around this type of activity and structure. The teachers need to regulate and care for the children's negative emotions to give the children the clear and repeated experience with adults who are reliably able to challenge them and provide empathic care and support.

Based on the different interactions and games that unfold and integrate the synchronization capacity of the autonomic system with the emotional exchange of the limbic system, the children can now begin to develop healthy internal representations of being with safe adults as a basis for developing regulated interaction forms with other children.

The role of dialogue and mentalization in shaping communities and group cohesion

The prefrontal cortex is a highly complex structure that plays a crucial role in preserving our emotional stability. The prefrontal cortex controls our primitive behaviour and basic emotions by inhibiting impulses and overriding our reflexive/instinctive systems and limbic structures. The area enables a sense of continuity between past, present and future and thus makes stable friendships possible. It is in this area that the experience of shame, embarrassment, remorse or regret resides. The development of the prefrontal cortex allows us to begin to mentalize, reflecting on ourselves and others and understanding others' inner states. The area contributes to our mental flexibility and is capable of modifying thoughts and acts based on associations. When the area matures, the result is an integration of cognitive and emotional areas that leads to a considerable development potential that continues to unfold for many years.

Because the prefrontal cortex is so complex and takes so long to mature, we need to address the maturation process in stages. The first growth period takes place between the ages of 1–2 years and is important for children's ability to engage in attuned interactions. The second growth phase occurs during the preschool age, 2–6 years, and is important for the development of friendships, the ability to play and group bonding. The third growth period, school age or 6–12 years, is important for group socialization, establishing social hierarchies, competition, the development of deeper friendships, self-reflection and the development of a conscience. The 'teenage' years, 12–20 years, are an important phase for the ability to see oneself from the outside, considering one's perceived self-image, who one would like to be, and the discrepancy between the actual and the ideal world. This phase in life is also important for the experience of group bonding and, not least, sexual maturation.

The first growth period of the prefrontal cortex, age 1–2 years

During the first growth period, when the child is aged 1–2 years, emotions of shame, pride and jealousy begin to emerge. This happens around the age of 12–14 months. The emergence of the capacity for shame and pride is important for the development of self-regulation and a superego structure, which enables children to stop a behaviour that offers immediate satisfaction but upsets others and also to feel pride when praised for their accomplishments. Around this time, the child develops the capacity for empathy, which allows the child to sense his or her own subjective state and project it onto another person or an object. From around the age of 1½–2 years, the child begins to be able to use language and play as a means of modulating and controlling emotional expressions and experiences and begins to be able to use private/inner speech to self-regulate (Emde, 1985, 1989; Sroufe, 1979). At this stage, children gradually begin to master symbols, expanding their play repertoire with symbolic play activities, such as pretend play. At this stage, children are only able to engage in parallel play, and their ability to bring new elements into the play activity is limited. To develop the ability to pretend to be someone else and engage in roleplay, the child first needs to be aware that other people have a different centre for their subjective experiences. This does not happen until around the age of 4 years (Neisser, 1993; Trevarthen, 1993, 1994).

The second growth period of the prefrontal cortex, age 2–6 years

During their second year of life, children begin to be able to distinguish between right and wrong. At the age of 2½ years, they are able to deny misbehaving even when they are obviously guilty

(Bruner, 1990). They begin to be able to adapt their behaviour – for example, by hiding emotions that they have learned are unacceptable in order to avoid criticism and harsh reactions from others. Around this age, children also begin to be interested in comparing their own abilities to others' and to construct rules. Reprimands increase the child's stress level at this age, and already from the age of 2 years, children tend to try to avoid reprimands – for example by denying their actions or by redefining them in order to appear blameless. Around the age of 2 years, children interact increasingly with peers, and around the age of 4 years, they begin to establish friendships and to prefer certain children over others. Their capacity for play develops, and from parallel play they now begin to take part in social play, which develops in a co-constructive process. Approximately half of all 4-year-old children will have a special relationship with one particular child, with whom they spend more than 30 per cent of their time. When external circumstances allow, these special relationships often last several years (Hart, 2012, 2013a; Hinde et al., 1985; Shonkoff and Phillips, 2000).

One of the most important competences to develop around the age of 3–5 years old is the capacity for mentalization, as children begin to be able to reflect on others' inner states and actions. Mentalization is the process that lets us realize, for example, that our own perception of the world is not necessarily identical to others'. This enables us to read other people's minds, in a sense, and it helps us predict and make sense of other people's behaviour. Because mentalization is such a crucial aspect of our social function, the development of mental structures for interpreting interpersonal behaviour is crucial for our development of social skills. In this sense, we become active contributors to our own development (Hart and Schwartz, 2008). This capacity for reflection allows children to inhibit a pleasure-driven impulse, for example, because they understand that acting on the impulse might hurt or upset others. It also enables children to engage in dialogue even when they do not feel like it, because they know that dialogue might help them make up with a friend. Mentalization expands our repertoire, so that instead of simply reacting to other people's actions, we can allow our response to be guided by our perception of the other's assumptions, emotions, convictions, desires, hopes, knowledge and ideas. Parental support helps children develop their mentalization capacity and their capacity for reality testing.

This in turn helps children accept and assimilate both pleasant and unpleasant emotions – a capacity that is further developed through play (Fonagy *et al.*, 2002; Hart and Hvilshøj, 2013).

The improvement of the mentalization capacity leads to the development of emotions such as guilt, embarrassment and envy, which emerge around the age of 3 years. Guilt requires an awareness of social norms and of the social expectation to comply with these standards. This understanding is fundamental for the later development of a moral sense. A sense of embarrassment depends on an awareness about how others might judge one's behaviour, which requires imagination. Similarly, envy presupposes an awareness of things that one does not have and which others might find attractive – this too requires a theory of mind (Øvreeide, 2002; Rutter and Rutter, 1993; Sroufe, 1979; van der Kolk, 1986). When the mentalization capacity begins to emerge, children will be able to come to terms with troublesome emotions such as guilt, embarrassment and envy (Dunn, 1996).

In groups, prefrontal impulse management is initially trained in play that does not contain a conflict element. This includes games where the teacher tells the children to stop an activity when they hear the word 'Stop!', or where they are required to do certain things, such as jumping on one leg from the middle of the room to the wall. The mentalization capacity is promoted by shared narratives about shared experiences and by descriptions of emotions and motives in imaginary animals, other children and adults. Symbolic play and narratives are used to create a safe space where difficult emotions and interactions can be explored without the risk of dangerous consequences. The teachers introduce games with symbols and little narratives that feature the children as actors, or they help put the children's own emotions into words. As in limbic, emotional processes the teachers need to be able to integrate the ideas and initiatives that the children come up with, without losing sight of the overall framework of the activity (Hart, 2011). When the group masters shared play narratives, and the children begin to be able to engage in roleplay in small groups, regulating misattunement themselves with occasional adult support, the teachers may begin to include shared narratives about previous shared experiences – for example, a group excursion, with elements of shared as well as individual experiences as support for verbal identity formation. As this requires a high degree of emotional maturity in the group, NASSA and other similar programmes save this for the final sessions (see Chapter 11).

The third growth period of the prefrontal cortex, age 6–12 years

Around the age of 8–10 years, children begin to develop a conscience. This means that they begin to be able to attach a negative emotion to their own actions and assess their own intentionality – for example, when their conscience is troubled by their thoughts about others. At this stage, children have no trouble telling perceived reality from fantastical stories shaped by the desire for social affirmation from oneself and others. They are also beginning to be able to deal with the fact that there are different sides to their own personality. At this stage, children are increasingly able to consider the intention behind an act and can handle having mixed emotions about others (Øvreeide, 2002; Tetzchner, 2002). This development enables the children to reflect on themselves and others from multiple perspectives and to consider and allow for different perspectives without taking a judgemental and rigid view of others. At this stage, the children are able to feel a sense of belonging and build group cohesion, which the teachers can draw on to create a safe space where the children can unfold their creativity without being held back by stated or tacit disapproval, contempt or exclusion. Creating such a space, however, still requires a teacher who is a good 'caravan leader' for the group.

It is not until the age of 9–10 years that children are able to understand that rules are social constructs or common human norms based on consensus and ethics, which are therefore always, in principle, up for negotiation. At this stage, children become increasingly aware that they affect other people's emotions with their actions as well as with their nonverbal expressions of emotions. Pride and guilt come to play a key role, not just in the form of other people's judgement but also in terms of one's own inner assessment. Reflecting on one's own emotions and thoughts is the driver of mentalization and becomes an integrated aspect of a more nuanced self-understanding. Language seems to be a key mechanism for this integration. For example, language combines actions with emotional sensations, and narratives connect sensations, emotions, thoughts and actions in ways that organize both an inner and an outer reality. Language symbols attribute meaning to emotional and perceptual experiences. Therefore, all children's groups should conclude with a final session where the children can reflect on their thoughts and emotions together, being curious about the other children's thoughts and emotions and being able to handle disagreement and integrate different experiential qualities with respect for the differences in the group.

As we have seen, groups have to have a high degree of maturity to achieve a high mentalization capacity, and it is always crucial to meet the children at their actual level rather than aiming too high and seeking to move on before the group is ready. Even if the children in a group may be quite different, this requires a structure that accommodates everyone and allows them to benefit on their own specific level of emotional development. For most children, friendship is a key goal in life. Throughout history, philosophers have studied the nature of friendship. For example, Aristotle stated that a friend is someone who wishes and does what is good, or seems to be good, for the friend's own sake, and who grieves and rejoices with the friend (Annas, 1977). The ability to see oneself from the other's point of view is crucial for the ability to form stable friendships. In order to understand why one's relationships look the way they do, one has to be able to see oneself from the other's perspective. A study by the National Network for Child Care (USA) of what children look for in a friend uncovered the following six implicit criteria (Williams and Asher, 1993):

- Is this child fun to be with?

- Is this child trustworthy?

- Do we influence each other in ways I like?

- Does this child help me achieve my goals?

- Does this child make me feel good about myself?

- Is this child similar to me?

Conclusion

The capacity to balance kindness, altruism, egoism, revenge, justice, etc. is acquired through play. Our moral principles are shaped by the combination of our own emotions and our awareness of how these emotions affect others. Mentalization is the difficult art of being aware of our own emotions and striving to understand both our own and others' emotions. As Erik H. Erikson (1972) pointed out, play is not a phase that children go through and leave behind but an inherent competence and urge that healthy, thriving children and adults carry with them throughout life. By encouraging children to play, we support their integration of social and emotional abilities. Play supports creative and innovative aspects of human life, and a cornerstone of play is that the adult is able to communicate via his or her facial expression that this is play, not real-life danger, for example. Many social skills are acquired in the world of pretend play (Cohen, 2006). Humans have evolved to feel a need for belonging and acceptance. Sometimes, this need clashes with the delicate balance between competition and cooperation, egoism and social needs, conflict and harmony; this balance is the focus of Chapter 3. As humans, we balance on a knife's edge between pursuing our own narrow interests and pursuing our need to connect with others. The two are related, and children learn to balance between these extremes through social activities with other children – through play. Emotional learning is a complicated affair!

For decades, many educators have sought not only to evaluate children's cognitive skills in specific subjects but also their emotional skills. Edward Zigler (Zigler and Bishop-Josef, 2006; Zigler and Trickett, 1978), who is now a professor emeritus of psychology at Yale University and who was one of the initiators of the American Head Start programme, argued 30 years ago that the assessment criteria for children should be expanded to include social skills as a key goal for success in schools. Already then, he saw it as essential to be able to assess both children's cognitive skills and their social skills with peers, school attendance, etc., as part of a global assessment of the full and diverse range of children's skills.

Children come into this world with an innate motivation for development and a drive to engage in interactions with their environment through play and other activities. This innate development capacity has to be met with relevant responses to optimize the child's development. What capacities the environment promotes, and how, is inherently a cultural project. The prevailing culture shapes the way parents respond to their child and the way that teachers and peers meet the child later in life. It is important to consider the interaction between the child's inherent potential and the cultural project – in other words, how parents and teachers perceive their own role and how they interact with the child. This context can either act as a source of conflict and stress or form the supportive context that facilitates the child's development (Hart and Bentzen, 2015).

References

Annas, J. (1977) 'Plato and Aristotle on friendship and altruism.' *Mind 86*(344), 532–554.

Bruner, J. S. (1983) *Child's Talk: Learning to Use Language.* New York, NY: W. W. Norton.

Bruner, J. S. (1990) *Acts of Meaning: Four Lectures on Mind and Culture.* Cambridge, MA: Harvard University Press.

Cohen, D. (2006) *The Development of Play* (3rd edn). London: Routledge.

Damasio, A. R. (1999) *The Feeling of What Happens: Body and Emotion in the Making of Consciousness.* New York, NY: Harcourt Brace.

de Waal, F. (2006) *Our Inner Ape: The Best and Worst of Human Nature.* London: Granta Books.

Dunn, J. (1996) 'The Emanuel Miller Memorial Lecture 1995. Children's relationships: Bridging the divide between cognitive and social development.' *Journal of Child Psychology and Psychiatry 37*(5), 507–518.

Ekman, P. (2003) *Emotions Revealed.* London: Weidenfeld & Nicolson.

Emde, R. N. (1985) 'The Affective Self: Continuities and Transformations from Infancy.' In J. D. Call, E. Galensch and R. L. Tyson (eds) *Frontiers of Infant Psychiatry* (vol. 2). New York, NY: Basic Books.

Emde, R. N. (1989) 'The Infant's Relationship Experience.' In A. J. Sameroff and R. N. Emde (eds) *Relationship Disturbances in Early Childhood: A Developmental Approach.* New York, NY: Basic Books.

Erikson, E. H. (1972) 'Play and Actuality.' In M. Piers (ed.) *Play and Development.* New York, NY: W. W. Norton.

Fagen, R. (1981) *Animal Play Behaviour.* New York, NY: Oxford University Press.

Flavell, J. H., Lindberg, N. A., Green, F. L. and Flavell, E. R. (1992) 'The development of children's understanding of the appearance-reality distinction between how people look and what they are really like.' *Merrill Palmer Quarterly 38*(4), 513–524.

Fonagy, P., Gergely, G., Jurist, E. L. and Target, M. (2002) *Affect Regulation, Mentalization and the Development of the Self.* New York, NY: Other Press

Harris, P. L., Brown, E., Marriott, C., Whittal, S. and Harner, S. (1991) 'Monsters, ghosts, and witches: Testing the limits of the appearance reality distinction.' *British Journal of Developmental Psychology 9*(1), 105–125.

Hart, S. (2008) *Brain, Attachment, Personality: An Introduction to Neuroaffective Development.* London: Karnac Books.

Hart, S. (ed.) (2011) *Neuroaffektiv Psykoterapi med Børn.* Copenhagen: Hans Reitzels Forlag.

Hart, S. (ed.) (2012) *Neuroaffektiv Psykoterapi med Voksne.* Copenhagen: Hans Reitzels Forlag.

Hart, S. (2013a) 'Det er en Køn Historie.' In C. Bendixen and H. Fischer (eds) *Psykologi i Skolen: Hvad Virker?* Copenhagen: Hans Reitzels Forlag.

Hart, S. (2013b) 'Sprog før sproget.' *Kognition and Pædagogik 23*(90), 40–58.

Hart, S. and Bentzen, M. (2015) *Through Windows of Opportunity: A Neuroaffective Approach to Child Psychotherapy.* London: Karnac Books.

Hart, S. and Hvilshøj, H. (eds) (2013) *Ledelse Mellem Hjerne og Hjerte: Om Mentalisering og Neuroaffektivt lederskab.* Copenhagen: Hans Reitzels Forlag.

Hart, S. and Schwartz, R. (2008) *Fra Interaktion til Relation: Tilknytning hos Winnicott, Bowlby, Stern, Schore and Fonagy.* Copenhagen: Hans Reitzels Forlag.

Hinde, R. A., Titmus, G., Easton, D. and Tamplin, A. (1985) 'Incidence of "friendship" and behavior toward strong associates versus nonassociates in preschoolers.' *Child Development 56*(1), 234–245.

Howes, C. and Matheson, C. (1992) 'Play sequences.' *Developmental Psychology 28*, 59–75.

Ladd, G. W. and Hart, C. (1992) 'Networking in the American toddler.' *Developmental Psychology 28*(6), 1179–1187.

Lewis, T., Amini, F. and Lannon, R. (2001) *A General Theory of Love.* New York, NY: Vintage Books.

MacLean, P. D. (1990) *The Triune Brain in Evolution: Role in Paleocerebral Functions.* New York, NY: Plenum.

Meltzoff, A. N. and Moore, V. (1977) 'Imitation of facial and manual gestures by human neonates.' *Science 198*, 75–78.

Meltzoff, A. N. and Moore, M. K. (1999) 'Persons and Representations: Why Infant Imitation is Important for Theories of Human Development.' In J. Nadel and G. Butterworth (eds) *Imitation in Infancy.* Cambridge: Cambridge University Press.

Neisser, U. (1993) 'The Self Perceived.' In U. Neisser (ed.) *The Perceived Self: Ecological and Interpersonal Sources of Self Knowledge.* Cambridge: Cambridge University Press.

Øvreeide, H. (2002) *Samtaler med Barn: Metodiske Samtaler med Barn i Vanskelige Livssituasjoner.* Kristiansand: Høyskoleforlaget.

Panksepp, J. (1998) *Affective Neuroscience: The Foundations of Human and Animal Emotions.* New York: Oxford University Press.

Panksepp, J. and Biven, L. (2012) *The Archaeology of Mind: Neuroevolutionary Origins of Human Emotions.* London: W. W. Norton.

Pellegrini, A. D. (2009) *The Role of Play in Human Development.* New York, NY: Oxford University Press.

Rutter, M. and Rutter, M. (1993) *Developing Minds: Challenge and Continuity Across the Life Span.* New York, NY: Basic Books.

Shonkoff, J. P. and Phillips, D. (eds) (2000) *From Neurons to Neighborhoods: The Science of Early Child Development.* Washington, DC: National Academies Press.

Sroufe, L. A. (1979) 'Socioemotional Development.' In J. D. Osofsky (ed.) *Handbook of Infant Development.* New York, NY: John Wiley.

Stern, D. N. (1985) *The Interpersonal World of the Infant: A View from Psychoanalysis and Development.* New York, NY: Basic Books.

Tetzchner, S. (2002) *Utviklingspsykologi: Barne- og Ungdomsalderen.* Oslo: Gyldendal Akademisk.

Trevarthen, C. (1993) 'An Infant's Motives for Speaking and Thinking in the Culture.' In A. H. Wold (ed.) *The Dialogical Alternative.* Oslo: Scandinavian University Press.

Trevarthen, C. (1994) 'The Self Born in Intersubjectivity: The Psychology of an Infant Communicating.' In U. Neisser (ed.) *The Perceived Self: Ecological and Interpersonal Sources of Self Knowledge.* Cambridge: Cambridge University Press.

van der Kolk, B. A. (1986) *Psychological Trauma.* Washington, DC: American Psychiatric Press.

Vygotsky, L. S. (1978) *Mind in Society: The Development of Higher Psychological Processes.* Cambridge, MA: Harvard University Press.

Williams, G. A. and Asher, S. R. (1993) 'Children without friends: Learning about a child's strengths and weaknesses.' *Day Care Center Connections 3*(2), 3–4.

Zigler, E. and Bishop-Josef, S. (2006) 'The Cognitive Child vs. the Whole Child: Lessons from 40 Years of Head Start.' In D. G. Singer, R. Michnick-Golinkoff and K. Hirsh-Pasek (eds) *Play = Learning: How Children's Play Motivates and Enhances Children's Cognitive, and Social-Emotional Growth.* Oxford: Oxford University Press.

Zigler, E. and Trickett, P. (1978) 'I.Q., social competence, and evolution of early childhood intervention programs.' *American Psychologist 33*(9), 789–798.

3

Should School Be a Place
for Fun and Games?

Susan Hart

Play exists among all mammals and in all human cultures. Regardless of where children live and what language they speak, they engage and are expected to engage in playful activities. Play is such a common and normal activity, especially among children but also among adults (e.g. in sports competitions, etc.), that some cultures consider play to be the 'job' or 'work' of childhood (Smith, 2010). The German-born pedagogue Friedrich Fröbel (1782–1852), for example, sought to foster his students' play impulse and self-agency by varying between play, crafts activities and outings, and he argued that children should receive age-appropriate support at every stage, and that childhood is not only to be seen as a preparation for life but as an important part of life itself. He believed that it was important to awaken the child's self-agency rather than instilling factual knowledge, and he viewed play as the highest achievement of child development (cited in Rusk, 1967, pp.60–61). In Chapter 1, Trevarthen and Panksepp described how children's desire to learn stems from an inherent capacity for curiosity and attention. This inherent capacity forms the basis of learning and should be supported by the teacher's structured, engaged approach, driven by understanding of the individual children's emotional and cognitive levels. Both the teacher's and the child's well-being depends on a mutual experience of attachment, of playful experimentation and the joy of shared meaning-making. Old knowledge is transferred to the next generation, and new ways of understanding one's world are generated in attachment-based communities, where no one needs to fear bullying or exclusion. We can only develop self-esteem and confidence if we manage to keep joy in our lives, and play is the perfect arena for doing just that. This chapter describes how teachers can tap into the potential of the human capacity for play, and how they can promote not only the children's cognitive competences but also their emotional, personal and social competences through playful activities.

Emotions as the 'glue' of human relationships

The human mind is hugely complex, and it gives us a clear survival benefit to enter into prosocial communities, which to a large extent develop through play. Thus, our emotions and our social skills are the 'glue' that binds us together in human communities, and they develop in a relational context. Already from the first day of life, the infant has inherent capacities for interacting with others. For a child to be able to unfold his or her innate potential, as described in Chapter 2, the caregivers have to have an intuitive capacity for synchronizing with the child and support the child's development process in a mutual sharing of experiences through early playful behaviour.

In school, cognitive and language skills play an important role, but the basis of emotional attunement is the interactive process that might be called 'language before language'. Thus, even though of course the teacher uses words, the emotional integration process lies in the symmetrical synchronization based on body language, facial expressions, tone of voice, the rhythmic quality of touch and the voice. In the engaging contact with a person that the child perceives as trustworthy, safe and calm, and who is able to synchronize with the child, the child begins to be able to regulate his or her nervous system (Hart, 2013).

When the child is unable to establish an interaction, he or she either loses control and acts out or withdraws and seeks to calm him or herself down by means of self-stimulation or passivity. As described in Chapter 1, Colwyn Trevarthen and Jaak Panksepp (see also Trevarthen, 1979, 1993) found that it is the precise match in the interactions and vitality of the contact that drive pleasant engagement. Moments of communicative exchanges through playful activities contribute to the child's capacity for forming and maintaining emotional bonds while also developing a capacity for self-regulation, which is ultimately what drives the development of the mentalization capacity. As described in

Chapter 2, the mentalization capacity lets us read other people's minds, in a sense; it is the process that lets us know that our own perception of the world is not necessarily identical to others'. The mentalization capacity also involves our ability to understand and reflect on our own emotions, that is, the ability to see ourselves from the outside while seeing others from the inside – understanding their emotions (Fonagy *et al.*, 2002). These competences develop at a high level in the brain hierarchy – in the prefrontal cortex – and they can only unfold once our emotional structures have matured. The adult's stance helps the child shape his or her self-perception and self-esteem. The child needs to feel that the world is manageable and that there is a clear authority figure in charge. If these conditions are missing, the world is perceived as unsafe and frightening.

Engaging activities contain pleasant stimulation, and variation enables the child to understand that surprises may be fun and that new experiences may be enjoyable. Engaging activities usually involve eye contact, potentially physical contact and attention to the other's reactions, and in many cases there are moments of shared surprise and enjoyment. Showing the child that one enjoys his or her company and that the child is a person it is a pleasure to be with helps strengthen the child's self-esteem and self-worth. We all feel a sense of joy and pride when we reach the goals we have set for ourselves, or when our needs are met, and we feel uncomfortable and frustrated when we fail to reach the goals that are important to us (Hart, 2013). It is important for us to have challenges that we can handle in order to develop feelings of competence, confidence and self-agency, and play is an important platform for acquiring these types of competences. By providing opportunities for physical, motor and sensory activity, early play offers an important precursor of pretend play and roleplay, which involves elements of planning, rehearsal, fantasy, problem-solving, social agility, language, communication and empathic processes, which are essential for all forms of human contact (Burghardt, 2005).

As Jerome Bruner (1983) points out, play helps the child acquire the social norms that form the basis of later communication through verbal dialogues. According to an old English motto, you have to play the games to learn the rules of life. The socialization that takes place in play prepares us to take part in the many exchanges and interactions of life. Thus, it is not the content of play that matters but the way in which parents and children engage in the many varied interactions.

The learning aspect of play is that the child is able to test his or her own and others' boundaries and learn new skills in a safe context, since, after all, it is only a game. In this process, smiles and laughter play a key role. They are important signals that tell the child that there is no danger or threat. The child needs to trust the adults and also be allowed to experience a certain sense of omnipotence – for example, by having the adults give themselves a handicap and creating a world where the child can pretend to be the stronger of the two. As the famous paediatrician and psychoanalyst Donald Winnicott (1964) explained, the potential space of play fosters self-worth in the child because it offers a space where the child can have his or her dreams come true in a relation context without hallucinating. As he also explains, it is easy to see that children play to have fun, while it is far more difficult to see that children also play in order to master anxiety or to master ideas and impulses that cause anxiety if they are outside one's control.

Svend Brinkmann (2011) points out that we can only develop self-awareness in relationships with others; one might add that relationships develop and mature through playful interactions. Emotions communicate what we need to do (e.g. withdrawing in case of fear, seeking comfort in case of grief, etc.) and they often helps us to maintain social ties. Emotions motivate us to act – for example, anger motivates fighting, guilt motivates us to apologize, joy motivates us to be helpful, etc. – and many of these emotions are trained in a playful pretend space. Without emotions, other people cannot mean anything to us in a deeper sense, and relationships with significant others are crucial for our ability to develop an own identity and self-awareness. We cannot avoid spontaneous emotions, but we can learn to become aware of them and to decide whether to act on them or not. This is an ability that takes time to develop as it presupposes the existence of a mentalization capacity. It is an ability we often take for granted in adults, although it is not always very well developed, but all forms of attention deficits and behavioural disorders can be traced back to diminished activity in certain parts of the frontal lobes. The training of our capacity to control needs and urges, attention functions, etc., takes place in playful activities. As David Cohen (2006) points out, active and energetic spontaneous physical play stimulates neural circuits in the frontal lobes, and as Jaak Panksepp (1998) points out, physical play contributes to our self-regulation capacity. All mammals, even rats, spend a great deal of time play-fighting and rough-housing. When the need for physical activity is met, the organism calms down again. Play helps children develop social skills, including turn-taking, roleplay, switching hierarchical positions, looking out for each other, expressing care and closeness, etc.

The importance of attachment processes

Children need appreciation and recognition to be able to develop emotionally, which means that the child's primary adults have to be emotionally accessible and able to empathize with the child's needs. This recognition gives the child a sense of being entitled to his or her own feelings, and it is a precondition for developing adaptive relational strategies and social skills (Hart, 2011b). We develop self-esteem and confidence by encountering tasks that we can handle, and which we receive recognition for dealing with. Whether we are children or adults, it helps us to feel happy and secure if we receive attention, interest and contact from our peers as well as others who have a higher position in the social hierarchy.

A growing body of research is demonstrating that children can overcome even massive neglect from their own parents. A classic study (Werner and Schmidt, 2001) followed a group of children born in 1955 for more than 40 years, focusing especially on the subjects who did well despite several social risk factors. A third of the children were born in at-risk families, including families characterized by instability and numerous conflicts. The study showed that most of the children and youths had developed behavioural disorders and learning difficulties and mental disorders when surveyed at the age of 10 years and again at 18 years. A third of the children, however, could be characterized as resilient: they grew up to be harmonious, well-functioning, happy and helpful adults. The study had three main conclusions concerning the resilient children: they were of normal intelligence; they had developed emotional attachment bonds to a near relative or significant other; and they had access to a system, such as school, which rewarded their competences and afforded them possibilities for cooperating with other youths and adults. As we see from this, parent–child interactions have a considerable impact on children's coping skills and their social interactions with others. For example, in a study involving families with 4–6-year-old children, Kahen, Katz and Gottman (1994) found that the children of positive parents who frequently engaged their child in emotional communication had a much easier time establishing friendships and engaging in creative play with their peers. Children whose mothers express many negative emotions or neutrality in their contact with the child often appear fearful and have limited facial expressions. Erratic parents who vary unpredictably between positive and negative communication, who constantly interfere with the child's actions or who use sarcasm often have children who are reluctant to engage in playful relationships – the children of these parents are more negative and experience more conflicts. The child's ability to engage in social interactions and, at a later stage, sophisticated roleplay seems to depend to a high degree on the parents' ability to stimulate the child in synchronized interactions (Pellis and Pellis, 2009).

The child's attachment pattern (i.e. whether the child has a secure or insecure attachment pattern with the parents) also seems to have a significant impact on the child's later ability to engage in roleplay. Roleplay is important for the child's ability to engage in adaptive cooperation relationships later in life. For example, research (Perner, Ruffman and Leekam, 1994) has found that when children are around 3–4 years old, their ability to engage in roleplay is the best predictor for their later capacity for engaging in cooperative relationships and embracing another person's perspective. In roleplay, children typically rehearse their ability to put themselves in someone else's place, also in order to achieve something for themselves. In a sense, children need to mentalize in order to build a balanced 'we'. In roleplay, they learn to negotiate a variety of roles. Several studies, including ones by Fonagy, Redfern and Charman (1997) and Meins (1997), have found that the child's mentalization capacities are already well developed at the age of 4 years, provided the caregiver has shown empathy, been receptive to the child's comments, actions and perspective and viewed the child as possessing independent agency. An Australian training study in a preschool class (quoted in Smith, 2010, p.192) looked at roleplay and children's ability to put themselves in someone else's place. Prior to the training study, the researchers had tested all the children's ability to engage in roleplay and put themselves in someone else's place. One group then received play training for four weeks, where the play was about starting up a pizzeria, and where the teachers initiated the play development. The control group continued with their usual activities. The children were then tested immediately after the training had stopped and again three weeks later. In both tests, the training group showed an increased capacity for engaging in complex roleplay and for understanding something from another person's perspective. The study demonstrated that social negotiation and verbal communication in social roleplay with others had helped the children develop mentalization skills.

As Bretherton (1989) and Gordon (1993) pointed out, pretend play and roleplay not only promote the mentalization process; through play, the child also learns to master difficult emotions, including more commonly occurring emotions such as being afraid of the dark, family conflicts, etc. Play is, indeed, the most common way for children to overcome fear, anger and grief; this means that children depend on being able to engage in social relationships and complex roleplay in order to regulate and process their emotions. Children with insecure attachment patterns, who have difficulty engaging in social relationships, are thus much more vulnerable when it comes to handling difficult emotions, because they are less able to benefit from pretend play and roleplay. Children with an insecure attachment pattern who have been subjected to emotional trauma are often more aggressive or depressive and may show more controlling and domineering behaviour when they play. They have difficulty finding solutions to handle negative emotional experiences in the themes that come up in play; they show less coordination with others; their play is often more chaotic; and there is less pretend play. There are thus strong indications to suggest that pretend play and roleplay promote the child's development of coping skills for emotional self-regulation (Smith, 2010). The core of empathy is the ability to match another person's emotion and show a synchronized response. Positive attunement generates mutual trust and drives the establishment of interpersonal bonds. A secure and empathic relationship generates an inner sense of security and enables us to create a safe environment. That requires a 'caravan leader' – a parent or a teacher who has to be involved and engaged and offer both verbal and nonverbal acknowledgement to be able to build the sense of safety that enables children to bring out their best.

Macro- and micro-regulation

Human development processes involved both macro- and micro-regulation processes. The regulation of macro-rhythms is about creating structures, frameworks and predictability – for example, eating patterns, diurnal rhythms, etc. Micro-rhythms are the near-invisible synchronizations that did not become visible until the invention of film and video cameras, and which are a key area of study in modern developmental psychology.

Back in the 1950s Louis Sander (Sander *et al.*, 2008) introduced the concept of biorhythmicity and microscopic aspects of the caregiver's interactions with the infant regulation. I combine these concepts in the concept of micro-regulation. Sander explained that it depends on the ability of the child's primary adult caregivers to engage in shared activity with the child. The sense of being connected or being on the same wavelength arises through the mutual influence on each other in the dyad. This sense of connectedness is established through mutual synchronized regulation, which plays a crucial role for the organization of the brain and the regulation processes of the central nervous system. The synchronized interaction may give rise to so-called 'present moments'. For example, when a mother and an infant engage each other in a well-regulated interaction, a certain smile from the child that the mother finds surprising or funny can make her look at the child with a big smile, which makes them both laugh. Most present moments are positive, and misattunements are rare. In fact, most misattunements are repaired so quickly that they are never registered on a conscious level, and in many cases, it is the repair of a misattunement (e.g. the surprise) that makes mother and child break out laughing and thus creates the present moment. The present moment is experienced as an authentic meeting, which provides nourishment and simulation for the nervous system to develop. Moments of meeting may also involve confrontations, however – for example, when the 1-year-old child needs to learn not to throw his or her food on the floor or open the door to the freezer. The beginning of this moment of meeting occurs when the parent connects with the child; the climax consists in a clear misattunement, where the caregiver shows that he or she is serious; and the end is when the caregiver distracts the child's attention and helps him or her escape from the unpleasant situation. All moments of meeting, pleasant as well as unpleasant, involve moving into the moment, sharing the moment and moving away from the moment. The transfer of emotional information is intensified in the present moments, which develop the nervous system's emerging capacity for self-regulation and attention control (Sander, 1988, 1992; Schore, 2003a, 2003b; Sroufe, 1996; Stern, 1977, 1990, 1998, 2004).

The micro-regulation processes, which are the real driving force of emotional maturation, are difficult to describe and require a trained eye to observe. They all include a beginning, a climax and an end, like a piece of music. As described by Trevarthen and Panksepp in Chapter 1, already during the child's first year of life, a rhythm develops between infant and caregiver based on the caregiver's intimate care, emotional expressions and his or her hands, eyes, face and voice. The authors call this mutual sympathy, which springs from shared body movements, 'synrhythmic'. Throughout the new development phases of life, there is a growing exchange of emotions related to joy-filled as well as frustrating emotions. The desire to enter into an intersubjective field with another is important for the formation relationships and is only possible in the moment. Psychological states are reflected through the child's and the caregiver's behaviour towards one another; and when they meet in this shared moment, the meeting expands the experience for both of them. Most people have the potential to build emotional connections. As Stern (2004) points out, we develop emotional skills by living in the present, through implicitly learned interactions.

In discussions about parenting, the focus tends to be on macro-regulation – how adults can use behavioural regulation to make children accept the given structure. Macro-regulation is very important as structuring, boundaries and predictable contact are the source of security and a stable self-image. In other words, teachers have to create a framework that is structured, clear, unambiguous, understandable and predictable, where the children are prepared for what is going to happen. Rhythms, predictability and structure foster a reassuring sense of security. The more insecure children are, the more maladaptive behaviour they display, and the greater is their need for structure and attunement. Many pedagogical approaches that are based on rewarding adaptive behaviour and punishing maladaptive behaviour completely fail to consider the child's emotional development level. If the parents have given the child more decision-making influence than the child can handle, this can make it difficult for the child to accept boundaries and structure. In that case, the child might benefit from clearer boundaries. It may also be necessary to introduce control measures to stop antisocial behaviour. However, micro-regulation is a condition for personal and emotional development, and it is not enough to regulate the child's behaviour without also addressing the child's relational capacity, which is needed to improve attachment and self-esteem. Macro-regulation without micro-regulation is brutal, but macro-regulation is a necessary condition for effective micro-regulation. If the child does not have a secure setting, a predictable external structure with specific expectations and recurring features and predictability, such as a regular bedtime, regular meals, etc., it is not possible to work on micro-rhythms. Thus, although macro-rhythms are not the source of emotional change processes, they are the condition for the establishment of micro-regulation rhythms (Hart, 2008, 2011b, 2013; Schwartz and Hart, 2013).

As mentioned earlier, macro-regulation is expressed through structures and boundaries and often involves clear consequences in case the boundaries are violated. Frans de Waal (2006) describes how even baby chimpanzees that have been reprimanded for bad behaviour will try to make up for their transgression. First, the chimpanzee sulks and whimpers until it cannot stand that any more. Next, it climbs on to its mother's lap and wraps its arms tight around followed by an audible sigh of relief when she comforts it. Today, we are living in a culture where many parents and educators find it difficult to set the necessary boundaries for the children they care for. When the children react by constantly insisting on their rights, they often encounter anger and rejection from adults, but cooperation and peace-making is something all primates have to learn, and that begins when the child is weaned and is framed by attachment and the early parent–child relationship.

As de Waal (2006) explains, even a chimpanzee mother will briefly push the infant away from her breast when it is being weaned but allow it to feed when it screams and objects. The interval between rejection and acceptance increases as the young chimpanzee grows older, and conflicts can grow into major dramas. Parents and children bring different weapons to this power struggle. The parents are stronger and smarter and more intelligent, while the child can muster vocalization and crying designed to soften the parents' resolve. The child will try to lure the parents in by showing signs of stress (e.g. with intense crying), and if that fails, the child may throw a temper tantrum where the child almost chokes on his or her own screaming. Weaning conflicts are the first negotiation with a social partner we encounter in life, complete with opposed interests and meetings of both a negative and positive character, which should ideally result in a compromise. Preserving the crucial attachment bond with one's parents despite disagreements forms the foundation for being able to resolve conflicts later in life.

The next step is to negotiate deals and achieve reconciliation with one's peers, another important skill that we acquire early in life. Any group strikes its own balance between competition and cooperation, and this applies both to humans and to apes. De Waal (2006) points out that the first cultural communication takes place in the meeting between parents and infant. In any parent–child constellation and in any culture it is important to consider whether one wants to teach the child to go for his or her own rights or to find mutually acceptable solutions and thus embrace a shared responsibility for the well-being of the group.

Micro-regulation processes enable children to develop a sense of attachment, care and acknowledgment but also awareness of others and the need to consider their needs. The importance of shared and attuned experiences can be illustrated, for example, with Tronick *et al.*'s (1978) famous 'still face' experiment, where infants first interact with their mothers in a mutual interaction, and then the mothers are asked to stop responding to the infants' initiatives and to render their faces expressionless in the middle of an interaction. In this experiment, the infant will take the initiative to revitalize the mother, trying various strategies to bring her out of her unresponsive, expressionless state. The infant's reactions when these attempts fail demonstrate the crucial importance of attunement. Even though the mothers in Tronick *et al.*'s (1978) experiment only remained expressionless for two minutes, the infants found the temporary breach extremely disturbing. When the child is denied a pleasant interaction, he or she loses interest in the outside world. The child is unable to engage in the external world without the caregiver's involvement (Hart, 2011b; Hart and Hvilshøj, 2013; Tronick, 2007). When infants do not receive adequate pleasant stimulation, they are not encouraged to engage in the mutual experiences that are needed for them to display and develop their creativity (Hart, 2011b). Children need engaged and authentic teachers, and the less confidence and self-esteem they have developed, the more external approval they will need, which is reflected in the micro-regulation processes.

From individual to dyad to socialization in groups

Children learn to play in asymmetrical relationships, but they train their play capacity in symmetrical relationships. Mutual playful interactions between parents and children, such as noisy play-fighting with dad, seem to play an important role in helping children constrain and control their aggression. In this context, children learn to regulate mutual exchanges with peers that do not lead to a higher level of frustration and aggression than they can handle. Children also learn to regulate their emotions in peer interactions. Kittens, puppies and children all run into trouble with their playmates and are met with rejection if they are consistently unable to inhibit their impulses (Pellis and Pellis, 2009).

Early play relationships develop many social life skills, and there are strong indications to suggest a link between children's ability to assess and understand others' thoughts and emotions and their ability to take part in shared pretend play. Children's understanding of social relationships develops when they engage in conflict resolution where they need to consider others' points of view and reconcile after a disagreement and through repeated experiences with sharing, arguing and negotiating in a pretend world where they encounter others' opinions and perspectives. Turn-taking, sharing toys, maintaining shared attention in play, incorporating each other's ideas in play, agreeing on ground rules, etc., are all experiences that promote children's social awareness and thus their emotional capacity and personality. The willingness to understand others, establish shared ground rules and tolerate and resolve conflicts incurs important skills for engaging in close and equal relationships in adult life. This development begins in dyadic parent–infant relationships, and throughout childhood it unfolds in larger groups. Initially, these important skills are trained in asymmetrical relationships, for example with the parents, but later, peer exchanges provide experiences with symmetrical interactions where children need to regulate their own nervous system and take responsibility for regulating shared arousal and interactions.

Group socialization involves symmetrical peer interactions with mutually satisfying activities, and the ability to develop good interactions, peer relationships and friendships that children learn in school is central for the formation of social relationships in their later adult lives. One example of this type of skills is checking that everyone in the group is included. This is crucial both in childhood and in adulthood and involves making sure, for example, that everyone is involved in a game or a conversation, that everyone gets their turn, that everyone participates more or less equally, etc. Group socialization is also about the issue of hierarchy and social status. Stable social hierarchies are important in social groups, because they provide 'traffic rules', determining who goes first, for example, which helps reduce the number conflicts and leaves more time for prosocial contacts and other types of activities (Shonkoff and Phillips, 2000).

Both the friendship aspect and the status aspect are important motivating factors in human communities, including families and collegial relationships.

Although play between parents and children is important, children can also develop social skills in prosocial play-based communities. For example, studies have found that maladjusted children may benefit from spending time with well-adjusted children, which is also the case for other highly developed social mammals. For example, Stephen Suomi and Harry Harlow (1972) put a group of maladjusted rhesus monkeys together with a group of younger, socially normal monkeys. They found that the older and stronger monkeys that had been raised by a surrogate mother and therefore were less socially competent than their younger playmates were able to develop better social skills by playing with the younger, socially normal monkeys. By engaging in playful interactions, both the older deprived and maladjusted monkeys and the younger monkeys were able to develop competent social skills such as turn-taking, including inhibiting aggressive responses, especially during rough-and-tumble play. Already in the 1960s, Harry Harlow suggested that social play enhances emotional regulation, and he pointed out that rhesus monkeys that play with their mothers and with peers (e.g. through rough-and-tumble play) learn to moderate their emotional responses to unclear and socially provoking behaviour. For example, they learn to tell the difference between intentional and accidental behaviour. Later studies (Pellis and Pellis, 2006) found that children similarly learn to regulate their emotional responses through play. One of the motivating factors in play, especially in social play, is its unpredictability – we never know what is going to happen next. When this unpredictability occurs in a safe environment, where the children know each other well and feel secure, the play relationship can handle a fair amount of unpredictability. This safe space gives the children the courage to take chances and accept risks (Pellegrini, Dupuis and Smith, 2007; Pellis and Pellis, 2006; Spinka, Newbury and Bekoff, 2001).

Conflict resolution

Conflict resolution is part of any social culture. Preschool and school teachers have to be able to tolerate conflicts, because the only way the children can learn from conflicts is if they have the chance to encounter them. If two rats are placed on a steel plate and simultaneously subjected to an electric shock, they will instantly attack each other, the moment they feel the pain. Rats never hesitate to blame the other. Baboons project aggression in a similar manner. For example, if a male baboon loses a confrontation, it will not hesitate to take its frustration out on a smaller baboon, which serves to reduce the loser's stress levels. Instead of withdrawing to lick its wounds, it is quick to pass the problem on to someone else. In mammal societies, this tendency seems to be more pronounced among males. Males prefer to give someone else an ulcer instead of developing one themselves. Humans do the same by finding victims to blame based on skin colour, religion, a foreign accent, etc. Learning to take responsibility for one's own wins and losses is a lengthy process, and apparently, reducing stress at the cost of fairness and justice is a deeply ingrained tactic (de Waal, 2006).

Chimpanzees, too, seek sympathy and soothing. An agitated or frightened chimpanzee seeks physical contact from others, and when it is successful, the soothing effect is instant. For example, a screaming, howling male chimpanzee may run towards other monkeys to touch, kiss and hug them in the throes of frustration, begging for support by holding out its arm. Both chimps and people seem to put a high price on reconciliation and repairing valuable friendships (de Waal, 1982, 2006).

Both chimpanzees and people form attachment bonds through humour and laughter. Laughter activates the brain's reward centres, which generates pleasant emotions. This even occurs if we simply watch someone else laugh, probably due to our many mirror neurons. Not surprisingly, people also begin to laugh when they are confronted with uncomfortable social situations, probably in order to feel more confident but also in order to show their counterpart that the confrontation is not so serious. Both laughter and humour probably evolved as a means of reducing stress and facilitating the process of attachment and bonding. Children often justify an inappropriate act by saying that they only did it in fun, in an attempt to defuse the situation and a loss of status (Pellis and Pellis, 2009).

Social hierarchies

The instinctive behaviour that drives the formation of social hierarchies emerged early in evolution. For example, fish and reptiles establish ranks, and ranking in social groups exists in all social mammals. A social hierarchy can be understood as a set of social norms that governs individuals' behaviour and rights, based on their social standing (Cummins, 2000, 2006; Hart, 2012). To avoid the punishment of exclusion, group members therefore have to find their place in the hierarchy with the rights, obligations, possibilities and prohibitions that come with that particular position. This sort of ranking requires continuous clarification and enforcement to work, and higher-placed individuals will punish behaviour that violates the norms, but they also often put a stop to conflicts between lower-ranking individuals or mediate between higher-ranking group members (de Waal, 1996; Hart and Hvilshøj, 2013). In all species, animals can achieve and maintain a high status in two ways: through aggression and threats or through prosocial contacts, which includes both direct exchanges and social control based on higher-ranking animals modelling good behaviour. In other words, high-status behaviour can be expressed both through ranking and physical or social aggression and through protection, generosity and conflict mediation. Among animals and people, those at the top of the hierarchy may rely on both aggressive and prosocial interactions; and while some prefer prosocial strategies, others will be quicker to resort to threatening or punishing behaviour.

Stable social hierarchies play an important role in social groups by modelling ways of being together. An example of this type of skill is the capacity for turn-taking, which involves both waiting one's turn, taking one's turn when it is time, ending one's turn again and, on a higher level of development, checking that everyone has been included. This involves, for example, checking whether all the children are included in the game, or, in adult groups, whether everyone is involved in the conversation.

Hierarchies and status-regulating behaviour form one of the two key interaction types that exist among many social mammals, and which reach an exceptional level of sophistication in human groups. The other type revolves around symmetrical peer interactions, which involve mutually satisfying activities such as playing or socializing, which are acquired through the human capacity for attachment. The ability to form good interactions and build friendship bonds is very important, and the social skills that children rehearse during their preschool and school years are central to the formation of adult social relationships.

In ordinary social groups, status relations and friendships are interwoven. Symmetrical friendship relations generally have a reassuring and stress-regulation effect. Howling, asymmetrical friendships also offer benefits. While high-status individuals derive social support from friendships and alliances with lower-status individuals and thus diminish the risk of losing status, lower-status individuals often enjoy protection against attacks from others in the social group. Both symmetrical and asymmetrical friendships are created and maintained through mutual obligations and favours (de Waal, 1982, 1996; Goodall, 1986) and are necessary for keeping order in the group. Children develop a sensitivity to social hierarchies while they are still very young. Imitation is one of the earliest contact forms that children use to initiate contact with other children, and already at the age of 2 years, children prefer to imitate higher-status children rather than lower-status children. Status-oriented behaviour, such as actions aimed at excluding individual children or deciding who can play with whom, is clearly evident in 3-year-old children, both boys and girls (Card *et al.*, 2008; Cummins, 2006).

Differences between boys' and girls' groups, and between male and female 'caravan leaders'

There appear to be differences in the way boys and girls play, generally. Boys are more likely to play outdoors and to play in large groups with a clear hierarchical structure. Their groups typically have a leader who tells the others what to do and how to do it, and he opposes other boys' suggestions. Boys negotiate high status based on issuing orders and by sticking together. Boys' play has winners and losers, and they set up systems based on rules that are frequently debated. In the boys' hierarchical world, status matters. The way to achieve and preserve status is to issue orders and make others follow them, and low-status boys are pushed around. The intensification of aggressiveness and the suppression of vulnerability enable boys to gain status in their peer groups, and reactions of vulnerability are often met with teasing and humiliating reactions from the other boys. Boys therefore check their relationships for subtle shifts in status by keeping tabs on who is leading and who is following. If the boys have a complaint about another boy, they tell him to his face, but when a girl has a complaint about another girl, it is rarely brought up while the targeted girl is present (Adler, Kless and Adler, 1992; Brody, 2000; Hart, 2012, 2013; Tannen, 1990).

To girls, intimacy seems to be far more important. Girls therefore check their friendships for subtle shifts in alliances and try to be friends with the popular girls. Popularity confers some sort of status, but it is relational in nature. Girls are not expected to brag about what they are good at or show that they are better than others. Girls do not give orders; they express their preferences as suggestions, and suggestions will usually be accepted. While boys are more likely to use expressions like 'Give me that!' and 'Get out of here!', girls tend to use expressions such as 'Do you think we should do such-and-such?' and 'How about we do this?' to avoid giving the appearance of being domineering. Girls enjoy spending time together, and girls often worry more about not being well liked. Even among 4–5-year-olds, girls' groups focus on group cohesion and do not wish to put any single person in charge. These different social structures are also seen in boys' and girls' typical play preferences. Boys tend to prefer competitive activities, such as soccer and basketball etc., and even when boys' activities are not *per se* competitive, they often join teams in order to promote competition. A typical boys' game might be about running and chasing each other in large groups or taking part in organized team sports. The girls are not interested in this type of organized activity but prefer group activities where everyone participates on an equal footing (Tannen, 1990). Girls' play often involves taking turns to engage in games with very few rules, and they typically compete in games with standardized rules instead of competing directly against each other. Detailed observation studies of girls have found that they organize in 'best-friend' pairs, which in turn are part of a larger, complex social network. Girls also seem to be focused on which other girls are best friends. They tend to prefer avoiding conflicts with adults and generally seek to avoid open confrontation and risky behaviour (Cairns *et al.*, 1989; Hart, 2013; Hart and Hvilshøj, 2013; O'Connell, Poplar and Kent, 1995; Thorne and Luria, 1986).

In play, girls try to include their girl friends, as they balance between engaging in competitive interactions versus being nice and avoiding openly excluding anyone. Competition has to take place within a framework of apparent collaboration. The girls' preference for avoiding direct confrontation results in a behaviour that is traditionally perceived negatively, as it involves talking about others 'behind their back'. Like the boys, the girls seek to control what happens in play. Both boys and girls want to have things their way, but they tend to pursue this desire in different ways. Among girls, sharing secrets is proof of friendship, and bonding is promoted when the listener responds as expected. Boys typically bond in competitive interactions (e.g. rough-housing and sports). In a study of 3–4-year-olds in a day care institution, Sheldon (1990) found that when girls and boys engage in activities where they are required to perform an individual activity in groups of three children of the same sex, unlike the boys, the girls maintain contact by telling each other what they are doing and responding to each other's remarks. Boys have a greater need to challenge authority and are more likely to resolve conflicts by aggressive means. They are much more likely than girls to need a clear hierarchy with an obvious leader. Girls, instead, need to feel good socially and avoid conflicts. They need consensus and intimacy and close groups of friends. Girls have a greater need for a directive authority to support their close interactions and help them form a close-knit group where they avoid talking behind each other's backs. The older the children in a group are, the more stable is the hierarchy and the status relationships. This means that it is harder to break up a well-established, relational hierarchy among older children compared to younger children. The older the child is, the more essential his or her status in the peer group is to the child's sense of self-esteem.

Research has also found sex differences, generally, between mothers' and fathers' roles in shaping the child's development, and the question is whether this knowledge could be brought into play in the classroom. Parents provide different kinds of care, and the child clearly benefits from the combination. Fathers 'nudge' the child more, and their behaviour with the infant invites more play. Fathers' behaviour intensifies the child's mood and arousal. Mothers give the child protection, while the father often holds his baby in a way that lets the child see what is happening in the environment. Generally, fathers seem to be more directive, while mothers allow the infant to control the interaction more. The father often takes more risks with the infant, including throwing the child into the air etc. The father's interactions invite the child to dare to take risks and become independent, while the mother's behaviour encourages intimacy, protection and nuanced emotions. The mother tends to be more verbal, while fathers are more physical and encourage wrestling matches and more rough-housing, especially with their sons. Through physical play, the child learns important skills for handling his or her own aggression; and when the child, for example, plays too rough or gets too excited, the father typically tells the child to stop (Brazelton, 1992; Hart, 2008; Sroufe, Cooper and Deltart, 1992).

The connection between status hierarchy and attachment pattern

There is a connection between attachment patterns and the way we engage in social relationships. A child with a secure attachment pattern often has a more flexible ability to find different positions in the group hierarchy, depending on the group's constellation, compared to a child with an insecure attachment pattern. A child's status may vary in different groups, and it may vary over time. The opposite is also common, however – that is, a child who has a low status and is excluded in class maintains this low status even if he or she moves to another school. Already in the preschool years, the child's status in the peer group appears to have a big impact on his or her sense of self-esteem, and since status and approval affect our self-esteem, children may conclude that there is something wrong, either with them or with the environment they find themselves in. Since humans establish hierarchies, and since there appears to be an evolutionary and biochemical reward associated with higher hierarchical status, lower status often involves a biological punishment. This is reflected in low self-esteem.

Low self-esteem is destructive both to creativity and learning, and it may of course stem from a variety of issues. A lack of secure attachment to caregivers and other family members can lead to low self-esteem, but the feeling of not belonging or of having a low status in the peer group can also be the main factor. Perceived low status may in some cases be purely a matter of group dynamics, but it may also be related to a lack of the particular social skills that are important in the given group. Finally, low self-esteem may arise from the experience of lacing specific skills or resources, such as language, education, housing or other concrete values that are associated with an acceptable social status in the environment that the child belongs to – or aspires to belong to (Hart and Hvilshøj, 2013).

Both in primates and humans, it appears that individuals often seek to form friendships with others who resemble them with regard to status and other key factors. For example, children (and adults) often underscore and emphasize these similarities, also in trivial areas such as dress style, hair style and favourite expressions. Friendships often develop on the basis of mutual services, and in long-term friendships this exchange is stabilized. Also, friends often develop a greater tolerance for differences in gains and losses in competitive situations that might otherwise lead to envy or anger. A new or less firmly established friendship may thus be threatened if one child feels that he or she is being unfairly treated in comparison with the other child, while the less fortunate party in a more stable friendship might find it easier to accept or may even rejoice in a friend's good fortunes. Similarly, the friendship makes it easier to accept behaviour that would cause irritation in other circumstances. In other words, the mentalization capacity is both acquired and challenged through friendship. The mentalization capacity is crucial for our social and mental flexibility and our ability to include others in the group – also in the face of considerable cultural differences. Groups of children or adults characterized by insecure attachment patterns and low mentalization capacities will often have a much higher stress level, because everyone is wary of each other, and those who are not fully included in the group will feel marginalized and lonely with a high stress level as a result (Shonkoff and Phillips, 2000). The person at the top of hierarchy has considerable power to spread both good and bad interactions, since primates, whether humans or apes, tend to copy each other, especially the actions of those that are seen as the highest ranking in the status hierarchy (de Waal, 2006; Hart and Hvilshøj, 2013).

Studies among preschoolers have shown what it takes for a child to enter into a game that other children have initiated, and where the group has already been established. These studies show that to be accepted into the group, the newcomer not only has to time his or her approach correctly but also has to balance between being too pushy versus observing for too long, and between being too dominant versus too submissive. In light of these demands, it is understandable why some children prefer staying close to the adults: being close to them offers protection and also gives the children a chance to pick up social skills from adults – whom most children, fortunately, view as being the highest placed in the social hierarchy. This protects the most vulnerable children from bullying or feeling that they are being bullied. Children who prefer contact with adults over peer contacts may lack the social skills required to engage in interactions with their peers (Pellegrini, 2009). The child's attachment pattern, cultural norms and own sense of fitting in without standing out too much influence how quickly he or she is accepted by the others.

The important role as 'caravan leader'

The altered educational style that found its way into schools in the 1960s and 1970s meant a huge change in the demands on the individual teacher's personal capacity for establishing him/herself as an authority in relation to students, building a relationship where the students had respect for the teacher but were also able to engage in creative learning processes. Today, it is not enough for a teacher to attempt to be a knowledgeable educator with the goal of conveying cognitive knowledge – the teacher has to be attuned with the student. For a child to achieve autonomy and independence, the adults have to embrace their leadership role. An Arabic proverb says, 'The dogs bark, but the caravan moves on.' The caravan leader has to know the way and make sure that everyone makes it to the next oasis before nightfall. Dogs might chase after lizards or other exciting things they spot along the route, but the caravan cannot stop every time, because then it risks being swallowed up by the desert. The teacher has to take the role of caravan leader. The only way children can really develop a sense of security is by having someone show them the way. When children feel secure, they have room for exploration, joy and creativity, and most teachers are able to integrate the role as caravan leader, enabling the children to find their own way or to find it together with the teacher (Hart, 2011a, 2013).

Authority has to be acquired and developed – it is no longer written into law. Since the teacher is responsible for creating a functioning relationship and a constructive affect attunement, regardless of the child's sex, the teacher has to be prepared to accept consultation and support when a relationship is not working. Thus, the teacher has to be able to observe the interactions in the relationship and interpret what is happening, and be ready to act on the basis of this knowledge and insight. The ability to distinguish observation from interpretation in emotional and relational aspects and to distinguish between the behaviour of boys and girls requires a high mentalization capacity. Mentalized curiosity can generate development, while unmentalized assessments lead to insecurity, impasses and rigidity, and the maladjusted student is often seen as an annoying troublemaker that it would be nice to be without, so that order might be restored (Hart, 2013).

Any asymmetrical relationship, such as mother–child, preschool teacher–child, teacher–student, etc., involves an unequal distribution of responsibility. Like the caregiver, teachers have to take responsibility for their educational goals and remain aware of the implications of the asymmetrical relationship. As in the caregiver–child relationship, the optimal development in the teacher–student relationship is that the child has an engaged relationship with the teacher but with an asymmetrical distribution of responsibility, where the teacher takes responsibility for boundaries, attunement and navigation.

The child brings his or her personality patterns to the class. The teacher needs to understand the child's emotional history and development level on an intuitive level but also needs a theory about the child's emotional development and an understanding of the relationship between the child and his or her environment. A child who has grown up in an environment with insensitive or chaotic caregivers often becomes wary or suspicious of others and lacks confidence. The lack of positive life experiences can lead to a fundamental and general sense of mistrust. A predictable emotional environment where the child develops a trusting relationship with the teachers and the other students can become an essential aspect of such a learning process.

When a student has maladaptive reactions, the cause of the problem does not lie with the individual student but is a product of the interaction between teacher and student. That is not to say that there are not individual causes for the student's actions, whether neurological or developmental – that is, either genetic or the result of an inadequate childhood environment. Regardless of the causal explanation, the teacher's responsibility is to create an optimal learning environment for the individual student. This involves the creative task of building an environment around the child where the teacher maintains his or her authority as teacher – the natural position at the top of the hierarchy which helps the student feel secure. The student needs encouragement to find motivation and confidence in his or her coping skills and unfold his or her capacity to engage in interpersonal attachment processes, which in turn drives emotional and personal development. Whatever the child does, the teacher is responsible for what happens. In other words, the goal is to create a symmetrical relationship with an asymmetrical distribution of responsibility. Thus, while every success is the child's success, anything that goes wrong is the teacher's responsibility. When the adults are in charge and carry the responsibility, the child is liberated from the burden of having to decide what the next step should be or exercise control and keep him/herself safe. The goal is to make sure that the student feels seen and noticed in engaging moments, which requires an engaged teacher.

One possible consequence of this is that teachers begin to pursue differentiated pedagogical approaches instead of differentiated instruction. Some children need a learning space with a high degree of (hierarchical) structure, boundaries, predictability, preparation and regular rhythms (see Hart, 2009, 2011a). When the child has difficulty with self-regulation, a structured and predictable context is the best way to promote a sense of security where the child can unfold his or her potential. Other children with better self-regulation skills, who are able to handle project-based learning, group work, etc., thrive with a looser framework that lets them unfold their creativity. In this light, inclusion requires each class to have an educational framework that is able to accommodate individual students' needs, meaning that one track may be structured around boundary-setting approaches while another is structured around project-oriented approaches.

As the head of this 'children's caravan', the teacher has to have strong self-esteem to act as a good 'caravan leader' and sometimes make bold and courageous decisions (Hart and Hvilshøj, 2013). Like parents, teachers have to be predictable and able to provide security, organization and regulation. The fact that the adults are in charge, even when the environment is unpredictable and chaotic, is reassuring and helps the child develop self-control. The teacher initiates interactions, organizes and regulates the child's experiences, sets boundaries and provides direction and guidance. If there is no structure, most of the child's energy is directed at preparing for unpredictable events and seeking to control the environment, especially the people in it. If the people who exist in their world are too frightening, children learn to control every single aspect of their own behaviour in order to submit to the adults or control them through power struggles.

The teacher has to give the children a relevant degree of control – not too much and not too little – a level of responsibility that needs ongoing adjustment. It is important to loosen the structure whenever it is relevant and, conversely, to maintain a stricter structure if that is required. Structure makes it safe to pursue a spontaneous interest. A flexible structure is a condition for releasing the potential in anyone's spontaneity and creative energy. Such a flexible structure requires the teacher to be simultaneously strong and receptive, well prepared and in control, constantly open to the children's signals but also prepared to point out new possibilities. The teacher has to show some degree of predictability but also has to be able to offer positive surprises when problems arise and always embrace asymmetrical responsibility (Hart and Hvilshøj, 2013).

From mammals' play to human play

For more than 150 years, researchers have sought to understand the importance of play in both humans and animals. There has never been any doubt that play is important. For example, Robert Hinde wrote in 1974 (p.227) that play takes up so much time and energy that it must have significant adaptive importance for development. Play does not need to be all fun and games. Much play is on the border between thrilling and frightening – although having fun and laughing together does seem to be the most natural play scenario. In his laboratory, Panksepp (Burgdorf and Panksepp, 2001; Panksepp, 1998, 2000) discovered that even rats laugh, with ultrasonic shrieks, when they are tickled in a playful way. Like children, apes also laugh when others tickle and play with them in an empathic way. Panksepp argues that these positive emotions contribute to the social attachment that we find in virtually all mammals. However, all play is sometimes less fun for the potential loser or for someone who is taken advantage of in play. Both in animals and humans, play can range from intense pleasure and enjoyment to surprise and intense fear, anger and sadness. In humans Sutton-Smith (2003), among others, has described how play can be a way of activating emotions in a pretend context that is not truly frightening but, ideally, safe and enjoyable. Much human play seems to be a means of experiencing virtual emotions in a safe context. Unfortunately, however, once the virtual emotion has been activated, the actual emotion can quickly be triggered too, which means that play can quickly turn serious (Burghardt, 2005).

As Panksepp and Trevarthen point out in Chapter 1, it appears that the human urge for play comes from the same origins as playful activities in animals. Panksepp (1998) documented the existence of a play circuit in the mammalian brain that makes it rewarding to engage in play. The main difference between humans and other mammals is our huge neocortex – the outer layer of the brain that enables us to think, symbolize, analyze and relate to both the past and the future. If the cultural resource of play is not associated with social enjoyment, it is difficult for us to unfold our humanity and our sense of self-esteem. Animal studies have shown that the neural circuits for social engagement and joy are located in the area between the limbic system and the prefrontal cortex. In humans, the corresponding area is placed underneath the neocortex, and our interpersonal interactions give rise to the emotional and cognitive circuits that enable us not only to think clearly but also to feel clearly, which is the essence of mentalization. As Panksepp and Trevarthen point out, play not only promotes sympathy, empathy and social skills but also our intellectual capacity. A culture that values creativity and innovation will therefore need to provide a learning space for play and creative expression.

Play is not expressed under all circumstances. For example, studies of animal play have shown that play behaviour only occurs when the animal is not hungry and when it is not preoccupied with mating, marking its territory, competing for essential resources or fleeing from predators or attackers. It has long been known that animals that are full and free from stress play more than animals that are hungry, too hot or too cold, sick, etc. Including play in school activities to stimulate creativity and problem-solving has proved to be most effective when the children feel secure and are with adults (Tegano, Sawyers and Moran, 1989). Like other mammals, children who have not played for some time have a greater need to engage in playful interactions. If the play activities are not organized and taken seriously by the adults, it may cause destructive or fearful behaviour, which might trigger an attention deficit hyperactivity disorder (ADHD) diagnosis. According to Panksepp (2008), this creates a vicious cycle, as the commonly used medical treatment of ADHD reduces the urge to play.

As children grow older, they are capable of containing growing arousal levels. This means that their capacity to contain and handle more intense emotions, including joy as well as fear, anger and sadness, increases, as does their capacity for handling growing amounts of frustration and aggression. Already at the age of 1 year, the child needs to begin to learn to inhibit impulses, and this is an important capacity for engaging in play interactions with peers. All highly developed social mammals rely on this capacity, and without it the child will not be able to inhibit aggression. A child who lacks both the capacity for impulse inhibition and the capacity for feeling shame or embarrassment may experience an attack on a smaller and weaker child as enjoyable and as play, and this may serve the purpose of exercising aggression to demonstrate power. This is seen, for example, when prison guards abuse prisoners and soldiers take advantage of the opportunity to kill, torture, rape and humiliate defenceless people – in the attackers, these acts may be a source of fun, excitement and temporary satisfaction.

As described earlier, the regulation of energy levels and emotions, and the capacity for impulse inhibition all develop through interactions with others, including play, and an important aspect of play behaviour is learned in asymmetrical relationships where parents accommodate the child's development level and create a context where play is fun and takes place on equal terms. The parent creates a structure where the child experiences success, which sometimes requires the adult to give him/herself a handicap. Play is only fun if the weaker participant also has a chance to win sometimes. Even if the child finds out, as he or she grows older, that these handicaps are self-imposed, they still help make the interaction enjoyable. This is also seen in other mammals, when the stronger and most dominant sibling uses less advantageous strategies, inhibits its behaviour and takes other measures to keep the other animal in the game (Burghardt, 2005). Play requires two participants who enjoy the interaction, therefore there has to be a certain degree of equality and an even distribution of cooperation and competition. The mammalian play circuits help children learn about social rules, including when to compete, when to cooperate, when to end the game in a positive mood and when to let others win. In mammalian rough-and-tumble play, if one animal wins more than 70 per cent of the time, the losing animal stops enjoying the game and does not want to play anymore. Children first learn about this balance in asymmetrical relationships when they are able to transfer it to symmetrical relationships – that is, when they need to find the right balance in interactions with peers. Through play with peers, children acquire valuable social skills, including the need for reciprocity and thus the need to sometimes give in to the other; if they fail to acquire these sensibilities, their playmates will begin to reject them. No one wants to play with a tyrant (Panksepp and Biven, 2012)!

Benefits of pretend play

The Greek philosopher Plato (quoted in Plato, 1957) considered play important and believed that children should be taught through play; and Friedrich Fröbel, who founded the kindergarten movement, developed play materials to prepare the children for the world that they were going to move into as adults. Both Plato and Fröbel were well aware that life is not all fun and games, and today we need to find the best ways to incorporate play into our education system. Training to become a creative human being is a life-long process that begins when we first draw breath. This development involves understanding the value of transferring play and learning to a challenging work context, making work fun, creative and innovative. Necessary and serious activities can feel playful – for example, when our work is so exciting and absorbing that we lose track of time and forget about the outside world.

One aspect of children's play involves risk-taking. If we look at children's play all over the world, challenges and risk-taking seem to be key development dimensions that are promoted through play. The play environment is an important context for testing our skills in decision-making, understanding the social implications of making certain decisions and assessing risk aspects in decision-making. In play, children need to take risks in order to test their skills in the social context with their peers and discover what is possible (Jambor, 1998). We get to know ourselves by playing a variety of roles where we test our own boundaries, which also involves an element of risk-taking. This requires the ability to engage in the type of pretend play that only emerges around the age of 3–4 years (Winnicott, 1971/2003). In humans, pretend play is crucial. Initially, young children assume that their thoughts and notions are the same as their playmates'. Through repeated social interactions in pretend play with peers, where different points of view collide, children begin to realize that their playmates sometimes see things differently. At this time, children begin to be able to suspend their own perceptions and seek and wish to understand their playmates' perceptions and desires in order not to spoil the game (Burghardt, 2005).

In addition, pretend play helps the child to handle pain and anxiety by allowing him or her to experience and rehearse unpleasant experiences in the safe context of play, as pointed out by many psychoanalysts, including Freud (1933/1959) and Winnicott (1971/2003). This helps children master the real world (e.g. by playing doctor, going to hospital, etc.), which is the rationale behind play therapy, a helpful psychotherapy method before the child has the capacity to put his or her difficulties into words.

Play as a way to rehearse good cooperation and healthy competition

Many researchers believe that the mentalization capacity has not just evolved as a way of strengthening friendships thanks to the ability to empathize with the other's needs but also as a means of personal gain by understanding how to avoid being caught or punished by a higher-ranking individual that one does not have an attachment relationship with. As described in Chapter 2, as humans we have not only developed the capacity for attachment but also the ability to negotiate sophisticated social hierarchies. This inevitably also involves dealing with play interactions where someone attempts to benefit from a situation at someone else's cost. These play experiences can result in serious fights or result in the child no longer being an attractive playmate. This phenomenon is seen in virtually all mammals. Rough-and-tumble play and playfighting require a grasp of reciprocity and fairness. Rough-and-tumble play is only fun if both parties achieve something, and if there is a certain degree of reciprocity. There has to be a certain degree of competition, but because the competition needs to be balanced and sometimes kept in check, there must be an element of cooperation. All play has to involve a balance between competition and cooperation.

The balance between cooperation and competition and the preservation of an element of fairness in play, whether among rats, dogs or humans, can be difficult to maintain. There appears to be a 50/50 rule, and the more rough-and-tumble play and play-fighting deviate from this balance, the likelier it is that the play will be suspended because the losing party does not feel like playing anymore (Dugatkin and Bekoff, 2003; Pellis and Pellis, 2009). The 50/50 rule means that one party holds back from taking full advantage of their superior strength, which leaves a certain possibility open for the roles of loser and winner to switch. Thus, play does not necessarily require a strict 50/50 distribution of wins and losses, but often, a child will introduce a certain self-imposed handicap in order to preserve the other child's interest in the game. This principle of fairness is built into any action in rule-free games. For all mammals, play appears to promote coping skills and the ability to handle a variety of unexpected social situations. Animal studies also show that animals that were reared in isolation and thus missed out on play stimulation are quicker to become stressed when required to learn something new (Pellis and Pellis, 2006).

Most humans are altruistic by nature, but the development of this capacity requires a delicate balance between looking out for our own and others' needs – a balance that we learn in playful interactions where we show mutual consideration to keep the activity going. Altrusim and cooperation require reciprocity, and before children, one hopes, mature and acquire this skill, they need to be in a group with a clear 'caravan leader' who is capable of supporting and directing the children's activity towards this development. As humans, we acquire altruism and cooperation by engaging in shared activities with other people. The group context is where we learn to cooperate and where finding the balance between our own selfish needs and altruism can serve everyone's interests. If the groups we experience are too big or are constantly broken up, we cannot develop the sense of community required to establish reciprocity. Reciprocal altruism only emerges in groups where we engage in many repeated interactions, and where we develop a culture and a memory of reciprocal altruistic interactions as well as sanctions against those who do not contribute (Trivers, 1971). Although the basis for friendship may vary considerably, a key aspect of equality in deep friendship relations has to do with our mentalization level. Often, imbalances in this dimension are not discovered until a conflict arises, since this is where mentalization is crucial for seeing each other's perspective, regulating one's own affect, acknowledging one's own share in the problems and finding a viable solution.

Should the parents be allowed to play too?

In homes where the parents, for whatever reason, have not managed to support the child's emotional, personal and social development, it may be absolutely crucial for the child to engage in relevant interactions with others. School can give the child this opportunity to be seen, contained and supported in developing social skills in interactions with other children and with teacher support. In many cases, it will be very relevant to include the parents, both in order to give them a chance to see the child in a new light and in order to help them develop the necessary skills for engaging in more developing interactions with their child. Parental involvement may take a variety of forms. Chapter 9 describes a combination of individual, family and children's group therapy, where the main teacher for the class plays a key role in providing full support for the child. Chapter 13, about the multi-family school, describes the more drastic step of establishing a class for both parents and children with several weekly sessions. Unfortunately, when a vulnerable child is unable to attune with his or her parents, the child is also unable to attune with his or her peers. Far too often, these children are therefore marginalized and isolated, and they need a learning space to be able to synchronize, attune with and be seen by others. This learning space enables them, eventually, to put their experiences into words and thus to develop their own identity. If the child is not able to receive parental support, it would be preferable to support the child in a context that promotes the development of attunement and thus emotional competences that may not be possible in the child's other contexts.

The development of social relationships always has to involve an element of affirmation and an element of challenge – sometimes, striking the right balance can feel like walking on a knife's edge. The more vulnerability there is in a children's group, the more challenging it is to find the right balance. In a social context, establishing a secure base is a crucial condition for any successful interaction; the teacher has to be reliable, which is a key requirement in groups of vulnerable children. Understanding the child and finding meaning in the child's actions is crucial for supporting a child's emotional, personal and social development. It is important for the child that both the parents and the teachers who see the child on a daily basis have this understanding. Neither the parents nor the teachers should ever wind up in a situation where they feel that they are out of their depth.

Children also need the teacher to have a trusting working relationship with the parents. Cooperation problems and tension between teachers and parents are very stressful for children. In fact, generally, it is very stressful for children when the people close to them do not get along. The teacher therefore has to try hard to develop or maintain a positive working relationship with the parents. This depends both on the way the teacher addresses the child and on the parents feeling that they are included, acknowledged and accepted. Positive statements about the child or positive, appreciative statements to the child not only make the child feel acknowledged and relaxed, they also put the parents at ease. When the child does something that is directed at an adult, such as calling the teacher a bad name, the parents often get nervous, thinking either the child is misbehaving or that the teacher is against the child. If the teacher responds by saying, 'It's okay', this helps the parents trust that their child is a 'good enough' child and that they are succeeding as parents. It is therefore important to know how to regulate both the child and the parents at the same time. Thus, in addition to the activities in the children's group, the teachers also have to bring the parents and the child into the same universe. For example, if the teacher manages to connect with the child, he or she has to make sure that this does not exacerbate the parents' feelings of inadequacy, if they have these feelings. The teacher always has to consider the parents, and someone has to help them develop their competences to become or remain the child's most important sources of security. This is one of the main goals of the multi-family school. For this effort to succeed, the therapists/teachers need to be sure that the parents are able to cope with and engage in the situation (Hart and Bentzen, 2015).

The teacher's responsibility is to be present in the moment, to be curious about who this child is and share this discovery with the child's parents. Homework for the parents and child in this situation might be that whenever the parents see the child enjoying a particular aspect of something that is happening in school, they have to try to recreate it at home. For example, the therapists at the multi-family school always consider how a positive situation that parents and child experienced together at the school can be generalized and transferred to the home environment. This is often done by giving the parents fun, simple everyday assignments, exercises or homework that are easy to work into the daily routines without becoming too demanding (Hart and Bentzen, 2015).

Conclusion

The origins of play probably date back to a time before mankind, and play makes life worth living. Still, play is often ignored as an aspect of children's development. Play enables us to adapt to our environment and develop self-esteem, form new ideas and soothe stress, in part by encouraging new social relationships. Children spend a great deal of time playing, and since they spend the first year of life mainly with their closest caregivers, play has its foundations in these relationships. This means that children who feel secure with their parents tend to be more curious, explorative and play more creative games (Cohen, 2006).

Our societies are never completely peaceful, never completely competitive or driven purely by egoism, nor are they morally perfect. We find kindness, evil, generosity and meanness – sometimes in the same person. People are full of contradictions, but usually these contradictions are kept in check. In order to succeed as human beings, we have to be neither a tyrant nor a doormat. Our success as a species is that we have carried the inventive urges and the curiosity that characterize young mammals with us into adulthood. The Dutch philologist and cultural historian Johan Huizinga (1872–1945) characterized mankind as *homo ludens* – playing man – and all around the world, children play, regardless of culture and place; and wherever children play, that is a sign of healthy development. However, the extent of children's play varies considerably across cultures. Play has a universal dimension as well as specific cultural aspects, and play gives children a wealth of experiences about their environment, where they learn about physical coordination, making and using objects, interacting with peers, etc. (Smith, 2010). Creativity, reflection and innovation have become crucial concepts in society, but they are not taught as a school subject because they cannot unfold through cognitive knowledge. They only unfold in the pedagogical framework and in play where children synchronize with their peers. Today, primary and lower secondary schools in many countries are increasingly required to include as many students as possible, yet there is little focus on anything besides improving the children's cognitive skills and knowledge.

As Panksepp and Trevarthen emphasize in Chapter 1, it would be desirable for schools to embrace a learning style that takes play seriously as an important aspect of life-learning aimed at achieving a balance between cooperation and empathically competitive relationships. Without this learning, we are probably going to lose in the competition with cheap labour and restrictive education systems that we see in many Asian countries. We need to understand the importance of playful, loving and more physical caring relationships in relation to children who are stressed, maladjusted, acting out or withdrawn, children who may have lacked close and secure relationships in early childhood or who are insecure in their relationships with others and excluded from peer relationships. These children need to become a part of synchronized communities, where they receive support to engage in appropriate interactions with others. It is through these experiences that they develop self-esteem.

The remaining chapters of this book describe group-based methods for children to meet the challenges they need to develop their emotional potential in a social context with other children. They also provide suggestions as to how this development can take place in the children's zone of proximal development. The various descriptions illustrate how targeted methods can help a children's group develop competences for reflecting and, ideally, mentalizing: reflecting on both their own and others' emotions. The descriptions contain examples of structured play that helps the children inhibit their urges or angry impulses and consider others' needs by putting themselves in another child's place to avoid hurting others and to be able to reconcile after a conflict.

References

Adler, P. A., Kless, S. J. and Adler, P. (1992) 'Socialization to gender roles: Popularity among elementary school boys and girls.' *Sociology of Education* 65(3), 169–187.

Brazelton, T. B. (1992) *Touchpoints: Your Child's Emotional and Behavioural Development.* Reading: Addison-Wesley Publishing.

Bretherton, I. (1989) 'Pretense: The form and function of make-believe play.' *Developmental Review* 9(4), 383–401.

Brinkmann, S. (2011) 'Følelser på Godt og Ondt.' In C. Elmholdt and L. Tanggaard (eds) *Følelser i Ledelse.* Aarhus: Klim.

Brody, L. (2000) 'The Socialization of Gender Differences in Emotional Expression: Display Rules, Infant Temperament, and Differentiation.' In A. H. Fischer (ed.) *Gender and Emotion: Social Psychological Perspectives.* Cambridge: Cambridge University Press.

Bruner, J. S. (1983) *Child's Talk: Learning to Use Language.* New York, NY: W. W. Norton.

Burgdorf, J. and Panksepp, J. (2001) 'Tickling induces reward in adolescent rats.' *Physiology and Behavior 72*(1–2), 167–173.

Burghardt, G. M. (2005) *The Genesis of Animal Play: Testing the Limits.* Cambridge, MA: MIT Press.

Cairns, R., Cairns, B., Neckerman, H. and Ferguson, L. (1989) 'Growth and aggression: 1. Childhood to early adolescence.' *Developmental Psychology 25*(2), 320–330.

Card, N. A., Stucky, B. D., Sawalani G. M. and Little, T. D. (2008) 'Direct and indirect aggression during childhood and adolescence: A meta-analytic review of gender differences, intercorrelations, and relations to maladjustment.' *Child Development 79*(5), 1185–1229.

Cohen, D. (2006) *The Development of Play* (3rd edn). London: Routledge.

Cummins, D. D. (2000) 'How the social environment shaped the evolution of mind.' *Synthese 122*(1–2), 1–26.

Cummins, D. D. (2006) 'Dominance, Status, and Social Hierarchies.' In D. M. Buss (ed.) *The Handbook of Evolutionary Psychology.* Hoboken, NJ: Wiley.

de Waal, F. (1982) *Chimpanzee Politics: Power and Sex among Apes.* New York, NY: HarperCollins.

de Waal, F. (1996) *Good Natured: The Origins of Right and Wrong in Primates and Other Animals.* Cambridge, MA: Harvard University Press.

de Waal, F. (2006) *Our Inner Ape: The Best and Worst of Human Nature.* London: Granta Books.

Dugatkin, L. A. and Bekoff, M. (2003) 'Play and the evolution of fairness: A game theory model.' *Behavioral Processes 60*(3), 209–214.

Fonagy, P., Redfern, S. and Charman T. (1997) 'The relationship between belief- desire reasoning, and a projective measure of attachment security (SAT).' *British Journal of Developmental Psychology 15*(1), 51–61.

Fonagy, P., Gergely, G., Jurist, E. L. and Target, M. (2002) *Affect Regulation, Mentalization, and the Development of the Self.* New York, NY: Other Press.

Freud, S. (1933/1959) 'The Relation of the Poet to Day-Dreaming.' In J. Riviere (ed.) *Collected Papers by Sigmund Freud* (vol. 4). New York, NY: Basic Books.

Goodall, J. (1986) *The Chimpanzees of Gombe: Patterns of Behavior.* Cambridge, MA: Belknap Press of Harvard University Press.

Gordon, D. E. (1993) 'The inhibition of pretend play and its implications for development.' *Human Development 36*(4), 215–234.

Hart, S. (2008) *Brain, Attachment, Personality: An Introduction to Neuroaffective Development.* London: Karnac Books.

Hart, S. (2009) *Den følsomme Hjerne: Hjernens Udvikling Gennem Tilknytning og Samhørighedsbånd.* Copenhagen: Hans Reitzels Forlag.

Hart, S. (ed.) (2011a) *Neuroaffektiv Psykoterapi med Børn.* Copenhagen: Hans Reitzels Forlag.

Hart, S. (2011b) *The Impact of Attachment: Developmental Neuroaffective Psychology.* New York, NY: W. W. Norton.

Hart, S. (ed.) (2012) *Neuroaffektiv Psykoterapi med Voksne.* Copenhagen: Hans Reitzels Forlag.

Hart, S. (2013) 'Det er en Køn Historie.' In C. Bendixen and H. Fischer (eds) *Psykologi i Skolen: Hvad Virker?* Copenhagen: Hans Reitzels Forlag.

Hart, S. and Bentzen, M. (2015) *Through Windows of Opportunity: A Neuroaffective Approach to Child Psychotherapy.* London: Karnac Books.

Hart, S. and Hvilshøj, H. (eds) (2013) *Ledelse Mellem Hjerne og Hjerte: Om Mentalisering og Neuroaffektivt Lederskab*. Copenhagen: Hans Reitzels Forlag.

Kahen, V., Katz, L. F. and Gottman, J. M. (1994) 'Linkages between parent-child interaction and conversations of friends.' *Social Development 3*(3), 238–254.

Martin, P. and Caro, T. (1985) 'On the Function of Play and its Role in Behavioral Development.' In J. Rosenblatt, C. Beer, M. Bushnell and P. Slater (eds) *Advances in the Study of Behavior* (vol. 15). New York, NY: Academic Press.

Meins, E. (1997) *Security of Attachment and the Social Development of Cognition*. Hove: Psychology Press.

O'Connell, P. D., Peplar, D. and Kent, D. (1995) *Gender and Age Differences in Types of Aggressive Behavior*. Poster presented at The Biennial Meeting of the Society for Research in Child Development, Indianapolis.

Panksepp, J. (1998) *Affective Neuroscience: The Foundations of Human and Animal Emotions*. New York, NY: Oxford University Press.

Panksepp, J. (2000) 'The riddle of laughter: Neural and psychoevolutionary underpinnings of joy.' *Current Directions in Psychological Science 9*(6), 183–186.

Panksepp, J. (2008) 'Play, ADHD, and the construction of the social brain.' *American Journal of Play 1*(1), 55–79.

Panksepp, J. and Biven, L. (2012) *The Archaeology of Mind: Neuroevolutionary Origins of Human Emotions*. London: W. W. Norton.

Pellegrini, A. D. (2009) *The Role of Play in Human Development*. New York, NY: Oxford University Press.

Pellegrini, A. D., Dupuis, D. and. Smith, P. K (2007) 'Play in evolution and development.' *Developmental Review 27*(2), 261–276.

Pellis, S. M. and Pellis, V. C. (2006) 'Play and the Development of Social Engagement: A Comparative Perspective.' In P. J. Marshall and N. A. Fox (eds) *The Development of Social Engagement: Psychobiological Perspectives*. New York, NY: Oxford University Press.

Pellis, S .M. and Pellis, V. C. (2009) *The Playful Brain: Venturing to the Limits of Neuroscience*. Oxford: Oneworld.

Perner, J., Ruffman, T. and Leekam, S. R. (1994) 'Theory of mind is contagious: You catch it from your sibs.' *Child Development 65*(4), 1228–1238.

Plato (1957) *The Republic of Plato*. New York, NY: E. P. Dutton & Co.

Rusk, R. R. (1967) *A History of Infant Education*. London: University of London Press.

Sander, L. (1988) 'The Event Structure of Regulation in the Neonate-Caregiver System as a Biological Background for Early Organization of Psychic Structure.' In A. Goldberg (ed.) *Progress in Self Psychology* (vol. 3). Hoboken, NJ: Taylor & Francis.

Sander, L. (1992) 'Letter to the Editor.' *International Journal of Psycho-Analysis 73*, 582–584.

Sander, L., Bianchi, I. and Amadei, G. (2008) *Living Systems, Evolving Consciousness, and the Emerging Person: A Selection of Papers from the Life Work of Louis Sander*. New York, NY: Taylor & Francis.

Schore, A. (2003a) *Affect Dysregulation and Disorders of the Self*. New York, NY: W. W. Norton.

Schore, A. (2003b) *Affect Regulation and the Repair of the Self*. New York, NY: W. W. Norton.

Schwartz, R. and Hart, S. (2013) *Barnet og dets Relationelle Miljø*. Copenhagen: Hans Reitzels Forlag.

Sheldon, A. (1990) 'Pickle fights: Gendered talk in preschool disputes.' *Discourse Processes 13*(1), 5–31.

Shonkoff, J. P. and Phillips, D. (eds) (2000) *From Neurons to Neighborhoods: The Science of Early Child Development.* Washington, DC: National Academies Press.

Smith, P. K. (2010) *Children and Play.* Chichester: Wiley-Blackwell.

Spinka, M., Newbury, R. C. and Bekoff, M. (2001) 'Mammalian play: Can training for the unexpected be fun? *Quarterly Review of Biology 76*(2), 141–168.

Sroufe, L. A. (1996) *Emotional Development: The Organization of Emotional Life in the Early Years.* New York, NY: Cambridge University Press.

Sroufe, L. A., Cooper, R. G. and Deltart, G. B. (1992) *Child Development: Its Nature and Course* (2nd edn). New York, NY: McGraw-Hill.

Stern, D. N. (1990) 'Joy and Satisfaction in Infancy.' In R. A. Glick and S. Bone (eds) *Pleasure Beyond the Pleasure Principle.* New Haven, NJ: Yale University Press.

Stern, D. N. (1977) *The First Relationship: Mother and Infant.* Cambridge, MA: Harvard University Press.

Stern, D. N. (1998) 'The process of therapeutic change involving implicit knowledge: Some implications of developmental observations for adult psychotherapy.' *Infant Mental Health Journal 19*(3), 300–308.

Stern, D. N. (2004) *The Present Moment in Psychotherapy and Everyday Life.* New York, NY: W. W. Norton.

Suomi, S. and Harlow, H. (1972) 'Social rehabilitation of isolate-reared monkeys.' *Developmental Psychology 6*(3), 487–496.

Sutton-Smith, B. (2003) 'Play as a Parody of Emotional Vulnerability.' In D. Lytle (ed.) *Play and Culture Studies* (vol. 5). Westport, CT: Praeger.

Tannen, D. (1990) *You Just Don't Understand: Women and Men in Conversation.* London: Virago Press.

Tegano, D. W., Sawyers, J. K. and Moran, J. D. (1989) 'Problem-finding and solving in play: The teacher's role.' *Childhood Education 66*, 92–97.

Thorne, B. and Luria, Z. (1986) 'Sexuality and gender in children's daily worlds.' *Social Problems 33*, 176–190.

Trevarthen, C. (1979) 'Communication and Cooperation in Early Infancy: A Description of Primary Intersubjectivity.' In M. Bullowa (ed.) *Before Speech: The Beginning of Interpersonal Communication.* Cambridge: Cambridge University Press.

Trevarthen, C. (1993) 'The Self Born in Intersubjectivity: The Psychology of an Infant Communicating.' In U. Neisser (ed.) *The Perceived Self: Ecological and Interpersonal Sources of Self Knowledge.* New York, NY: Cambridge University Press.

Trivers, R. (1971) 'The Evolution of Reciprocal Altruism.' *Quarterly Review of Biology 46*(1), 35–57.

Tronick, E. (2007) *The Neurobehavioral and Social-Emotional Development of Infants and Children.* New York, NY: W. W. Norton.

Tronick, E., Als, H., Adamson, L., Wise, S. and Brazelton, T. B. (1978) 'The infant's response to entrapment between contradictory messages in face-to-face interaction.' *Journal of Child Psychiatry 17*, 1–13.

Werner, E. E. and Schmidt, R. S. (2001) *Journeys from Childhood to Midlife: Risk, Resilience and Recovery.* London: Cornell University Press.

Winnicott, D. (1964) *The Child, the Family and the Outside World.* Harmondsworth: Penguin.

Winnicott, D. (1971/2003) *Playing and Reality.* New York, NY: Basic Books.

4

Infectious Joy

A Neuroaffective Perspective on Sensorimotor Processes in Groups of Children

Marianne Bentzen and Christine Lakoseljac-Andreasen

In this chapter, the two authors combine their different experiences with encouraging children's development processes. Marianne is a somatic psychotherapist and trainer; besides her trainings and private practice she has used psychomotor approaches in children's groups and with adults with intellectual disabilities. Marianne is also in a decades-long collaboration with Susan Hart about developing the neuroaffective theory on personality development. Christine is an occupational therapist and has worked with children's groups for many years. The case study vignettes in this chapter are taken from her collaborations with therapists and preschool and school teachers. We will offer some glimpses of Christine's practice combined with reflections from Marianne's neuroaffective perspective.

The growing emphasis on evidence-based methods in recent years makes it easy to overlook a crucial insight: in biological terms, personal and social maturation is not a technical training programme. It is a fundamentally *interpersonal* project, driven by mutual attunement, enjoyment and satisfaction – a form of emotional and often joy-filled infection. Educational methods, whether they focus on sensorimotor processes or literacy, frame the interaction by providing a 'macro-structure'. A clear macro-structure that matches the children's competence levels is the first step in a good learning process because it lets everyone know exactly what the interaction requires of them. This gives the children good conditions for finding satisfactory ways of cooperating. The quality of the cooperation begins with the gaze contact, tone of voice, facial expressions and body posture that the adult displays in conveying the macro-structure, and it continues in the countless micro-interactions among the children and with the adult. These interactions form 'micro-structures' in the way they are together. In a sense, the macro-structure could be described as 'what' we do, while the micro-structures define 'how' we do it.

From birth, we humans prefer to be in a mutually synchronized and emotionally attuned contact (Sander, 1988; Trevarthen, 1994), as long as it is offered at the level that we are capable of perceiving and engaging in – that is, our 'zone of proximal development'. This synchronized attunement is the core of the joy and infectious engagement that characterizes a motivated learning process. Infectious engagement between people is primarily bodily and emotional in nature. In this chapter, we are therefore going to take a closer look at the conditioning macro-structures in the work with sensorimotor integration in children's groups and at some of the interactions that form the micro-structures that promote maturation.

Body-based ego formation

Already in the early 1900s, Freud (1923) stated that the initial formation of the ego is completely dependent on the body. Later research has found that this body-ego is shaped by the infant's interactions with his or her caregivers (Hart, 2008, 2011b; Sander, 1988; Stern, 1999; Trevarthen, 1994), which come together to teach the child the feeling of 'being in the world'. Extensive research in the fields of developmental psychology and neuropsychology has shown that all infants, as well as older children and adults, are infected and affected by other people's inner states: their joy, interest, sorrow or indifference (Keysers, 2011; Lewis, Amini and Lannon, 2001; Stern, 2004; Stern et al., 1998). Feelings and emotions are infectious, and they are fundamental to our motivation and energy. Throughout life, this infection is mainly conveyed nonverbally, through attitudes, behaviours and tone of voice, and it shapes the meaning of our very existence as well as the meaning of our environment in everything we do. However, bodily and emotional integration after infancy takes place under the level of awareness – we tend to take it for granted and give it little thought. For instance, the feeling of 'being in the world' is so basic that few normally functioning adults are able to attune to dysfunctions at this level.

Occupational therapy also views the body as crucial for our personality development. We experience ourselves and our environment through the continuous processing of sensory stimuli, as we sort through impressions and prioritize what is important to us and ignore what we perceive as irrelevant. Engaged and joy-filled sensorimotor integration is seen as the basis of personality development, interaction and learning and thus also as a way of understanding the child. During early childhood, the brain learns to gather, sort and organize stimuli from the body, other people and the environment, and this process continues throughout life, mainly under the level of awareness. The result of effective sensory integration is adaptive behaviour: behaviour that seeks to meet our needs in ways that match the conditions and possibilities of the context. This may involve motor behaviour, social behaviour or psychological/emotional behaviour. Dysfunctional sensory integration may lead to difficulties in all these areas – for example, in the form of over- or under-reacting to touch and other sensory impressions, balance problems, angry outbursts, sadness, anxiety, social withdrawal or rigid and controlling behaviour in interactions. One of the key goals for working with children is to promote healthy body/mind development by supporting their engagement in everyday activities, whether these are social relations, activities of daily living or play.

During childhood, the body-ego develops its ability to sort and prioritize, based on thousands of caring, meaningful and engaged interactions, initially with the primary caregivers and later with other adults and children. It is through this emotional attunement in countless interactions that children learn to sense themselves, regulate their energy level and experience meaning, comfort and discomfort.

Macro-regulation: framework and structure

In the following, we will address the way macro-structure frames a safe context for working with sensory integration.

Case study 4.1

Christine: When I invite children into our playroom, it is very important that I first prepare the room to make sure that it promotes the intended activity and purpose. The surroundings have an important impact on children's play impulses. If the children are going to engage in a particular activity or game, only the items we need are left out. The light is on, to let the children know that we are here to play. I speak clearly, and I usually have pictures of the activities I have planned. The setting is always a source of 'potential opportunities and resources, demands and constraints' (Kielhofner, 2002, p.21) that influence the child's reactions. The physical space and the objects in the room are an important part of the macro-structure. We often bring the children's groups into our motor skills room, a large space with lots of room to romp and play. That room clearly encourages active play. The following is an example of how the design of the room encourages certain activities – just not at all in the way we expected!

Five children ran into the motor skills room. They had arrived a little early, so they began to run around and keep each other entertained. When it was time to start, we had a hard time capturing their attention. They did not want to sit down on the circle of cushions laid out on the floor where we had planned to explain what we were going to do during the next two hours. Instead of sitting on the cushions, they began to throw them around and, get into each other's space and they did not pay any attention to what we were saying. As a result, our session got off to a frustrating and uncoordinated start.

After the lesson, we knew that we had to change our start-up framework. After all, the motor skills room encourages play, so once the children are in there with all our toys and the lights on, they quickly switch to a high activity level and find it difficult to calm down again. So after some reflection, we found a solution:

We decided to start our next lesson in another room, which had tables and chairs and not much else. Again, the children showed up slightly early, but this setting did not encourage physical activity. We had the children sit down, with one chair each, spaced well apart, facing the whiteboard. This time, they were calm and ready to receive a message about the day's activities. Next, we went to the motor skills room together, and the children calmly and collectively started on the first game, cooperating nicely.

In the first situation, the macro-structure was not sufficiently contained. Therefore, the children's arousal level became so high that the adults could not regulate them and they could not attune with each other. As a result, the children infected each other with unregulated arousal. This is a good example of how important a good macro-structure is for arousal regulation, and it illustrates that if the macro-structure fails, we lose focus and also the infectious shared engagement that drives development. In the following lesson, the adults established the necessary framework for focusing the children's attention on the information. That also helped the children co-regulate afterwards; they were able to create continuous tiny micro-regulating contact sequences in their activities. In the next section, we will outline how these contacts unfold at the various neuroaffective levels of experience.

Three neuroaffective levels of interaction and co-regulation

As mentioned in Chapter 2, the neuroaffective development theory is inspired by Paul MacLean's theory (1990) about the evolution of the brain with the emergence of three functional levels, corresponding to three developmental stages of the human brain during childhood. Susan Hart has used this structure, with its three hierarchically organized personality levels – sensing, feeling and mentalization – as a device for systematically evaluating children's developmental resources and challenges (Hart, 2008, 2011a, 2011b) (see Figure 4.1).

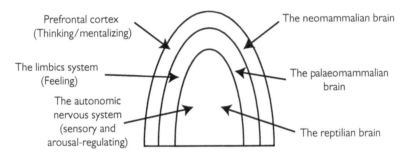

Figure 4.1: *The triune brain*

In the next paragraphs we will take a closer look at how co-regulation and attunement change according to the neuroaffective level of experience, and how various sensorimotor activities invite the child to discover new possibilities at the different levels.

At the autonomic, sensing level, which develops mainly from the prenatal period until the age of 3 months, co-regulation takes place through sensorimotor synchronization of movement and breathing, gaze contact, imitation, mirroring, gentle touching, reassuring repetition and physical care. It is important to understand that as humans we never 'outgrow' this synchronization, just as we never 'outgrow' breathing, even though our capacity for breathing matures before we are born. Co-regulation at the autonomic level has two objectives. One is to regulate arousal, the inner energy state, to prevent the child's energy level from getting so high that the child cannot be regulated or so low that the caregiver cannot reach the child. The other objective is to help the child distinguish between different kinds of sensory impressions and notice when something is pleasant or unpleasant, which is a prerequisite for being able to regulate one's own inner state.

At the limbic, emotional level, which develops mainly during the first year of life, all basic emotions mature. Co-regulation now involves various emotional states and energy levels, and the infant develops emotional patterns, complex interaction habits and expectations. In playful activities, it generally seems natural to create a shared build-up of tension or to introduce surprises at a level that is exciting or even slightly scary, but still fun – for example, by playing 'tag'. All good play also involves moments of meeting, where the children and perhaps also the adult have fleeting or slightly more prolonged experiences of contacts that feel especially important. In many cases, this feeling arises in connection with a shared focus on a third element: the shared project in play. In very high-energy activities, co-regulation should also include 'breaks for digesting', where either the children or the adult introduce calmer play elements, such as yoga or a foot massage. Co-regulation processes consist of all the little initiatives from the play partners that 'fit into' the play, along with the necessary emotional adjustments in relation to others' initiatives, and also of reattunements, which are attempts at reconnection and re-establishing the sense of rapport in the game after a loss of contact or misattunement. When children experience negative emotions, such as anxiety or sorrow, they often need the adult's containing care and help in the form of a diversion or distraction; however, children may also co-regulate with other children, showing emotional sympathy followed by an invitation to take part in an enjoyable activity after a suitable interval. The interaction habits that children develop through emotional co-regulation are internalized as expectations of interactions. Co-regulation at the limbic level trains and integrates the impulse to switch one's awareness focus between oneself and someone else, and later this develops into the capacity for a 'we-feeling' and for shared attention on a third element. Another key aspect is the capacity for experiencing both positive and negative emotions and moods and to receive help with containing them. These are particularly important skills for children in the quick-changing interactions of peer play. Children develop empathy as they practise shifting their attention between self and other, which supports security in their emotional interactions and leads to a realistic and secure inner 'map' of themselves and their interactions of the world around them.

At the prefrontal, mentalizing level, co-regulation takes place through play that involves cues to make a certain movement or to stop an activity, as well as turn-taking, symbol play, verbal agreements about games, roles, rules, verbal invitations and proposals and support for the children's spontaneous empathic care for other children. Mentalization is the capacity to grasp others' experiences and thinking and to see oneself from someone else's perspective. As children develop the initial aspects of the mentalization capacity, their conscious and verbally explicit understanding of their own and each other's inner states and motives become more nuanced and realistic, which can make it easier for them to deal both with external conflicts and inner dissonance. At the prefrontal level, co-regulation aims to develop a capacity for impulse management and for mentalization. Impulse management involves the ability to control needs and urges and to carry out tasks, even if one does not feel like it. Mentalization involves the basic ability to understand oneself in relation to the surrounding world, the ability to shape coherent inner narratives and the ability to adopt other perspectives. It is an extensive and incredibly nuanced capacity, and even though it develops in childhood and adolescence, it generally continues to develop well into adulthood, and ideally throughout the lifespan.

Sensorimotor activities at the three neuroaffective levels

From a neuroaffective perspective, various types of sensorimotor games can be used to promote a natural development and connection of the three neuroaffective levels (Bentzen, 2011) and thus support the children's capacity to self-regulate based on what they have already mastered.

At the autonomic level, the first step involves capturing and briefly holding the children's spontaneous curiosity and attention. Play at this level is simple and involves sensory experiences, imitation and shared rhythms. It may involve examining faces, imitating each other's (exaggerated) facial expressions or body postures and inventing games that stimulate the organization of innate reflexes and impulses, such as quickly or slowly sucking juice through a straw and swallowing it. It may utilize games with rhythmic standing, walking and cycling movements or marching in step with the adult (symmetrical and asymmetrical leg stretching reflex), where the level of difficulty can be varied by varying the pace, and other games involving rhythmic movement that alternately raise and lower the children's arousal level. Generally, it is paced so that quick and active games alternate with calm, soothing activities such as playing 'nap time', singing a song in whispers or getting a foot massage to practise regulating changing arousal levels.

At the limbic level, emotional impulses are expressed and contained in sensorimotor play. At this stage, children have a more stable attention capacity and are able to be absorbed in games and activities for slightly more prolonged periods. This is experienced as a 'state of flow', a concept we will return to later. Joy-filled surprises and challenges in play and showing care for anxiety and pain create moments of meeting that expand the children's capacity for recognizing and tolerating many kinds of emotions in themselves and others. Games with complementary physical 'roles' are used to induce more rapid shifts in arousal as well as the essential balance between emotional security and exciting thrills. Typical games are peek-a-boo, or the adult pretending to be a 'monster', chasing the children but later becoming nice and tame. It should be noted, however, that games with limbic 'roles' rely on motor activities with exciting and surprising behaviour elements, not on fantasy elements or symbols, as they do not come into play until the prefrontal level matures.

At the prefrontal level, games are about volitional control and symbol play. Stop games help train impulse inhibition and, in combination with verbal instructions (e.g. 'Find a red carpet triangle to stand on NOW!'), these activities train the coordination of impulse inhibition, volitional compliance with instructions and, later, the rules of games, sensory orientation and language. Any type of controlled movements (e.g. yoga exercises, gymnastics or rule-based ball games) will train the prefrontal regulatory capacity. Games of make-believe, where the children can become various animals (or, in a later example, aeroplanes) or play-act a story and need to cooperate in order to have fun, also train impulse control and the ability to coordinate with one or more other children.

As described in this section, macro-regulation in the form of specific tasks and activities invites development at specific levels. However, it is micro-regulation, both with the adult and among the children, that creates the countless moments of meeting (Sander, 1988; Stern, 2004; Trevarthen, 1994) and brief or more enduring states of flow and thus helps the individual child mature. We are therefore now going to take a closer look at specific classroom situations involving micro-regulation and co-regulation.

Mutual micro-regulation among the children

In a typical development process, the child masters basic social skills in contact with caregivers around the age of 1½ years. Although children at this age continue to need significant adult regulation, support and macro-structure to create an inviting framework in interactions, they are increasingly able to attune with other children in play and interactions. Children with sensorimotor issues often have age-appropriate interaction skills and interests as well as obvious shortcomings in their basic interaction skills, learned during the earliest years of life. Based on their early interactions with caregivers, the more skill children have in interacting, the better they are at finding solutions in the fascinating but also frequently frustrating contacts with their peers. And the less skill a child has developed in his or her early interactions, the more adult structure and support he or she needs in order to be able to co-regulate with other children.

Case study 4.2

Christine: In a group where children and parents normally received individual instruction, we wanted to see what sort of difference it might make to have the children see each other and see themselves reflected in others in the first session. We aimed to develop the children's engagement and motivation and had established a macro-structure to match this objective. For example, the parents had been instructed to follow their child's initiative, and we put out toys that would appeal to the children as well as challenge their motor skills.

Sam and Tina, who were both 4 years old, had motor challenges in the form of cerebral paresis, low muscle tone and reduced proprioception. They walked with difficulty and only with support, and they preferred to sit on the floor when they needed to concentrate, because that gave them a wider base and greater stability.

Initially, both Sam and Tina were focused on playing with a ball track – a sort of roller coaster for marbles that stands on the floor – which is tall enough that the children had to stretch to put the marble into the chute at the top.

Both children were so absorbed in putting marbles into the chute that even though this was the first day, they completely forget about being shy around each other and the other children. At first, Sam stretched to reach the chute, but he did not have sufficient control over his legs to be able to reach that high. Tina had discovered the trick of moving from a seated to a kneeling position, and that gave her enough reach to place her marble in the chute. In their shared engagement and joy over this victory, they smiled at each other and arrived at a shared intent of getting more marbles up to the chute. Sam tried to imitate Tina's successful manoeuvre. His mother helped him get up on his knees, and this time he too was able to place his marble in the chute.

After this one session, the mother noticed that Sam had begun to seek new challenges on his own initiative, and that he was much happier, which naturally made her happy too.

This example shows a spontaneous autonomic and limbic resonance and shared attention between Sam and Tina, based on their focus on this simple activity with a predictable outcome, which is that a marble rattles down the track. They developed the shared goal of placing the marble in the chute at the top of the track. This joint limbic engagement let Tina share her joy and pride over reaching a difficult goal with another child who shared the same challenging goal. The interaction gave Sam the added spark that helped him too achieve the challenge and allowed him to share his accomplishment with his playmate. 'Look what I did!' became 'We did it!' This example demonstrates the naturally developing limbic resonance that emerges when children with a similar skill level are together in a safe setting with appropriate challenges. Children are motivated and inspired by their similarities to a degree that does not occur when they play with adults.

Both Sam and Tina moved a small step further in their sensorimotor development – but equally important, they gained an important experience about themselves in joy-filled play with another child. This experience occurred because the two children co-regulated in a framework of autonomic, limbic moments of meeting and flow. Although in a situation like this the attunement happens between the children, the adult still has overall responsibility for framing the macro-regulation and supporting the micro-regulation that sustains the tender meeting. The adult stays in the background, 'propping up the walls', as it were, but always ready to step in. However, to create precise macro-regulation and micro-regulation, the activity and the interaction both need to challenge the child to the edge of his or her current capabilities, and the process must capture the child's enjoyment and attention. We will discuss this in more depth in the next section, as we look at Vygotsky's theory of the zone of proximal development.

The zone of proximal development in groups

The Russian psychologist Lev Vygotsky's (1978) understanding of the zone of proximal development, which was described in Chapter 2, is an excellent tool for identifying the development potential in any learning process. Originally, the term was used in relation to language acquisition, but it is also well suited for finding and structuring appropriate challenges and tasks in motor, personality and interpersonal development, also in groups. The model is presented in Figure 4.2 and shows that the zone of proximal development, which is the area where a child or a group of children can learn new skills, on the one hand overlaps with what has already been mastered by the child or children and, on the other hand, partially overlaps activities or skills that lie beyond reach.

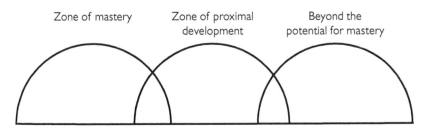

Figure 4.2: Vygotsky's three zones

Experience shows that if children are offered an activity they have already mastered, they are bored and lack engagement. On the other hand, if the activity is too challenging, it lies outside the learning horizon, which leads the children to feelings of defeat. Conversely, in the zone of proximal development, the 'Goldilocks zone' between these two extremes, there are many promising possibilities, from fine-tuning existing skills to taking on brand-new challenges. Although many school and preschool teachers and psychologists are familiar with Vygotsky's model, in our experience it takes a fair bit of sensitivity and precision to actually utilize it. First, the macro-level has to be in place: With knowledge of each child's zone of mastery and problem-areas, and drawing on sensory integration theory, it is possible to develop a programme for the group that matches each child's zone of proximal development. Naturally, this is easier to do with children who are largely at the same level, like Sam and Tina in Case study 4.2, so classes and groups are usually made up of participants at approximately the same level. Once the macro-structure is in place, the music of micro-regulation can unfold and be supported as the children play. Thus, in any given situation, the adult has to 'co-sense' the children's interactions – that is, track them with felt engagement – in order to discover where each of them is today and in this moment. This attunement enables the adult to facilitate a continuous attunement process in the children's activities and time support or step in as an appreciative witness to the child's or children's steps towards new discovery and mastery. Also, this attitude and engagement naturally inspires the adult to reshape or introduce new macro-structures in the form of new tasks, when necessary.

Another important principle is to ground the process first and foremost in skills that the children have already mastered, rather than on skills that they need to learn. One of the most frequent mistakes in working with the zone of proximal development is to look at what the individual 'needs' to learn. What a child or an adult needs to learn is the long-term goal, but the challenges we can joyfully lose ourselves in here and now are found in the zone of proximal development. An old joke plays on this distinction. A man passing through a small town in Texas stops his car and asks a local, 'What's the best way to get to New York from here?' The local thinks for a while, then replies, 'Well, see, if I was going to New York, I wouldn't start from here!' Following a similar logic, educators often choose to start the process in a place that makes it easy to reach the target. That makes sense, because in many cases the children are in a place fraught with challenges. But no one can start from any other place than where they are. This means that we must find ways to use the children's mastery and their zone of proximal development as our point of departure. When all is said and done, that is where we are at, and that is the space of possible growth. Every day. In every meeting.

Flow

Activities that match the zone of proximal development create the conditions for children to be able to experience flow states, which are those profoundly meaningful peak experiences that an individual can achieve during an activity. Flow is a mental state where one is completely absorbed in an activity, completely engaged and enthusiastic and with full control over the activity. In this state, we lose our sense of time and place. Several factors have to be present for a state of flow to emerge (Nakamura and Csikszentmihalyi, 1975):

- The task has to match the child's capabilities – that is, it must lie within the zone of proximal development.

- The activity must have a clear goal; a vague goal will fail to motivate the child.

- The child must receive constant feedback that he or she is getting closer to the goal.

If the challenge is too daunting, the child may be overwhelmed and anxious; if the challenge too small, the child is likely to get bored. It is these edges – the experiences of anxiety and boredom, respectively – that motivate the child to adjust his or her actions and challenges to be able to return to a state of flow (Nakamura and Csikszentmihalyi, 1975).

In personal and social development, it is particularly interesting to focus on prolonged states of flow that involve micro-attunements and co-regulation. Afterwards, people often describe these states using terms like 'we just clicked', 'we had a really good rapport' or 'the chemistry was perfect'. As we shall see later, children tend to express the state nonverbally – for example, by giving each other 'high-fives'.

However, it is not always possible for flow to occur in the activity that the adult has planned. For example, some children with sensory integration issues have difficulty reaching a state of flow without substantial external support. States of flow spring from the limbic and autonomic system in a spontaneous engagement, so it is important for the adult to be on the look-out, to spot exactly when the children reach this deep level of shared attention, either during the structured tasks or in spontaneous play 'outside' the planned structure, as in the following example.

Case study 4.3

Christine: It was a Thursday morning, and we had started the third session for a motor skills group of five boys with two adults present. The children had been introduced to the activities when they came, and we were in the middle of the third activity. This activity was a 'stop game', where the children had to look at the adult when the music stopped and then listen and look to receive instructions for the next step.

The boys had a hard time focusing, and it was difficult to maintain their attention. Jack was wearing a T-shirt with an aeroplane on it, and when Mark noticed this he began to talk about aeroplanes and took off 'flying' around the room, arms outstretched while he made engine noises with his mouth. Loudly, and in a surprised tone of voice, I said that he had almost flown off! Then the others began to fly too. For the next five minutes, the five boys 'flew' to different parts of the country. Eventually it was time to land, and they all landed – safe and sound on the landing strip – on their bellies.

With great agility, Christine switched here from her own structure to a game that emerged on the spot, and the children went from an unfocused partial participation to a shared flow on several levels. The 'stop game' invited the children to play with prefrontal control over motor impulses. The spontaneous flying game involved simpler motor demands than stopping on cue and also offered a rich opportunity for getting into a limbic emotional play community, based on many moments of bodily autonomic imitation and synchronization. At the same time, Christine remembered her role as the holder of the macro-structure, although the game she was now structuring was the children's own invention. The adult has to strike the right balance between being able to follow the children's own initiatives while also maintaining leadership.

Although it is easier to frame the zone of proximal development and inviting states of flow in a relatively homogeneous children's group, it is also often possible to make the most of the differences in competence that occur naturally in a group of children. We are going to look at this in the next section.

Challenges at different levels for different children in the same group

Until adolescence, play and social interactions among children involve a great deal of physical activity, so it is important to ensure that the children have enjoyable experiences using their bodies, and that they receive support to engage in social relationships with other children.

Case study 4.4

Christine: A group of boys met for a 1½-hour-long motor skills group. There were six children in the group, aged 4–5½ years. The children all had gross motor, fine motor or sensorimotor challenges in addition to other issues, and therefore each child was accompanied by a special needs teacher. The macro-structure was a pre-planned motor skills programme that included a number of group games and activities involving gym equipment. The agenda of group games included a song game with accompanying movements, a 'stop dance' with various tasks and finally a skateboard relay activity, where the children took turns in teams to go out, pick up puzzle pieces and put together a puzzle.

All six boys and their special needs teachers were instructed in the 'stop dance' game. This dance involves carpets patches in blue, green, yellow and red triangles, squares and circles. These patches are spread out over the floor. When the music stops I call out a shape or a colour, and the children have to hurry over to stand on a matching patch. When the game begins, everyone is focused and quickly finds the right shape or colour. After a couple of rounds, the game is taken up a notch as I call out both a colour and a shape – for example, blue triangle. This new task was a little challenging for one of the boys, but he soon found a solution by following one of the other boys over to the right patch.

For most of the children, this game is too simple and boring if it is not expanded to include both colour and form. The children who are quick to pick it up can be challenged further by being allowed to lead the game, so that they now take turns calling out the cue.

Here again, the macro-structure offered a play activity based on prefrontal impulse control, initially with the simple instruction of hurrying over to a particular shape or colour. Since most of the children mastered this challenge, Christine sought to challenge them in their zone of proximal development by making the task more complex, requiring them to find both a particular colour *and* a particular shape. For one of the boys, the activity now lay outside his zone of mastery, but he soon found his own creative way of keeping up.

Case study 4.5

Christine: A later activity in the group was called 'skateboard relay activity'. In this the boys worked in pairs, taking turns to lie face down on a skateboard to skate over to pick up puzzle pieces and bring them back to put together a jigsaw puzzle. I knew that the skateboard was going to be a challenge for one of the boys. Therefore I paired him up with a boy that I knew found this task easy. The boys were still at an age where they did not spot this little regulation – if there had been an odd number of children, I might have added another member to their team.

The boys took turns lying down on a skateboard and picking up two puzzle pieces each. Eventually, the children collected enough puzzle pieces that they could begin to assemble the jigsaw puzzle. They decided that one boy should go for more pieces while the other boy worked on the puzzle. They quickly completed the puzzles and everyone proudly presented the result.

This activity gave the children a flow experience and challenged them in their zone of proximal development. If the children had had very diverse skill levels, I might have put all the fast boys on one team and given them a bigger, more challenging puzzle.

This activity contained a purely autonomic, sensorimotor element in the skateboard trips. At the same time, there was limbic and prefrontal co-regulation and flow in the boys' cooperation as they took turns to wheel themselves over to get more puzzle pieces. At a prefrontal level, they were focused on the common task of completing the puzzle. Christine's macro-structure accommodated the different competence levels, because the activity was designed to allow the two boys to keep switching tasks. This let her structure the game to make sure that the weaker boy was not a burden to the faster boy, and instead they both achieved a shared state of flow and an experience of challenge and mastery in their zone of proximal development.

Case study 4.6

Christine: Later, the session involved individually coordinated activities using six types of gym equipment. Everyone was given a piece of equipment, and we switched around during the activity, so that all the boys tried all the different kinds of equipment. The children used the same equipment in different ways to match their individual level.

One boy used an ordinary swing seat suspended from a hook in the ceiling, swinging gently back and forth. For another boy, this was too boring and simple, and at first he wanted to jump off the swing, but instead he found a way to lie on his belly and play being in an aeroplane. A third boy kept a big stack of bean bags in his lap while he swung and tried to hit a ring on the floor with the bags.

Again, Christine had created a macro-structure that offered several different levels of motor challenges, this time involving gym equipment. It is remarkable that the boys were able to work independently at this stage of the group process, showing a joy and engagement that characterizes good autonomic and limbic regulation. They also showed good prefrontal self-organization in their ability to handle shifts in activities without mutual conflicts or disruption. From a neuroaffective perspective we concluded that the boys had spent so much time during the session with enjoyable shared flow and co-regulation that they had achieved an overall shared regulation in the group as a whole. With some amount of structuring adult support, this helped the boys self-regulate their arousal and engagement in their zone of proximal development.

Case study 4.7

Christine: Many of the children who come to sensorimotor training have sensorimotor challenges but function well socially, while others have difficulties in both areas and therefore find it difficult to participate in the day-to-day activities in preschool or school. Some children have a slight developmental lag compared to their age or a low level of confidence and are therefore quick to give up on new activities. Some have a low activity level. Others have dyspraxia or similar symptoms, giving them an innate problem with coordinating their movements. Others have developmental difficulties in sensory or motor integration etc. These diverse issues prevent the children from taking part in day-to-day activities and cause social problems in their interactions with other children, and in many – but not all – cases, they also suffer from low self-esteem. In these groups, many of the children have the experience of being 'on par' with other children and of being given challenges that they are able to master. These success experiences give them the necessary confidence to take on new experiences, and they appear happier and more willing to take on challenges in mainstream groups as well. Children naturally strive for flow when they play together, and carefully matched physical activities give them optimal opportunities for experiencing a state of flow.

Through sensorimotor training we aim to help the children transform their lives, unfold their potential and become the unique individuals they can be, despite their difficulties.

In a group of four 9-year-old boys with a variety of challenges, one of the boys, Ben, wanted to be better at using a push-scooter. He had difficulty balancing, and his physical reluctance showed that he was afraid of falling. He was very timid compared to the other boys, who enjoyed rough-housing. He did not have many friends in school but was very close to one of the other boys in the group. Where Ben was cautious, Brian was virtually fearless – so they complemented each other well. After practising 'falling' and balancing many times, the day came when it was time to use the scooters. We set up a course where the children could go down a wooden ramp, around some cones and then back up the ramp. The other boys queued up and looked forward to their turn. Ben stood a little apart, watching the others. After the other three boys had completed the course, it was Ben's turn. He stood at the top of the ramp, just looking and afraid to get started. Brian, who was good at using the scooter and who had completed his first round, moved up to stand next to Ben. Brian could tell that it was difficult for Ben, and he had tried to explain how much fun it was – but his words did not get through to Ben. Instead, Brian then stood next to Ben without saying anything, and together they rolled down the ramp. I filmed Ben on his way down the ramp. He looked a little scared – rapid breathing and big, round eyes – but he got down the ramp nevertheless. When he reached the bottom of the ramp, he was very relieved – I showed him the video, and he began to smile proudly. Now he wanted to go again. On his next ride, I walked next to him – I encouraged him as we went, saying that he was doing great, while someone else filmed him. At the end of the ramp he was all smiles and was keen to go again – on his own! I filmed his solo-ride, and he was so proud that he asked us to show it to his mum. He went a few more times – and there were lots of high-fives! He was given a copy of the video to take home to show his family.

This happened just before the summer break. After the summer break, I was keen to hear how he was getting on with the scooter. His mum told me, proudly, that he was an avid scooter-user now and had begun to do stunts on it with his friend Brian. She saw a new level of motivation in him: he challenged himself more than before and had also begun to talk to the other children in his neighbourhood as they now had a common activity to talk about. Brian grew in other ways. His mastery lay in being able to help his buddy through a tough spot, and after this experience he repeatedly showed his awareness of situations where he was able to help someone else with encouragement or support.

Here, Christine thoroughly prepared the children for the big challenge. The boys had practised falling, which trains the reflexes that are normally developed in the period from 6 to 18 months, and the prefrontal balancing skills required to use a push-scooter. In the tense situation where Ben tried to get up the courage to ride down the ramp for the first time, Brian reacted with an empathic, prefrontal impulse to help. At first, Brian offered verbal (i.e. prefrontal) encouragement but noticed that this did not help Ben master his fear. In this moment of truth, language lay beyond Ben's zone of proximal development. Spontaneously, Brian found the level where he was able to reach and help Ben: the limbic, autonomic wordless partnership of standing side by side and then going down the ramp together. Both boys had now mastered a maturity-building challenge. Ben overcame his anxiety, completed the course – eventually on his own – and entered the community around scooter activities. Brian used his prefrontal integration of empathy and mentalization to engage in helping his buddy, and he did not give up even though his initial attempt was unsuccessful.

This example also indicates another key aspect of working with children, which we do not address anywhere else in this chapter: the integration of parents and family. By taking the recording home, Ben was able to share his accomplishment with his parents, and one hopes that Brian and his parents might have found a way to share Brian's joy over his share in Ben's accomplishment. Ben's parents were well-functioning and supportive, but if the parents of a child find it difficult to manage their role as parents, it would be helpful to invite them to watch this kind of recording with their child and his teacher or therapist, as this might help the parents give their child the parental response that he or she needs.

In the situation described above, the adult's structure and macro-framing created the perfect conditions for the boys' maturation process in their zone of proximal development. However, no teacher or therapist gets it right every time, and from a developmental perspective, that is an advantage. One of the most important confidence-building experiences a child can have is that misattunements, with the discomfort they produce, can be turned around by a shared effort and attunement to create the flow and the vital interaction that drives the child's development. We will take a closer look at this mechanism in the next section.

From adult leadership to the children's improvisation

Any teacher or therapist will sooner or later be confronted with a situation where children are decidedly unexcited about one's brilliant macro-management and planning. The best solution is to draw out and incorporate the children's own activities as a new framework and structure, as Christine did in the following example:

Case study 4.8

Christine: I instructed a group of children in yoga as part of a motor skills course. Some of the boys observed and others lay on their mats, losing focus, while a few of them took part and did their best. I could tell that I was not going to engage them unless I changed my approach – they were not self-motivating. One boy bent his body into a funny posture. I seized his initiative and said, 'Hey, David, that looks fun, how did you do that?' and tried to copy his position. The other boys watched and laughed; in fact, we all laughed because I looked silly. Then I asked David what the name of the yoga pose was, and he said it was the Dinosaur. Now everyone tried to do the Dinosaur. Soon all the boys were trying to come up with new yoga poses, and we all tried them and gave them names.

Suddenly everyone was involved in a third activity, which we co-created and decided on together. As we made the shift into new ground, it was important that we stayed close to the initial activity of yoga, which was my agenda, and it was also important that the boys used their bodies at the level that each of them could handle and enjoyed.

In this situation, Christine captured the boys' limbic playful initiatives while also creating the necessary framework for channelling the playful activity into the original task, to prevent the group from descending into chaos or simply falling apart. The limbic moment of meeting emerged as the result of a surprise: Christine directed the group's attention to the funny pose and imitated it. Next, she incorporated the boys' playful engagement into the structure by pretending that the new position was a *bona fide* yoga pose with a name. With a number of micro-regulations she injected energy into the macro-structure, and the boys had the experience that 'boring' prefrontal tasks can be transformed into playful limbic, autonomic attunement.

These sensible and boring prefrontal tasks, which may even lie beyond the children's zone of proximal development, are often initiated by the adults; but not always. The expectation of what is 'the proper thing' to do may also emerge in a sort of unwitting conspiracy between the adult and a child – usually, a slightly older child.

Case study 4.9

Christine: In this group, we were two adults working with four boys around the age of 10 years, all with a variety of diagnoses and motor challenges. Three of the four boys were also overweight. The purpose of the group was to focus on body enjoyment and movement. When we asked what their goal was for the group, all four boys wanted to be better at running (i.e. faster) in order to do better at soccer. So the next time we met, we decided to go for a run together. That was not a success.

We got out the door all right, but the boys kept complaining and had difficulty even dragging their feet along. 'It's boring!' and 'It hurts!' they kept saying. When we finally gave up and went back inside, they were unfocused, threw themselves on the floor, teasing and disturbing each other. We adults did not understand what had gone wrong. After all, running was the boys' own idea. We took a short break, and one of the boys started talking about his brother, who played floor hockey. This piqued the other boys' interest, and they thought it sounded like fun. We said that we had some hockey sticks and a ball lying around! We split the boys into two teams and agreed on the ground rules; and then the game began. The next 15 minutes they were running around, laughing, yelling with excitement and really pushing themselves. When they stopped, they had nice red cheeks and slapped each other high-fives.

In hindsight, we could see that running was simply too hard for the boys. They were not motivated about running, and every step they took was a reminder of their failure. While they were playing hockey, they forgot all about their surroundings and were able to lose themselves in the game.

At the end of the course we talked to the boys about what it was like to be in the group. We were keen to hear their thoughts and whether they felt that they had reached their goal, which was about being better at running. Their verdict was that it was difficult to judge – but they also did not think it really mattered. They thought it was fun to be part of the group and get to know the other boys.

In this example, the adults and the boys had both walked into the prefrontal trap we described at the beginning of the chapter. At the beginning they all agreed what they needed to learn – running –

instead of beginning in their zone of proximal development, focusing on what was within reach in the situation. Fortunately, the boys' limbic, emotional objection was strong enough that the sensible project had to be abandoned, and in the midst of the frustration and bad behaviour that often emerges, a new idea popped up spontaneously: a game where the boys had all the skills they needed to have fun. At the same time, they were able to improve their running skills without being confronted with the prefrontal inner critical judge. Hockey was an age-appropriate team activity, where the prefrontal rules would be combined with limbic, autonomic enjoyment and coordination.

The importance of infectious engagement

In this chapter, we have used examples from Christine's sensorimotor method to highlight a key aspect of inclusion: the delicate balance between the adult's responsibility to provide a macro-structure and the responsibility to support the micro-processes between the children. In addition, we have sought to bring in the science of developmental psychology to offer a new and (we hope) refreshing metaphor for sensorimotor and personal maturation as something that happens through a sort of ongoing interpersonal infection. Adults infect children on a daily basis – and they in turn infect each other – with a sense of their own value and the value of their environment. This infection occurs through our emotional responses and through our mutually attuned engagement in everyday activities. Children are born with the seeds of competences, ready to develop ever more sophisticated skills in co-regulation, self-regulation, emotional presence and expression, capacity for attention, frustration threshold and empathy – and much later, a capacity for reflection. Shared joy is a crucial carrier wave in this maturation process, and we hope that this chapter may help to generate more infectious joy in education, regardless of the underlying method that shapes the educational macro-structure.

References

Bentzen, M. (2011) 'Sproget før Sproget.' In S. Hart (ed.) *Neuroaffektiv Psykoterapi med Børn*. Copenhagen: Hans Reitzels Forlag.

Freud, S. (1923/1994) *Das Ich und das Es: Metapsychologische Schriften*. Frankfurt am Main: Fischer Taschenbuch Verlag.

Hart, S. (2008) *Brain, Attachment, Personality: An Introduction to Neuroaffective Development*. London: Karnac Books.

Hart, S. (ed.) (2011a) *Neuroaffektiv Psykoterapi med Børn*. Copenhagen: Hans Reitzels Forlag.

Hart, S. (2011b) *The Impact of Attachment: Developmental Neuroaffective Psychology*. New York, NY: W. W. Norton.

Keysers, C. (2011) *The Empathic Brain: How the Discovery of Mirror Neurons Changes our Understanding of Human Nature*. Groningen: Social Brain Press.

Kielhofner, G. (2002) *Model of Human Occupation: Theory and Application* (3rd edn). Baltimore, MD: Lippincott, Williams & Wilkins.

Lewis, T., Amini, F. and Lannon, R. (2001) *A General Theory of Love*. New York, NY: Vintage Books.

MacLean, P. (1990) *The Triune Brain in Evolution: Role in Paleocerebral Functions*. New York, NY: Plenum.

Nakamura, J. and Csikszentmihalyi, M. (1975) 'The Concept of Flow.' In M. Csikszentmihalyi (ed.) *Beyond Boredom and Anxiety: Experiencing Flow in Work and Play*. San Francisco, CA: Jossey-Bass.

Sander, L. W. (1988) 'The Event Structure of Regulation in the Neonate-Caregiver System as a Biological Background for Early Organization of Psychic Structure.' In A. Goldberg (ed.) *Progress in Self Psychology* (vol. 3). Hoboken, NJ: Taylor & Francis.

Stern, D. N. (1999) 'Vitality Contours: The Temporal Contour of Feelings as a Basic Unit for Constructing the Infant's Social Experience.' In P. Rochat (ed.) *Early Social Cognition: Understanding in the First Months of Life*. New York, NY: Lawrence Erlbaum.

Stern, D. N. (2004) *The Present Moment in Psychotherapy and Everyday Life*. New York, NY: W. W. Norton.

Stern, D. N., Sander, L. W., Nahum, J. P., Harrison, A. M. *et al.* (1998) 'Non-interpretive mechanisms in psychoanalytic therapy: The "something more" than interpretation.' *International Journal of Psycho-Analysis 79*, 903–921.

Trevarthen, C. (1994) 'The Self Born in Intersubjectivity: The Psychology of an Infant Communicating.' In U. Neisser (ed.) *The Perceived Self: Ecological and Interpersonal Sources of Self Knowledge*. Cambridge: Cambridge University Press.

Vygotsky, L. S. (1978) *Mind in Society: The Development of Higher Psychological Processes*. Cambridge, MA: Harvard University Press.

5

Group Theraplay™ in Classrooms

How Playful Engagement Fosters
Social and Emotional Growth

Phyllis Rubin and Marlo Winstead

Outside a classroom door with 24 students aged 10 and 11 years, shouts of glee and laughter are heard. Students and their teacher, Mrs. Fitz, are lifting three balloons in a blanket and counting how many lifts they can do before a balloon leaves the blanket and floats to the floor. All together, they say, '1-2-3-Go!' and synchronize their movements to lift the balloons in a cooperative effort. When one balloon eventually flies away and falls, some turn to their classmates and give high-fives, saying, 'Good try. Let's do it again!' Such glee and cooperation is not always found in schools, and certainly was not the case at the beginning of the year in Mrs. Fitz's fifth grade room. Something happened to turn things around in a major way.

Welcome to Group Theraplay™, an experiential, relationship-based method that is lively, spirited, caring, and 100 per cent interpersonally interactive. Participating in a Theraplay Group is a unique experience in which everyone – including you – is emotionally connected and expressive. It is through experiencing this unique form of adult-guided play with others that children can grow in self-esteem, self-care, and empathy for others, in confidence and assertiveness, and in the ability to cooperate with peers and adults. Group Theraplay in classrooms can build more cohesion, and thus make managing the classroom easier. A final benefit of Group Theraplay is that it addresses the often ignored human need for joy – the spirited joy that can erupt between friends who are enriching their relationship by sharing a moment of delight. Joy can go a long way in lightening stress and relieving social tensions, allowing children's brains to reset themselves for learning (Brown and Vaughan, 2009).

Group Theraplay™ began when Phyllis Rubin – then a school speech-language pathologist, now a clinical psychologist, Theraplay and Group Theraplay therapist, supervisor, and trainer – was working in schools with children with special needs and was challenged by teachers to adapt individual Theraplay to classroom groups to reach more children. (More about individual Theraplay in a moment.) Phyllis proceeded to develop the Group model described here, co-authored a book about it (Rubin and Tregay, 1989), and began teaching teachers, therapists, speech-language therapists, occupational therapists, and psychotherapists to lead Theraplay Groups in their settings. Marlo Winstead is a licensed clinical social worker, Theraplay and Group Theraplay therapist, supervisor, and trainer who works with children, families, and groups who have experienced relational trauma. Marlo has lead Theraplay Groups with children in after-school groups, schools, community centers, hospitals, churches, head start programs, and residential treatment centers for children aged 2 years to early adulthood. She has co-authored several chapters on the subject, trained many professionals in the Theraplay model, and created a multitude of activities that promote the spirited, cooperative, and caring atmosphere of Group Theraplay.

Basics of Theraplay

While Group Theraplay led by a teacher in schools is not therapy,[1] it is based on parent–child Theraplay, an experiential attachment-based therapy guided by the therapist. Theraplay is framed around five types of experiences that have been observed to lead to healthy attachment in children: Structure, Engagement, Nurture, Challenge (Booth and Jernberg, 2010), and Playfulness (Mäkelä and Hart, 2011). These experiences – in Theraplay, we identify them as dimensions (Booth and Jernberg, 2010) – are a natural part of parent–child play that help develop healthy neurological and emotional functioning and, among other things, prepare children for school. The first dimension is *structure* that involves setting rules and limits and providing thoughtful

---

1   When teachers lead groups based on Theraplay Groups, we recommend including them in the social-emotional curriculum.

guidance to children. Like authoritative parenting (Alizadeh *et al.*, 2011; Baumrind, 1978), clear, firm limits and boundaries in adult–child relationships, along with warmth and logical explanations, contribute to social and academic competence and healthy behavior patterns. The second dimension, *engagement*, involves sharing joyful in-the-moment experiences during which the adult is deeply attuned to the child's emotions and state of alertness (Hart, 2011; Stern, 1985; Sunderland, 2006; Trevarthen, 2001). Attuned engagement helps to regulate a child's state so that it is not too high or too low, but 'just right' for thinking and doing. The third dimension – *nurture* – involves the adult caring for the child's basic needs (e.g. feeding and soothing). Such experiences calm a child's distress and anxiety, help regulate the nervous system and emotions, and contribute to a secure base (Bowlby, 1988; Cooper, Hoffman and Powell, 2009), all associated with the ability to problem-solve and cooperate with others (Sroufe, 1988; Sroufe and Fleeson, 1988). The fourth dimension is *challenge*, which involves encouraging the child to grow, learn, and take the next step in development (Chrousos, 1998; Vygotsky, 1978). Challenge, with associated feelings of mastery, increases motivation. The fifth dimension is *playfulness*, which has been called the 'joy juice' (Sunderland, 2006, p.90), and helps a child feel the bond of positive emotions with others (Schore, 2001) – including teachers! Because 'laughter is fundamentally a social phenomenon' (Panksepp, 2001, p.155) that draws people together for the good, being the bearer of joy can result in children being more responsive to you.

Theraplay™ is built on the belief that children have an underlying need for a balance of these dimensions within adult–child relationships. When children have received healthy combinations of these dimensions with their parents and other adults, they go out in the world armed with self-confidence, a *joie de vivre*, and trust that they will find supportive friends and teachers. They will also have the ability to learn from and share ideas with others. The attachment literature suggests that these children will be more prepared for life than those who have missed such experiences and have not had these needs met (Bowlby, 1988; Rubin, 1996; Schore, 1994; Sroufe, 1988; Sroufe and Fleeson, 1988).

Group Theraplay™ framework

To facilitate these healthy experiences within groups of children, the five dimensions of structure, engagement, nurture, challenge, and playfulness are translated for Group Theraplay into three explicit rules and one implicit rule: No Hurts, Stick Together, Have Fun, and (silently) the Adult is in Charge. These simple rules, perfect for the classroom, shape the focus of your groups. The leader does not just talk about these rules. Rather, the leader acts on these rules and helps the children respond to them as well. By embodying these rules, the leader creates the powerful Group Theraplay atmosphere: a safe, accepting, and emotionally connected experience. Here's how to create it:

1. *No Hurts:* No Hurts represents the nurturing dimension in Theraplay. When you announce the No Hurts rule, you are saying that you will care for and respect each person in the group, and that hurting others' bodies and feelings has no place in building positive and cooperative relationships or in healing emotional wounds. You, the leader, follow the No Hurts rule by 'repairing' any hurts that happen during group time – whether intentional or unintentional. No Hurts functions to provide the nurturing that everyone needs and to keep everyone physically, emotionally, and psychologically safe – particularly hurt, scared, or traumatized children. No Hurts is built into the opening ritual of Check-Ups (described in the Purple Butterfly Ninja Group vignette later in the chapter) and is activated when someone gets their body or their feelings hurt. At these times, the leader notices the hurt, acknowledges it, and *does something* to help the hurt child feel cared for. Examples of 'doing something' are: gently rubbing lotion around an outside hurt; dabbing a hurt with a cotton ball or feather; giving a hug. Most important, the leader *responds emotionally* to the hurt by putting concern into voice and face. It is this non-verbal communication of the rules – in this case, No Hurts – that creates the emotional connection unique to Theraplay. You will see through the case vignettes how the rules are carried out in practice.

2. *Stick Together:* This rule represents the structure and engagement dimensions of Theraplay. As much as possible, you don't start an activity until the whole group is present. If, during your group,

two kids start interacting separately from the group in a way that is distracting and disrupting, you would *do something!* You would notice their separateness and say, 'Hey guys, stick together! We want you with us!', structuring the children to stay connected to each other. As your group matures, the children may invoke the rules as well, reminding a peer who has strayed, 'Hey, stick together!' This is good peer pressure! Remember to respond emotionally when children go off 'on their own'. Rather than showing irritation or reprimand, you convey in your voice and on your face a genuine wish for them to be part of the group. Practicing the Stick Together rule tells the children that each one of them is welcome and wanted in the group, and that you want to be engaged in an attuned, attentive and emotionally connected experience with each of them. This 'rule' not only gives them the message that they are important to you, but helps draw them closer to each other in a therapeutic experience that addresses their emotional and social needs.

3. *Have Fun:* This rule represents the challenge and playfulness dimensions. You practice this rule by bringing fun activities to your group that challenge the children to stretch themselves socially and emotionally. If an activity you start is not fun, you would *do something!* You would notice the upset or the 'we-have-to-do-this-anyway' feeling – in your kids or in *you* – and you would stop the game, saying, 'Oh my! This isn't fun, is it? Let's do something else.' (Or you would change the game in some way.) Bringing fun to your children and joining in tells them you genuinely want to *be with them.* Have Fun may seem like the easiest rule to practice. While it can be, it all depends on you and your state of mind while you are with your group. You, first and foremost, need to be having fun with your children. Tricky, because you are also leading the group! You have to be in charge *and* also participate totally in the activities. We'll describe how the leader does this in the next section and later in this chapter.

4. *The Adult is in Charge:* This is the 'implicit' rule – not spoken but carried out nevertheless. By putting you in charge, this rule also provides structure, but you structure in a rather unique way. Your

Theraplay Group is neither free play nor is it teaching. Your role is both to lead *and* to participate. For example, for Check-Ups (described in the Purple Butterfly Ninja Group), you would lead by saying, 'I'm going see how Sammy [child next to you] is today.' After you have checked Sammy, you guide him to check Sarah (next to him), and the Check-Ups go around the circle of children until it gets to you. Then the child at the end, next to you, checks *you* and cares for any special spots or hurts. This is an important part of Group Theraplay™ because the children see how you handle receiving care and engage in fun activities. You are showing them that these experiences are positive and healthy among friends and you are also showing them how trust looks. You lead but don't participate when it is necessary to apply the rules – for example, if a child gets bumped. In this instance, you stop the playing and, with No Hurts in mind, say, 'Uh oh, Tommy got hurt. Tommy, we have to make sure you're OK. Let's see. Oh, I think you need some cream on that elbow.' Remember that you don't announce The Adult is in Charge rule.

Special characteristics of a Theraplay™ Group

Watching a Theraplay Group, you will see that it is full of playful activities that involve appropriate, healthy physical contact and explicitly caring acts. *Why physical contact?* Children need to know how to have appropriate physical contact. To learn this, they need experiences with appropriate touch. Group Theraplay activities do not avoid touch. We clap hands with friends, draw shapes on each others' backs, hold hands, have thumb wrestles, and may touch elbows-to-elbows or toes-to-toes. Appropriate physical contact will help children know when there has not been appropriate contact. Should hurtful touch occur, we use the No Hurts rule to correct the inappropriateness and convey that we take such violations of boundaries seriously. *Why explicitly caring acts?* What we do always speaks louder than when we simply say, 'I'm sorry.' Treating people respectfully and in caring ways shows that we are truly sorry and that we want to make amends to make sure the other person feels better. It shows we mean what we say. *Why playfulness?* Playfulness engages spirit and emotions. The person is totally *in* the relationship, heightening the experience of connectedness. Playfulness can lift a person out of self-absorption and isolation and bring the person into the classroom community. It can reduce stress and lighten one's load, facilitating resilience so that one can better manage the challenges and stressors of life (Sunderland, 2006).

Unique characteristics of the Theraplay™ Group leader

The Theraplay Group leader must be playful and engaging, comfortable with closeness, touch, and nurturing, and must be able to stay with the children emotionally and maintain a positive attitude toward them despite the difficult behaviors that they may present. The leader must accept a wide range of behaviors during the group and not punish or consequence infractions, but instead, employ group rules to manage problematic behaviors in a positive and sometimes even playful manner. The leader has to maintain a balance between being in charge of and participating in the group, and make mastery appealing by challenging the children to stretch themselves and, then, enthusiastically delight in their efforts.

Research

Two studies have been completed on the effects of Group Theraplay: one with children and the other with adults. Group Theraplay was found to decrease *internalizing problems* (self-blame) in children after only eight weeks of Group (Siu, 2009) and to increase self-esteem in depressed adults living alone (Kim, 2011). Both these studies support the lessening of depressive tendencies after a course of Group Theraplay. For teachers, it may be obvious that lifting children's depression would have a positive impact on school functioning.

How to present to children and parents

Introducing Group Theraplay to children is quite simple. The first time you sit in your circle, explain the purpose: 'We're going to do some special things together to help us get along better with each other, with other kids outside of our group, and with adults. And we're also going to play and have fun.' Then, after singing a song and introducing each child, explain the group rules: 'There are some special rules about playing together. First, No Hurts! That means that if someone does get hurt, I want to know and we will take care of you.'

For parents or other caregivers, you can have a meeting or send them written information about Group Theraplay™. They should know the purpose of Group Theraplay – for example, 'This is a social skills group to help improve peer relationships as well as your child's relationships with adults.' Give parents a description of what the group will look like: 'We will sit in a circle and do caring and fun activities.' Provide examples of activities that you plan to do with the group and include some that are explicitly caring, fun, and involve touch. Present the rationale for these characteristics, much as we have stated above. If you have developed more specific goals for your group of children, include these as well. If the parents come to a meeting, demonstrate some activities with them and allow for a discussion about how they experienced them. You can also invite them to think about how their child will experience and respond to Group Theraplay.

Group examples[2]

In this section we will be describing two Group examples to demonstrate the practical application of Theraplay Groups.

The 'We Can Do It Group'

Remember Mrs. Fitz's 10- and 11-year-olds lifting balloons in a blanket? The start of the school year was very different. This experienced teacher quickly recognized that she was in for a challenging year. Many of her students were struggling academically and behaviorally – not a good combination for learning. The school principal provided Mrs. Fitz with support through an educational specialist and a behavioral specialist during the first semester. The team, including Mrs. Fitz and the specialists, worked very hard to help the children understand why they were there and who was in charge.

At first, behavior charts seemed to work. For the first two weeks of using them, most of the kids completed their assignments and earned tickets to spend at the 'store'. The biggest problem occurred when students didn't earn the number of tickets they aimed for and they

---

2   Information in all case examples has been disguised to protect the privacy of group participants. The examples we are sharing with you include challenging behavior to enrich your understanding of how we manage resistance, but many groups take place without these types of difficulties.

weren't able to 'buy' what they wanted at the store. New problems arose in the classroom – students were stealing tickets from their peers, trying to buy tickets with money or food at lunch time; and when those strategies didn't work, two of the students, Elisio and Quinton, started saying, 'If you don't give us your tickets, we're going to wait for you at the bus stop and beat you up.' Mrs. Fitz was very discouraged, and on top of the daily issues, the majority of her students were testing two to three grade levels behind academically.

The team stopped using the behavior charts because they were causing too many problems. They tried to implement other strategies, such as small group learning, centers, additional academic focus time before school, during recess, and after school, but they weren't sure what else to do. The problems in Mrs. Fitz's room were also very worrisome for the principal. When he heard about 'play groups' at another school that were 'helping kids get along better', he thought, 'Well, might as well give it a try. Nothing else is working.' The principal contacted me, explained the difficulties in the classroom, asked if I thought Group Theraplay™ would help, and requested that I meet with him and Mrs. Fitz. From our meeting I gathered that Mrs. Fitz had a very good reputation for managing challenging children, and she ended up with a classroom full of them. She was exhausted and said, 'I'm feeling hopeless about most of these kids passing [the 5th grade], and I don't think that I can take another semester of this. I appreciate you coming, but I don't think that a group where the kids play [Theraplay Group] will help them. It's nothing personal, it's just not going to work, and I don't have the energy to do another thing that won't work.' I could tell that Mrs. Fitz cared for her students, and that she was very committed to helping them succeed. I valued and respected her dedication.

I left the meeting under the impression that Mrs. Fitz was not interested, so the groups would not take place. Then I received a call from the principal the next day asking when I could start doing the group in Mrs. Fitz's classroom. I was surprised, nervous, cautious, but also delighted because I truly thought it would be helpful for Mrs. Fitz and her students. I met with Mrs. Fitz to prepare her to participate in the group and found out that she did not want to do the group but was told by her principal that it was going to happen – not the best way to start a therapeutic intervention. After several classroom observations and Mrs. Fitz introducing me to the kids as someone coming to help them behave (a less than ideal introduction), it was Thursday morning and time for our first group.

'Okay everyone, we're going to carefully move our desks to the sides of the room so that I can put this blanket on the floor and we can have some fun,' I said. 'Everyone with blue on, move your desk carefully... Okay, good... Now, if you are wearing anything with yellow, move your desk safely.' As the children looked at each other's clothes, searching for blue, yellow, green, pink, etc., the atmosphere started to change just a little bit. To get organized, I announced, 'Now, everyone sit down on the blanket in a circle.' Two students, Quinton and Melody, were arguing about where they should sit. I caught a glimpse of Mrs. Fitz, whose tense body language and exasperated facial expression seemed to be saying, 'Here we go again.' I walked over, put my hand out to shake their hands, and said, 'Hi, I'm Ms. Marlo. What's your name?' Melody quickly reached out and said loudly, 'I'm Melody!', but Quinton, in a skeptical way, looked at my hand, folded his tightly against his chest and said, 'I'm Q.' I replied, 'It's nice to meet both of you. I'm going to be right here so that I can get to know you better,' as I assertively squeezed between the two of them.

I took a seat on the blanket, motioned for the students to do the same, and introduced myself: 'Hi Mrs. Fitz's fifth grade class. My name is Ms. Marlo, and I'm so glad to be here. I have one of the coolest jobs in the world. I get to play with kids! Now, we're going to play together on Thursday mornings every week for the next 14 weeks. We're doing this to help you get along better with each other and with adults, and to exercise your brain in different ways. Thank you for letting me come and play with your students Mrs. Fitz, and thank you for being a part of our play group too.' As I mentioned playing, the students' eyes got bigger and I could hear little giggles of pleasure throughout the room, with the exception of Q, who was very stoic and unimpressed. I continued, 'There are only three rules when we play together. The first one is "No Hurts". Say that with me and do this hand motion on the count of three: one, two, three,' and in unison we shout, '"No Hurts!"' 'That means with our bodies and our words.' I introduced the second rule, Stick Together, and the third, Have Fun, in the same manner. In a playful way, and to reinforce the rules I said, 'Let's practice them all together now, one, two, three,' and 26 voices said, 'No Hurts, Stick Together, Have Fun!' along with hand motions.

'Now we're going to do a rhythm together to say "hello" and practice each other's names. Follow me,' I said as I tapped the floor in front of me twice and then clapped my hands together twice and repeated the rhythm. After four repetitions everyone was in sync so I added the words, 'Hello, We Can Do It Group,' and the students repeated, 'Hello, We Can Do It Group.' I continued, 'Hello, Melody,' and the group echoed, 'Hello Melody.' This continued all the way around the circle: 'Hello, Melissa,' 'Hello Melissa'; 'Hello Mrs. Fitz,' 'Hello Mrs. Fitz'. I shouted each member's name and the group copied me. *[The Hello Rhythm was a ritual that signaled the start of the group and provided a moment for each member to be noticed individually. As presented in Chapter 1 by Trevarthen and Panksepp, rhythmic synchrony has been shown to promote calmness in the brain as well as bonds between people.]*

I took some lotion out of my bag, squeezed a big glob onto my hand, and said, 'We're going to see how many times we can send this blob of lotion around the circle. I'm going to pass it to Q, and then he's going to pass it from his hand to Megan's hand, and it will go all the way around the circle. Now after Q passes it to Megan I will check and see if there is any lotion left on his hand and make it disappear by rubbing it in, and then he gets to check Megan's hand and rub it in, and on around our circle until everyone has had a turn.' Q certainly wasn't excited about the activity, but he cooperated and seemed to soften a bit after I rubbed in the leftover lotion on his hand. *[Playfulness can be a way to disguise the nurturing children so need and make it palatable for kids like Q who deny this need.]* The children waited anxiously as the glob of lotion made its way around the circle. A few times it seemed like the lotion was going to slide off of someone's hand and onto the floor, and each time the recipient caught it, Elisio would say, 'You have saved the day my fair prince/princess,' and the whole group erupted with laughter. Not only the children, but I too was surprised when Elisio, the former sticker stealer and bully, added such a congenial comment showing that he valued his peers. This blew our minds! When the glob of lotion made it back to me, I said, 'Wow, we made it all the way around and we have lots left. How many times do you think we can make it around the circle?' There were shouts from around the group, 'Four times,' 'Seventeen times,' 'Nine times,' and more. As I passed it to Q again, I said, 'Those are a lot of good guesses. Let's keep going and see how many circles we can do.' We passed the glob of lotion around the circle four and a half times, and I said, 'Hooray, four and a half, that's awesome! Let's have a cheer. On the count of three we're going to say "We are awesome" three times in a row. One, two, three.' I'm sure our shouts 'We are awesome, we are awesome, we are awesome' could be heard down the hallway. The We Can Do It Group was off to a great start.

This is an account of the introduction and first four activities (Rules, Hello Rhythm, Lotion Pass, We Are Awesome) in the first group of Mrs. Fitz's fifth-grade class. While Q and Melody posed a minor challenge at the beginning, this did not impede the group's success and joy. The children were cooperating with each other and with me as the group leader; they were having fun, laughing together, working as a team to accomplish something, and participating in an uninhibited manner. Mrs. Fitz was glad to see the children having fun, and said that she had a little fun too, but she did not understand how rewarding the children with playtime would improve their behavior or their learning in the classroom.

I acknowledged Mrs. Fitz's concerns and discussed the importance of psychological, emotional, and physical safety in the environment for children to learn. I also referenced the five dimensions of Group Theraplay™ that we discussed previously and I pointed out relevant examples. For instance, I mentioned various Structure activities and described how they helped the children to accept adult direction in a fun way so that they would be able to accept her directions when it wasn't as much fun. *[Because, in Theraplay, structure and playfulness go together, children experience limit setting as part of something pleasant rather than suppressive or demanding. As a result, they are often more cooperative when the situation is more serious. And remember that, as said earlier, being the bearer of joy can help children be more responsive to you.]* I also shared how activities that incorporated Engagement and Challenge facilitated teamwork and collaboration so that competition between students would decrease, including 'catty' behavior, put-downs, and the bully–victim behaviors.

I continued to meet with the We Can Do It Group, and each week the level of cooperation, fun, collaboration, and regulation increased. I also noticed that Mrs. Fitz was genuinely more involved: she smiled more, laughed more, and was more playful with her students. Just before we moved the desks for Group on week three, I noticed a handful of students in the corner having an argument. I walked over and said, 'Friends, remember Stick Together. Come on, we can't have fun unless we're all sticking together.' The group quieted, but as I started to walk away I saw them motioning toward each other and making faces. The argument wasn't over. *[First, I used the rule to manage the situation. But I was attuned to a problem that I needed to understand better in order to help the children stick together.]* I turned and said, 'What's going on you guys?', and a clamor of six voices responded: 'I said I was going to sit next to Mrs. Fitz'; 'No, last week I said I was going to sit next to her this week'; and 'I haven't gotten to yet so that's not fair'. I looked at Mrs. Fitz, who very surprised by her students' desire to be close to her. I settled the argument by saying, 'Okay, you two, Latisha and Alexis, haven't had a turn to sit next to Mrs. Fitz. You get to sit on either side of her this week and then two other people can sit by her next week.' After Group I asked Mrs. Fitz how she felt during this exchange and she said, 'I felt special. Like my students finally wanted to connect with me. I'm still not saying this is working, but something good is happening.' *[Sharing fun with others does promote feelings of emotional closeness and cooperation!]*

We continued to meet together each week. Gradually Mrs. Fitz became more and more involved and animated with her students, and in turn the students were more responsive and cooperative. Now, they all were excited when I arrived on Thursdays. The playful synergy between Mrs. Fitz and her students increased as they enjoyed bopping balloons around the group, making a group hand stack, and sending a hula-hoop around each child in the circle without letting go of each other's hands. The children's desire to cooperate with each other and Mrs. Fitz continued to grow. At the end of the Group sessions Mrs. Fitz reported that the behavioral issues were close to non-existent, and the students' willingness and capacity for educational learning increased as well.

The 'Purple Butterfly Ninja Group'

This is an example of a Theraplay™ Group in an after-school program outside of school, without the children's teachers, and with children who were not from the same classroom. The kindergarten-age group – 17 boys and girls aged 5 and 6 years – were known to be extremely playful, rowdy, and in need of clear limits and boundaries because they had trouble managing their excitement. The complaints from the staff about this group included difficulty listening to instructions, lack of empathy for peers, frequent incidents of verbal and physical aggression between students, and an overall feeling in the adults of stress, anxiety, and unpredictability when the group was together.

The group appeared to be extremely challenging at first. Many of the children exited the bus upon arrival in a highly aroused state, shouting, running, and bumping and crashing into their peers, the floor, the walls, and adults. However, when I looked more closely, I noticed there were a few ringleaders inciting most of the unwanted behavior. When the children arrived, the staff attempted to corral them into their classroom by holding their hands and saying, 'Come on everyone, come on, we need to go into the purple room...come on, we do this every day, you know what we need to do,' but many of the children continued to shout and play without paying much attention to the instructions. By the time the children were wiggling in their chairs, the staff looked deflated and exhausted.

I started their group two weeks later, but not before preparing the staff. Prior to the first group, I met with the staff members in charge of the kindergarten group, Ms. Cathy and Mr. Jon. I asked them what skills the students needed help with. I explained the purpose of a Theraplay™ Group and demonstrated their role in the group by engaging them in a group experience. Mr. Jon and Ms. Cathy were skeptical that this would work, but they tried to keep open minds and listen carefully to what I was saying. When I demonstrated a group with them so they could experience what it felt like, there was much laughter and playfulness as well as collaboration, teamwork, and a general sense of fun and enjoyment. During the discussion afterwards Ms. Cathy said, 'I haven't had this kind of fun in a long time. I can't remember the last time that I played with balloons,' and Mr. Jon chimed in with, 'Yeah, playing should be fun, not stressful and dangerous. Playing with these kids always makes my blood pressure go up, ha!' I said, 'What do you think the kids in your class will experience in a group like this?' Mr. Jon said, 'Well, *if* they can sit down and listen for long enough to participate, which I'm not sure they can, I think that they will feel accepted and, like you said, nurtured, and maybe more like they're a group that can work together instead of fighting all the time.' Ms. Cathy shook her head in agreement and added, 'AND, I hope they will listen better!' *[Sometimes just a few children can send a whole group into chaos, so I needed to learn more to see if this was the case for this group of children.]*

On a Tuesday Ms. Cathy, Mr. Jon, and I started our first group with the kindergarten class. I walked onto the bus before the class exited and said, 'Listen up kindergarten friends,' and then I said softly, 'We're going to go to our classroom as quiet as little mice and see if we can make it past the front desk without Mr. Rashad noticing us,' while I physically demonstrated how a little mouse would walk. 'Then, we're going to eat our snack and play some games together.' The 'little mice' filed off the bus behind me, all of us tip-toeing like a mouse. Mr. Jon joined the line in the middle and Ms. Cathy brought up the caboose, both pretending to be little mice. *[This is an example of the adults leading and also participating.]* There was some minor pushing as Anthony and Jeremiah raced to get to the front of the line, but Ms. Cathy and Mr. Jon were both amazed by how quickly and organized the transition was. *[Theraplay™ Group techniques can be used effectively for classroom – and bus! – management and not just during Group time.]*

'Okay, I put some glue on every chair in this room, and I'd like to see how sticky it is. So, if you have a missing tooth, go find a seat and show me how sticky the glue is. If you have bobbles in your hair, find a sticky seat,' and I continued until each child was in a seat. Jasmine found her seat and said, 'Mine ain't got no glue, see!' as she bounced up and down on her seat. I decided to ignore her challenge since the rest of the group was engaged and participating. I provided structure by giving them clear and simple instructions: 'Mr. Jon will give everyone in their sticky seat a snack, and Ms. Cathy is passing out milk to everyone in their sticky seat. After snack we will be playing some games together.' The children gobbled up their snacks, and Anthony and Jeremiah charged toward me and said, 'We know a game, we know a game, let's play dog pile, let's play chase, oh, no, no, no, let's play musical chairs.' I quickly, but calmly, put my hands on their shoulders and guided them back to their seats while saying, 'You both have a lot of great ideas, but I have prepared the games that we're going to play today so you don't need to worry about that part. You just focus on having fun.' *[I took charge and used playful structure to help the children Stick Together.]*

I needed to use some creativity to smoothly transition the children from eating snack at tables to sitting on a blanket on the floor: 'Kindergarten friends, I'm moving the glue from your seat to the wall. The group at this table [while tapping lightly on the table top] is ready to move to the wall.' As I tapped on each table, Ms. Cathy and Mr. Jon moved the tables to the side of the room. I intentionally chose Anthony, Jeremiah, and Jasmine's table last so that they would not have to wait on the wall for very long with the increased freedom that standing allows. I laid a king-size sheet out on the floor and invited all of the little mice to come and join me in a circle on the floor. Then I introduced myself and the group: 'Some of you I know, and some of you know me, but I'm a new person for a few of you, and a few of you are new to me. My name is Ms. Marlo, and I have one of the coolest jobs in the whole wide world... I get to help kids learn things by playing with them.' Many of the children had large eyes and excited expressions when I said this, so I continued: 'I know that this group likes to have fun and run around and laugh and do fun stuff, so we're going to do some of those fun things. I also know that sometimes it's been tough to get along with each other and with Ms. Cathy and Mr. Jon and follow instructions, so we're going to work on that together in fun ways.' As I mentioned the 'tough' times, Anthony and Jasmine rolled their eyes and sucked their teeth in disdain while Jeremiah's shoulders slumped and his head hung slightly.

'We'll meet together 12 times to play; usually on Tuesdays. When we play together, there are three rules,' and I introduced 'No Hurts, Stick Together, and Have Fun' in the same way as I did with the We Can Do It Group. 'We're going to decide on a group name and then I'm going to teach you our Hello Song. What should we be called?' Shouts from around the room included 'fabulous,' 'gummy bears,' 'blue,' 'butterflies,' 'NO! RED!' (Jasmine's contribution), 'Teenage Mutant Ninja Turtles,' 'thug life,' and more. I said, 'Wow, so many great ideas. I'm putting them in my pot and I'm stirring, I'm stirring, I'm stirring... AND, out comes... *The Purple Butterfly Ninja Group.*' Jasmine quickly retorted, 'No, I said red, not purple. I'm not going to play!' as she quickly scooted off the blanket with a pouty look on her face and started sucking her thumb. I responded, 'Jasmine, you said "red" and someone else said "blue", so if we mix those together we get purple. That's why I chose purple. So, we are *The Purple Butterfly Ninja Group.* I can tell that you're not happy with that, so you're welcome to take a little break and re-join us when you're ready.' Jasmine stayed right where she was and stared at me angrily, but I had 16 other children to tend to, so we moved forward. *[Although Stick Together means you seek to have all the children together, you also don't want one child to prevent the others from experiencing the health benefits of your group. So I was giving Jasmine space and continuing with the group.]* 'Now, everyone gently hold your neighbor's hand and follow me.' I swung my arms gently as I started to sing, 'Hello Purple Butterfly Ninja Group, Hello Purple Butterfly Ninja Group, Hello Purple Butterfly Ninja Group, we're so glad you're here to play. Now join in with me on this part. Hello, Loraine, hello Jesse, hello Destiny,' and we acknowledged each person's presence by saying their name as we went around the circle. Although Jasmine was still sitting out of the circle sucking her thumb, we said 'hello' to her because she was a part of our group.

Transitioning to Check-Ups, I motioned with my hands as I said, 'So, these six friends will be with Ms. Cathy, these six friends will be with Mr. Jon, and Anthony, Jeremiah, Jasmine, Sam, and Jamie will be with me. Adults, we are going to notice a few things about each member of our group. I will demonstrate with Jeremiah.' Turning to Jeremiah, I held his hand as I said, 'I see that you brought your nose, and your toes, and a great big smile. Ms. Cathy and Mr. Jon, you'll do that with each child in your group.' *[This engagement activity provides a brief moment of individualized attention for each child to feel noticed and valued.]* Most of the children enjoyed the one-on-one attention they received, and when the adults would notice their smiles, their grins grew even wider. The activity piqued Jasmine's interest, but she remained on the fringe of the small group with her thumb in her mouth as I did the Check-Up with her classmates and with her, from afar. Anthony rolled his eyes and said, 'This is so stupid. We all have a nose and toes and whatever else you're gonna say.' I responded by saying, 'I see that you've brought something else with you too. You DO have a nose, you DO have toes, and, you brought your eye rolling with you too. Go ahead and show the whole group what a great eye roller you are.' Anthony was not expecting my response. He was taken aback for a moment and then decided to take the challenge and show his classmates the best eye roll he could muster up. Everyone laughed and tried it themselves. I said they were all the best eye rollers! *[Prescribing the unwanted behavior is an example of the Theraplay™ way of managing a child's resistance. If I tried to control every behavior, it would pit me against the children and we'd frequently be in power struggles that would push us apart instead of bring us together, this being the goal of a Theraplay Group. So, still leading, I accepted Anthony's behavior and drew him in.]*

Moving to the next activity, I said, 'Now, we are going to take a look and see if each student has any hurts or special spots on their hands or arms for us to put lotion on. Let me demonstrate with Sam, and then Ms. Cathy and Mr. Jon you will do this with each one of your students. Okay Sam, let me take a look at those hands. Wow, you have a little bruise here on your pointer finger. I'm going to put some lotion on that, and I see that you have a few freckles on your wrist, I'm going to put a dot of lotion on each one of those. And last but not least, it looks like your elbows could use a little bit of lotion. Now we'll take care of each member of the Purple Butterfly Ninja Group.' *[The nurturing ritual of Check-Ups is one of the important ways we practice No Hurts with our Group.]* When I turned back to my small group, I was surprised to see that Anthony and Jeremiah were missing. When I demonstrated the lotion activity with Sam, I heard a bit of movement behind me, and I now realized it was Anthony and Jeremiah moving themselves out of the group and underneath a desk. I heard them saying, 'Let's take this apart, yeah, let's unplug 'em all.' I reminded the boys of our Stick Together rule and verbally asked them to return as I physically made my way closer to them to provide a guiding touch for them to re-join the small group. As I got closer to them Anthony started disconnecting each wire he could grab while looking at me with an indignant expression. Jeremiah kept his eyes on me, but seemed frozen.

It was clear that Jeremiah would respond to a firm but accepting tone, which he did, and he re-engaged with the group. However, Anthony's defiance would be more challenging to deal with. For the remainder of the first group Anthony crawled back and forth from one desk to another desk, attempting to gain attention from the adults or other children. Fortunately, the children were engaged and participating in the group activities and Anthony and Jasmine's behavior only caused minor distractions. Unfortunately, the ratio of 17 children and three adults made it difficult to respond to Jasmine and Anthony in ways that would help them participate while maintaining the flow of the group.

After the first session, the leaders discussed the challenges that we experienced with Jeremiah, Anthony, and Jasmine. We came up with a plan to provide structure and grounding support for them, and I demonstrated various techniques for engaging the children when they were struggling. I planned the next session with an emphasis on Engagement and the importance of regulation and proximity for Anthony and Jasmine. The second session was very similar to the first. Most of the children experienced connection with the other members in the group through playful interactions, and enjoyed being cared for by the leaders. Jeremiah's second Group Theraplay™ experience was much smoother than the first week. It helped that we seated him next to Mr. Jon and farther away from Anthony. Anthony and Jasmine responded a little better when we were divided into three small groups, but they struggled just as much when the whole group was involved. When Anthony and Jasmine were being disruptive, several of the other children expressed their frustration and anger toward them, which was healthy and appropriate, but not effective.

Anthony and Jasmine's disruptions interfered with the group goals, and the children were not getting maximum therapeutic benefit from the group. I realized that I had to first meet Anthony and Jasmine's needs before they could better participate in the group. To do that, I divided the group into two smaller ones, split the allotted time in half, and, following the same plans, led two separate groups for four weeks. This separation allowed us to do several things for Anthony and Jasmine specifically, and also for the other children: increase the amount of adult support, attention, and care they received; and help them to actively participate and embrace the rhythm and rituals of the group. The two more needy children were in separate groups to minimize the negative influence they had on each other during the first two weeks. The plan was to bring the whole group back together for the remaining weeks. Jasmine and Anthony made significant progress in the smaller groups. Mr. Jon said, 'Whoa, Anthony seems like a totally different kid. I would not have believed you if you had predicted this when the group started.' Anthony and Jasmine actively participated and positively contributed. *[Smaller group size can be crucial for needy or troubled children who can get their needs met so that they can return to a larger group.]* On week six, I prepared both groups for re-integration of the whole group the following week. I also spoke with Anthony and Jasmine individually to let them know how proud I was of their progress, how much fun we were having playing with them, and that we (adults) would be there to help them if they struggled the following week in the group.

The seventh session was wonderful. Each child gladly participated in the activities and supported their peers by encouraging and helping one another. I intentionally sat Anthony next to me, Jasmine next to

Ms. Cathy, and Jeremiah next to Mr. Jon so that we would be able to recognize and respond quickly if they needed extra care. Throughout, Anthony leaned on my leg to stay physically close. *[Some children need to be physically close to a trusted person to help them interact with others.]*

For the remainder of the 12 sessions, all 17 students took pleasure in playing together, collaboratively achieving goals, and taking part in caring for their neighbors. During session ten I said, 'Okay everyone, we're going to see how many bubbles the Purple Butterfly Ninjas can pop. We [the adults] are going to blow them and we'll see if you can pop them before they hit the floor! Remember rule number one?' And in unison they said, 'YES! NO HURTS!' After the group shout, Anthony turned to me and said, 'We don't want to hurt our friends with our hands or our words, right Ms. Marlo?' He was internalizing the Theraplay™ Group culture.

Conclusion

Theraplay Groups seek to improve one of the foundational elements of life: *relationships*. Group Theraplay facilitates social and emotional growth through active, nurturing, and fun experiences that help children feel cared for, more connected to each other, safe to be themselves, and supported to be more engaged and compassionate with others. Theraplay Groups have benefits for healthy children as well as troubled and traumatized children. This is a group in which everyone wins. There is amazingly great power in the classroom fun of Theraplay.

Where to be educated and qualifications of trainees

Group Theraplay training is available through courses provided by The Theraplay Institute (www.theraplay.org). Training in Group Theraplay currently consists of a beginning class. To be certified as a Group Theraplay Specialist, you would enter into a practicum with a Group Theraplay supervisor assigned through The Theraplay Institute. Supervision involves submitting videotaped sessions that can be sent electronically. You and your supervisor will watch the video and you will receive constructive feedback. There is a midterm and final, supervised by a different supervisor. Teacher qualifications in your country are sufficient for entering the practicum.

References

Alizadeh, S., Abu Talib, M. B., Abdullah, R. and Mansor, M. (2011) 'Relationship between parenting style and children's behavior problems.' *Asian Social Science* 7(12), 195–200.

Baumrind, D. (1978) 'Parental disciplinary patterns and social competence in children.' *Youth and Society 9*, 229–276.

Booth, P. B. and Jernberg, A. M. (2010) *Theraplay: Helping Parents and Children Build Better Relationships Through Attachment-Based Play.* San Francisco, CA: Jossey-Bass.

Bowlby, J. (1988) *A Secure Base: Parent–Child Attachment and Healthy Human Development.* London: Routledge.

Brown, S. and Vaughan, C. (2009) *Play: How It Shapes the Brain, Opens the Imagination, and Invigorates the Soul.* New York, NY: Penguin Group.

Chrousos, G. P. (1998) 'Stressors, stress, and neuroendocrine integration of the adaptive response.' *Annals of the New York Academy of Sciences 851*, 311–335.

Cooper, G., Hoffman, K. and Powell, B. (2009) *Circle of Security Parenting: A Relationship Based Parenting Program* (facilitator's manual).

Hart, S. (2011) *The Impact of Attachment.* New York, NY: W. W. Norton.

Kim, Y. K. (2011) 'The effect of group Theraplay on self-esteem and depression of the elderly in a day care center.' *Korean Journal of Counseling 12*(5), 1413–1430.

Mäkelä, J. and Hart, S. (2011) 'Theraplay: Intensiv, Engagerende, Interaktiv Leg som et Middel til at Fremme Psykisk Udvikling.' In S. Hart (ed.) *Neuroaffektiv Psykoterapi med Børn.* Copenhagen: Hans Reitzels Forlag.

Panksepp, J. (2001) 'The long-term psychobiological consequences of infant emotions: Prescriptions for the twenty-first century.' *Infant Mental Health Journal 22*(1–2), 132–173.

Rubin, P. (1996) *Understanding homeless mothers: The dynamics of adjusting to the program of a long-term shelter* (unpublished doctoral dissertation). Chicago, IL: Illinois School of Professional Psychology.

Rubin, P. B. and Tregay, J. (1989) *Play with Them: Theraplay Groups in the Classroom.* Springfield, IL: Charles C. Thomas.

Schore, A. N. (1994) *Affect Regulation and the Origin of the Self: The Neurobiology of Emotional Development.* Mahwah, NJ: Erlbaum.

Schore, A. N. (2001) 'Contributions from the decade of the brain to infant mental health: An overview.' *Infant Mental Health Journal 22*(1–2), 1–66.

Siu, A. (2009) 'Theraplay in the Chinese world: An intervention program for Hong Kong children with internalizing problems.' *International Journal of Play Therapy 18*(1), 1–12.

Sroufe, L. A. (1988) 'The Role of Infant-Caregiver Attachment in Development.' In J. Belsky and T. Nezworski (eds) *Clinical Implications of Attachment.* Hillsdale, NJ: Lawrence Erlbaum.

Sroufe, L. A. and Fleeson, J. (1988) 'The Coherence of Family Relationships.' In R. A. Hinde and J. Stevenson-Hinde (eds) *Relationships within Families: Mutual Influences.* Oxford: Clarendon Press.

Stern, D. N. (1985) *The Interpersonal World of the Infant: A View from Psychoanalysis.* New York, NY: Basic Books.

Sunderland, M. (2006) *The Science of Parenting: Practical Guidance on Sleep, Crying, Play, and Building Emotional Well-being for Life.* London: Dorling Kindersley.

Trevarthen, C. (2001) 'Infant intersubjectivity: Research, theory, and clinical applications.' *Journal of Child Psychology and Psychiatry 42*(1), 3–48.

Vygotsky, L. S. (1978) *Mind in Society: The Development of Higher Psychological Processes.* Cambridge, MA: Harvard University Press.

6

Inclusion, Children's Groups, Music Therapy

Music and Communicative Musicality

Ulla Holck and Stine Lindahl Jacobsen

Music has a rare ability to affect us directly. Pulse and rhythms make us move, and notes and harmonies inspire and express our inner emotions in a direct and immediate way that goes beyond what words or even other art forms can rarely achieve (Panksepp and Trevarthen, 2009). Music creates a delightful build-up of tension or soothes us, and its narrative character gives rise to mental imagery or memories. Music brings people together and helps to build communities across languages and common divides. And – not least – music captures children's immediate attention, so when the music starts, so do the children! Initially, this is by rocking in time to the rhythm, and then with dance moves or spontaneous singing.

In this chapter, we demonstrate how music and music activities can be used as a means of including vulnerable children in preschool or school settings. Based on experiences from music therapy, we have selected six case stories from Denmark to illustrate how musical interplay can promote attention, concentration, emotional attachment and social skills in groups and, in the last of our case stories, also the quality of parent–child interactions. The specific cases were selected because they involve fairly simple musical activities, some of which can be used by preschool, school or music teachers without requiring additional instruction, while others require supervision or collaboration with a music therapist. With this chapter, we aim to offer specific ideas for inspiration but also a more general portrayal of the qualities of musical interplay that promote well-being in group settings and, thus, the inclusion of vulnerable students. Therefore, we open the chapter with a focus on musicality and on the importance of applying a musical approach in relation to the children.

Communicative musicality

There is a certain general tendency to view musicality as a unique and personal capacity for singing or playing an instrument: something reserved for the lucky few. However, this somewhat elitist view of musicality is not borne out when we consider the broad appeal of music. This is reflected both in the immediate joy of singing and dancing, which expresses *a general musicality* regardless of others' assessment, and in the innate *communicative musicality* that is activated when we engage in mutual interactions, regardless of language skills or age.

The concept of 'communicative musicality' (Malloch, 1999) was originally introduced by infant researchers in their analyses of early interactions, which demonstrated the capacity of infants to engage in *timed*, synchronized interactions with their parents by means of vocalization and movement: a capacity that is crucial for early attachment and the child's neurological development (Hart, 2008; Stern, 1985). The broad and lifelong appeal of music is probably directly associated with this early – and vitally important – ability to engage in interpersonal interactions, in concrete terms by means of simple basic musical elements (Holck, 2014; Malloch and Trevarthen, 2009).

In later interactions (play, conversations, meetings, etc.), communicative musicality is probably best described as the underlying message behind the words – for example, the emotional tone of the voice (regardless of the words), whether there is a common pulse in terms of turn-taking, whether the overall pace is calm or hectic, whether there is a mutual attunement in relation to waves of tension build-up and relaxation, or whether there are tiny (micro-) pauses in the interaction without a disruption of the contact. Few people notice these dynamic features in the process, unless the vitality has disappeared completely from the interaction. Nevertheless, when the interaction is characterized by warmth and emotional engagement (regardless of sorrow or joy) and/or of back-and-forth exchanges, dynamic spontaneity and creativity, the communicative musicality swings, and we are neurologically attuned.

Thus, people might possess a high degree of communicative musicality, whether or not they have ever learned to play an instrument. And if we combine communicative musicality with our general musicality – that is, our joy of music, of singing and dancing – we have already come a long way in terms of using musical interplay to promote well-being in a group. Musical training, from choir singing to playing an instrument, obviously has an important impact – for example, on the sorts of activities a teacher is prepared to engage in. The key point, however, is that relating to children with musicality is a crucial condition for using music to promote good group dynamics.

Music in school settings

In primary and lower secondary school, music is often viewed as a fairly non-essential cultural discipline (see Chapter 1), whose potential justification stems mainly from its role in cognitive learning – for example, in relation to language or maths – despite the huge role music plays in our life (see also, Bonde, 2008; Nielsen, 2008). Unfortunately, this debate often tends to overlook the social, emotional and relational impact of music, although this knowledge is far from obscure. A large-scale longitudinal school study in Berlin that ran for six years (1992–1998) found convincing indications that classes that received two music lessons per week, combined with ensemble playing and (individual and group-based) lessons in a musical instrument, developed a far better social climate than the control classes, which only had one music lesson per week and no ensemble playing or instrument lessons (Bastian, 2000, 2001). In the experimental classes, which had additional music training, the children displayed far less dismissive behaviour towards each other and were much more skilled at social reflections. Socially disadvantaged children with less cognitive stimulation in the home also profited from the expanded music training (Bonde, 2008; Nöcker-Ribaupierre and Wölfl, 2010). In light of what is known about communicative musicality, it is a central point that the added music training consisted of activities where the children engaged in shared musical activities (Holck, 2008a). If ensemble playing is done *in a way that is fun for the children*, it results in automatic rhythmic and dynamic attunement and in a sharing of common dynamic time sequences with waves of tension and relaxation.

In the United Kingdom, Germany, the United States, Australia and New Zealand there have been good experiences with using music therapists in school settings with a view to strengthening youths who are emotionally and relationally vulnerable (McFerran and Campbell, 2013; Nöcker-Ribaupierre and Wölfl, 2010; Rickson and McFerran, 2014; Tomlinson, Philippa and Oldfield, 2011), or as a means of supporting and guiding classes and music teachers, therapists and families in the basic use of music to promote inclusion processes (McCarrick, 2013; Rickson, 2012; Tomlinson *et al.*, 2011). In a Danish context, the experiences are more limited, but in the following we bring selected examples of initiatives where music therapists have worked directly or indirectly in school settings with a view to applying and conveying knowledge from music therapy as it pertains to vulnerable children.

Two case stories about musical interplay, attention and concentration

As a result of a new law about inclusion in Danish primary and lower secondary schools that came into effect in 2012, children with minor brain injuries are now included in mainstream classes. Some of these children, however, have difficulty taking part in an ordinary school day with its varying arousal levels and shifts in attention focus. The following examples illustrate that a small effort can make a big difference in terms of optimizing interactions in class and the teacher's classroom management. The musical activities are described in some detail as they are widely applicable in classes struggling with disruptions or poor well-being.

Case story 6.1

Six-year-old Frederik was in a reception class. He had mild cerebral palsy (congenital brain injury) and was included in a mainstream class without any special support measures, although the parents and the school had been granted a series of sessions with a special-needs advisor to help ensure a good school experience for Frederik.

During his first months in school, Frederik had difficulty concentrating and sitting still during lessons. He rarely took in group messages, and it was difficult for him to transfer learning from the board to his own individual work tasks. The classroom environment was somewhat chaotic. The students spoke loudly, disturbed each other and had a strong need to be the centre of attention. They were also hard on each other. They reprimanded each other and often paid more attention to whether the others followed instructions than to their own role in class and during recess.

In order to address the classroom dynamic rather than focus on Frederik's challenges in isolation, the school engaged a music therapist to support the class, including the class teacher, in a unit involving activities and methods from music therapy. The unit included three lessons at approximately one-month intervals, and in the time in between the unit lessons, the teacher incorporated the activities that she felt comfortable with, and which she felt that she could work into the everyday activities in class. A common feature across the musical activities was a focus on *body sensations*, *shared pulse* and *synchronicity*, and on the children's ability to *listen to each other* without offering any verbal assessments. The activities were sequenced to begin with a high level of activity to match the level of noise and turmoil and the high arousal level in the class, followed by activities that required more focused concentration and listening and concluding with the following calm, inwardly focused exercises:

- *Start song:* We sing a children's song that the children already know while clapping during the chorus, introducing an offbeat, a little rhythm sequence in between verses, etc. To make the clapping slightly more challenging, the children are instructed to clap their own stomach, buttocks, thighs, etc., instead of simply clapping their hands, as this helps to focus their attention and increases their sense of learning.

- *Drumming games:* Next, we move on to drumming games, which produce a common pulse and attention focus in the group. The drum is the children's own body, preferably the thighs, because they can sustain the slapping. To ensure the common pulse, I (or the teacher) lead the singing without necessarily requiring the children to sing along. We scratch the 'drum', stroke it, tap its sides, and finally we give it a big boom! Using our index finger, we tap the drumming thigh, and then we use all our finger tips to tap the thigh. Then we gradually play faster and louder while using our voices to produce an 'Aaahhhh' on a rising note. It should end on a high note but not in a scream. Then we say, '1-2-3-4, hear us play (stomp, sneak…), 1-2-3-4, hear us now' and again end on a rising 'Aaahhhh.'

- *Clapping passed around:* We stand in a circle, and I (or the teacher) clapped my hands once, then the child standing next to me claps once, and so on, until we have completed the circle. The clapping should follow a common pulse. Next, I clapped twice, fast or slow, etc. This activity requires the children to focus on themselves and on each other in order to be ready in time to clap. Make sure the group is not so big that each child has to wait too long for his or her turn to clap.

- *Instrumental round robin:* The children stand in a circle; each child gets a simple percussion instrument. Now, they have to alternate between playing the instrument, stopping and passing the instrument on to the person standing to their right without saying anything. I (or the teacher) play the guitar and sing a home-made song about how they are now playing, and soon they will have to pass on the instrument. When I stop, the children have to stop playing, pass the instrument to the right and receive a new instrument from the left – all without speaking or breaking the chain. Then I resume playing, and in my song I comment on their success and mention that soon it will be time to practise again, and so on, until the next pause. In this exercise, the children engage in a group interaction with common rules, group messages and self-focus (instead of focusing on whether the others succeed or follow instructions), and they have a success experience. The activity can be carried out using just a couple of chords on a guitar or by singing while keeping the beat on a drum with a low note.

- *Relaxation:* To give the children a chance to calm down and turn their senses inward, we conclude by having them lie down on the floor while they listen to my singing or recorded music. Initially, the group is doing well if everyone manages to lie down without getting fidgety or restless. Many children feel more secure and focused lying on their stomach or side, while more secure children/groups will be able to relax to the music while lying on their back.

For the class teacher, these simple musical activities offered new, helpful and exciting ways of working with attention, concentration and the children's self-focus. She would often bring the children out onto the floor in the middle of a lesson and also developed her own ideas for expanding on the activities. She mostly used the exercises when the class was worked up or 'hectic', as they helped the children to calm down. Instead of reprimanding the children, she could now focus on reminding them to turn their senses inward, to listen, etc.

As a result of this therapeutic experience and the class teacher's follow-up, the class began to see Frederik as a fellow participant in joint activities. The activities gave him a sense of calm, familiarity and joy about taking part and succeeding. The class as a whole became calmer and more focused, and the individual students were clearly more focused on their own participation than on reprimanding or correcting their class mates.

Hilde Skrudland, MA, Music Therapy, Denmark

The activities did not change the fact that Frederik continues to have special needs that have to be met for him to function in a mainstream classroom. However, the unit and the inclusion of methods and activities from music therapy did have a positive impact on the classroom environment, the group's capacity for self-regulation and thus on Frederik and the other children's well-being and conditions for learning.

The direct learning situation between the music therapist and the class teacher allowed the class teacher to see, hear and experience the music therapist's musical way of relating to the children. It is one thing to know a set of musical activities and incorporate them into the group's repertoire, and another thing entirely to do this in a way that strengthens the group's communicative musicality and social and emotional competencies in practice. It is worth noting here that the music therapist only had to be present for three sessions before the class teacher felt at ease with the concept and was able to come up with new activities and approaches.

When planning a unit that involves therapeutic music activities, it is important to pay attention to the overall arousal curve in the activities – for example, to open with physical activities and a relatively high arousal level and to conclude with a low arousal level. In the practical execution it is important to use one's communicative musicality, which in practice means being present in the moment, having a playful stance, finding the interactions with the children enjoyable and meaningful, and remembering that music unfolds in time, which means that (micro-) pauses are musical too – indeed, it is music to the ears, especially in a group that is generally noisy and chaotic!

Engaging in interactions where an adult takes the responsibility for varying between heightened and reduced arousal, as in this case story, gradually raises the child's neural maturity level in terms of being able to handle stimuli and, thus, stress. Play and physical activity are often used in therapeutic work with children, but as described by Trevarthen and Panksepp in Chapter 1, the self-regulating (autonomic) maturation process does not take place until body awareness is linked with the innate capacity for synchronizing with others through arousal-regulating and emotional interactions (see also Hart and Bentzen, 2015). Case story 6.2 describes experiences from a process with a group of 9–10-year-old school children with attention deficit hyperactivity disorder (ADHD)-like features. With support from the arousal level, form and pulse of the music, these children were able to calm down and be present in the moment, which in turn promoted humour, emotional sharing, imagination and relational experiences (Magnussen *et al.*, 2013; and personal communication, 2015).

Case story 6.2

In the school where I was attached as a music therapist, we decided to set up a number of theme-based groups that class teachers could refer students to. Some of these groups consisted of children with ADHD-like features who lacked the stamina to deal with a whole school day. Musical activities offer a meaningful outlet for motor restlessness. For example, I taught the children some rhythms on the drums, which they then used to accompany a song that matched their energy level. We were also able to work with changes and maintaining a pattern over time by following the form of the music and varying between intro, verse and chorus. For example, a big Danish pop hit from 1986, 'Jutlandia' (Kim Larsen), which has a characteristic rock-intro, has proved popular with many of the boys I have worked with. Almost invariably, they join in, spontaneously, on the characteristic rhythm in the riff that the song opens with. Carried by the drive from this initial rhythm, they gradually learn to play a different rhythm for the verse and a third rhythm for the chorus. On a basic level, this is a way of working with the concept of 'structure', but it happens in a shared musical space, *where the structure of the music is in charge*, and where the children strive hard to make the song and their mutual interaction work. Over time, this creates a calm and focused space, and many children gradually open up to each other and to me – for example, some of them bring in poems they have written, which we then expand on and put to music in the group.

It requires heightened attention to tune in to the shift from pure rhythm playing to making the children gradually feel secure enough to open up emotionally and use their imagination – together. Being part of a group is helpful for the children, and I facilitate the process with music therapy activities *that invite musical play and humour*. For example, we have created a musical story about 'going on a picnic together', and musical role plays and games where we 'speak' to each other without words, each using a musical instrument instead.

The key goal with musical interplay is for the children to have experiences where they are successful and capable, where their contribution matters, and where they are valuable – in contrast to: 'Aw, that's too hard, I can't do it, and now it's all going to end up being stupid or misunderstood or lead to conflicts and stuff – again.' They are able to return to the classroom with a different sense of calm and openness, and that rubs off on the way they relate to others. Some of the children want to continue with music and join the school choir or take music lessons. They have discovered that they are able be part of a social community based on music, and that music is an interest they can continue to develop and build on.

Bente Østergaard Callesen, MA, Music Therapy, Denmark

As described in the case story above, musical interplay can take a familiar song as its point of departure, and especially with slightly older children it may (at least initially) be important to maintain the outer focus on the music to keep them from judging the activity as *too childish*. However, even if the stated goal is, for example, to train a common rhythm for a familiar song, the adult's awareness of promoting communicative musicality and the sense of bonding in the group is crucial in determining whether children with low self-esteem take a sense of joy and mastery with them from the musical activities or, instead, a sense of frustration and defeat. A deliberate use of musical humour, as in the case above, is essential, because humour captures the attention, breaks fear and promotes playful interactions. Children's natural insecurity about a new adult or a new situation can be eased if the adult suddenly makes a fun or surprising noise, is reluctant to play or, by contrast, gets it completely wrong when he or she begins to play. A good, shared laugh can provide a shared and liberating 'now moment', but less dramatic variations between a build-up of musical tension and calmer passages can also give the children a shared experience of waves of arousal. Dynamic communication and positive relational experiences strengthen the children's identity and self-worth (Irgens-Møller and Bjerg, 2004).

In the case story above, the music therapist used song-writing techniques that are typically used in music therapy to boost self-esteem, identity and bonding in groups. Some schools already include song-writing in the music curriculum. However, when the goal is to bolster a weak sense of self-esteem, as in this case, it is a good idea to bring children with similar difficulties together in a smaller group where they can develop a sense of security with each other – in this case, enabling them to share poems with a personal content.

Case story 6.2 included the use of musical games or ground rules, a music therapy technique where the children are introduced to brief role plays or exercises. In it, an example is the idea of having a 'conversation' without words, using musical instruments instead (Holck, 2008b; Wigram, 2004). Other games that focus on concentration and dialogic interactions could be to ask the children to take turns playing one at a time, perhaps in the format of Follow the Leader. You can also ask them to take turns leading the interaction, using clear cues to let the others know whose turn it is to play or sing (see Case study 6.6). Games can also have a bigger component of pretend or make-believe, as in the example of 'going on a picnic together', where the group improvises music together. Finally, a game format can also revolve around emotions, as illustrated in the following two case stories.

Two case stories about musical interplay as a facilitator for emotions

Music and emotions are irretrievably linked, whether the music is used to express and evoke dynamic forms of vitality (Stern, 2010) or basic emotions such as joy, sorrow, etc. Therefore, music also offers a direct path to emotional phenomena such as playfulness, excitement, sadness, etc. In Case stories 6.3 and 6.4, music is used in different ways to move into and out of dangerous or difficult emotions and to dramatize or express them. Both case stories feature musical game formats that are adapted to the children's age and backgrounds. And in both examples, the adults secure opportunities for emotional attunement processes that develop the children's emotional resilience.

In the first case stories, music is used in combination with play with a group of 5-year-old socially at-risk bilingual refugee children. In children who may have a severely dysregulated nervous system, it is necessary to pay special attention to attunement and waves of arousal (Hart and Bentzen, 2015), that is, the build-up of tension versus relaxation in connection with emotionally supportive play (Bjerg and Jensen, 2014). Attunement is achieved when the adult dynamically matches what the children do – for example singing more loudly when the children stomp their feet or singing more softly when they tiptoe around, pretending to be tiny little mice. In addition to promoting shared attention, this also facilitates shifts between varying levels of arousal – for example, by introducing quieter passages (relaxation) after a very active or dramatic sequence (tension). Music can support this type of game and make it more fun and dramatic, but music is a powerful medium that might overstimulate a vulnerable or highly susceptible nervous system. Before initiating a game with musical accompaniment, it is therefore essential that the adult leader knows how to lower the arousal level without losing touch with any of the individual children in the group. However, adults who have knowledge and experience with working with refugees will be able to combine play with a deliberate use of music to express basic emotions in a way that makes the experience fun, captivating and a tiny bit dangerous – and in a way where the children can overcome the danger together.

The Danish School Readiness project, which is organized by the Danish Refugee Council, is aimed at helping socially at-risk bilingual refugee children. The goal of the project is to improve the 5-year-olds' language, social, behavioural and emotional skills to prepare them for school. Children of traumatized parents often show signs of a failure to thrive already in preschool, in the form of aggressive behaviour or withdrawal, and therefore the project is aimed to address these signs at an early stage. In connection with the project, music therapist and then project manager Mathias Granum described concrete suggestions for group activities and games aimed at improving the children's social and language skills (Granum and Siem, 2013):

Case story 6.3

The children meet in small groups for one hour a week to work with social learning, language stimulation, music therapy and physical games. Some of the children we work with have difficulty playing with other children. However, play is an important way for the children to develop social skills and to process unpleasant experiences together with an adult. In this capacity, music is used in a variety of ways to promote focus, highlight emotions and add drama or as a means of nonverbal communication. All the games involve two adults: one is the group leader (the music therapist), who tells the children what is going to happen and provides the music, while the other adult joins in alongside the children, so that they always have an adult by their side as they play.

'Focus activities' are brief games that only last a few moments, but which quickly generate a shared focus in the group as a condition for carrying out some of the other activities. For example, we start by tiptoeing into the room together in order to keep the children in this mode instead of letting them rush in and begin fiddling with all the musical instruments. Sometimes, as we move from one activity to the next, the children may be requested to do a drum roll while I (or the group leader) fetch something we need for the next game. That pulls the group together and creates a shared focus and is far more efficient than verbally asking the children to be quiet!

It is important for the children to be able to recognize and sense emotions in themselves and others – and to put them into words. Some of the children we work with have a limited vocabulary for emotions – for example, the word 'mad' is often used to describe a rather diverse range of emotions. The first step in this process is aimed at distinguishing between emotions and recognizing them in oneself and in others. To that end, we use a variety of devices, including recorded music with a distinctive emotional expression as a basis for guessing games where the children are asked to pick the emotion they think the music conveys. For example, sadness can be expressed with 'The Death of Åse' (from Edvard Grieg's *Peer Gynt*), and sullenness can be exemplified with 'The Imperial March' (from John Williams' *Star Wars*).

One of the children's favourite emotions turned out to be 'scared', and here we use a variety of effects to create a spooky mood, including making the room dark or using scary music (*Close Encounters*, Suite by John Williams). We also use scary games, depending on how brave the children feel. For example, we have a game where the children have to help each other cross 'Crocodile River' without being eaten by the crocodiles. To cross the river, they use a series of stepping stones, and as the starting signal for the game, we use the musical theme 'Jungle Trek' (by Alan Silvestri) from the film *Predator* to create a sense of drama, danger and excitement as they cross Crocodile River. We always make sure that in the end, the children overcome the scary challenge together. When we work with basic emotions we also use the kazoo, a small instrument that is easy to play for everyone, and which can be used to express a wide range of emotions by direct, nonverbal means. We use game formats with guessing games, where some of the children perform while the rest have to guess which emotion they are expressing. The kazoo can also be used to practise turn-taking, where the rule is that only one person can play at a time.

Mathias Granum, MA, Music Therapy, Denmark

When introducing games with potentially frightening emotions, as in this case, it is important to do it in a way where the adult is able to attune emotionally with the children continually. This is always true when working with children's groups, but for children who may have had traumatic experiences, it is especially important to avoid making the children so frightened that they are re-traumatized. Therefore, the adult may never act as the scary element in the game – for example, by using gestures or facial expressions to appear scary; the scary element has to come from something else, in this case Crocodile River, the dark room and the music. This lets the adult share the scary experience with the children and attune with them emotionally in the process, perhaps adjusting the mood slightly, calming the children down or giving them a friendly wink if some of them are a little too frightened. This opportunity to share a potentially scary experience with an emotionally attuned adult, followed by a shift to calmer passages, will help the children develop emotional resilience.

As in the previous case story, Case story 6.4 also uses musical game formats where the children try to have a conversation without words. Most children have immediate access to their communicative musicality when they are asked to represent a nonverbal pretend argument using only their voice or a simple instrument like the kazoo. In this case, the game further introduces a guessing game about the expression of basic emotions, and the more the children are able to empathize with the emotion in question, the easier it is for them both to convey it and to guess it. In this way, a simple game format can help these preschoolers not only develop clearer nonverbal communication but also develop a greater capacity for empathy with regard to decoding others' emotional expressions.

With older children, game formats can be used similarly to focus on emotions, but here, the activity would typically revolve around emotions that are expressed in the group. Case story 6.4 is from a music therapy process with a group of tween girls, whose parents had difficulty meeting the girls' emotional needs.

Case story 6.4

At the school we decided to establish a theme group for 'little adults' that the class teachers could refer their students to. The group came to include four 11–12-year-old girls who completed a 12-week music therapy course together, with one lesson a week. The girls were all bright and did well on their school work, but they were often so preoccupied with events in the home that they were unable to live up to their potential. They showed symptoms of stress: headaches, lack of concentration and a sad look in their eyes. All four girls were little adults, who took on far too great a responsibility for the family's well-being. Music therapy offered them a space to talk about things that were important to them and to engage their vitality and joy of life, to be children and to share their dreams and fantasies in a playful community of peers.

Halfway through the music therapy course, we had a talk about the parents' mutual quarrels, backbiting and conflicts. This led the girls to talk about what they could do to treat each other right, and how they could help and support each other instead of bringing the conflicts into the school. In order to embody these insights and help the girls sense themselves in their shared space, I developed a game format where each member of the group had to pick a musical instrument, and together, we would then express the sense of loathing and disgust we had felt in the conversation, allowing ourselves to make ugly and unpleasant sounds without paying any special attention to each other. After a while, we would replace this with a kind of music where we listened to each other, supporting each other and bringing everyone together in a shared expression.

It was a highly rewarding improvisation, which demonstrated how difficult it was to express all the ugly and unpleasant aspects, if one is used to being very proper and well behaved. At first, the music was quiet, with sporadic sounds, the girls eyeing each other with uncertainty. But gradually they allowed themselves to cover a wider range and make more powerful sounds on their instruments, and they were inspired by each other's displays of ugliness to find the nerve to be ugly themselves in the music. The improvisation then segued into the second part, ending in a closely aligned session, where everyone found a common pulse and notes that harmonized, as well as responding to each other's little rhythmic figures and strands of melody. One of the girls spontaneously began to play 'Little Ida's Song' (by Astrid Lindgren, from the film *Nye løjer med Emil fra Lønneberg*, 1972). The final verse begins with the words 'Little me, little me, sweet little Ida' (translated to English). As soon as the others recognized the tune, they began to play and hum along, which gave rise to an emotionally charged 'now moment'. Afterwards, the girls' eyes were smiling, and the atmosphere in the group was good, and one of them said, 'It's great that *we* all get along.'

The conclusion to the activity was touching and very telling. With the shared melody and the reference to Little Ida, all the girls appeared to agree to let go of their responsibilities *together* and to allow themselves to be the little girls they also were. The most important aspect, however, was to witness the girls' mutual emotional attunement and testing in both the first and second part of the improvisation, to see them become aware of the way they listened to each other and how they imitated each other and to see how they gradually allowed themselves to play together in the interaction.

Initially, my role as a music therapist was to guide the conversation and make sure that everyone was allowed to speak and sometimes to ask follow-up questions. During the improvisation, I supported their expression musically by imitating and mirroring the sounds they produced, thus promoting acceptance of everyone's contributions. Sometimes I linked together several co-existing expressions in the music by combining one girl's melody with another girl's rhythm, and in the final section, I pulled the overall expression together by filling in with harmonies in between their notes and sounds.

Bente Østergaard Callesen, MA, Music Therapy, Denmark

In this case story, the game format presented an emotional contrast between expressing loathing, disgust and ugliness on the one hand and listening to each other, striving for a common expression, on the other, which spontaneously fed into 'Little Ida's Song'. Furthermore, the game format also produced a *playful interaction at an age-appropriate level*, making room for the important attachment qualities of play without causing the situation to be too childish for the girls: serious notes, humour, shared reflection, a sharing of emotions, synchronization and affect attunement came together in a shared 'now moment'.

The second part of the case story brings up a number of music therapy improvisation techniques including imitation, mirroring, tying together the girls' different musical-dynamic expressions and tying the whole expression together (Wigram, 2004). These techniques are used to create synchronization and mutual attunement in groups, and they require an improvisational use of music for this purpose.

Rather than engaging in a direct therapeutic interaction with the children, as this case story demonstrates, the music therapist can instead create a musical setting for interactions between children and significant adults in their life. The final two case stories illustrate the direct involvement of teachers and parents in musical interplay with the children.

Two case stories with the involvement of teachers or parents

Music therapy with highly vulnerable and at-risk children has a growing focus on the importance of involving the children's closest caregivers in the musical interplay to ensure that what happens in music therapy can potentially be transferred to the children's everyday life (Jacobsen, 2013; Jacobsen, McKinney and Holck, 2014).

Typically, the music therapist provides a carefully tailored musical framework around the child's and the teacher's or parent's interactions to leave the adult free to focus on engaging in the interaction with the child. Music is an effective medium for bringing children and adults together, because it can facilitate play and mutual synchronicity and attunement. Taking part together with the children may further strengthen the adults' faith in their own musicality and their ability to relate to the children with musicality in interactions. Group settings are a good place to practise this, because they allow for mutual mirroring and reflection (Bonde, 2014).

Case story 6.5 takes us to a remedial class with eight students with a variety of social and learning challenges. The children's difficulties range from congenital developmental disorders to attachment disorders as a result of abuse or neglect. Several of the children have a history with a reactive attachment disorder or a disorganized attachment pattern, which makes it difficult for them to function in a group setting. In order to improve interactions in the class, the music therapist has organized a twelve-week unit with one weekly lesson. The unit also includes two teachers who work closely with the children every day.

Case story 6.5

Martin is 7 years old. Due to severe socio-emotional challenges, he has difficulty engaging in activities and in interactions with other adults and children. He is quick to lose faith in himself, and if it is his turn to come up with something in a musical game, he soon gives up, either by throwing himself down on the floor or by pacing restlessly around the classroom.

One of the recurring music activities in the unit is a song accompanied by maracas that varies between a sing-along verse, where everybody keeps the beat with their maracas, and a solo verse, where the children take turns to come up with something for the others to imitate. When it is Martin's turn to be a soloist, his initial inclination is to give up and throw his maraca on the floor, as he usually does. But then the remedial teacher, Louise, holds his hand lightly and guides him to shake the maraca in time with the music, and that enables Martin to continue.

Immediately after this exchange, Martin requests support by making eye contact with Louise. *While he continues to shake his maraca in time with the music*, he holds her gaze – quite unlike his customary fleeting, nervous glances. Louise calmly returns his gaze. Suddenly something happens with

Martin. He looks pensive, and then he begins to keep the beat by hitting the maraca alternately against his head and his hand. At first, he concentrates hard on playing in the new way he came up with, and while he does that the music therapist repeatedly sings, 'Martin strikes the maraca against his head and his hand.' Shortly after, Martin looks up and sees that the other children in the group are copying his pattern. Now, Martin takes eye contact with Louise. This time, he has a triumphant twinkle in his eye and looks both happy and a little shy, in a good way. Meanwhile, the children and the adults in the group seem particularly focused on following Martin's lead, and an intense shared moment arises in the whole group. Everybody seems to be aware how special it is to have Martin be part of the group instead of opting out.

Over the course of 12 weeks, Martin was gradually able to engage in more secure interactions with the other children through the music activities. Generally, there continued to be many school lessons where Martin had difficulty taking part in group contexts, but the experiences from the unit and the therapeutic music activities made it possible for Martin's teachers to support him in a development process, where he was able to experience himself as a valuable member of the class. The motivation that Martin had from his enjoyment and the recognition of the songs was another important contributing factor.

Maiken Bjerg, MA, Music Therapy, Denmark

As in the story about Frederik in Case story 6.1, a unit with methods and activities from music therapy cannot change the fact that Martin continues to have special needs that have to be met if he is to function in a mainstream setting. Nevertheless, the case story exemplifies how music therapy can help support a development process through carefully designed musical activities that create *a framework for potential attunement* between Martin and the day-to-day remedial teacher in class.

Ensuring that the lessons use recognizable songs from time to time, a regular pulse, a regular pace and clear instructions gives the children something concrete and predictable to relate to. That makes the group setting feel safer and more secure for children with socio-emotional challenges and may calm down their jittery nervous system. With help from the persistent pulse, the adult may connect with a child such as Martin in a gentle yet clear way – first in concrete terms by providing physical-rhythmic support to help him continue to tap out the pulse and then by meeting his gaze in a calm and containing way. When dealing with a child like Martin, who has had many experiences of human contact associated with chaos and violations of his personal integrity, it is essential to proceed cautiously when the child opens up to contact and interactions. That requires a highly attentive and nonverbally clear partner, who is able to 'read' the child and offer the right amount of emotional support. To support Louise's meeting with Martin, the music therapist provided a persistent pulse to keep both Martin's and the group's music-making going. Later, the music therapist worked Martin's initiative into the song she was singing, thus validating his initiative both to Martin and to the rest of the group.

When parent–child interactions are faced with severe challenges, it is rarely sufficient to create a musical framework for the interaction. That situation requires much more explicit instruction – verbal as well as nonverbal – and the music therapist has to encourage positive interactions in a more active manner by interacting musically with the group, being clear in his or her expression and, for example, demonstrating clear and effective turn-taking (Jacobsen and Killén, 2014).

The final case story, 6.6, is set in a family institution for at-risk families. The families had been referred to the institution due to suspicion of neglect and the child's failure to thrive. In this setting, the chapter's second author, headed a weekly activity called 'Let's play', where parents and their children met to play music, do cooperation exercises and sing together. One of the teachers at the institution took part in the activity to support the families in the activity and to act as a role model when new exercises were introduced. The purpose of 'Play to your heart's delight' was to improve the parent–child interactions by inviting them to engage in positive interactions and strengthening their relationship and emotional bond, in part by training both parties' social and communicative skills. The purpose of bringing several parents and their children together in a group was to improve the sense of community at the institution and to give them an opportunity to mirror and learn from each other. In a subsequent conversation that did not include the children, the parents had the opportunity to describe their parenting experience based on the specific activities that go into creating the musical interplay.

Case story 6.6

'Let's play' has a recurring, recognizable structure, where the five parents with their five respective children take turns to open the session by picking a song from a booklet. On the floor next to the singing circle, there is a selection of musical instruments to be used in the subsequent music activities. I introduce a game format with a focus on cooperation and on following and leading.

Today, I ask the whole group to follow or imitate the individual group member's expression, so that the whole group follows one group member, who thus sets the tempo, the dynamic and the pauses using a musical instrument of his or her own choosing. Subsequently, each parent–child pair does the same in a more concentrated form, where they take turns to follow or imitate each other's expression as a way of improving the parent's ability to listen, follow, read and attune with the child's expressions and needs. One pair in particular is having difficulties, because the 6-year-old boy is not used to following his somewhat introvert and vague mother. The boy keeps trying to control the process with his tin whistle, but when he sees that I am clearer in my interaction with another child, he pauses, looks at them and spontaneously says to his mother, 'You have to play louder, Mom, then it's easier for me.' The mother smiles at her son, looks at the teacher and the other pairs and beats her drum a little louder. Eventually, the boy is able to follow his mother's deep, rhythmic beats on the drum, and when they suddenly play a completely synchronized pulse together on the drum and whistle, they both laugh with surprise and relief.

In another exercise, I introduce a simple ground rule to the families, which is that everyone has to take turns playing. This exercise improves basic nonverbal communication skills, but I have also often found that it can strengthen a relationship, whether between parent and child, teacher and child or among the children in a group. By practising their ability to send clear nonverbal signals, the individual can make themselves easier to understand for others. Misunderstandings in the communication between group members become very apparent, both to the sender and to the receiver, in this sort of exercise, and the group discovers the importance of clear and explicit signals for successful communication. The group members become familiar with each other's signals, which helps them firm up group cohesion and good communication.

Stine Lindahl Jacobsen

This case story comes from a family treatment institution, so the specific example with the boy and his mother is not representative of an ordinary teacher's responsibilities with regard to the school–home relationship within the context of a mainstream class. However, the case story is relevant for schools cooperating with parent training or other initiatives that include the parents and/or the whole family in an effort to adjust a development that has begun to run off course.

Some of the game formats might be appropriate for a mainstream setting, however, provided they are used in a playful way – free from judgement or assessment. Thus, it makes good sense to let new groups of children get to know each other through musical interplay that promotes relationships and social skills. In special cases with bullying, maladaptive classroom dynamics, a poorly functioning class environment or mainstreamed children with special needs who require special attention from the teachers, it will also be helpful to invite parents or teachers to take part in the musical interactions aimed at promoting good classroom dynamics, as exemplified in Case story 6.1 about Frederik.

Conclusion

So far, the experiences of using knowledge from music therapy to promote group well-being and inclusion of vulnerable children in mainstream classrooms are few but promising. The examples we have mentioned here contain elements ranging from the instruction of music activities to actual music therapy with the use of clinical improvisational techniques. The latter requires music therapy training, which in most countries is acquired at university or conservatory level. In Denmark, music therapists have traditionally worked with groups of children with severe issues that require extensive treatment (e.g. Holck, 2011, 2013; Jacobsen, 2013; Malloch and Trevarthen, 2009), but as we have shown, the field has generated knowledge that can be helpful in contexts where the focus is on group well-being in mainstream classes. The six case stories thus illustrate how musical interactions can promote attention, concentration, emotional interactions and social skills in groups. The case stories involve fairly simple musical activities, some of which can be used by preschool, school or music teachers without requiring additional instruction, while others require supervision or collaboration with a music therapist.

In addition to the specific musical activity, relating to children in a musical way has a significant potential to promote well-being in the group and thus promote the inclusion of vulnerable children. Some readers may recognize their own work in some of the case stories, and the chapter is thus also an acknowledgement of all the professionals who spontaneously bring their own communicative musicality into the interaction with groups of children but who may have never had a concept to describe what they do – the way they use their voice, timing, attunement and dynamic waves of tension and relaxation. The point is that an engaged adult who is present in the moment can use simple musical activities to generate opportunities for synchronization, attunement, sharing and humour in children's groups. The key indicator to look out for is that the children have fun participating. When that is the case, there is an automatic mutual rhythmic and dynamic attunement as well as a sharing of dynamic sequences in time with waves of tension build-up and relaxation.

Inclusion obviously requires a broad and interdisciplinary effort that may also involve special-needs counselling and support. This chapter has described how musical interactions can be a part of the total effort, in various ways, as a measure that can help the students or classes that need to work with nonverbal, affective and arousal regulation processes in a medium, music, that appeals to most children and adults.

References

Bastian, H. G. (2000) *Musik (Erziehung) und Ihre Wirkung: Eine Lang-Zeitstudie an Berliner Grundschulen.* Mainz: Schott.

Bastian, H. G. (2001) *Kindern Optimal Fördern – mit Musik: Intelligenz, Sozialverhalten und Gute Schulleistungen durch Musikerziehung.* Mainz: Atlantis Musikbuch-Verlag.

Bjerg, M. and Jensen, C. (2014) *Smerter hos Børn: Indsigt, Mestring, Lindring.* Copenhagen: Frydenlund.

Bonde, L. O. (2008) 'Musik og transfer: Kan musikalsk læring overføres til andre lærings- og livsområder?' *Kognition og Pædagogik 70*(8), 42–55.

Bonde, L. O. (ed.) (2014) *Musikterapi – Teori, Uddannelse, Praksis, Forskning: En Håndbog om Musikterapi i Danmark.* Aarhus: Klim.

Granum, M. and Siem, M. (2013) *Ud på gulvet. Lege, der styrker børns sprog og sociale færdigheder* (metodehæfte). Published by Integrationsnet, part of the Danish Refugee Council, the Ministry of Social Affairs, Children and Integration and the City of Aarhus. Available at www.flygtning.dk/media/1902204/ud-paa-gulvet.pdf, accessed on 11 July 2016.

Hart, S. (2008) *Brain, Attachment, Personality – An Introduction to Neuroaffective Development* (e-book). London: Karnac Books.

Hart, S. and Bentzen, M. (2015) *Through Windows of Opportunity: A Neuroaffective Approach to Child Psychotherapy.* London: Karnac Books.

Holck, U. (2008a) 'Kommunikativ musikalitet.' *Kognition og Pædagogik 70*(8): 68–77.

Holck, U. (2008b) 'Spilleregler anvendt i musikterapi i børnepsykiatrien: Tværgående analyse af 10 forløb.' *Musikterapi i Psykiatrien 5*, 48–74.

Holck, U. (2011) 'Forskning i musikterapi: Børn med en autisme spektrum forstyrrelse.' *Dansk Musikterapi 8*(2), 27–35.

Holck, U. (2013) 'Forskning i musikterapi: Børn med fysiske og psykiske funktionsnedsættelser.' *Dansk Musikterapi 10*(1), 3–12.

Holck, U. (2014) 'Kommunikativ Musikalitet: Et Grundlag for Musikterapeutisk Praksis.' In L. O. Bonde (ed.) *Musikterapi – Teori, Uddannelse, Praksis, Forskning: En Håndbog om Musikterapi i Danmark.* Aarhus: Klim.

Irgens-Møller, I. and Bjerg, M. (2004) 'Positiv relationserfaring for børn i musikterapi: Relationsorienteret musikterapi med børn med udviklingsforstyrrelser i sammenhæng med tilknytningsforstyrrelser.' *Dansk Musikterapi 1*(2), 4–14.

Jacobsen, S. L. (2013) 'Forskning i musikterapi: Familier med børn med særlige behov og udsatte familier.' *Dansk Musikterapi 10*(1), 21–31.

Jacobsen, S. L. and Killén, K. (2014) 'Clinical application of music therapy assessment within the field of child protection.' *Nordic Journal of Music Therapy 24*(2), 1–19.

Jacobsen, S. L., McKinney, C. H. and Holck, U. (2014) 'Effects of dyadic music therapy intervention on parent-child interaction in families with emotionally neglected children: A randomized controlled trial journal of music therapy.' *Journal of Music Therapy 51*(4), 310–332.

Lindgren, A. (1972) 'Lille Ida's Sang.' In Nya hyss av Emil i Lönneberga (Olle Hellbom, dir.) [English translation: New Mischief by Emil]. AB Svensk Filmindustri (film).

Magnussen, B., Nordseth, C., Nielsen, J. B. and Møllegaard, A. (2013) *Musikterapi, ADHD, inklusion* ((Student project from the half-time programme Applied Music in Social, Educational and Health Care Settings). Aalborg: Musikterapiuddannelsen, Aalborg University.

Malloch, S. (1999) 'Mothers and infants and communicative musicality.' *Musicae Scientiae* (1999–2000 theme issue), 29–57.

Malloch, S. and Trevarthen, C. (eds) (2009) *Communicative Musicality: Exploring the Basis of Human Companionship.* Oxford: Oxford University Press.

McCarrick, P. (2013) 'Behavioral and Interpersonal Problems in School Children.' In M. Hintz, (ed.) *Guidelines for Music Therapy Practice in Developmental Health.* Gilsum, NH: Barcelona Publishers.

McFerran, K. and Campbell, C. (2013) 'Music therapists' use of interviews to evaluate group programs with young people: Integrating Wilber's quadrant perspectives.' *Nordic Journal of Music Therapy 22*(1): 46–68.

Nielsen, F. V. (2008) Musikalitet: I et musikpædagogisk og legitimerings- og dannelsesperspektiv.' *Kognition og pædagogik 70*(8), 30–41.

Nöcker-Ribaupierre, M. and Wölfl, A. (2010) 'Perspectives on practice: music to counter violence: A preventative approach for working with adolescents in schools.' *Nordic Journal of Music Therapy 19*(2), 151–161.

Panksepp, J. and Trevarthen, C. (2009) 'The Neuroscience of Emotion in Music.' In S. Malloch and C. Trevarthen (eds) *Communicative Musicality: Exploring the Basis of Human Companionship.* Oxford: Oxford University Press.

Rickson, D. (2012) 'Music therapy school consultation: A unique practice.' *Nordic Journal of Music Therapy 21*(3), 268–285.

Rickson, D. and McFerran, K. (eds) (2014) *Creating Music Cultures in the Schools: A Perspective from Community Music Therapy.* University Park, PA: Barcelona Publishers.

Stern, D. N. (1985) *The Interpersonal World of the Infant.* New York, NY: Basic Books.

Stern, D. N. (2010) *Forms of Vitality.* Oxford: Oxford University Press.

Tomlinson, J., Philippa, D. and Oldfield, A. (eds) (2011) *Music Therapy in Schools: Working with Children of All Ages and Special Education.* London: Jessica Kingsley Publishers.

Wigram, T. (2004) *Improvisation: Methods and Techniques for Music Therapy Clinicians, Educators and Students.* London: Jessica Kingsley Publishers.

7

The Emerging of Empathy

Dorothea Rahm

This chapter will describe group therapy with children previously assessed as unreachable by therapy, children presenting severe degrees of psychosocial impairment. Most of these children have a migration background. The work presented here focuses on a group of children whose interests are rarely defended by any advocacy groups in Germany.[1]

The starting point which led us to develop the therapy approach presented here was the question: is there anything we can do for children who seem to be doomed to fail in our social and cultural systems as well as in the school system? Is there anything we can do for children whose parents do not seem to be able to provide 'good enough parenting' (Winnicott, 1975) due to traumatizations of their own on one hand and their lack of language skills and cultural knowledge on the other? Is there anything we can do for children who will not get to benefit from the standard therapy programs available for various reasons – because their prognosis is too poor and their symptoms seem overwhelming, or because their parents seem not really willing to cooperate or are not really reliable, or are equipped with very limited language skills, or because it is easy to overlook the child and the trouble he or she is in since often the child is by far not the biggest problem that the family is struggling with?

So this was the question we discussed in a task force meeting with representatives from the youth welfare office, a child guidance office, a school teacher and a school social worker.

---

1   Dedicated to Maggie Kline, who inspired me to write this chapter.

It was brought up since the participants knew that I had worked successfully with groups of children and teenagers in a department of child and adolescent psychiatry for many years and that I had also instructed multiplicators like students and professionals (and gave trainings in group psychotherapy with children for the Bundeskonferenz für Erziehungsberatung as an organizer).

To cut a long story short: the answer to this question is a clear 'Yes' – we *can* do something. Considering the severity of the baseline symptoms and condition of these children, the input required to shift things is relatively small and its success rate quite remarkable. From the short-term perspective of a potential sponsor, however, it is a fairly costly and time-consuming endeavor.

Case study 7.1: Josip

Let me begin with a case study. Josip, whom we will continue to hear about in this chapter, is 8 years old, the third child out of five born into an immigrant family from Kosovo. The family has merely been granted tolerated residence status, which implies they are at risk of being deported to their home country at any time. Some relatives of Josip's family have become victims of massacres. Neither of the parents speaks German. The part of town where the family lives is exclusively inhabited by people who feel alienated and are excluded from the rest of society. It is a neighborhood inhabited by hardly anybody who would deliberately choose to live there. The predominant atmosphere is one of lack of prospects – a neighborhood in the so-called social problem area of the city. Josip's mother tried several times – and in the presence of her children – to swallow pills to end her life. After each of these episodes, she received short-term inpatient 'treatment' in a psychiatric ward. In line with customary practice in their culture, Josip's parents are strict in bringing up their children and also use corporal punishment. The parents love their children.

Josip has been assessed as 'practically unschoolable'. He seems to be devoid of any impulse control, and calling him hyperactive would be a flattering description of his behavior. He immediately tends to start hitting others blindly if something makes him angry or if others come too close to him. Wherever he is, he leaves a trail of destruction – for example, by grabbing some hydroculture pellets from the plant container in the break hall of his school in passing and hurling them across the hall.

In his first group therapy session, Josip boasts, 'It's my birthday tomorrow and I invited all my friends over, the entire class.' When asked in the next session how his birthday went, he mumbles almost inaudibly,

'Nobody came,' and hurls a stuffed animal against the wall. A year later, after the termination of the therapy group, the school social worker will share what his next birthday has been like: Josip invited one girl and two boys from his class, and they celebrated his birthday with him.

Development of a therapy concept

It was clear from the outset that we would develop a group therapy program which was to be anchored in the school setting. We wanted teachers and the school social worker to vicariously take over some of the tasks, which in other therapy programs would be taken on by the parents, such as ensuring regular attendance on the part of the children. If, for example, a child does not attend school on the day for which therapy has been scheduled (maybe because he or she needs to accompany his or her mother on a visit to a doctor or on a visit to the authorities as an interpreter), the school social worker can try to find another solution which will enable the child to participate in the group therapy session.

The concept for this group therapy was not designed by me alone – it is the result of an exchange I had had with many professionals involved in fostering the development of the children we are talking about here, in particular with my friend and colleague Carola Kirsch, the head of the Youth Department of the City of Wolfsburg, headmistress Brigitte Walkling, and the school social worker, Margrit Bittner.

And, of course, it was the children themselves – working closely and engaging with their respective group leaders – who were involved in developing the concept. Since every group brings its own gestalt, its own themes and coping challenges, the children in every new group will also continue to contribute to this developmental process in the future.

The depth-psychological and social search for meaning

I originally acquired my skills in group therapy in the early 1980s in training with Bruno Metzmacher and Helmut Zaepfel at the Fritz Perls Institute for Integrative Therapy (Katz-Bernstein, 1996a; Metzmacher, Petzold and Zaepfel, 1996a; Metzmacher, Petzold and Zaepfel, 1996b). In addition to group therapeutic play, the focus of the work was on depth-psychological and social sense-making, or more specifically on the search for answers which would nurture understanding, with a fluid transition between these two aspects.

Let me give you an example of these from our therapy group:

AN EXAMPLE OF THE DEPTH-PSYCHOLOGICAL SEARCH FOR MEANING

One child in our therapy group, Marvin, is maltreating his hand puppet, a lion, hitting it against the wall again and again, yelling at it: 'Here you are! You are getting what you deserve!' From the perspective of depth psychology, one explanation for his behavior might be that, in doing so, Marvin was using 'identification with the aggressor' as a defense mechanism, probably identifying with a battering and maltreating parent. I am shocked by the duration and intensity of this outbreak, by the hatred written all over his face. An attempt on my part to protect the lion and to voice the compassion I feel for the lion aggravates Marvin's rage even more. So I simply remain standing next to him silently becoming a – temporarily helpless – observer. Fortunately, I come up with something to say, namely that, right now, I cannot think of anything that might help here and that we, the group leaders, will consider what might be a good option in our team debriefing session.

By putting things that way I take into account that there are no easy and fast responses to big and difficult problems and questions. Instead, they are the result of a sometimes strenuous process. At the same time, I am letting Marvin know that despite my momentary helplessness, I can contain the situation and that I am confident that we will come up with something helpful. Also, I am signaling to him that I find it worthwhile to start looking for a strategy and that I will do so together with my colleagues.

As almost always in the case of calls for help (in other words, in implicit inquiries about solution options), the demonstration of the conflict – in this case the way the lion gets treated – continues until a conflict solution has been found. Marvin keeps hitting the lion during the following hour, giving me challenging looks in between, and I provide him with an answer which he can take in by commenting, 'Feels really good to beat the lion and feel your power. So good that you don't have to feel how it hurts him.' This formulation is what my colleagues and I had come up with in our debriefing session. It addresses both the fact that it is painful to be beaten as well as the urge to identify with the aggressor in order not to feel the pain. Acknowledging the defense response and the pain at the same time enables him to develop empathy with the lion – and with himself.

Marvin looks at me with a grin and keeps hitting, though the way in which he is hitting the lion has changed a little. Rather than hitting it grimly, he does so in a pleasurable way. He is no longer a beater who is at a loss to understand himself and his hatred. Instead, he is becoming a beater who understands what he is doing. Rather than getting stuck in his involvement in the act of hitting, he is simultaneously able to assume the role of an observer. From this vantage point, he gets a vague idea of what his behavior and this protective mechanism are about – they begin to make sense. This in turn paves the way for understanding his own motives and for having self-respect.

Moreover, this moment establishes something very special between Marvin and myself – an unspoken sense of mutual understanding; and with this understanding, we have become allies.

Whenever rich *Now* moments of this kind become possible within a group process, they tangibly impact the atmosphere for the other children, too. There is a little irritation, a minimally increased attention, a hint that something new just happened which might inspire hope and curiosity. This hint of something new is also experienced by the other children – including Josip, who happens to be observing the scene from close by. The fact that I had succeeded in making the process of me searching for an answer transparent, rather than offering an answer right away in the previous session, reinforced its impact further.

Initially, the children involved in the group therapeutical process tend to reject the search[2] for a depth-psychological and social understanding before they gradually begin to accept it. Only much later do they become curious and even adopt it with a sense of relief. Consequently, interpretative formulations should be used sensitively in the first sessions. At the beginning, they tend to sound unfamiliar and have an unsettling impact on the children, who will react by commenting 'blah, blah, blah,' being noisy, covering their ears or becoming aggressive. Curiosity will only evolve once some of the children have experienced such moments of truly meeting themselves

---

2   Peter Fonagy (Fonagy *et al.*, 2008) calls this a search for empathic mentalization, and Marianne Bentzen and Susan Hart (2013) describe it as a movement on the prefrontal cortex compass shifting from 'low reflection' to 'high reflection'.

and the therapist and have been able to share this experience with the others atmospherically.

AN EXAMPLE OF THE SOCIAL SEARCH FOR MEANING

While the other children are frolicking in the room, Josip and I are sitting next to each other on one of the windowsills. It is one of the rare moments in which he is quiet. With no apparent purpose, I hear myself saying, 'Watching the evening news, I sometimes feel reminded of you.' He gives me a puzzled look, all calm and attentive. I continue, 'Seeing these terrible pictures (of massacres) in your home country, I find myself wondering how your parents feel watching this.' Period. That is the one moment in our dialog that matters. The shift, however, is mindblowing. Josip continues to be quiet until the end of the session, and the stillness around him seems almost tangible. His class teacher accosts us one week later, commenting that Josip had suddenly become quiet and able to pay attention; even the other children in his class were thrilled, she says.

What happened? Obviously this condensed moment of dialog with me had helped Josip understand his own situation as the son of emotionally frozen parents – to a point of being able to relate to what they were going through. Together, we had encountered a moment in which empathic mentalization around his own state of mind and his family's situation had been generated in me – and then he had been open to taking my answer, my resonance with him, in with all of his senses. Subsequently, Josip became willing to learn in class and developed more and more self-agency.

Attachment and protective and risk factors

In addition to basing our development of child therapy approaches on the concepts of a depth-psychological and social search for meaning, we increasingly started drawing from the findings of attachment research and on the protective and risk factors involved since the 1980s (Ainsworth, 2014; Bowlby, 1990; Brisch, 2003; Dornes 1993; Rahm and Kirsch, 2000, 2005, 2010, 2011; Stern, 1995, 2000; Stern et al., 2010).

It was known that children growing up with many risk factors and thus exposed to highly stressful risk conditions tend to develop successfully only if they have access to, or develop, some vital protective factors. The most important core protective factor is a *longer-term positive relationship with an attachment figure and the secure attachment arising from it*. Among the other core protective factors are the following:

a) A realistic belief in self-agency: This belief evolves on the basis of the remembered or memorable experience of successfully completing a task or tackling a challenge. It is contingent on a realistic and appropriate self-perception and perception of the situation as well as on learning problem-solving techniques.

b) Reflectivity: This protective factor implies the capacity to reflect and understand oneself, the other person and relationships as well as the current and past situation or the capacity to imagine them as potentially understandable, both as a cognitive and as an emotional, empathic insight.

c) Solidarity: Solidarity is understood as the ability to establish and enjoy good, reliable, robust, pleasurable peer relationships (relationships with people in similar life stages and situations). Development of solidarity is contingent on the ability to experience empathy for yourself and others. For children with sub-optimal early attachment experiences, developing this capacity is an important second chance.

d) Androgynity: In this context, androgynity is seen as the acquisition of skills primarily viewed as associated with the opposite sex, namely verbally and physically assertive or even aggressive behaviors for girls, and empathic and caring skills (both related to self-care and care for others) for boys. These androgynous skills seem to matter only for those children growing up under high-risk conditions. For children with so-called 'normal' biographies, however, they don't play any major role.

Let me use the following example to illustrate how empathic mentalization of a denied conflict initiates the development of protective factors a), b) and c). After multiple surgical interventions attempting to correct her clubfoot in the first years of her life, Iris has maintained some mild motor impairment. She starts to boast loudly about her being able to jump over a wall made of foam blocks that the children had erected. As was to be expected, she ends up knocking the wall down and gets laughed at by the other children. Only very gradually and with the help of our support and the human kindness she is able to experience, she learns to become aware of herself without denying her own physical disability. She thus acquires a kind of empathic mentalization which enables her to understand that there is a reason why jumping is more difficult for her than it is for other children – namely a medical condition and many operations. Standing next to some other children performing high jumps a few weeks later, she starts to look somewhat sad and mumbles, 'I can't do that.' Another girl approaches her, asking her, 'Shall I show you how I learned to do the high jump?' Both of them begin to practice jumping with great focus. At first, they have fun successfully jumping over ridiculously low objects, but gradually their expectations and the height of the hurdles start to become more realistic, and Iris begins to become aware of her little successes and to savor them as achievements. The other children are following the process closely and give beaming Iris a big applause at the end of her explorations (Rahm, 2004, 2015).

From our experience, children who are out of touch with themselves while crying – in other words, who lack mentalization skills – are frequently made fun of by other kids and sometimes get treated downright cruelly. Children who are in touch with themselves while crying (thus demonstrating empathic mentalization skills), however, tend to be comforted or supported in other ways by other children.

With the exception of the protective factor of attachment, the development of which can primarily be supported indirectly, the remaining protective factors (a– d) mentioned above can be learned directly – at least to some degree (e.g. through processes involved in group therapy). Against this background, we defined the development of these skills related to protective factors as goals of our group therapy and focused on the developmental potential in this area.[3]

Affect regulation and mentalization

The findings of research on protective and risk factors and attachment science have largely become part of today's research on affect regulation and mentalization processes (Fonagy et al., 2008; Hart, 2011; Ogden, Minton and Pain, 2006; Rahm, 2015; Schore, 2003).

---

3   In previous publications (Rahm, 2004, 2010), I provide examples for measures that specifically stimulate and support the development of protective factors.

Affect regulation skills begin to develop in a co-regulative interaction process between the child and the mother (or primary caregiver) from the time of birth at the latest. Soon afterwards, initially rudimentary mentalizing skills begin to develop with the help of an exchange between the mother and the child based on resonance and mirroring phenomena. Empathic mentalization is the process of attempting to understand emotions and needs – both our own and others'. Mentalization relies on the moment of meeting while being in an alert and responsive affective state. This, however, tends to be impossible if there is either hyper- or hypoarousal.

Generally – but not always – mothers succeed in supporting their babies in developing these capacities. The better the mother's own regulation and mentalization skills – that is, the more she has been able to process and integrate difficulties and traumatizations in her own life – the more successfully she will master this task.[4]

All the children in our therapy groups share a lack of good compensatory protective factors and thus the positive impact they would have. All of the children lack a secure attachment relationship to a non-traumatized attachment figure equipped with certain regulation and mentalization skills. And what all of them have in common is that they have not had any role models for good affect regulation skills and helpful mentalization skills.

The absence of experiences of this kind cannot be compensated directly and fully, although it is possible to set the course in a way which initiates some development in a new direction. This process becomes possible through the combination of two factors:

- offering specific games in the context of group therapy which are fun and stimulating

- the role model effect of the therapist's personality and the attachment he or she offers, as well as his or her self-regulation

---

4   Rahm (2005) describes parallels between the mother–child and the therapist–patient dyads and their implications for the therapeutic process. Alan Schore (2003) compares the impact of the mother–child dyad to the impact of the patient–therapist dyad, stating that the ongoing social-emotional stimulation of the brain in the patient–therapist dyad helps to develop new processing options, and that the relationship between the patient and the therapist can support patients in establishing a new, more mature way of dealing with themselves and others. In this context, he rightfully points out that the therapist's own regulation capacity plays a major role by providing the resonance for the patient's facial, prosodic and gestural signals.

capacity, and his or her empathic mentalization skills including the ability to engage in a depth-psychological and social search for meaning.

Such a setting of the course through therapy is roughly comparable to the influence of the twelfth fairy in the fairytale *Sleeping Beauty* (Grimm, 2014). The impact of the prophecy made by the thirteenth fairy is offset by the promise of the twelfth fairy: although intended otherwise by the curse, Sleeping Beauty will not drop dead after injuring herself with a spindle on her fifteenth birthday; instead, she will fall into 100 years of sleep, from which she will wake up when conditions are favorable.

From our standpoint, the overarching goal for the children in our therapy groups is to help them develop affect regulation and empathic mentalization skills. Our understanding is that these skills are fundamental for developing protective factors and a capacity for relationships and that they will have a kind of favorable snowball effect in this respect. Our role in this, as we see it, is to create optimal conditions for fostering these processes in our group therapy settings.

Survive moments – thrive moments

Daniel Siegel (Siegel and Bryson, 2013) uses these two concise terms as a guideline in his wonderful book *The Whole-Brain Child: 12 Revolutionary Strategies to Nurture Your Child's Developing Mind*. He writes, 'the moments you are just trying to survive are actually opportunities to help your child thrive' (p.9). This is exactly the principle we get to experience over and over again in group therapy. Survive moments are those moments in the group when we as the group leaders feel powerless, confused, shocked, incompetent, sad, angry, disgusted, guilty and many things more. They are not just unpleasant – they are 'at the same time…opportunities – even gifts – because a survive moment is *also* a thrive moment, where the important, meaningful work of parenting takes place' (Siegel and Bryson, 2013, p.8). If this is something we bear in mind, we will be less tempted to ignore these moments or to get them over and done with quickly. The good thing about this type of awareness is that we end up feeling less at their mercy. This perspective helps us to feel more secure and able to take action – that is, we feel only relatively powerless, relatively confused or relatively disgusted. It makes affect regulation easier for us if we can use mentalization to see that this situation is a request by the children to us which is born out of desperation and that we will grow together if we embark on the search for answers.

In our therapy groups, the joint debriefings of the group leaders are an important element of this search. As we will see, the children grasp or sense very quickly that there is this valuable interplay between unresolved conflicts in the therapy group on the one hand and our search and cognitive processes in the debriefing on the other. Over the course of a group process, they tend to become more and more curious about aspects fed back to them from the debriefing.

Specification of the concept

The practical implementation of group therapy based on the concepts outlined above can be summarized as follows.

Framework conditions at the schools involved

Anchoring children's group therapy successfully in a school is contingent on creating the necessary preconditions. Both the principal of the school as well as the school social worker and the teachers who will send their students to a therapy group must back this educational measure without reservations. To this end, every party involved must receive extensive and specific information on the contents of the therapeutic work ahead of time. They must be made aware of the ways in which they will be required to contribute and be willing to make this contribution. It is worthwhile to talk about options of dealing with friction points which are to be expected and also to raise awareness about the fact that it sometimes requires a great deal of effort to generate appreciation and respect between people performing different roles (teachers and therapists). One of the teacher's specific responsibilities is to ensure – in cooperation with the school social worker – that the children attend the groups regularly and to advise the group leaders of any changes in the families promptly if required.

Team of therapists

The group is led by two therapists – ideally by a man and a woman. Their professional and personal skills must meet high standards. Moreover, physical fitness is important for this type of work.

At least one of them should be experienced in leading child therapy groups. Also, at least one of them should have a background in either depth-psychology or in a similar course of study, with well-founded knowledge in working with unconscious processes and with defence or protective mechanisms, respectively. Both of them need intercultural sensitivity and previous experience with different cultural conditions involved in socialization or at least the readiness to learn about them. Also, they need to be aware that the way they embody their gender traits and gender role will have an impact on how open the parents and the children will be to cooperating. They need enough imagination to consider that there might be some hard-to-understand behaviors on the part of parents and children originating from socialization conditions and life experiences which German group leaders without any migration background might tend to find strange. For example, it often becomes easier to comprehend some parents if we understand their tremendous fear of German institutions – and of the school system as an institution – from which they expect the exercise of power, sanctions and demands which can hardly be satisfied.

More than anything else, the therapists need sound self-regulation skills, which they can also successfully maintain in insecure, chaotic and challenging situations. Moreover, what is required from them is the ability to be aware of and clarify misunderstandings, to be aware of their own mistakes and faults and to be willing to apologize where appropriate, to ask others for help and support, to set clear boundaries, to preserve their curiosity, to maintain hope even in temporarily hopeless-seeming moments or to retrieve hope time and again.

Furthermore, the therapists need to have protoconversation skills (Fonagy et al., 2008), a mirror-neurons-driven choreography around encountering and communication. This kind of playing together goes way beyond comprehension on the level of speech. It also includes facial expression, gestures and affect regulation processes. When we find ourselves working with children who seriously lack mentalization skills and who did not pick up the German language from native-speaker parents, it is absolutely essential that what we offer to them on the level of language is explicitly accompanied by this type of protoconversational play. If children are not familiar with words such as 'comfort' or 'cradle', they need therapists who are aware of that and include protoconversation – for example, by jointly nursing the child's favorite soft-toy animal together with the child.

In addition to the two chief therapists, we have two trainees (social pedagogues, educators, psychologists) working in our therapy groups. They undertake to stay for an entire school year and, like the therapists, view themselves as learners in this process. From these trainees, too, we expect a high level of personal skills.

This composition of group leadership takes up a lot of manpower, but it has proved to be extraordinarily successful. It enables us to perform different functions and roles and, in the presence of the children, to be role models talking about topics with each other which are absolutely fascinating for the children and demonstrate unfamiliar possibilities of cooperation. We address topics such as: How can I as a learner (e.g. as a trainee) ask somebody else (another group leader) for help in a way which demonstrates how to do so while at the same time safeguarding my self-esteem? How do those with experience demonstrate respect towards the learners who are less experienced? How do I ask for support? How can I remain independent and self-confident when accepting help from others? How do we deal with different opinions and beliefs? How can we support each other and lessen others' burdens in situations of chaos and uncertainty? How do I treat myself and others if I happened to forget or overlook something or if I made a mistake? How do I apologize in a way which enables me to maintain my self-respect while at the same time experiencing heart-felt dismay?

Since there are four of us, we can guarantee the kind of continuity and reliability which is so important for the children: the therapy group can always take place, even if one of us is unable to attend.

In case both chief therapists are of the same sex, it is imperative to have both men and women in the team of four.

Selecting the children and composition of the group

For the therapy, we select children with a similar developmental age. The second grade of elementary school has turned out to be a particularly suitable age group. Age variability there is between 6 and 10 years of age.

The teachers propose those children for the therapy group with whom they have experienced the biggest difficulties. There are two main selection criteria:

- These should be children for whom there are no conceivable alternatives to this form of group therapy.

- The children present severe psychosocial impairments (usually associated with known or suspected traumatizations in their history) and at the same time an extremely negative development forecast.

Since the number of children suggested as participants by the teachers always exceeds the number of available therapy slots, the final selection is coordinated between the teacher, the school social worker and the principal. We work with six children in mixed-gender groups, preferably comprised of three girls and three boys. There should always be at least two children of the same sex per group.

In most cases, at least two-thirds of our children have a migration background. The children reach high scale values on three to five of the five axes and with reference to their global ratings for psychological disorders based on the Multiaxial Classification of Child and Adolescent Psychiatric Disorders (ICD 10; Remschmidt and Schmidt, 1994).[5] Consequently, they present profound psychosocial adjustment disturbances.

Cooperation with the parents

In the first therapy runs we tried out various forms of cooperation with the parents and then decided in favor of a single consultation of approx. 60–90 minutes with them before the start of the therapy group. Our further cooperation was based on more or less random encounters in fairly relaxed frameworks such as during school events and festivals. On these occasions, the parents felt comfortable to approach us. I will share a great subtle and indirect form of cooperation between us under the heading of 'messages' later.

The initial consultation takes place with one of the group leaders and the school social worker (whom the parents already know). In many cases, an interpreter joins the meeting. In these consultations, there are four topics, which are particularly important:

---

5   By comparison, children in conventional therapy groups in educational counseling centers usually present disturbances on one to two axes.

- We tell the parents in great detail about the therapy groups, providing examples for their potential content, and we share (strictly anonymous) experiences of other children. We deliberately choose examples which the parents can relate to, sometimes to the point of almost seeing their own child reflected in them. We tell them that the teacher selected and suggested their child for the therapy group because the teacher believes that this child has the capacity to make use of the group for the benefit of his or her own development *and* because the teacher has observed that their child currently does not really feel at ease when in class.

- We explain our confidentiality policy, assuring the parents that the group leaders will not disclose any private information related to the family vis-à-vis the school. This fact seems to be vitally important. For us as group leaders it sometimes involves a tricky balancing act. We need to consider carefully what we can disclose and what we are not allowed to share, and in which direction we would like to direct a teacher's imagination without giving away a secret. The fact that we are taking confidentiality so seriously is definitely one of the reasons why parents trust us, and why there have been no dropouts.

- We limit taking the child's case history to a minimum. For example, we try to find out something about the family's country of origin, their experiences associated with leaving their country and their degree of integration as well as about the personal situation and the skills and resources of all members of the family. We do not want the family to feel like they are being interrogated. It must be obvious at all times that our focus is on learning something about the potential of the child and ways to support him or her within the family.

- We explicitly ask the parents – in writing – to provide their consent to the child participating in the group therapy. At the same time, we signal to them that we are prepared to respect their decision in case they refuse to do so and that we will not try to persuade them otherwise. This is the attitude we actually arrived at in the course of multi-perspective discussions in which we deliberately tried to empathize with the given situations of the parents and their possibilities. Probably it is thanks to this approach that all of the parents we asked agreed.

- We assure the parents that the teachers will take care of everything with regard to their child's participation in the therapy group – for example, the teacher will take the child to the first sessions and the parents will not need to bother with anything.

Of course we asked ourselves why the compliance rates among these parents might have been so high. We feel that the point is that we do not impose any demands on them and that we do not overtax their willingness to change. Besides, we might be the only 'authority' who does not criticize their children and their family. And then there is also the miraculous impact of the 'messages' (see later in the chapter).

Time frame of the group therapy

The entire group therapy program comprises 26–30 sessions. We start with the preparatory selection interviews at the beginning of the school year (i.e. after the summer holidays). The group terminates one to two months before the end of the school year. The group does not meet during the school holidays. Over the course of the therapy, there are three two-hour meetings with everyone involved in the children's professional network. A therapy session lasts 60 minutes. It is followed by a 60-minute debriefing session (see later in the chapter).

In cases where the group therapy sessions take place during school hours, we recommend the provision of some transition between class and therapy – a kind of air-lock chamber enabling the child to mentally 'switch over'. What we have found particularly suitable for this purpose is a relatively small protected room in which the children might be offered something to eat and to drink.

Setting up the therapy space

The optimal therapy space would be a 550–750 ft^2 unfurnished room equipped with a hard-wearing wall-to-wall carpet. Recommended items would be eight woolen blankets, many cushions, two gym mats, plenty of soft toys (hand puppets), a foam ball and white chalk (easily removable with a vacuum cleaner) with which the children can make drawings on the floor. As needed, and depending on the development of the group, additional items, such as large foam cubes and read-aloud children's books can be added.

Content

Over the entire course of the therapy, we ensure a secure containment and provide the children with clear and dependable information and a reliable structure. In the first group sessions, we command lasting respect by being relatively authoritative and we only allow ourselves to approach them with our depth-psychological understanding once this respect has been established, since it is a precious commodity we do not want to squander. Most of our children grow up experiencing that the strongest is always right. They have taught us that they first need to convince themselves that we are strong before they dare to engage with something as unsettling as empathic understanding.

We start punctually and finish on schedule. We frequently orient the children to continuity, for instance by saying, 'We will meet in our therapy group two more times before the autumn holidays...and right after the holidays, the therapy sessions will resume...' Or three sessions before we reach the end of the therapy we say, 'Next time we will sit together and think about what you would like to do in our closing session and next time we will take farewell photographs of you with one of your favorite stuffed animals.'

In the first session, we welcome the children. For this purpose, we prepare in advance a circle made up of six blankets and seat cushions. We tell the children a bit about what games we will play during group time and show them our 'feel-good corner' and our 'not-participating area' for those who temporarily wish to withdraw from joint activities – each of them has a gym mat, and the feel-good corner is equipped with extra blankets and cushions. We tell them about the process which led up to them having been chosen for this group by saying something like, 'You have been selected because your teachers trust that you will be able to learn something here which will make you feel good. Also, you have been picked because every single one of you has something you are having a hard time with. For instance around making friends...or what you can do if you are angry...or how you can become a better student.'

We then propose the first game. We declare the blankets are protected islands which others must not set foot on unless expressly permitted or invited to do so. Every child is given the opportunity to pick one of the available animal hand puppets and take it with him/ her to the island. Often the initially selected animal stays with the same child over the entire therapy course, whereas others might be swapped, fought over or temporarily left with a caretaker who kindly looks after them; but there are also animals which are neglected or abused, which implies heaps of challenges for our work. We use chalk to write the name or chosen name of its inhabitant and his or her stuffed animal around each island (e.g. 'Shark-Dennis-Superman-Island'). We use these labelled islands in our beginning ritual for the group process as a whole. This sitting circle is often used to share important comments, wishes and specific sensitivities. From the second session, the children will also find their 'messages' (see later) on their respective island. This island game is a good starting point for developing further activities such as 'getting-to-know-their-animals-visits', for which the children take a seat on blankets and cushions (i.e. in water taxis and on dolphins) and have great fun allowing themselves to be transported from island to island by us. This in turn results in other games which sometimes get repeated in more than ten sessions since they are fun and contain a cause for conflict which needs to be coped with. For example, we might have all kinds of fights around boundaries: defending the boundaries of an island, asking others for help and support in doing so, and taking on help and support; stepping over others' boundaries; dealing with the 'victim' and the 'perpetrator' following a transgression of boundaries. Or we play out scenarios such as falling off the water taxi, almost drowning and being saved, getting good care in the hospital (feel-good corner) or – verbally supported by the therapist and cheered on by the other children – vomiting everything out: all the water and all the undigestible stuff swallowed during the near-drowning experience and during a lifetime; everything which is mean, yucky or unfair is to be expelled. We, the adults, strongly support the children in feeling, describing and exploring the bodily sensations involved in this exaggerated 'vomiting game'.[6]

After exhausting activities of this type, we offer the children something quiet and nurturing to allow things to settle: one of our

---

6   Fonagy calls this picking up and modified echoing of affect 'marked mirroring'.

favorites is a massage 'given' by the child's favorite animal (or a 'pizza fragrance massage' or 'carwash massage')[7] in the feel-good corner; or a wind massage for which a blanket is used as a fan. Over the entire course of the therapy, we offer games involving a lot of scuffling and romping around, trials of strength and being really noisy and tracking their bodies. These games are usually great fun for the kids and include physical activities they enjoy. They can be games that the children know and would like to play, or they can be exercises originally intended to foster psychomotor development, or else they can be self-invented games emerging from the process. Some examples are the 'protector ball game' or the 'body guessing game' with the children buried under blankets and cushions, or games which are about defending their territory, or pushing or pulling adults out of a chalk circle.[8]

After each of these activities, we invite the children to rest and relax in different ways while sensing their bodies. After a wrestling match, for example, we might initiate a towel massage for the wrestlers which we comment on by making all kinds of sounds to demonstrate how good it feels for the wrestler's back when all the power which had been mobilized in the wrestler's muscles can finally be released, or how the wrestler's breath can become nice and quiet again, or how we can sense our own hearts beginning to beat more slowly again.

---

7   In a pizza massage the child's back is imagined to be a griddle. The ingredients of the dough are kneaded and massaged on the back. The dough gets rolled out with both underarms. According to the child's wishes favourite food goes on top together with cheese and spices by slight touching. Both enjoy the fragrant smell and silently wait until the pizza is done and then admire the delicious taste. A carwash massage follows the same principle. The child imagines him or herself to be a car moving through the carwash. There might be a massage rubbing off the dirt, extended washing with delicious smelling shampoo, stroking to become shining and beautiful, wind-drying by waving a towel, kneading and polishing to give a protective layer against any rigour that might occur during the following week.

8   In the 'protector ball game' one child chooses a protector. Both stand in the middle of the circle. The child hides behind his or her protector and makes efforts to stay protected while the other children try to hit him or her with a soft ball. When they succeed, all applaud the child that was able to take the protection, the child that has protected and the one that threw the ball that hit. This one – in the next turn – starts with choosing a protector. In the 'body guessing game' one or more children hide under some blankets. Two children have to find out who they are by touching, exploring and naming, for example, 'this is a shoulder, a head, a big foot, is this a knee?... is this Jossip?' For a detailed description of these games, see Rahm (2004, 2010).

Tracking and commenting on physical sensations and body signals (associated both with arousal and with calming down) fosters the development of improved regulatory capacities – and at the same time goes far beyond that. Maggie Kline (Kline, 2008)[9] once described this process as follows:

> The integration between the neocortex and the brainstem happens by becoming aware and describing sensations. This integration triggers the growth of the insula region and – along with that – an increase in the ability to experience self-empathy, compassion and social empathy.

Most of the time, it is during these moments of calm and wide-awake attention that the children are particularly receptive to little communications and messages from our side – for empathic, supportive or also intriguing, slightly irritating mentalizations. If I am giving children – while they are identifying with their favourite car in their favourite color – the opportunity to relish the enjoyable experience of a car wash, it might sound like this: 'Ahh, so wonderfully clean...all the dirt and all the filthy stuff has been washed away; it can flow away, never to be seen again. The dirt is gone! All of this looks so shiny and feels so nice and clean under my hands. Can you feel it, too? Shall we polish it with impregnator once again; shall we provide it with a special layer which will protect it from accidents and crashes? What scent do you want the polish to have? Can you smell, too, how delicious this car smells? Ahh, now this Josip car is ready. Wonderful. This will last until next week. Maybe the Josip car will take good care and maybe not get any dents from jostling with other cars...' The kids greatly enjoy these elaborations. Often they cheer us on while we are making these things up and have fun if the ideas are particularly preposterous. This game is accompanied by such a sense of joyful harmony and ease that it does not even become threatening for the children if it is interspersed with minor suggestions around behavioral changes, such as: 'Maybe a Josip car with that special protective coating can become aware of a Marvin car hurtling toward him at great speed. Actually, does your car have hazard warning lights?' Josip giggling: 'They are broken!'

When we use massages in our work, the point for us and the children is to be very precise and mindful – mindful in exploring boundaries, mindful in dealing with boundaries, and also mindful in

---

9   For further reading see Levine and Kline (2006, 2008).

becoming aware that the needs of other children might differ from their own needs quite a lot. With children who always want to get a massage no matter what, it is sometimes about becoming more sensitive and learning to differentiate between what makes them feel good and what doesn't. With children who do not dare to express their longing to receive a good kind of touch or who do not dare to take it in, it is about initiating new explorations and new experiences. For example, for a child who tends to find touch scary we might initially affirm that it is a good idea to be vigilant. Later in the process, we might invite him or her to sit near another child receiving a massage or to watch the massage from some distance away. Another wonderful option in this context consists in the hand puppets. We can teach the shark soft toy to share how it wants to be massaged and to nod 'yes' or say if something feels good. We can teach it to say 'stop' or 'no' and to try out how well saying 'stop' works. In the complementary role, the children have the opportunity to empathize with the experiences of the toy animal and to investigate new options by way of identifying with it.

Apart from games suggested by us, the children increasingly begin to invent and design their own games over the course of the group therapy. Usually, these are games which give them great pleasure and which convey multiple indirect queries about how to process particular conflicts. Usually the children tend to play them over many therapy sessions. These experiences and creations also contribute to the children experiencing our group therapy as something of their own making, their own achievement. This process contributes to the development of 'self-agency', which is a protective factor.

I would like to outline an example, which shows exactly that. After multiple attempts and a lot of insistence and demonstration of solidarity, the children just about manage to convince us adults to do something which we definitely don't feel like doing: namely to carry very heavy tables from the break hall into the therapy room. With the help of blankets, the children then use them to create castles, caves, prisons and spaces used for social exclusion, for setting clear boundaries and for creating meeting places. At the end, this even evolves into a game, which never would have occurred to grown-ups: The children end up inventing an abuse scenario which involves a highly complex liberation from this situation, including imagining being protected and becoming whole and healed (Rahm, 2004, 2010).

We always end the therapy session with the same farewell ritual: Together with his or her stuffed animal, each child allows herself/ himself to be rocked on blankets by us adults. We do this ten times. This is – at least frequently – another good moment of attention to mentalization. It is an opportunity to verbalize subtle windows of opportunity we observed in the child. Of course we limit ourselves to just a few words and refrain from giving a lecture. Another less energy-sapping farewell ritual consists of pulling the children, together with their toy animals, through the room on their blankets, complete with an 'in-built back massage' (i.e. pulling them over self-chosen obstacles such as cushions or foam cuboids).

Case study 7.2: Josip

To end this section, I would like to share another episode with Josip: In a chaotic situation, I get hit on the back of my head from behind with a kids' fencing cudgel. It hurts a lot. In a surge of emotion, a mix of shock and pain, I lose control. I find myself grabbing the child who is standing behind me, Josip, and start to yell at him and shake him. Josip breaks away from me and escapes to the toilet. Gradually, I come to my senses again. The pain begins to lessen. The other children are talking agitatedly about what just happened. They are not used to this kind of behavior from me. They are confused, but also curious and eager to see how this will continue. I tell them both sides of the story: that I don't feel good about my behavior and that I am sorry (especially since it becomes obvious that he had not intended to hit me), *and* that I find my own reaction understandable. This is a kind of reflection, which the children rarely encounter in adults. It intrigues them that an adult person can reflect about her own fault while *at the same time* be secure in her self-esteem and remain in control of the situation. Josip still hasn't returned, and the children are beginning to speculate about how he might be doing, what he might be thinking, how they might view things if they were him and are wondering whether we should go get him. Right at this moment, he enters the door. Everybody starts talking simultaneously, wanting to share with him what has been discussed while he was absent, and I also want to have a word with him to apologize. Suddenly we all fall silent: Josip is just standing there having no idea what we are talking about – he has forgotten everything and is completely dissociated. Once the children comprehend that he really has no recollection of the event, they start telling him about the outrageous thing that just happened, every single one from his or her own viewpoint, again and again, until he gets an inkling of what just happened and what he did to protect himself. Josip is able to smile again – because the others are near him, because they managed to grasp something about him, because he is able to understand that part of himself now, and because, for a little while, he has become the hero of the group.

What just happened? A situation has developed which from the children's perspective is extraordinary and fascinating. Since the kids themselves are neither responsible nor directly affected, the secure environment they find themselves in, the group, enables them to reflect on the behavior and psychological processes from the position of witnesses. They get an idea that there is more than one possible perspective and that there are psychological processes which are 'beyond comprehension' (Josip's dissociation) but nevertheless make sense. The children are exposed to the pleasant, though for them rather unusual experience of mentalizing, and in doing so, of being able to feel empathy for another child: *the emerging of empathy*. It is this group's twenty-sixth session. During the first half of a group process, experiences of this kind would be inconceivable.

Debriefing session

Our 60-minutes' debriefing, which we always record in writing, and the interplay between the group process and the debriefing are an essential part of our work. In view of her role as a mediator between the team of therapists and the school, the school social worker also attends these debriefing sessions. Our way of being and working together is based on the principle of 'reflecting team' (Andersen, 1990) in the form of a multi-perspective unbiased brainstorming (Rahm, 2007). The questions and ideas that have come up remain present and spark new ideas and perspectives on the part of the others. Our joint work helps us to expand our professional, intercultural and personal horizons. Its benefit for the children lies in the fact that they learn that we value and discuss conflictual issues and questions from the group (the 'survive moments') and that we make our own learning process transparent by sharing it with them. We now do this even more consciously since the children themselves started to show us how intent they are on this kind of work – for example, by frequently asking us, 'What did you learn in the debriefing?'

Some of the most frequent themes of our debriefing sessions are:

- how we feel and get along with each other as a team, clarification of misunderstandings, anger and things not understood

- focus on every individual child, in particular on positive developments and abnormal, difficult situations

- comments and attempts to understand the process, as well as aspects to be considered about the next session

- networking issues and initiating particular measures (e.g. cooperation with the day care center or youth welfare office) related to the school social worker's responsibilities

- formulating 'messages' to one child or several children (two to three per therapy session).

One aspect we have to deal with in every group is 'projective identification as a group process' – in most of our groups this happens between the tenth and the twentieth session. The children tend to stand together in engaging in so much mischief that we, the group leaders, occasionally find ourselves helpless, lackadaisical, running out of ideas and a little confused. This situation always changes as soon as we begin to see this behavior as a defense mechanism of the entire group: the children are making us experience first-hand how they themselves feel in this world – and they are asking us how one can deal with things of this kind.

Messages

Our messages are documents. They are empathic mentalizations of developments and of the growth of protective factors. Every child receives her or his message in the form of a dated letter signed by all four of us and slipped into a nice envelope which we place on his or her island blanket to be read out by us at the beginning of the session. For each session we formulate about two or three of them. We make sure that all children receive approximately the same number of messages during the year.

With these messages, we place our focus on precious little moments frequently related to events occurring where 'survive and thrive' moments meet (Siegel and Bryson, 2012). Of course we do not want our messages to come along as something 'pedagogical', but rather as a small – slightly confusing and therefore intriguing – gift or acknowledgement. Some moments, however, are so delicate or so much associated with shame and so private that we can only hint at them in our message rather than referring to them explicitly. Here are some examples:

'You covered your ears when there was some difficult thing you did not want to hear. That's a smashing idea.'

'In our last session you had a lot of fun with Olga jumping across the little foam blocks. The audience was clapping. You brought joy to them, too.'

'In the last session you gave your kangaroo a really nice massage. You could feel exactly what it liked and what it did not like. You also taught it to say "stop it" when there was something it did not like. That is an important thing.'

'In the last session you have learned a lot in dealing with your lion. And the lion also has learned something.'

'You managed to say "no" to Ms. Rahm when she wanted to explain something to you while you were sitting on the window sill. You paid very close attention to what you wanted and what you did not want.'

'Last time all of you together demonstrated to us what it feels like to be constantly disturbed and interrupted while playing. Only when we had our debriefing, we understood how important it was that you showed us these feelings. We considered what might help in moments where you can't think of any solution.'

'Last time, all of you together succeeded in asserting yourselves towards the adults. We did not feel like carrying these large and heavy tables into the group room at all. But you insisted, and that was good. You invented a wonderful game around building table caves, and all of us enjoyed it a lot.'

When we began to give messages as little gifts to the children, we had no idea how significant they were to become. Hearing Josip comment one day how his mother would put all of the messages he received up on a pinboard, the rest of the children started sharing how the messages were kept in their homes.

Ever since, we always consider how each particular message might be received in the family when formulating it. In wording some messages, we actually primarily have the parents in mind. Probably the parents are able to accept these messages and take them in because they are not directly addressed at them. After all, these are messages to the children, so they can remain relaxed – they do not need to challenge or defend themselves; instead, they can secretly become curious and participate in their child's development.

At the very end of the group therapy, each child receives a booklet which contains the entire collection of messages and any photographs the child wants to have: Josip with the kangaroo, Josip with Iris, Josip with the entire group, Josip riding piggyback on the trainee's back.

Looking back, we can see again and again that the collection of messages documents the central theme in each child's development in the group process.

Network meetings and continuity

Over the course of the group therapy, we arrange three two-hour meetings with everybody involved in the kid's professional network – with the team of therapists, with all the teachers of the six children, the caregivers from the day care centre, the school social worker and the headteacher. Experience has shown that the best time for the conferences is three weeks before the therapy course starts, approximately in the middle, and two to four weeks after the end of the therapy. The discussions are structured and moderated in a way which ensures that we have 15–20 minutes to talk about each child. We use this time to exchange information – at the same time ensuring confidentiality – to clarify any questions and confusion, to appreciate developmental steps and stagnation alike. We give ourselves permission to develop visions for every single child's future development. Moreover, we specify which tasks the school social worker will take on for each of the children over the next school years, whether it is paying a visit to the local thrift shop to get some new clothes for them, mindfully monitoring some particular developmental aspects, or the idea to integrate a girl into a girls' group led by the social worker by the time she has reached puberty.

Almost always, when we take stock of our group therapy work, the result is impressively positive: all of the children have accomplished developmental steps which are clearly noticeable for everyone involved. For some children, one of them being Josip, the changes that have occurred are little short of a miracle, whereas for others they actually started out quite slowly – here, the child's further development remains to be seen and we will keep an eye on it.[10]

Apart from the changes we have observed in the children, we have also been able to witness a change process at the school over the years. More and more teachers have begun to develop empathy and respect for the – seemingly – 'hopeless cases'. They have become more self-efficient, more confident and have developed new skills, which are not only beneficial for these difficult children, but also for the entire atmosphere in the school.

The continuity of the group therapy and the fact that it is held in very high esteem at the school also contribute to its effectiveness. Thus, we occasionally experience former group children stopping by asking whether they can join the group again. When they get the 'no' they expected, they happily withdraw, proud of being ex-group kids who now do not need a group and leave the field clear for others. The children currently in the group, on the other hand, are just as proud of how attractive and important 'their group' obviously is for the older kids.

Group therapy with children in the form described here is an enormous challenge. It is hard work, which can be frustrating here and there and repeatedly stretches you to your limits. Only enthusiasm and love for these children make it possible.

At the same time, this kind of work is a gift for us as well. Hardly anywhere else in our professional life are we exposed to so much pleasure, joy and vitality, nor can we collect so many new and gratifying experiences. This kind of work enables us to experience first-hand how the developmental opportunities for children with very bleak development prospects can improve significantly within a short period of time.

References

Ainsworth, M. (2014) *Maternal Sensitivity: Mary Ainsworth's Enduring Influence on Attachment Theory, Research, and Clinical Applications*. New York, NY: Routledge, Chapman & Hall.

Andersen, T. (ed.) (1990) *Das Reflektierende Team. Dialoge und Dialoge über Dialoge*. Dortmund: Modernes Lernen.

---

10 Unfortunately, we did not have the means to perform follow-up studies to document the efficiency of the group therapy described here.

Bentzen, M. and Hart, S. (2013) *Neuroaffective psychotherapy*. Coesfeld, Germany. 10–14 September 2013.

Bowlby, J. (1990) *Secure Base: Parent-Child Attachment and Healthy Human Development.* New York, NY: Basic Books.

Brisch, K. H. (2003) *Bindungsstörungen. Von der Bindungstheorie zur Therapie* (5th edn). Stuttgart: Klett-Cotta.

Dornes, M. (1993) *Der Kompetente Säugling. Die Präverbale Entwicklung des Kindes.* Frankfurt: Fischer TB.

Fonagy, P. *et al.* (2008) Markierte Affektspiegelung und die Entwicklung eines affektregulierenden Gebrauchs des Als-ob-Spiels.' In P. Fonagy *et al. Affektregulierung, Mentalisierung und die Entwicklung des Selbst* (3rd edn). Stuttgart: Klett-Cotta.

Grimm, Jacob and Wilhelm (2014) *The Original Folk and Fairy Tales of the Brothers Grimm.* Princeton, NJ: Princeton University Press.

Hart, S. (2011) *The Impact of Attachment.* New York, NY: W. W. Norton.

Katz-Bernstein, N (1996) 'Das Konzept des "Safe-Place" – ein Beitrag zur Praxeologie Integrativer Kinderpsychotherapie.' In B. Metzmacher, H. Petzold and H. Zaepfel (eds) *Therapeutische Zugänge zu den Erfahrungswelten des Kindes von Heute. Integrative Kindertherapie in Theorie und Praxis* (vol. 2). Paderborn: Junfermann.

Kline, M. (2008) 'The Ordinary Miracle of Healing: Somatic Experiencing with Children and Adolescents.' Steyerberg, Germany. 25–27 April 2008.

Levine, P. and Kline, M. (2006) *Trauma through a Child's Eyes: Awakening the Ordinary Miracle of Healing.* Berkeley, CA: North Atlantic Books.

Levine, P. and Kline, M. (2008) *Trauma-Proofing Your Kids: A Parents' Guide for Instilling Confidence, Joy, and Resilience.* Berkeley, CA: North Atlantic Books.

Metzmacher, B., Petzold, H. and Zaepfel, H. (eds) (1996a) *Therapeutische Zugänge zu den Erfahrungswelten des Kindes von Heute: Integrative Kindertherapie in Theorie und Praxis* (vol. 1). Paderborn: Junfermann.

Metzmacher, B., Petzold, H. and Zaepfel, H. (eds) (1996b) *Praxis der Integrativen Kindertherapie: Integrative Kindertherapie in Theorie und Praxis* (vol. 2). Paderborn: Junfermann.

Ogden, P., Minton, K. and Pain, C. (2006) *Trauma and the Body: A Sensorimotor Approach to Psychotherapy.* Santa Monica, CA: W. W. Norton.

Rahm, D. (2004) *Integrative Gruppentherapie mit Kindern.* Paderborn: Junfermann.

Rahm, D. (2005) 'Bindungsentwicklung – über parallele Aspekte der Entwicklung von Bindungssicherheit in der Mutter-Kind-Interaktion und im therapeutischen Prozess.' *Beratung Aktuell 3*, 140–160.

Rahm, D. (2007) 'Hoffnungsfähigkeit: Anregungen, Gedanken, Impulse und Übungen für die therapeutische Arbeit mit Kindern.' *Beratung Aktuell 1*, 4–25.

Rahm, D. (2010) 'Kindergruppentherapie zur Förderung von Schutzfaktoren und Bindungssicherheit.' In M. Vogt and F. Caby (eds) *Ressourcenorientierte Gruppentherapie mit Kindern und Jugendlichen.* Dortmund: Borgmann.

Rahm, D. (2011) *Gestaltberatung. Grundlagen und Praxis Integrativer Beratungsarbeit* (10th edn). Paderborn: Junfermann.

Rahm, D. (2015) 'Vom Wunder der Resilienz. Hilfe für Kinder mit Traumafolgen.' *Erziehungsberatung Aktuell 1*, 2–15.

Rahm, D. and Kirsch, C. (2000) 'Entwicklung von Kindern heute.' *Beratung Aktuell 1*, 17–40.

Remschmidt, H. and Schmidt, M. (1994) *Multiaxiales Klassifikationsschema für Psychische Störungen des Kindes- und Jugendalters nach ICD-10 der WHO.* Bern: Huber.

Schore, A. (2003) *Affect Regulation and the Repair of the Self.* Santa Monica, CA: W. W. Norton.

Siegel, D. and Bryson, T. (2013) *Achtsame Kommunikation mit Kindern: 12 revolutionäre Strategien aus der Hirnforschung für die gesunde Entwicklung Ihres Kindes.* Freiburg: Arbor Verlag. (*The Whole-Brain Child. 12 Revolutionary Strategies to Nurture Your Developing Child's Brain.*) London: Bantam.

Stern, D. (1995) *The Motherhood Constellation: A Unified View of Parent-Infant Psychotherapy.* London: Karnac Books.

Stern, D. (2000) *The Interpersonal World of the Infant.* New York, NY: Basic Books.

Stern, D., Bruschweiler-Stern, N., Lyons-Ruth, K., Morgan, A.C., Nahum, J.P. and Sander, L.W. (2010) *Change in Psychotherapy: A Unifying Paradigm.* New York, NY: Persea Books.

Winnicott, D. W. (1975) *Through Paediatrics to Psychoanalysis.* London: Karnac Books.

8

My Pain Turned to Gold

Eldbjørg Wedaa

Many say that life entered the human body by the help of music, but the truth is that life itself is music.
(Hafiz, Persian Sufi poet, 1320–1389)

I had a vision, which was to teach children what I thought of almost as a secret that I had discovered for myself: play is bigger than us.

In the course of my life, I have seen my wounds turn into my biggest strength. I have seen my pain turn to gold, opening doors for me to see and help others. Although much was lacking in my childhood, I knew something essential. I knew how to open up and let play come to life. How to let the song, which is bigger than us, sing inside; and letting life, which is bigger than us, live inside. I wanted to share this wonderful experience with others. That was the cornerstone of Pinocchio Music and Drama.

Pinocchio is a music and drama school for children aged 3 months to 12 years. It is offered as a leisure activity, independent of the schools. The school is based at my house in the centre of the Norwegian city of Bergen. The children come here once a week for an hour or an hour and a half. A season lasts 14 weeks and is concluded with a performance where the children present what we have worked on to their family, friends and other students.

When I opened Pinocchio Music and Drama in autumn 1982, I drew on my training at the music conservatory in Bergen, where I trained as a preschool music teacher, as well as my vocal studies in Wiesbaden/Mainz, Germany. I also have a bachelor's degree in dramaturgy from the University of Bergen. After encountering children who needed special assistance, I chose to pursue therapeutic training. I am certified as a bodynamic analyst by the Bodynamic Institute in Copenhagen. I chose to specialize in shock and trauma treatment with a certificate in Somatic Experiencing. In addition, I have training in psychodrama from the Norwegian Moreno Institute (previously *Norsk Institutt for Psykodrama*). Working with vulnerable children does not necessarily require a background in psychotherapy, but it is helpful to seek inspiration from the experiences of professional psychotherapists. My knowledge and my years of working with therapy have taught me much, including giving me basic insight into psychological theory, anatomy and group dynamics. But for me, that is not even the most vitalizing effect. The most vitalizing effect for me and, not least, my students is the emphasis on possibilities, growth, balance, expression, play, music, rhythms and joy. I love to see timid or dispirited children open up, to see children who act out find new ways to use their strength, to see groups discover new forms of interaction. Music and rhythm have helped open new channels of sensing and intuition. I have seen many students find new direction in life by working with music and rhythm. Maybe it is not that music makes life richer; perhaps life itself is found in music?

When I opened my school, I advertised in the newspaper and assembled a small group of students. There I was, pounding heart and sweaty palms, with a typed-up manuscript and only an intuitive grasp of my skills as a teacher. At the time I could not possibly imagine that my school would blossom into a living institution in Bergen, which over the years has contributed to thousands of children's personal growth and development. I was 31 when I set out, and I had no idea of the possibilities that lay ahead. I also did not know what I see now: that I became my own life path that the pain and lack of contact I had experienced early in life was to drive me forward and eventually form the basis of my life.

So, what happened? How did I develop my method, and how can it be passed on to others? How can the method be used to help children who have experiences that are quite different from mine? In this chapter, I describe the main components of my method in detail and present exercises that others can use. I also outline the priorities in my work with different age groups and explain how music and rhythm can be used to set us free. But first of all, I want to offer a brief outline of the experiences that shaped me.

The backcloth

I was born and raised a single child in Bergen, Norway. My dad was a sailor who spent much of his time away from home, and my mum was unstable in her ability to connect and relate to me. I loved to play in the big hazelnut tree outside our house. Standing on a branch, I was able to swing, sing and send my voice out across the valley where we lived. Then, as now, I found singing a source of healing, comfort and growth.

Mum worked as a seamstress at a Catholic hospital. The nuns looked after us well, and when I was with them, I was allowed to take part in their work and prayer. They sang, played and mirrored me in a good way. Combined with profound experiences in Sunday school, the biblical stories and hymns had a deep impact on me. I felt loved by a great and loving God. That has remained a foundation for me ever since. In school too, I felt that music was a liberating force. Back then, every lesson started with a song. In addition, we played the recorder and had a rhythm section, and the class was like a choir. I felt what I also recognize in many of my groups today: that when I synchronize my breathing with others, we are lifted up, held by a sense of community. When our voices mingle, the individuals become a 'we' that is filled with vitality and joy. This is the source of expressions like 'on wings of song' (from Mendelssohn's eponymous song). Today, when the aesthetic subjects have such a diminished standing in school, I often think that without them my personal development would have been a very different story from how it actually turned out. My teachers in primary and secondary school taught us traditional Norwegian songs, rhymes and singing games. I am very grateful for that. In my childhood in the 1950s, playing in the street was everyone's venue for expression and development – together with other children. Preschool facilities and organized leisure activities were in short supply. Play in the street came with its own set of rules and roles. We were ourselves, with our talents, our strengths and our weaknesses. We faced challenges and grew with them. At Pinocchio, children can similarly take part as fully rounded individuals – as who they are.

A grandmother of one of my students wrote to me:

> In the street, there was no Eldbjørg. Eldbjørg at Pinocchio sees the big picture, and I find that she sees all the children as individuals. With her gentle being she guides them into and through the rules and roles of play to help them all receive stimuli for growth and development.

They feel safe and have fun; that is absolutely fundamental. At the same time, they face challenges and have to stretch.

I applied to the music conservatory and trained as a preschool music teacher. The approach was holistic, with fairy tales, rhymes, pictures, props and body movement. We learned to teach music to children, but even then I thought that if I were ever to work with children's groups, I would adopt a more experimental and less controlled approach. My goal was to allow them to experience and sense what music and music drama experiences can be like. As a child, I had found that spellbinding. It might in fact have been my salvation. I knew that once a person has been able to open their creative channel, that person holds a trump card. But the healing power of music that I had experienced so intensely was not on the curriculum. I had to keep searching.

Personal growth through classes in aesthetic subjects

My own upbringing had suffered under inadequate structures and the lack of support for learning or work routines. However, the fact that the school was so full of singing and joy in the 1950s helped strengthen my already wide-open senses and made me aware of a world of knowledge that was there for me, ready to embrace.

The opportunity for personal growth through artistic and aesthetic school subjects is under severe threat today. The 2012 Pisa (Programme for International Student Assessment) study found that Norwegian 15-year-olds perform around average for the countries we typically compare ourselves to in reading, mathematics and science (see Furholt, 2014). The politicians call this a crisis for maths and science and argue the need to enhance these subjects. Recent years have seen large-scale efforts in regard to literacy, maths and science, but the positive results have failed to materialize. The Knowledge Promotion Reform (*Kunnskapsløftet*) specifies the educational principles for Norwegian schools, as defined by the Ministry of Education and Research in June 2006 (Furholt, 2014). In this reform, aesthetic competences are not defined as fundamental to learning and insight. Practical and aesthetic subjects are no longer mandatory subjects in teacher training.

Naturally, this means that there are now fewer competent teachers for aesthetic subjects in schools. The emphasis has shifted towards a few prestigious subjects at the cost of diversity and a varied curriculum. The Pisa report does state one interesting finding, which is that Norway has the lowest score among 65 countries when it comes to creative activities in school. The report also states that creative activities can promote both cognitive and non-cognitive abilities. The Knowledge Promotion Reform guidelines state: 'The purpose of education is to enhance the ability of children, young people and adults to insight and experience, to engagement, expression and participation' (Furholt, 2014).

According to the Norwegian government, new generations need to achieve this understanding of the world without the benefit of the aesthetic dimension in education. There are many of us who find this utterly wrong. Even 'hard-core' subjects can incorporate new understanding and awareness by involving the arts. But it takes practice to embrace this capacity for rich sensory experiences – and even more practice if these experiences are to be linked up with abstract learning. Such a capacity takes training. And this kind of training is something the aesthetic subjects can provide; yet in the public debate, these subjects are widely portrayed as somehow less demanding. Thus, we now have few trained teachers with qualifications and competences in creative methods, and we are seeing a reduction in classrooms and school facilities suited to creative activities. Many schools no longer have these spaces – this despite the link between school performance and education in aesthetic subjects.

One aspect of this issue is the refinement of our ability to sense and reflect on our environment. Anyone who has tried will know that practice makes perfect. And the feeling of mastery itself is a source of motivation. It teaches the value of investing time and effort in practice – persistent practice. It teaches us that ultimately, talent is surpassed by the capacity for persistence. This knowledge is not available to everyone. In Norway, courses in aesthetic subjects mainly take place in municipal music schools, the so-called 'culture schools'. However, the typical music school student is recruited from the middle class and up. Some 75 per cent of the students are girls. Thus, children from minority cultural backgrounds and children with special needs rarely take part in these courses – and, of course, the boys are missing too. This is a paradox we live with. As the children grow older, their participation rates decline. In physical education, the emphasis on measurable performance scores has replaced the focus on body awareness that prevailed when I was growing up. I was even lucky enough to have a teacher who was inspired by the Laban approach.

Rudolf Laban (1879–1958) was a Slovakian dance theorist and choreographer. He was a pioneer in the development of modern dance. His philosophy was that dancers should base their expression and movements on their own inner life. He rejected the achievement-oriented teaching and training in movement, where everyone was pushed towards the same form of movement. In England he managed to develop modern dance as a school subject for everyone! My teacher was Inger Kalgraf. She taught gymnastics in a mainstream youth school, but she gave us lessons for life. Her teachings focused on body awareness in relation to our own body, in relation to others and in relation to space. Above all, she focused on the joy of movement! She gave us the most wonderful images – images that held a profound appeal for me. For example: 'We are in a crowded place. You are now going to move through the crowd. Let your shoulders and arms lead you and move you, and move with lightness.' Then she set a pulse rhythm on the small hand-drum she often used. Or, we would be on the floor, and she would say: 'You are hiding. Make yourself as small as you possibly can. Make sure that no one can discover you…hold on. But now you can expand. Now unfurl slowly, and expand to your full size. Fill up your lungs with air, and feel how great that feels. Now move among the others, and notice…'

Right there, I knew that this was life – life in abundance.

My training in aesthetic subjects was my salvation. That is what gave me life and gave me the confidence to seek knowledge. The parents of my students regularly tell me that the children's school performance improve after they have spent some time at Pinocchio. Music and the arts hold a special power to promote the discovery of and our contact with the creative power in the world and in ourselves.

The beginning of Pinocchio

When I opened Pinocchio Music and Drama, my goal was to invite children and adults into a unique creative landscape that spanned the different art forms. Previously, the various expressions were more strictly separated. The children received dance lessons in one context, played musical instruments somewhere else and expressed themselves through drama in a third setting. I wanted to offer a non-elitist platform where everyone was welcome, regardless of so-called 'talent'. What I really liked about the Pinocchio character was that he came to life through play and life experience. I wanted to help children experience everything that play has to offer, especially from a creative perspective – in order to foster sufficient joy and confidence that they could become playful adults. Today, achievement alone is not enough. *At its essence, this path is about love.*

The philosophy of Pinocchio Music and Drama, as I described it in 1982 is this:

> Childhood is the time when we are most in touch with our creative force. Many of us lose this connection over time. I want the 'Pinocchio children' to know that they have a creative force, and that it can be developed into an essential, life-long resource, whether they choose to become technicians, bureaucrats or artists. The child participates fully and intensively throughout life with his or her experiences and expressions. In interactions with adults and other children, the child's life drama is expressed in play, music, imagination, images and emotions. Through these interactions, the child develops his or her self experiences and environment. It is the educator's responsibility to offer guidance and provide the conditions for growth. In practice, this requires knowledge of the various stages in the child's development and the ability to stimulate the child to take on new areas of development continually.

> To me – and to the children – music and drama are inextricably linked. When we work with drama, theatre, music and movement we develop our thinking, emotions and imagination and our ability to cooperate. Much of the work is aimed at the children's social skills: individual development in a group setting. The children work on their personal expressive repertoire, building confidence and the belief that 'my contribution has value too.' In moments of intense experience, the child engages fully in the activity with his or her entire person, body and soul, living out his or her innermost creativity. Thus, the educational approach is driven by engagement, immersion and expression. (Wedaa, 1982)

Personal qualifications for teachers or therapists at Pinocchio

The key requirement is being in touch with your inner child. You have to enjoy playing. You have to be genuinely curious, flexible, patient and, not least, empathic. You have to dare be stupid, leaving your senses and your intuition wide open, and being in touch with your heart. This also means that you have to lay down the shield that therapeutic or educational terms and jargon can provide. At the same time, you have to possess authority, be able to set boundaries and know where you want to go with your work. The teacher sets up targets and provides perspectives for the direction of the group. Even though it is not always easy, leading with a light, kind and positive spirit makes for an optimal setting.

Another key element is wordless instructions. I do not say much about what we are doing now, or why. I also spend very little time transitioning from one activity to the next – I like to surprise the children. I do this in a light and playful way, losing myself in the process, which I enjoy as much as the children do. I take charge by letting go and trusting the process.

Teaching groups has given me insight into aspects of myself that I was not previously aware of. My own patterns with regard to planning and boundary-setting and the way I claim my space in a room were brought to the surface. At first, I carefully planned every single group lesson in a series of numbered steps, as I had learned at the music conservatory. Every single minute of the lesson was planned. Still, time and time again, I found myself doing something else once the children entered the room. Subsequently I spent a long time kicking myself because I saw this deviation from the plan as a lack of structure and control. Nevertheless, what I came up with in contact with the group was superior to my initial plans. It took time to shape a structure that matched the more experimental approach I wanted to adopt. I needed different management tools. It also took time for me to trust my own inner authority. Today I think of it as my two toolkits. One is my 'hardware' – my professional knowledge, acquired at the conservatory and in therapeutic training. My other toolkit is my 'software' – my intuitive empathic awareness, which unfolds in dialogue with myself and with the children in the group, including the sensory input and images I receive from the group. This makes it easier for me to grasp the needs of the group in the given moment. To have a shared experience in the group, first the children's eyes and faces have to light up.

This shared experience cannot get off the ground until everyone is sufficiently affirmed and engaged.

We are dependent on each other. That aspect was never included in the lesson plans I developed initially. It was only once I began to follow the group's impulses that surprising things began to happen. I never show up for a lesson without a basic plan – a framework – within which the magic can emerge in the given group.

An invitation to express ourselves

To what extent can I be *myself* in my interactions with you? That is the unspoken question that children ask in their encounters with others. To a small extent? To a bigger extent? Can I perhaps be fully myself in my interactions with you? When we answer this question through our actions, I find that the children open up. This involves respecting the individual child for the potential he or she holds simply because he or she exists. Above all, a teacher should be him/herself, as this allows the child to be who he or she is, as much as possible. The most important thing is to be genuinely interested. It is not necessary to be perfect.

Learn the children's names. This may sound like a trivial point, but time and time again, I have seen how the very first connection follows this exact path: name and gaze. I look directly at each individual child and actively use the child's name. If there are any parents present, I look at them too, because the child tends to copy what the parents do. This lets the entire group feel seen and welcomed in the room. But how do I go from that to creating a sense that here the children can be exactly who they are, wholly and fully? When some of the children begin to dance during the welcome song, we clap along. Not in the form of applause but as a rhythmic encouragement to the child's own impulse, as I have experienced it first-hand in countries like Burkina Faso and Ghana. If someone moves his or her body in time with music, someone else immediately responds, showing support and affirmation by clapping along. Similarly, the child should be seen in the group, in stark contrast to our high-efficiency culture, which does not always appreciate spontaneity. In this encounter, I frequently see the child respond by cheering or saying things like 'yeah, yeah, yeah!' Children who follow their individual urge to dance should be encouraged. Often, the lessons feel like being at a party, especially when the adults open their voices and set them free. Many adults come into the situation with the notion that they are simply accompanying their child to a music lesson. I want to show them that music and song are universal. It is about immersion and expression for our children as well as for the adults' inner child. I create a safe space for them by modelling this behaviour – we learn more from what we see than from what we hear.

My groups

As previously mentioned, my groups range from babies, about 3 months old, to drama groups where the oldest children are around 12 years old. Describing everything that we do would go beyond the scope of this chapter. Therefore I have chosen to focus on some main themes that permeate my teaching and on my work with two groups:

- children's groups without parents: 4–5 years of age
- drama groups: 6–12 years of age.

Empathy and nurture

Children's groups without parents: 4–5 years of age

For many children, this is their first experience of being in a children's group without the support of participating parents. During the lesson, some of the children need to check whether mum and dad are still there for them in the waiting room. Others test what will happen if they hide, while others may refuse to follow instructions in the group. My vision is to create a group that is attentive and receptive, and where everyone pays attention to and looks after one another. That is no easy task at this age. Every single child needs to feel seen and welcomed. The content of the lesson has to capture the children's attention without generating too much arousal. Everyone needs to feel included. I have specific rituals for opening and ending the lessons.

At this age, children's development undergoes many and intense phases. There is a high level of energy, many emotions and a great deal of creativity to be unfolded, adapted and regulated. The child has to experience saying 'yes' and 'no' and the consequences of both. The children develop increasingly complex motor skills and combinations of words. I also see how the children develop a growing social complexity. They become more adept at standing up and expressing themselves independently. In the rhythmic realm, they move from simple to more challenging rhythms.

We open the lesson with singing, movement and rhymes, often using instruments. Next there is a drama section. This may be based on something I have prepared ahead of time – for example, a circus show, dragon hunting, a trip to the bottom of the sea, etc. Afterwards, I let them talk about their experience, and new stories emerge from the original experience. Spontaneous developments arise in the moment. Some of them we continue to work with for an extended period. There have to be positive sensory experiences, and everyone has to cooperate and participate. There is a serious side to our play here. Over the course of the lesson they will have a shared experience of fluctuations in their energy level. I make sure they calm down again after high-arousal stimulation, and this teaches them something about containment. The children participate with every aspect of who they are and get to know each other well. This also helps them discover and take an interest in each other's individual differences. When it is somebody's birthday, we sing to the birthday child, and afterwards there is time for someone to say a few words to the birthday child if he or she wants to. Sometimes, this brings out really good messages, illustrating how good children are at 'reading' each other.

Case study 8.1

When the Romanian dictator Ceausescu fell and the borders were opened, the images of the horrendous conditions in the orphanages were among the first we saw in the West. Andrew came to Bergen from one of these orphanages. Shortly after his arrival he joined the group of 4-year-olds at Pinocchio without his parents. His mother told me that he could be a little 'wild' sometimes, but that she would be in the waiting room if we needed her. Other than that, I knew nothing about his background. Andrew really was a wild child. He was almost constantly in motion and sometimes he would get a running start and then throw himself directly at the wall. That was an amusing sight, and the other children cheered with delight. He was different but no outsider. The pain and traumas he carried from his young life were obvious, but he was a good boy and he was easy to love.

His group was guided in a framework based on appreciation of the individual group members, with activities revolving around rhythms, social structures and body awareness. Gradually, he was able to contain more of his own energy and calmed down. A strong source of creative openness and wisdom was revealed in him. When the children were invited to say something to a birthday child, he would sometimes offer real gems. I think that the lessons affirmed him on a profound level. He took drumming lessons from us for several years.

When he turned 12, he continued at another drama school, where he launched right into teaching the other students about the instruments of the body, giving stomp an d drumming courses. At the age of 14, he was much in demand as a drummer. I am still in touch with him and his family. I see how his profound learning has become a sought-after commodity. Now he is nurturing others.

Much of my work is about seeing the child's essence and potential and giving the child value and importance. When children learn to be in touch with their own heart, they grow wise.

From shrinking violet to head of the student council

Andrea, one of my students, told me, 'Before I began to come here, I would blush if the teacher called on me in class. Now, I am head of the student council at school.' I know that many other children have had a similar experience. We have fostered many student council presidents. These children have received support and learned to express themselves in a variety of ways. They have learned to use senses. They have developed confidence and learned to understand nonverbal communication. I have never deliberately aimed for Pinocchio children to improve their school performance, but I continually hear that it happens. This creative field, this playful interaction, seems to hold a tremendous potential, and regardless of children's differences, their shared experience becomes an emotional carrier wave, which in turn stimulates interaction competences.

From inner fantasy images to expression

Many children only relate to the group in indirect ways. A random impulse may be enough for them to stop relating to the group or the teacher. Sometimes all it takes for them to disconnect is an object in the room or a remark that captures their attention. Now, increasingly often I face a challenge that has become clearer over the years than I recall it being when I first set out. A growing number of children lose interest as soon as the focus is not specifically on them. They may have a burning desire to play the lead role in a drama, but they do not prepare very well if they get the part. They also lack the ability to enjoy others' ideas and expression. It bores them. Anything that is not about 'me' is mindless waiting time.

How can the children discover their own inner world and learn to take an interest in that of others? I can lead the children into a fairy tale, and everybody pays attention. But we could also tell 'the story about me' or 'the story about my day'. For example: What happens in my body? How do I sense it inside? I might say: 'Can everybody take a deep breath, pulling the air all the way into their belly? Does the body feel light/heavy, cold/warm? Do I find anything when I look inside – any images, any colours?' Their faces take on a look of deep concentration when we talk about the various findings. Then we take an interest in that, stretch a little, stomp our feet and do a dance. Imaginary journeys are an exciting way in. Afterwards, when the group makes drawings of the mental images they saw and describe their experiences, it is like discovering a new world. That is a way for children to learn about what is happening here and now, in their immediate world and surroundings.

Another good exercise *is word associations*: I will tell the children to say the first image that comes up on their inner mental screen – for example, if one of them says 'rock', I say 'moss'; the next child might say 'water'; the next one after that, a 'troll's foot'.

When the group becomes a safe and secure space, it can be an arena where the children dare to show more of themselves. I divide them up into small groups. The task may be quite simple: Define where you are, who is present, and what sort problem needs solving.

The focus may also be on sensitive topics, such as not fitting in, anger, loneliness and experiences with bad alliances. When the children mirror and make room for each other, I see how their capacity for mutual empathy and nurture is strengthened. We mirror each other's nervous systems.

Play also generates knowledge about narratives: how we can create a variety of stories about me, about us, about what is amazing and interesting. This in turn stimulates the children's desire to read, to seek knowledge and explore a larger world.

Sometimes I encounter children who are frightfully shy, who have a hard time entering a room with many people and who find it even more overwhelming to speak up in a group. Being the centre of everyone's attention is daunting. Learning to be grounded, both feet planted firmly on the floor, finding one's balance, breathing with the group and adding one's own voice to theirs causes the room to open up. In fact, the world opens up. The child calms down, feels a healthy sense of curiosity, seeks contact and is more at peace within him or herself.

Contributions from the children are always welcomed – they are usually so much better than the ideas that we adults come up with. The children have privileged access to magic, poetry, power and energy (although this is always there for us when we seek it, regardless of age). I have a programme, but the most important programme is us, here and now. The children sense that, and they know intuitively that this is because they are valuable.

I can be whoever I want to be
Drama groups: 6–7 years and 8–12 years of age

Over several years of therapeutic work with adults I have noticed how few are fully aware of the many polarities we carry within. Most are content to explore just a few of the possibilities a life holds. For example, many adults live their workplace role most of the time. But it is liberating to be able to move through multiple layers of one's personality. A more fully unfolded role-self is an invaluable resource for children as well as adults.

Certain elements from groups with young children are also important in groups for these age groups. I continue the effort to build the group and promote a sense of cohesion. We use drama and awareness exercises and inspire the children to tell stories that we subsequently perform. Recognizing their own idea in a drama performance is especially rewarding and empowering for the children. If I were to point to one primary message from my work with the theatre groups, it would have to be role development.

I let the children work with the characters in the play. They play the fox, which is cunning and vigilant. The cat demonstrates how soft and light it is. The predators dare to let their power shine through, even in their eyes and through their skin. The mouse is small and cute and is often attributed great wisdom. These drama exercises give the children insight into the many polarities that dwell in us all. This is a preliminary stage to transferring these elements to human characters. Do I have a predator inside or perhaps a little squirrel?

Maybe both but at different times? How about a cat or a monster? We can put that to the test – adding sound. At first, when the roles are distributed, everybody wants to be one of the nice characters. But the bad characters undeniably have more vitality, and that can be very entertaining. Eventually, everybody wants to be bad. But then we realize that we need both sides, and more, to make things work. Life is a stage.

If I come on stage expressing the attitude that 'I am little and stupid', the audience accepts that. Our surroundings believe what we communicate, and that is why it is so important to be who we want to be. I have included some exercises below, which I have used throughout the years and never tired of.

EXERCISES

The blue chair

I have a blue children's chair, which I sat on as a child when I used to sing all the songs I could think of, one by one, as if they were my treasures. Towards the end of the lesson I ask if someone would like to sit on the chair and sing us all a song or tell a story. Somebody always does – some children do it with great confidence. Others step up, sense the light from the others' eyes and then return to their place with the adult who is accompanying them. When that happens, they are applauded for having the courage to step forward. Next time, another child may step forward with an adult and have help singing. This is always followed by applause and thanks for their contribution. There is no evaluation. Here, the children practise being the centre of attention and being seen and heard. We often hear that they later performed in front of family and friends or got up on a public stage as if it were the most natural thing in the world.

The flower

Each child has a chiffon shawl that they crumple up in their hands.

> **Poem:**
> I'm a little flower,
> I'm a little flower.
> When the sun shines
> And warms my cheeks
> – I unfold.

Everybody shows what they have in their hands: so many different colours!

The fantasy animal

The children sit on the floor. We have seen each other and spoken to each other. I ask them to close their eyes, breathe calmly and pay close attention to their 'inner film'. They place their hands in their laps, palms facing up. I say: 'Now you notice a tiny bit of foam in your hand. Gradually, the foam begins to develop. It is not dangerous. Now it begins to turn into a tiny animal. It might be an animal that no one has ever seen before, but it could also be an animal that lives here in Bergen. Can you see the eyes? Notice everything. Does it have fur or a smooth skin? Does it have a tail, and if it does, what does it look like? Notice the colours, perhaps the animal has very special colours. Try to notice how you can play with your animal… Now it's time to say goodbye to the animal, because it's about to disappear… Now it's getting smaller, disappearing back into the foam. Now there's just a tiny speck of foam left, and now it's gone. When you open your eyes again in a little while, you should draw the animal you saw. Later we'll tell each other about it, but for now it's your own personal secret.'

The red flame

First, everyone connects with their legs by stomping or by patting them with their hands. Everybody has to stand comfortably. I show the children how to lay a hand flat against the front of the pelvis. We breathe in, pulling the air into the place where the hand is resting. I tell them: 'Make a sound that comes from there, like the boats in the harbour. Inside us, inside the place where the hand is resting, lives the tiny red flame. As long as we are just standing there calmly, the flame is tiny. But sometimes, the predator awakens. It can rise up, all the way up to here [I point to my chest]…and if it wants to, it can rise up all the way and get into our eyes and into our skin. Release the predators!'

Sensing your presence

Half the children (Team A) are standing still with plenty of space between them. Their eyes are closed. The light is dimmed. Now each of the children in the other half of the group (Team B) walks over to a partner in Team A. The children who are standing with their eyes closed do not know who is coming. Without touching, the children in Team B now have to check the space around the their partner's body, checking for any variations in the other child's temperature or energy. The Team A child meanwhile tries to guess who their Team B partner is.

The lung

The children are standing in a circle, holding each other's hands. Very slowly, we move towards the middle while everyone breathes out. Immediately, we go back out again while everybody breathes in. The group is like a lung, contracting and expanding.

Here I come

We are standing in two lines, facing each other with a passage through. One of us walks in between the two lines acting 'poor little me' or 'strong and happy'. Now the group respond to that acting by cheering 'Yes' or 'Oh, no! Poor you'.

Birthday

The birthday child stands in the middle of the room. The group forms a circle around the child. We sing one or several birthday songs. Then we move closer to the birthday child, and now the floor is open to anyone who wants to say a few good words to the child. I usually say something too, but I let the children go first. Often, we conclude with a big group hug.

Closing remarks

Over the years and during the various stages of my own personal development, there has been something deep inside me, like a watermark: the profound joy of sensing and playing. I have had a need to create something beautiful, spiritual and fun around me. My joy has come from seeing it mix with other's need for the same. No one's life is free of worries, injuries or pain. But music, rhythms and creativity can be a channel for reaching out to others. There is no 'them' and 'us'. We have a common denominator in our shared humanity. I discovered it through my love of music and creativity.

A former student of mine, who is now a mother herself and has sent her three children to Pinocchio, wrote this to me:

> The biggest reward of all is the development of social relations, sensing moods and expressions – one's own and others'. After many years at Pinocchio, as a child and as a mother, I think that I have developed my ability to empathize with others' thoughts and feelings. In my work as a teacher, I find this to be invaluable knowledge that has helped me tremendously. My daughter is happy to take up challenges like piano recitals, solo singing – for example, at weddings – and roles on

stage. She shows concern for others and offers nurture and security. I think that much of her strength for doing that stems from Pinocchio Music and Drama. Thank you for this world of hers – a world of song, dreams and music.

References

Furholt, A. (2014) 'Politisk styrt kunnskapsfall' ('Political directed decline in knowledge') *Bergens Tidende*, 10 January, 2014.

Wedaa, E. (1982) 'Pinocchio Musikk & Drama.' Bergen: A/S Repro-trykk.

9

Playing with Possibilities

Sensorimotor Psychotherapy with Younger Clients in Individual, Family, and Group Psychotherapy[1]

Bonnie Goldstein and Pat Ogden

All children will experience trauma and attachment challenges to varying degrees. Bromberg (2011) writes:

> If we accept that developmental trauma is a core phenomenon in the shaping of personality then we also accept that it exists for everyone and is always a matter of degree. If that is so, then the stability achieved by even secure attachment is also a matter of degree. That is to say, everyone is vulnerable... (p.14)

Each child's development, vitality, and well-being are impacted by the accumulation of both positive and adverse experiences at home, with peers, and at school. The personal meaning children make of these experiences is revealed not only through words but also through physical actions. Even infants express the meaning of their interactions with others through physical action and especially through the procedural organization of their posture and action sequences (Beebe, 2006; Tronick, 2006). When particular actions are consistently ineffective in eliciting the desired response from the people important to them, children will abandon such actions – for example, they will stop reaching out if no one is there to reach back or such overtures were not responded to in an attuned manner; they will slump and keep their heads down if standing upright with heads held high brought unwanted attention, criticism, abuse, or shame (Ogden, 2013).

---

1   The authors wish to thank Deb Banowetz for her contribution to this chapter.

By the time a child reaches the age at which emotions and meanings can be verbalized, such procedural habits are already well established. A child's patterns of physical tension, movement, gesture, posture, physiological arousal, gait, and other action sequences form a 'somatic narrative' that tells a story of both trauma and attachment inadequacy. These physical habits, in turn, constrain a child's 'capacity to make new meaning and respond flexibly to the here and now and turn the future into a version of the past' (Ogden and Fisher, 2015).

Sensorimotor Psychotherapy utilizes both verbal and somatic interventions to treat younger clients, aiming to identify and understand the somatic narrative, in addition to any available verbal narrative, so that the non-conscious procedural patterns can be directly addressed. It should be noted that many children are unable to discuss what has happened for a variety of reasons: language centers of the brain are not developed; they cannot formulate the words, they are ashamed, they fear retribution, and so on (Ogden, Goldstein and Fisher, 2012). By not relying solely on language for its efficacy, a Sensorimotor Psychotherapy approach can directly target the non-verbal legacy of childhood trauma and relational difficulties (Ogden, Goldstein and Fisher, 2012; Ogden, Minton and Pain, 2006).

Through the focus of Dr. Goldstein's work, clients learn to navigate life's complexities addressing relationship and developmental challenges as well as trauma, grief, and loss issues. She has co-authored various papers with Dr. Ogden applying this treatment modality, and has a private practice in West Los Angeles offering individual, group, and family therapy.

Dr. Pat Ogden, Founder and Educational Director of the Sensorimotor Psychotherapy Institute, was an elementary school teacher at a low-income inner city school in the 1960s. She also worked at a local day care center, where the children taught her the chants and dances that so clearly helped them regulate arousal and cope with community, family, and individual traumatic experiences. During the desegregation of American schools in 1970, she taught at one of the first integrated elementary schools in Louisville, Kentucky, addressing the challenges of racial diversity. Pat left teaching to pursue a career in psychotherapy, beginning by working with psychiatric in-patients, where her duties included conducting groups for adolescents and adults in art therapy, yoga, and dance. These pursuits reinforced her interest in the importance of physical action in regulating arousal and recovering from trauma and attachment inadequacies. Her experience with these children, families and patients, was the early inspiration for Sensorimotor Psychotherapy.

This chapter describes a Sensorimotor Psychotherapy approach implemented during a long-term therapeutic journey with David, who was 5 years old at the beginning of treatment with the author (Bonnie Goldstein). David's treatment included individual therapy, family therapy, and eventually weekly group therapy. We will illustrate how addressing David's physical sensations and actions led to significant shifts in the context of child/therapist, child/child, child/group and family interactions, positively influencing his social engagement. The analysis of symptoms and somatic interventions described herein will help to educate teachers about the difficulties that children, and especially children diagnosed with an autism spectrum disorder (ASD), face that can lead to undesirable behavior in the classroom. These children often experience difficulty integrating sensory stimuli and regulating their impulses. The source of such difficulties typically lies in an inability to regulate physiological and emotional arousal, rather than in intent to misbehave, which highlights the limitations of typical classroom discipline and provides an explanation for why such discipline is sometimes ineffective. This chapter emphasizes basic somatic skills that help children take action to regulate their arousal. Although we do not directly address how teachers might integrate regulatory skills into their daily schoolroom activities, we hope that it will spark curiosity as to how simple breathing, movement, and other somatic exercises might assist children to regulate their arousal and thus promote adaptive behavior in the classroom.

Introduction to David

David's journey learning to self-regulate, develop self-awareness and shift consciousness began after his preschool director and his kindergarten teachers voiced their concerns about the following aspects of his behavior: not sitting in class; walking around the room; standing on one leg; not following or understanding directions; talking back to the teacher and otherwise challenging her; and asking multiple questions before figuring out an assigned task. Interpersonally, David's poor boundaries manifested as his touching and hugging other kids on the playground and in class, following classmates around against their wishes, and responding inappropriately when asked to stop.

David's school counselor recommended psychological testing, and David was evaluated by a neuropsychologist who identified the first indications of a probable ASD. The assessment indicated that although his schoolwork was on track for his age, his social and emotional difficulties rendered him unable to continue at his current kindergarten without therapeutic intervention. Because of his aptitude (testing suggested that he was in the gifted range), he was not a candidate to repeat kindergarten. Hence, in order to move forward in school, which required a remediation of his disruptive behavior, he started intensive twice-weekly individual therapy and bi-monthly family therapy in the spring of his kindergarten year, with the addition of group therapy several months later.

David experienced several early attachment disruptions. His mother's week-long hospitalization due to an emergency C-section occurred when David was almost 2 years old. Both his mother and his baby sister were hospitalized for a week following her premature birth. Additionally, his mother returned to hospital due to post-partum depression, leaving David with a caretaker. Following years of marital conflict, his parents divorced when he was 2½ years old. David experienced the divorce as a profound loss and frequently asked his parents when they would be getting back together. These early-childhood disruptions, combined with his diagnosis of high-functioning ASD, affected David's capacity to engage well in relationships, as evinced by his problematic behavior at home and at school.

David's parents had hoped that he would outgrow his behavioral and developmental difficulties, and grappled with the limitations indicated by his diagnosis. They reluctantly realized that they, and David, needed help. An initial family therapy session illuminated the impact of myriad family struggles on David, and his parents began to understand that David's difficulties are characteristic of children who have early attachment disruptions as well as diagnosis of ASD. David started weekly individual therapy, adding additional family sessions every other week. Family treatment was essential to David's progress. Through psychoeducation during family sessions, his parents became part of the treatment process, helping to integrate therapeutic goals, validate large and small steps achieved, and aid in their son's improving participation in the family milieu.

After seven months of individual and family therapy, David joined a newly formed weekly children's group, continuing his individual sessions as well. Over the year of individual and group therapy, family sessions were intermittent, usually scheduled when David was having difficulty at home or at school. David continued in a group for a second year, with his individual sessions becoming less frequent (at first every other week, then monthly 'check-ins') and with family meetings as needed.

David's first therapy session

David's therapist first met with him after a playground conflict in which he was sent home mid-day and subsequently brought to therapy under duress. David promptly told his mother how sorry he was about pushing his classmate; he even apologized to the therapist, to which his mother replied in an exasperated tone, 'David, you're the Apology King, always saying 'I'm sorry'...but it's not OK unless you change your behavior.' David looked at his therapist and woefully said, 'I'm the Apology King.' Unfortunately, for David, his peers, and his parents, he had learned to say that he was sorry without understanding how his behavior needed to change. He was able to apologize, and genuinely felt distress when his behavior displeased others, but he was unable to change his behavior at school or at home.

David's inability to connect his actions with consequences or pair his apology with a new action is characteristic of ASD. Neurobiological studies on the autistic brain suggest an 'underconnectivity' between its parts. For example, the mammalian brain (responsible for feelings of empathy or guilt when apologizing) does not work well with the neocortex (responsible for understanding when apologetic words are necessary to maintain social engagement). In addition, children with ASD commonly demonstrate difficulty in planning, controlling impulses, focusing attention, and problem-solving, executive functions of the neocortex (Kunzig, 2004; Russell, 1997), all of which worked against David in his social interaction at school. David's mother's plea to him to change his behavior, attempts to help him, and the punishments he received at school made little impact on his impulsivity. Without the ability to integrate information from different regions of his brain, and without the tools to help mitigate his impulses and problem-solve, David's disruptive behavior surfaced again and again.

Learning to pay attention to his experience – that is, to understand his own impulses, physical sensations, and non-conscious procedural action patterns – and develop skills to self-regulate in interactions with others were David's challenges. The following treatment goals were established collaboratively with the family and carried out across individual, family, and group therapy:

- developing greater awareness and sensitivity to other children

- becoming more 'in tune' with himself and his peers

- establishing and following through on appropriate boundaries regarding self and other

- learning ways to self-regulate impulsive and disruptive behavior

- engaging his own natural curiosity, playfulness, present moment awareness, and drive for mastery.

Beginning somatic resources

It is critical that children diagnosed with ASD be allowed the time to develop a connection with their therapist, without too much emotional intensity, which can cause further dysregulation (Turkington, Davidson, and Carson-DeWitt, 2012). Thus, David's earliest individual sessions focused on developing rapport with his therapist and learning resources for regulating the arousal and frustration that he experienced on the playground during recess and lunch times, which often led to disruptive behavior.

At school, the play-yard tetherball game was a constant source of interpersonal conflict for David, who would throw his entire body into other players, landing upon them or stepping over them in order to win the game. When his foot landed on the windpipe of a classmate, who screamed at David to get off, he shouted, 'I won, I won,' apparently not registering that his classmate was writhing in pain. On one occasion, when his shoulder hit the nose of another classmate, it was only the deep red color of the blood that oriented him to the pain he had inflicted, as his goal – to master the game – superseded awareness of the distress of his peers. Many children with a diagnosis of ASD can be described as 'systemizers' (Kunzig, 2004) who become obsessed with the intricate details of logical systems, often at the expense of empathy (Kunzig, 2004). Indeed, David had been focused on the game and how to win it, at the expense of empathizing with his peers. Because of his behavior, David was reprimanded, punished, placed on a 'reward' system, and provided with a behavioral shadow (a teacher who would accompany him during play time), with little result. In fact, David often lashed out verbally and physically in response to these interventions.

While describing these incidents to his therapist, his breath became more staccato (short and quick) as his arousal and anxiety mounted. Often, children with ASD have an overactive amygdala, which is the part of the brain associated with anxiety. Clearly, David needed to learn skills that would help him both improve his social awareness and calm his arousal. As David's anxiety increased and his breathing became ragged, he was encouraged to bring his attention to his breath, which he willingly did, taking a huge breath. Working with breath can be particularly useful for regulating dysregulated arousal, decreasing emotional intensity, or providing energy or fostering relaxation (Caldwell and Victora, 2011; Ogden et al., 2006). David was able to notice that after breathing deeply, he could better discuss his distress.

In fact, deep breathing became a resource on which David came to rely, particularly when he was triggered to act out. Learning to pause and breathe deeply proved particularly helpful in shifting states of consciousness, calming himself and containing the uncontrolled outbursts that were ill-suited to a particular situation, difficulties typical of children with ASD (Turkington, et al., 2012).

During one of the monthly family sessions that paralleled his individual therapy, David's therapist encouraged him to model deep breathing for his parents. He assumed his favorite position, with hands resting on his lap, legs crossed, sitting aligned with spine elongated, then moving his hands in an arc with elaborate upper body movement; his hand gestures spontaneously emerged as he encouraged his parents to follow his guidance. As David instructed his parents, who attentively mirrored his movements, his enjoyment of his role as teacher instead of as the target of disapproval was obvious in his big smile and eager participation. Additionally, as he taught the movement and explained its effect, his own learning about his resources of using breath was enhanced.

At a subsequent family session discussing a previous conflict David had with his younger brother during which David became physically aggressive and was punished, breathing again was useful in regulating David's arousal. As he retold the conflict, he grew quite agitated, repeatedly kicking his foot against the back of the couch, wiggling and squirming. He paced the room, expressing his outrage at his mother for 'unfairly' doling out consequences, unable to settle himself. He then stated how exhausted he felt in our session and collapsed onto the couch. In a short period of time, David's arousal escalated to hyperarousal and then plummeted into hypoarousal, as illustrated in Figure 9.1.

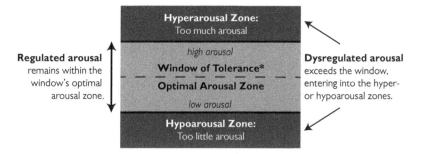

Figure 9.1: *Window of Tolerance*
(*Ogden and Minton, 2000*)

David's therapist reminded him of how much he had been helped in previous sessions by deep breathing, and encouraged him to select a small stuffed animal from those available in the office, and to place it on his belly as he lay on the couch, watching it gently go up and down as he breathed in and out. David enjoyed the playful nature of balancing the animal on his belly and felt a sense of satisfaction when he succeeded in doing so. This intervention immediately helped his arousal return to a window of tolerance so that he could participate in the discussion of the conflict without undue dysregulation.

The use of mindfulness

Children's internal reactions to stimuli happen rapidly and unconsciously, and are often translated immediately into action. Teaching mindfulness and developing consciousness of internal reactions can help them identify the somatic precursors to action, giving them tools to notice the indicators of dysregulation prior to action. Most definitions of mindfulness include an attitude of openness and receptivity to present moment experience, as a 'quality of attention which notices without choosing, without preference' (Goldstein and Kornfield, 1987, p.19). Sensorimotor Psychotherapy uses particular mindfulness techniques to provide specific tools for helping children become aware of their bodies, emotions, and thoughts within the context of the therapeutic relationship. Specific 'directed mindfulness' (Ogden, 2007, 2009; Ogden, 2014) interventions guide children's awareness toward particular elements of present-moment experience considered important to therapeutic goals. Siegel (2010) notes: 'When we focus our attention in specific ways, we create neural firing patterns that permit previously separated areas to become linked an integrated. The synaptic linkages are strengthened, the brain becomes more integrated, and the mind becomes more adaptive' (p.43). With the use of focused mindful attention toward new elements of internal experience, we hope to help children develop new mental capacities that can interrupt old patterns of reaction.

From the initial session using Sensorimotor Psychotherapy, David began to acquire the skill of directed mindfulness. To clarify, non-directed mindfulness would be a general question: 'What do you notice?' An example of directed mindfulness might be: 'What do you notice in your chest right now as you tell me about being punished?' The second question is based upon the therapist's specific tracking of the child's physical response (i.e. tightening in his chest that restricts his breathing) to the verbal narrative. David learned to identify several somatic signals (e.g. his heart beating faster, a knot in his stomach, tension around his heart, short and shallow breathing) that indicated distress and increased arousal related to interactions with others.

Critically, mindfulness in Sensorimotor Psychotherapy is not a solitary activity, but is firmly embedded in what occurs within the therapeutic dyad. In conversation, children tell their story by 'talking about' rather than noticing their bodies. With the use of embedded relational mindfulness™, therapist and client both notice how the experience of the story unfolds in the present moment, through changes in the body, emotions, and thoughts. This is not a solitary endeavor; both parties are attending to the ebb and flow of the child's present-moment experience. Taking place within an attuned dyad and group, mindfulness activates not only the child's experience of the effects of trauma and attachment inadequacies but also increases the engagement and connection between the child, therapist and other group members.

It is imperative that mindfulness is employed in a way that increases patients' experience of relational safety and fosters their ability to connect to and engage with others. A significant element of this process in individual therapy was that David and his therapist worked together, as she helped him become mindful of his body. Utilizing such collaborative, mindful suggestions as 'It is as though we can sense the sound of our breath' and 'Let's feel our breath together as it comes in and goes out' helped David learn to sense his breath and subsequently shift his energetic state while staying in close contact with his therapist.

In school, David often had difficulty regulating his arousal during transitions, especially from play-yard to 'quiet time'. Through the use of mindfulness, he learned to recognize 'wiggles that had no place to go', which often occurred right after play-yard, when the children were instructed to get their mats and pillows for a short break. Invariably, he was the one who was admonished by his teachers for not settling down. As he spoke of this in therapy, his agitation emerged anew, expressed with wiggling feet, one leg bobbing up and down before he abruptly stood upright with his fist clenched. He and his therapist capitalized on this moment to help David pay attention to these bodily signals that would otherwise go unrecognized, signals that often led to admonishment and punishment. With instruction from his therapist, he scanned his body from top to bottom, starting with the top of his head, then down toward his shoulders, arms, hands, heart, tummy, legs, and feet, noticing what thoughts and feelings accompanied his sensations. David soon discovered that his aggressive impulse was connected with his fists, and his impulse to bolt was preceded by a tingling in his feet, expressed in wiggling movements. David learned to describe the sensations in his body, using words like 'tingling', 'pulsing', 'throbbing', and 'jarring'.

David began to recognize that these sensations indicated an escalation in arousal, coupled with emotional reactions that were the precursors to his impulsive behaviors (e.g. impulses to step on another's foot, kick someone, or grab items that aren't his). Learning to recognize these signs, and learning to implement his deep breathing resource at those times to calm himself, were primary treatment goals throughout the course of individual and group therapy.

When teaching children to become mindful of their bodies, a playful atmosphere becomes an important element that not only facilitates mindfulness, but also activates the child's play and the social engagement systems (Ogden *et al.*, 2006). In group work, mindfulness was included spontaneously as incidents occurred. For example, when David apologized to the group for his behavior, his therapist said to the group, 'Let's find out what comes up when you hear David say the words, "I'm sorry".' This was followed by the question: 'Maybe you feel relieved or happy or mad. I'll bet something changes in your body – can you tell us what changes? Maybe your body tightens up or relaxes, or maybe your breathing changes.' Directing mindfulness in this way helped the children notice things like muscle relaxation and tension, changes in facial expression, movements such as backing away or turning toward, changes in breathing, and so forth. Playfully saying, 'Let's all be like Dora the Explorer, and see what happens inside our bodies' led to robust conversations wherein the children were able to enliven each other's burgeoning self-awareness.

Group therapy

As David gained awareness of his body, developed self-regulation skills, and gained confidence in his relationship with his therapist, expanding from individual and family therapy to a weekly group experience became possible. David, like many children diagnosed with ASD, had difficulty making friends (Frey and Carson-Dewitt, 2012), Although he wanted friendships very much, he did not seem to comprehend that basic implicit social cues are necessary for interacting with other children, a characteristic difficulty of children with his diagnosis (Turkington *et al.*, 2012). Group therapy using Sensorimotor Psychotherapy offered David another theater in which to explore social engagement, increase his self-esteem, challenge his newly developing body awareness and somatic self-regulation skills, and learn how to recognize and respect his own and others' boundaries. Group Psychotherapy offers a particularly effective format for treating the multifaceted issues of children, especially those with ASD who typically have difficulty reading social cues. Group experiences help such children to explore how they react to social situations and to begin to understand that others have perspectives different from theirs.

At school, as at home, David was given the message, both overtly and covertly, that he was a problem. He came to believe that 'there's something wrong with me' and change felt insurmountable because he deeply believed he was defective. Due to David's history, particularly his experience in school, shame became a deep assault on his developing psyche, and one goal of group work was to ensure that further shame was not elicited. Thus, shame was an important emotion to identify for David early in the group experience because his underlying fears made it hard for him to feel comfortable and safe with others. David learned to identify his feelings of fear and shame and their ensuing sensorimotor correlates. Because David keenly felt that he was flawed, reframing his difficulties while fostering self-compassion and empathy along with enhancing awareness of others were all necessary. In group therapy, opportunities arose for David's peers to model the type of reciprocal social support that David needed both to experience, and to learn how to provide to others.

David's introduction to the ongoing weekly first-grade co-ed group was set up carefully to minimize any shame and maximize the chances for him to feel empowered and gain the respect and admiration of the other members. He was encouraged to take a role as a kind of co-leader, directing other group members to experience and discuss the breath work he had mastered. He modeled deep breathing, as he had already done with his parents, and the other children were instructed to mimic his actions of opening his chest by spreading his arms and straightening his posture. Teaching his fellow group members to do this enhanced his own self-understanding of the breath and offered an opportunity for him to experience pride and empowerment in interaction with others.

David's group therapy also included listening to the echoing reverberations of a gong or a singing bowl. Children with ASDs often exhibit hypersensitivity to sound (Stiegler and Davis, 2010), although studies showing that the physiology of hearing of this group does not differs from that of those who are not sensitive to sounds (Stiegler and Davis, 2010). Koegel, Openden, and Koegel (2004) demonstrated success in treating this sensitivity through exposing children with ASD to disturbing sounds over time. Similarly, in the group, as each child took a turn tapping the gong, they were guided with prompts to become mindful, such as 'Let's quietly listen to the sound and notice what happens inside each our bodies' or 'Let's see how long you can hear the sound as it rings, listening to the sound as the ringing fades.' As the children listened, they also practiced the deep breathing somatic resource that David had taught them. Adding the breathing helped David in particular regulate his arousal so that he could remain calm as he listened to the gong.

He loved the breathing exercise and gradually began to request it, particularly when interpersonal conflict arose in the group. Thus, breathing exercises were used often, not only when David's arousal increased, but also when group members spoke about themselves, which helped David become more centered, reflective, open, and curious about his peers' perspectives and experience. By using breath to quiet the anxiety-driven sensations and movements that had caused him strife with peers in the past, he was able to increase his interest in others and maintain social engagement even in times of conflict. It can be surmised that through these exercises the three levels of his brain – cortex, mammalian, and reptilian – began to work together in a more integrative way, rather than his subcortical brain hijacking his cortex.

Setting and respecting boundaries

A somatic sense of boundaries is an essential resource that many children need help to embody (Kepner, 1987, 1995; Levine and Frederick, 1997; Macnaughton, 2004; Ogden et al., 2006; Rosenberg, Rand and Assay, 1989; Rothschild, 2000; Scaer, 2001). Our younger clients often have difficulties appropriately setting boundaries for themselves and respecting those of others, and David was no exception. His 'under-bounded' style manifested in difficulty saying 'no', identifying his own needs and desires, and invading the boundaries of others. He found that the boundaries he had set ineffectively were often violated, and he was unaware that his body frequently was collapsed and his posture slumped, often signs of weak boundaries (Ogden et al., 2006; Ogden and Fisher, 2015).

Sensorimotor Psychotherapy can help children establish non-verbal boundary setting through exploring simple physical actions, including:

- the use of facial expressions like frowning or grimacing
- crossing arms in front of the chest

- making a 'stop' sign with the hands

- building a tangible boundary through the use of rope, pillows, or other objects

- integrating proximity seeking actions (e.g. reaching out or beckoning another person to come closer).

(Ogden *et al.*, 2006; Ogden and Fisher, 2015)

David often provoked interpersonal conflict by physically disrespecting the boundaries of others – stepping purposely on a group member's foot, taking chairs or sitting on laps without permission, following and poking classmates even after they asked him to stop, and, in one session, stealing another child's private diary to read selections aloud (much to her consternation). To help David learn more about his own boundaries and the boundaries of others, he and another group member explored physical distance and proximity. Guided by the therapist, Tami and David, both 6 years old at the time of this session, stood facing one another on opposite sides of the room, with the other group members quietly observing. David was instructed to ask Tami to come forward towards him, using both words and gesture, until he felt that she was 'just the right distance' from his body, at which point he was to ask her to stop. As he said the words, 'come closer,' he made a beckoning motion with both hands. When he felt that she was at the right degree of closeness and that she should not come any closer, he indicated this with a 'stop' gesture by placing his hands in front of his chest, palms facing outward, along with verbally asking Tami to stop.

Characteristic of weak boundaries, David did not experience Tami as too close until she was nearly on top of his toes. Then he finally said, 'OK, stop there.' His therapist asked, 'What happens in your body that lets you know that this is just the right distance?' David pointed to his tummy, his feet, and the top of his head, saying, 'My tummy knows and my feet, they say it, and they tell my brain the same.' These words and gestures illuminated his growing capacity for self-reflection and also reflected the collaborative work that had transpired in both his individual and group sessions in which David had been guided to acquire skills to scan his body in order to gain insight about himself.

When it was Tami's turn to beckon David closer, he failed to heed her words or body language indicating that he had reached 'just the right' distance for Tami, and instead ran impulsively very close to her, causing Tami to move backward, and cry out, 'Too close!' As the exercise was repeated, David was instructed to look for somatic cues from Tami (leaning back, movements such as making a small 'stop' gesture, facial expression of discomfort, looking away, a downward tilt of the head) that indicated she did not want him to come any closer to her. As he noted these cues, he gradually began to gain the insight that Tami's boundaries were different than his own.

In order to foster David's ability to look, listen, and become curious about Tami's experience, his therapist instructed him to approach her 'much slower, as if making a slow motion movie.' As David again moved closer to Tami in response to her beckoning gesture from across the room, he heartily engaged in this activity, saying, 'I must move very, very slowly' and he made large, slow movement of his arms and legs. This slow movement, coupled with reminders to pause and notice Tami's non-verbal communications and hear her words, such as 'stop', 'wait', or 'back up', allowed the time for David to respond appropriately. David's drive for connection was powerful, and he eagerly complied with exercises such as these; but repetition is key to developing a felt understanding of boundaries, so this exercise was repeated many times, in a variety of contexts.

In subsequent sessions, the group members explored boundaries in other ways, with leaders reiterating the importance of setting one's own boundaries and noticing and honoring the boundaries that others established. In one such exercise, each child took a turn to establish his or her own personal space by using pillows, jump-ropes, and other props to mark a tangible boundary. They were guided to find the words that represented their boundary, such as 'This is my space' or 'Don't come here' or 'Please ask before you cross my boundary'. Similar to his interactions with Tami, David would impulsively invade others' physical boundaries, despite their words or signaling with a 'stop sign' that they were not receptive to his proximity and wanted him to maintain distance. It is important to note that in Sensorimotor Psychotherapy, the times that David did not respect a boundary were communicated to him and to the group as opportunities to practice skills, rather than as failures. Since David often found it challenging to honor these tangible boundaries of the other children, he was provided myriad opportunities to practice this essential skill.

Exploring proximity and distance through exercises such as those described above provides a venue for discussion about boundaries and promotes understanding, empathy, cooperation, and consideration of others. Each participant's ability to sense the other's experience is increased. Over time, with practice and reinforcement, David became better at both reading and respecting the somatic and verbal boundaries of his peers. He learned to track and appropriately interpret non-verbal cues, and take those cues into account; this limited his impulsive actions, helped him remain connected with the other person, and led to less reprimand for upsetting others. His progress continued outside of group therapy, as evidenced by subsequent reports from his school teachers of his improved behavior.

Use of video

Group sessions were often videotaped and reviewed by the group later so that all members could learn from observing their own behavior and the behavior of their peers. Because viewing oneself in conflict-laden or high arousal moments in group therapy, especially in the presence of that group, has the potential to be upsetting, frustrating, or shaming, group members were shown short, edited clips, followed by empathetically attuned discussion. Hearing from peers that they too have felt embarrassed or ashamed at times helps to ameliorate these potentially negative feelings, and enhances the safety and learning possibilities. Video segments can thus provide transformative opportunities by highlighting critical moments and observing and discussing inevitable interpersonal challenges. David's initial response when he saw the video playback of the group therapy in which he stole the diary was to laugh; however, his body appeared tense and anxious, his posture rigidly upright, but with his feet wiggling rapidly. Viewing the moments before stealing the diary, he and group members noticed that his body lurched upward and that there was an almost imperceptible shaking of his arm – somatic signs had gone unnoticed during the session but were evident as the session was viewed. The group explored early indicators of arousal in their discussion, noticing together in a playful, interactive, and collaborative dialogue. Some members recognized and shared similar experiences of getting in trouble for taking something (e.g. stealing cookies before dinner even though they knew they were off limits, or grabbing their sister's pillow at bedtime) and the children collaboratively brainstormed about the somatic resources they might use to curb such impulses. For example, one member said that when he tried to stop himself 'doing something naughty' he would 'suck in my breath', which he then demonstrated by taking in a very large gulp of air. David said that he could take a 'super big breath' and he then demonstrated as well, his arms extending widely, his mouth opening and closing, and a chorus of laughter broke out as fellow group members mimicked him to take their own big breaths.

Following the conversation, playful opportunities for practicing were created in the group. A few members role-played having an object that David might want to grab, and David took his 'super big breath' as a regulating action to curb his impulse to take the object. There was much laughter as David role-played with his peers, taking many large gulps of breath, adding a hand movement of drawing large circles with his arms in the air.

All members experienced encouragement and support throughout David's practicing of his 'super big breath'. Others group members also were afforded opportunities to share times that they got in trouble or broke a rule and to find resources that might help them inhibit impulsive behavior. These discussions, accompanied by members role-playing their experiences, allowed David and all the members to learn together and experience safety in the commonality of sharing. For David, this was evidenced by his posture visibly relaxing, his breathing spontaneously deepening, and his wiggling feet becoming still.

An important element of this exercise was to discover and practice new resources the children could use to curb the impulses that got them into trouble. Each child was encouraged to find gestures or movements that were their own, perhaps inspired by one another, yet germinating from their own experience. During each member's role-play, mindfulness questions such as 'What happened in your body the moments before…' and 'Let's notice what's happening right now, as you describe this…', or 'What can you do first to help you calm down or curb your impulse…' led to collaborative brainstorming of somatic resources to self-regulate. One child said, 'I can stretch my arms widely, reaching way up to the sky like David did,' while another reported, 'I can melt into the chair and relax,' and yet another said, 'I can feel my feet plant onto the floor like glue.' Together, the children tried out each other's resources, learning new regulatory skills from each other.

During individual therapy, other opportunities for therapeutic integration unfolded as David was able to deepen his understanding of the rich array of movements and gestures and postures available, and we discussed what he had seen from his fellow group members. David was encouraged to reflect upon insights about his group members' actions, as they might be useful to him. For example, David said that he could try on Sammy's 'sticky feet' as he reflected on his peer's use of 'foot glued to the ground' as his way of curbing impulsive behavior. David then role-played a scenario where he would forgo taking a toy in the office that was deemed off limits. David placed his feet firmly on the ground (sticky feet), his body posture shifting to upright and purposefully rigid, saying, 'See, just like Sammy, I'm not going to take the toy.'

At a family meeting one week later, David's parents learned about the targeted goal of preempting impulsive or problematic behaviors and actions through David's sharing of the events, the antecedents, and the outcomes. David talked about his initial anxiety when he viewed the videotape of his taking the diary, speaking about noticing how his foot or arm wiggled, his body posture tensed, and so forth. He spoke of the regulatory resources of the 'super big breath' and 'sticky feet' that were co-created through the group process. The coherence of self-understanding as he described these sessions offered yet another 'teachable moment'. There was a shift wherein David was no longer the problem but rather part of the solution, a certain self-esteem builder. This shift was confirmed in the following weeks, as his teachers reported David's behavior on the playground had improved markedly with fewer conflicts and no reports of physical skirmishes or violations of personal property. David's parents reported that David often practiced 'gulping super big breaths' and 'sticky feet' and, with the reminder of his parents, would be able to utilize these resources to help regulate his arousal and behavior.

Integrating therapy into David's school and home life

David, his therapists, and other group members learned to recognize the somatic signs of David's escalating arousal, and were able to remind him to implement resources, such as deep breathing, to great success. However eliciting his parents' or school teachers' full support for his newfound skill proved challenging. At home, his parents easily slipped into old patterns of shaming admonishment and punishment, failing to help David assess his behavior or use his resources. At school, once David grew flustered or frustrated at an interpersonal challenge, he had difficulty accessing the skills that he had been learning in therapy. He needed the initial support of his teachers to help him to recognize the somatic signs of his dysregulation and remind him to breathe, until, over time, he was able to internalize these skills on a more consistent basis.

As a result, violating boundaries and the personal space of others continued to be a challenge for David. The tetherball game at school, in particular, was a consistent source of interpersonal conflict in which David had difficulty drawing upon the skills he had learned in therapy to regulate his disruptive behavior. However, over time he attained better awareness and his impulsivity diminished. At one group session, David proudly reported that he played tetherball for an entire period: 'No one got hurt... My teacher gave me a happy face sticker that I got to wear all day on my shirt...and when my mom picked me up, she told me how proud she was.' These positive responses to his success on the play-yard, and the support and compliments of the group members as he reported his success, were encouraging to David in his efforts to change problematic behaviors. As he reported his successes in subsequent therapy sessions, his pleasure was evident by his huge beaming smile. As he looked in the full-length mirror in the office, he could see remarkable differences in his body and posture. Enthusiasm and self-confidence seemed to bubble from his tall, elongated stance, replacing the slumped posture that had been his norm.

Though David had made marked progress in reading social cues and resonating empathetically with others, it remained one of his biggest challenges. Seeing himself through the eyes of another remained especially problematic and he often seemed confused about why his behavior had 'hurt' another child. He desperately wanted to be accepted and was very willing to say 'I'm sorry,' but increasing his understanding of how his behavior affected his parents, teachers, classmates, and group members continued to be a goal of treatment. Slowly, over time, both maturation and practice led to increasing success. His progress report at the end of his first-grade year stated 'consistent attempts to regulate behavior with increasing success; room for improvement.' Those simple remarks held both a sense of achievement and hope for David. Not only had he taken conscious effort to change his behavior, he now had at his disposal a set of resources and skills that would help him to continue improving.

Conclusions

Patterns of behavior may become so familiar and habitual that they interfere with the establishment of new neural pathways and subsequent novel patterns of behavior. Working with younger clients early in life provides an opportunity to teach self-regulation skills that can mitigate problematic behaviors (and before they become ingrained). Through the use of directed mindfulness, embedded in relationships, we hope to capitalize on the neuroplasticity of the brain by teaching children to notice the internal somatic indicators that comprise their automatic reactions, and then purposefully direct mindful attention to something they typically do not notice, like deep breathing, thereby creating a new experience.

A Sensorimotor Psychotherapeutic approach to working with younger clients aims to integrate mind and body through teaching body awareness, helping children understand procedural learning, and enhancing existing regulatory skills and teaching new ones. Through the mind–body integration that developed in individual, family, and group treatment, David was afforded an opportunity to engage his natural curiosity and playful nature in the service of these aims. His own and his peers' capacity to listen to one another, establish and respect boundaries, to 'feel felt' as each of the members was changed, for the better, by the others, grew as therapy progressed. By learning somatic resources to quiet his anxiety and high arousal, and with practice reading and responding to social cues, David gradually began to develop self awareness and form stronger and more satisfying relationships with others.

References

Beebe, B. (2006) 'Co-constructing mother–infant distress in face-to-face interactions: Contributions of microanalysis.' *Infant Observation* 9(2), 151–164.

Bromberg, P. (2011) *The Shadow of the Tsunami: And the Growth of the Relational Mind.* New York, NY: Taylor & Francis.

Caldwell, C. and Victora, H. K. (2011) 'Breathwork in body psychotherapy: Toward a more unified theory and practice.' *Body Movement and Dance in Psychotherapy 6*, 89–101.

Frey, R. and Carson-Dewitt, R. (2012) 'Asperger Syndrome.' In K. Key (ed.) *The Gale Encyclopedia of Mental Health* (3rd edn, vol. 2). Detroit, MI: Gale.

Goldstein, J. and Kornfield, J. (1987) *Seeking the Heart of Wisdom: The Path of Insight Meditation.* Boston, MA: Shambhala Publications, Inc.

Kepner, J. (1987) *Body Process: A Gestalt Approach to Working with the Body in Psychotherapy.* New York, NY: Gardner Press.

Kepner, J. (1995) *Healing Tasks: Psychotherapy with Adult Survivors of Childhood Abuse.* San Francisco, CA: Jossey-Bass.

Koegel, R., Openden, D. and Koegel, L. (2004) 'A systematic desensitization paradigm to treat hypersensitivity to auditory stimuli in children with autism in family contexts.' *Research and Practice for Persons with Severe Disabilities 29,* 122–134.

Kunzig, R. (2004) 'Autism: What's sex got to do with it?' *Psychology Today 37*(1), 66.

Levine, P. and Frederick, A. (1997) *Waking the Tiger: Healing Trauma.* Berkeley, CA: North Atlantic Books.

Macnaughton, I. (2004) *Body, Breath, and Consciousness: A Somatics Anthology.* Berkeley, CA: North Atlantic Books.

Ogden, P. (2007) *Beyond words: A clinical map for using mindfulness of the body and the organization of experience in trauma treatment.* Paper presented at Mindfulness and Psychotherapy Conference, UCLA/Lifespan Learning Institute, Los Angeles, CA.

Ogden, P. (2009) 'Emotion, Mindfulness, and Movement: Expanding the Regulatory Boundaries of the Window of Tolerance.' In D. Fosha, D. Siegel and M. Solomon (eds) *The Healing Power of Emotion: Perspectives from Affective Neuroscience and Clinical Practice.* New York, NY: W. W. Norton.

Ogden, P. (2013) 'Technique and Beyond: Therapeutic Enactments, Mindfulness, and the Role of the Body.' In D. J. Siegel and M. Solomon (eds) *Healing Moments in Psychotherapy.* New York, NY: W. W. Norton.

Ogden, P. (2014) 'Embedded relational mindfulness: A sensorimotor psychotherapy perspective on the treatment of trauma.' In V. M. Follette, D. Rozelle, J. W. Hopper, D. I. Rome and J. Briere (eds) *Mindfulness-oriented Interventions for Trauma: Integrating Contemplative Practices.* New York, NY: The Guilford Press.

Ogden, P. and Fisher, J. (2015) *Sensorimotor Psychotherapy: Interventions for Trauma and Attachment.* New York, NY: W. W. Norton.

Ogden, P. and Minton, K. (2000) 'Sensorimotor psychotherapy: One method for processing trauma.' *Traumatology 6*(3) 149–173.

Ogden, P., Goldstein, B. and Fisher, J. (2012) 'Brain-to-Brain, Body-to-Body: A Sensorimotor Psychotherapy Approach for the Treatment of Children and Adolescents.' In R. Longo, D. Prescott, J. Bergman and K. Creeden (eds) *Current Perspectives and Applications in Neurobiology: Working with Young Persons Who are Victims and Perpetrators of Sexual Abuse.* London: Karnac Books.

Ogden, P., Minton, K. and Pain, C. (2006) *Trauma and the Body: A Sensorimotor Approach to Psychotherapy.* New York, NY: W. W. Norton.

Rosenberg, J., Rand, M. and Asay, D. (1989) *Body, Self, and Soul: Sustaining Integration.* Atlanta, GA: Humanics Limited.

Rothschild, B. (2000) *The Body Remembers: The Psychophysiology of Trauma and Trauma Treatment.* New York, NY: W. W. Norton.

Russell, J. (1997) 'How Executive Disorders Can Bring about Adequate Theory of Mind.' In J. Russell (ed.) *Autism as an Executive Disorder.* Oxford: Oxford University Press.

Scaer, R. C. (2001) 'The neurophysiology of dissociation and chronic disease.' *Applied Psychophysiology and Biofeedback 26*(1), 73–91.

Siegel, D. J. (1999) *The Developing Mind.* New York, NY: Guilford Press.

Siegel, D. (2010) *Mindsight: The New Science of Personal Transformation.* New York, NY: Random House.

Stiegler, L. and Davis, R. (2010) 'Understanding sound sensitivity in individuals with autism spectrum disorders.' *Focus on Autism and Other Developmental Disabilities 20*(10), 1–9.

Strand, E. (2004) 'Out of sync?' *Psychology Today 37*(6), 26.

Tronick, E. Z. (2006) 'Self and Dyad Expansion of Consciousness, Meaning-Making, Open Systems, and the Experience of Pleasure.' In G. B. La Sala, P. Fagandini, V. Lori, F. Monti and I. Blickstein (eds) *Coming into the World: A Dialogue Between Medical and Human Sciences.* Berlin: Walter de Gruyter.

Turkington, C., Davidson, T. and Carson-DeWitt, R. (2012) 'Autism.' In K. Key (ed.) *Gale Encyclopedia of Mental Health* (3rd edn, vol. 2). Detroit: Gale.

10

Getting Together, Playing Together, Healing Together

How to Craft a Somatic-Based Activity

Alé Duarte

The earth roared beneath my feet, deafening and awful. The windows – already weakened from the last devastating earthquake – shuddered. I was standing in the center of a school courtyard in Sichuan, China, waiting for colleagues to finish a session with children and teachers, when I saw the land ripple broadly, forging its way towards me. Hordes of desperate children poured, screaming, out of the school doors and dashed towards the road. The noise of the building, shaken, as if like a toy; the windows practically spat out. The wave passed beneath our feet, undulating through our bones.

At that moment, motionless and alone in the courtyard, I did my best to find my own centre in the midst of the chaos. I scanned my surroundings for anyone in immediate danger, appraising the risk of falling debris. From my vantage point, I observed the behavior of those around me – adults and children staggering, the shine of terror in teenagers' eyes, their bodies frozen in shock; the crying of small children. An orchestra in chaos. Then, as a tropical summer storm dwindled into a light drizzle, the quake's wave softened and faded into a momentary hush. The stillness was so deep I could feel my bones vibrating and a slow dissipation of energy.

Then something unexpected happened – a phenomenon so striking that it came to inform the very core of my work with children. I watched as almost all the children resumed the very same activities they were engaged in before the earthquake struck. A group of girls returned to sing and clap palms, others resumed a game of hopscotch. A knot of small boys enveloped a young and shocked-looking doctor, clamoring for him to sing a karaoke song. Now the vast majority of children – who only moments ago had been running, frenzied, across the schoolyard – resumed their play and interactions *as if nothing had happened.* Some 20 per cent of them, however, remained in shock, requiring support from nearby adults. A young girl ran to her teacher, whose outstretched arms embraced and comforted her. A teenager, paralyzed by shock, briefly accepted support from another adult before rejoining his peers. Fortunately, no one was physically hurt. The event stirred some important questions in me:

- Why did the vast majority of children return to their earlier activities as if nothing had happened?

- How might one capitalize on the body's innate ability to self-regulate following a traumatic event?

- How might one best facilitate this process of self-regulation?

Through reflection, analysis, and practice, I have refined my answers to these questions, creating a set of principles that enables adult facilitators to harness children's innate capacity for self-healing through play.

Prioritizing safety

Safety is the foundation of self-regulation and homeostasis. In somatic work, reconnecting with the experience of safety is essential for the stabilization of autonomic nervous system processes. Thus, when it comes to engaging groups, facilitators may be tempted to try to establish a semblance of order, by requesting that the group assemble in a particular manner, settle down, be physically uniform, etc. However, this does little to influence the felt sense of safety within the group and may in fact mask levels of internal dysregulation, containing them only superficially. Unless children are at risk – in which case I would ask them to stop doing whatever they are doing – I make my presence felt by more implicit means.

On meeting a group of children, I am conscious of the degree to which it is I who is, quite rightly, being evaluated by the children – they are quick to read my face, my eyes, my body language, my tone of voice; the speed of my movements, the predictability of my gestures, the quality of my alliances. I imagine that at every glance, they are asking themselves: 'Is this adult reliable? Will he protect me in the group? Is he open to my ideas and needs?' My intention is always to answer these questions with my presence, and in the warmth, curiosity and acceptance manifest in my relationship with the children.

When children feel safely held, their arousal level automatically drops, internal unease and discomfort decreases, and they begin to express their needs – a far more important aim. As I observed in the aftermath of the quake, children quickly took advantage of the restoration of physical safety to create opportunities for self-healing.

The importance of this insight cannot be overstated: for self-regulation, we must make the sense of safety as tangible as possible. While workshop leaders and participants already acknowledge the importance of safety, it has become clear to me that, as facilitators, we can do better in practice at making safety real for the child. This requires an active approach, which makes use of physical presence, tone of voice, receptive gestures, congruence between internal states and external expressions/actions, clear commands, and – above all – eye contact. This is such an important part of valuing and acknowledging each child within the group. For example, after ensuring that all children were physically safe after the tremor, I paused to check my own impulses, ensuring that I myself was well grounded and oriented and in touch with my own internal sensations, in order that I could be a genuine source of safety for the children. Only then could I assume leadership. In approaching individual children and small groups, I made direct visual contact to assure them that all was well, and to communicate that I could be relied upon to respond to their needs: I affirmed the activities that they were already engaged in, acknowledged their enjoyment or worry; in short, I made my presence felt to them.

Harnessing the body's instinctive drive to self-regulate through play

In *Waking the Tiger*, Dr. Peter Levine (Levine and Frederick, 1997) recounts the story of a mother cheetah and her three cubs in the African savannah. The mother goes out to hunt for food, leaving her cubs unprotected and vulnerable. Soon a hyena arrives and makes a play for the cubs, which instinctively clamber up a tree to escape and cower in the branches. They remain there until their mother returns, and sees off the hyena, which flees and is eventually lost from sight on the horizon. The cubs, realizing the presence of the mother, feel a renewed sense of safety and descend the tree. They are clearly excited and joyful at their mother's return. The cubs then begin to play.

At first glance the cubs simply appear to be enjoying spontaneous fun. However, Levine (Levine and Frederick, 1997) realized the deeper purpose of this interlude: spontaneous play was a means of reorganizing and rebalancing the autonomic nervous system at a biological level; it was, in effect, an indispensable mechanism of survival following the potentially traumatizing event. Instinctively, the cubs took it in turns to role-play both predator and prey (hyena and cub), and thereby released the build-up of fight-or-flight responses that were inhibited while they sought refuge up the tree. In doing so, the cubs re-experienced a potentially lethal situation, this time incorporating opportunities for them to fight, defend themselves, and ultimately to triumph – all the while exposing themselves to manageable doses of risk – in the non-threatening realm of play.

Two important dynamics at work in this episode require emphasis here: (1) the re-establishment of the sense of safety on the mother's return, and (2) the cubs' innate impulse to play soon after the traumatic event – a behavior that restored equilibrium in the autonomic nervous system (ANS). These concepts have important parallels in children's functioning.

Just as the adult cheetah's return reassured her young that the danger had passed and that they could play freely, thereby facilitating the process of self-regulation, the presence of a reliable, attuned adult gives the children the requisite sense of safety that enables them to play, whilst also co-regulating them at the level of nervous system arousal. This reinforces the importance of facilitators remaining as calm and present as possible and is especially essential for any group activities that provide the containment for children's self-regulatory processes. The conditions must allow the children to express freely the defensive/attack behaviors (so long as they are not harmful to others) inhibited during the moment of threat within the safe structures of the game or activity.

The children's almost immediate resumption of their pre-quake activities was a powerful reminder not to interfere with children's innate capacity for self-healing and resilience. Resuming their games, which had been interrupted by the tremor experience, was key to the healing process. The children's systems needed not only to resume the inhibited action, but also to express the spontaneous behaviors which are unavoidable in the discharge of residual energy. Playing allowed this to happen for most children, but not all, which is why interventions are required at times.

Typical group composition: balanced, hyperactive, and apathetic children

In my role as facilitator I pay close attention to the level of ANS activation evident throughout the group. Who are the busiest children? Who are the quietest or most apathetic? Who are the most engaged? Who are the most raucous? This focuses my attention on the energetic, rather than behavioral, profile of the group, and gives me a specific picture of what needs to be stimulated or contained within a session. These are all considerations when determining the choice of activities or approaches and it requires skill to appraise many aspects of the group presentation simultaneously.

In my experience, three distinct groups tend to emerge during group interventions: the *balanced*, the *hyperactive*, and the *apathetic* children. The balanced group comprises 60–80 per cent of the children – those who are easily engaged in the activities without experiencing overwhelming arousal. While they are not homogeneous, their dynamic is neither chaotic nor disruptive; they appear balanced rather than anxious or lethargic.

About 10–20 per cent fall into the hyperactive category: running, knocking things over, upsetting others. Given their more aggressive behaviors, they are likely to be experiencing more intense ANS activation (with stomach contractions, chest anxiety, and/or discomfort in the head region) and require a facilitator's immediate presence and attention.

The remaining children, perhaps 10–20 per cent, comprise the third group. These are the quieter, introspective children who show very little movement or participation. Restrained and inhibited, they tend to receive less attention than the most active group members. However, it is important to focus more directly on them and to offer increased opportunities for contact in order to facilitate their involvement within the group. Otherwise, such children may be tempted to drop out of the activities altogether. From a somatic perspective, I have found that such children generally show little energetic activity in the arms and legs, report an empty feeling in the stomach and tightness in the chest near the throat, as well as discomfort in the head that can bring a state of confusion and dizziness.

Harmonizing energy levels within the group

As facilitator, it is my responsibility to foster an environment that permits a child to express spontaneous impulses since their repression only increases the likelihood that they will emerge later on. I intend not only to let these impulses emerge but to escort children all the way to integration by increasing their awareness of their bodies and encouraging their orientation to the outer world. This is the process that anchors them and re-establishes their connection with safe external resources as well as with internal resources (e.g. positive sensations in the body, feeling their feet rooted on the ground, the regularity of their breath).

Rather than insisting on organization from the start, I aim to move the group towards ever-greater synthesis through the intervention. As we saw, the same stimulus – the quake – elicited very different reactions across the group of children. Different interventions will also provoke varied responses that should not be overlooked or minimized. I observe each child, appraising each one's activation level or internal collapse, attentive to the quality of their responses to each stimulus. Facilitation thus requires a stance of continual responsiveness as I seek to harmonize the energy levels of the group – always seeking harmony rather than uniformity. During this process, a child's behavior should not be seen as symptomatic of their state per se, but rather as part of a larger pattern that is still unfolding.

Many facilitators prefer to work with the core, balanced group, finding the apathetic or hyperactive children disturbing. The tendency is to marginalize or exclude these children, leading to a gradual fragmentation of the group. Recognizing that the core group is already functioning well and comfortable allows me to focus my attention on the groups at either extremity, and to trust that the stabilizing influence of the core group will ultimately support the integration of the other children. Inviting a group of children to play a game has proven to be a remarkably effective way of drawing a group of children into a state of collective readiness.

HYPERACTIVE CHILDREN

The energies of the more hyperactive children, whose tendency is to leap impulsively into action and bypass the Readiness Phase (see later in the chapter) altogether, I attempt to hold longer in a state of expectation. These children find it difficult to tolerate waiting due to the excess of activation, which is relentlessly thrusting them into action. I help them to linger in a state of readiness just long enough to ensure an opportunity for them to make contact with their own internal sensations. Before I release them into the next phase, I pause and invite them to notice what is happening in their body. This allows them to be more closely attuned to the nuances of the energetic trajectory that culminates in action. By pausing I am seeking to draw their attention to the 'tipping point' between states, inserting an interval of awareness between impulse and action, which helps them to channel their energies more constructively.

APATHETIC CHILDREN

The apathetic children, conversely, wish to avoid action and interaction because of its attendant anxieties and are often arrested in the Settled Phase (see later in the chapter). It is my role to escort them across the threshold of fear or hesitation into the Readiness Phase (see later in the chapter). I do this in part by shielding them with my physical presence from the overbearing energies of the more hyperactive children, creating a zone of safety around them. I adapt my approach, softening my tone. Often I will whisper, conveying a sense of privacy and intimacy that assures them they will not be exposed, as this may be one of their greatest fears.

Making use of play: what's 'under the hood' of all activities

By making full use of play, we can provide children with opportunities to re-enact elements of traumatic experiences in a safe environment and so facilitate the natural process of self-regulation. Almost any activity or game with a defined structure and rules can become a perfect vessel to help a child find internal comfort.

The emergence of undesirable behaviors[1] usually signals reactivity to an aspect of the game structure that needs altering. Structural shortcomings to be remedied are any that deny sufficient time or opportunity to escape, that provoke a feeling of being trapped, or that leave a child feeling unprotected. Similarly, a game that makes a child feel they lack the necessary skills to perform well will impede the self-regulation process.

Before delving into further details of structuring activities, facilitators will benefit from a conceptual map designed to orient them through the group somatic intervention process from start to finish. This schema (see Figure 10.1) represents the core of my work. It also serves as a tool for quickly assessing the energy level of each child, whatever the diversity of the group make-up.

The five phases of the self-regulatory process

Every game orchestrated by children repeats a simple structure, which turns out to be instrumental in strengthening the ANS's ability to self-regulate and self-heal. The key lies in the structure's sequence of organized phases – phases characterized by experiential states that parallel those of the fight-or-flight sequence. Consider the simple game of 'tag': the group leaves a safety point, moves into a zone of action and interaction where the energy and stakes are higher, and culminates in their return to a place of safety where they may recover before beginning the next cycle.

This play sequence can also be observed in the animal world in the dynamics of predator and prey: the two parties start from an energetic baseline – a 'neutral' somatic experience associated with physical ease, and the ANS at rest. When the predator becomes hungry, an instinctive signal induces an alert-and-search state; the readiness phase is ignited, and the animal assumes the pre-attack position. When the time is ripe, the predator's accumulated energy fuels real action directed at the prey, whose own energy is focused on defending or escaping. The parties begin to interact, evaluating each other's speed and power, relative abilities, and environmental resources. Afterwards, regardless of outcome, energy levels taper off. Respite is necessary for

---

1   For example, impatience, sense of urgency, deflection and avoidance of the activity, clinging, defensiveness, hesitance, fear, insecurity, over-control of the activity, constant need for changing of the rules of the games.

the replenishment of energy in preparation for future attempts and escapes.

Understanding this great cycle of fight and flight and its components is the key to facilitating successful interventions. Each cycle comprises five distinct, well-marked sequential phases, which I have named *settled, readiness, action, interaction,* and *integration.* Each has its own identifiable characteristics.

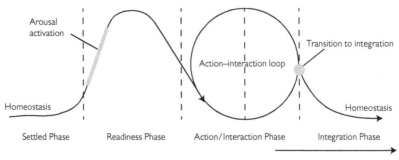

Fight-or-flight response – full cycle

Figure 10.1: *The five phases of the ANS self-regulatory process*

PHASE 1: THE SETTLED PHASE

The Settled Phase is the beginning of the cycle: the child is not yet engaged with the task or activity. They might be quietly observing or looking around as they assess new possibilities, browsing for anything that might pique their interest and generate sufficient energetic arousal to move them towards the desired activity. In this state their activation level is mild to moderate, the heart rate low, and muscle tone relaxed. If this child accepts an invitation to play a game, for instance, their whole physiology will shift as arousal and excitement levels rise, characterizing the transition to the next phase (see Figure 10.2).

PHASE 2: READINESS

The Readiness Phase, one of the richest phases of human energetic experience, precedes action. It marks the period for preparation, for defense or attack, during which the body tightens, the spine lengthens, the focus narrows, and heart and breathing rates accelerate. Meanwhile, the mind seeks to process very rapidly any new information regarding threat or excitement. Stored energy is transformed into action, congruent with self-preservatory instincts. Although children deliberately seek excited states when playing, very strong excitement provokes a myriad of bodily sensations that can be misinterpreted as external threats, leading to fear and insecurity.

At the invitation to play, the child's body moves into the Readiness Phase, with a concomitant adrenaline rush, as expectation is aroused. The increase in overall bodily energy sends a warning signal to the brain to find out what is happening (or what will happen) in order to prepare for action (to accept the invitation or flee). Behavioral disturbances (e.g. climbing, running around) during this phase signal that the child feels out of their comfort zone and is dysregulated.

PHASE 3: ACTION

As the invitation becomes reality, the child directs their energy towards playing and interacting, seeking out activities that involve fight and flight – defending their territory, their physical integrity, their friends, and their own self-image. Characteristics of the Action Phase include flow of arousal energy, euphoria, muscular expansion and contraction, fight-and-flight behaviors, and increasing contact with the outside environment.

PHASE 4: INTERACTION

During this phase the child is processing bodily activation, experiencing excitement and surprise in their interactions with objects and people. They are also in a state of perpetual expectation with regard to their contact with others. The Readiness Phase is the preparation, or rehearsal, for the 'show time' of the Action/Interaction Phase.

PHASE 5: INTEGRATION

Finally, the operation loses strength: the child's interest in the activity declines, and they move towards disengagement. Energy levels drop, and the child needs to refuel and rest, ushering in the Integration Phase. It is as if the body is indicating that one experience must be digested before the cycle starts afresh. The ANS activation is evident in the behavioral and energetic characteristics of this phase: nesting, desire for food or drink, desire to go to the toilet, feeling calm or sleepy, a sense of satisfied completion. One common mistake is to stop paying attention to the child at this point, as this phase presents an unparalleled opportunity for the adult to reflect back to the child their calmer state; they might do this by sighing or yawning, thereby welcoming the child's own impulses towards rest and renewal and deepening their experience of the integration process. I have found that these shared moments of integration can feel quite magical to both parties.

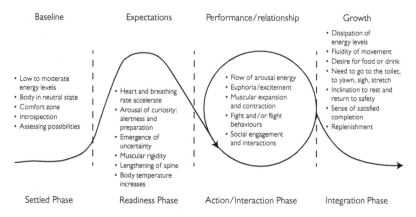

Figure 10.2: *Characteristics of each phase*
of the ANS self-regulatory process

The restoration of missing elements through play

When children experience a shock, such as a natural disaster or an attack, the body can become trapped in a state of perpetual alertness, or readiness, continuing as it is in order to defend against the unexpected, and frightening, event. This inefficiency creates undue demands on the ANS, as seen in the looping action in Figure 10.1, much as if one were stepping on a car's accelerator and brake simultaneously.

Species survival has depended on ANS defense mechanisms. When these natural defenses are swamped by a sudden and intense threat, trauma occurs, as Levine (Levine and Frederick, 1997) observed. A traumatic experience is one that is too intense, too soon, and too fast, he explains, overriding the body's inherent ability to defend itself and then stabilize. In other words, trauma results when critical elements are missing: the person experiences a deficiency of time (for thinking and coping); a deficiency of options (to make good decisions), a deficiency of skills (to successfully escape or defend). Further, they may lack a safe person to provide the requisite support. In crafting somatic interventions that optimize self-healing, we must restore these lacking elements by providing (1) enough time, (2) choices, (3) opportunities for skill development, and (4) reference for safety.

Successful facilitation involves optimizing these four fundamental elements to help children find playful ways to escape threat and build their confidence. Many children's games already include them – for example, 'hide-and-seek' and similar games involve an interval of counting that gives children a chance to run away and elude their captor. Children themselves often make adaptations, inventing rules of immunity or invisibility to give themselves additional opportunities to succeed. Rather than seeing this as a form of cheating, we might regard these adaptations as a child's resourceful means of meeting their needs and compensating for perceived disadvantages. If necessary, I tend to make similar adaptations to games when facilitating groups, as follows:

1. *Minimize urgency, maximize time:* The child must perceive that there is sufficient time for them to learn the skills necessary for the task. Demonstrate that you will follow the child's pace. Count aloud in anticipation of the task to build a sense of readiness. While this generates its own pressure, the child becomes aware of the time frame and can thus manage it better than if surprised by an unexpected demand for action, as occurred at the moment of trauma. Use delay tactics to stretch time – for example, in tag, introduce a round of the game 'Scissors-Paper-Stone' when a child is tagged, providing a second opportunity for escape.

2. *Offer choices:* The facilitated activities must allow the experience of choice in order to prevent a rise in stress levels. Choice may involve any number of factors – for example, the direction in which to run, the difficulty level, etc. Decision-making can be stressful and children are often afraid of 'getting it wrong'. When a facilitator helps a child choose, by providing both a sense of perspective and a way to figure out the best option, the child feels freer to use skills already at their disposal, and more confident that they will be able to respond decisively in the moment. Identifying the options available to them ('Are you going to catch the ball with your right or your left hand?') and helping them to distinguish the merits of each ('You've got a few options here – which one do you prefer?') is also supportive.

The child who lacks confidence can easily become disoriented, and the facilitator's encouragement and assurance, and even (especially with younger children) assistance in orienting them decisively towards their target, can help the child strategize and develop trust in their decisions. Identifying hesitant children and offering them a safe, encouraging connection will promote the effectiveness of the intervention.

3. *Develop skills:* This element has two distinctive purposes: (a) to ignite the system so the child moves out of their frozen or hesitant state, and (b) to increase real capabilities to help a child overcome the concern that a task is too difficult. When a child perceives that their abilities do not meet the situational demands, and they fear being exposed as inadequate, their body starts to shut down and freeze. The facilitator can use the Readiness Phase to build skills (e.g. running, skipping, pulling, pushing, rolling, etc.). This developmental step is vital for the child, since by rehearsing, they move beyond the freeze and into the next phase. Practice assures them 'I can do this, I just did this: it is possible'. Even otherwise well-functioning children may freeze at times when invited to play.

4. *Provide a clear reference for safety:* Children often wish that a protector had been present at the moment of trauma. Even during playful activities, a child may experience stress and loneliness, and be unable to interact. This is when an invitation to 'buddy up' with another child works well. The presence of another child, an encouraging adult, or even a transitional object (e.g. a teddy bear) allows a child to share their failures and successes. Encouraging comments can help foster a sense of safety: 'It will be okay if you make a mistake, I'm here for you'; or perhaps 'If you need me, I'll be here'. Some children will take greater risks when accompanied, providing an important counter to the sense of isolation experienced during the traumatic event.

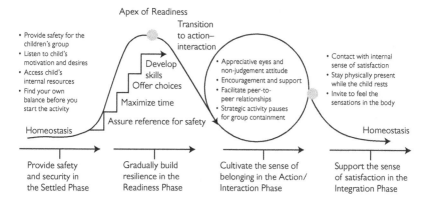

Figure 10.3: *Strategies to facilitate a child's ANS self-regulatory process during a playful activity*

Case study 10.1: Getting unstuck and letting the cycle flow

Out of nowhere, the hammer smashed through the car window, followed by a hand that reached in to snatch the handbag from the front seat. Startled from her nap in the back seat, 5-year-old Sofia awoke with alarm. 'We were helpless,' Sofia's mother told me. Since then, Sofia had suffered from tics and nightmares. She was now extremely cautious about starting any activity, would strive to be in control and avoid any challenge. This informed me that Sofia's system was in shock: her instinctive fight-or-flight response to the abrupt noise had been interrupted as she lacked the necessary time to orient herself and choose the best defense. Group play with her parents and siblings, I explained, could help re-initiate the sequence in a manageable way that would allow her to move beyond the Readiness Phase in which she was stuck and integrate the pent-up survival energy that was constantly alerting her brain to danger.

I invited the group to make a circle and take the edge of a colorful parachute, stretching it taut. 'At the count of 10,' I announced, 'we will start shaking the parachute' (Readiness). As I began to count, Sofia became apprehensive, her tics intensified and she began to blink rapidly. Her arms stiffened and she appeared confused. Evidently, this pre-action Readiness Phase contained more energy than she was able to manage. Noticing her apprehension, I stopped counting and asked her to look at her parents (Action/Interaction) in order to orient her with her source of safety. During the pause, I observed that her symptoms decreased in intensity and I tracked signs of integration in her body: a big intake of breath, followed by discernible release in her shoulders as she relaxed more fully.

Even though we had not yet shaken the parachute, Sofia's system had now made an initial passage through the five phases. It is important to ensure that – even if it lasts only a few minutes or seconds – you support the body to complete a full five-stage sequence at least three to four times. I resumed counting and asked Sofia to keep her focus on her parents as my counting ramped up the suspense and thus intensified her sense of readiness. Following this second attempt, there was a considerable improvement in her symptoms.

On the count of ten, I paused again (maximizing time) and proposed that we should have a little practice session during which we shook the parachute between us. By interrupting the growing sense of readiness, I aimed to restore a sense of safety to the proceedings, reducing Sofia's performance anxiety and granting an unexpected opportunity to build skills and confidence. The switch from 'show time' to 'rehearsal' saw a significant shift in Sofia's anxiety levels: she was able to enjoy the activity. It also allowed me to track her once more and I asked her to tell me about any bodily sensations she was experiencing. Again, we continued through the entire five-phase sequence. As Sofia showed no attempts to control the rules or others' behavior, I began to count again, stopping once more at ten – the apex of readiness. Then I introduced a little playfulness by shaking the parachute more vigorously, thus engaging the family more actively in the mood of the game (the Action/Interaction Phase). On the final count, it was not necessary to pause before shaking the parachute and Sofia entered into the spirit of the play, laughing with exhilaration. She wanted to play again and that informed me that she was becoming more comfortable with the activity and with the sensations in her body, suggestive of increased resilience.

After finishing the game, when everything had become more peaceful – ushering in the Integration Phase – Sofia sat beside her mother. I asked her to notice any positive sensations in her body. She responded that her belly was quieter and that she wanted to lie down and sleep on her mother's lap. The next day her parents called me to tell me that Sofia had slept very well and that her tics had gone.

Conclusion

Most children, when left to their own devices, find ways of restoring their self-regulation organically; those who don't will benefit enormously from the methods described above. These can be used with any children, not only those who have suffered a trauma, and are especially effective for working with children who are regarded as 'difficult to engage' because of the emphasis on playfulness. It is not the game or activity itself but the engineering beneath it that matters – namely the importance of the activity providing opportunities to progress through the five phases and arrive at a state of integration. This is a versatile model and can easily be adapted and used with many art forms such as theater or storytelling. In a society overwhelmed by electronics, by perpetual stimulus and information, children can easily be distracted from their organic processes. To reconnect, through play, with their own internal wisdom is at the core of healthy development.

References

Levine, P. A. and Frederick F. A. (1997) *Waking the Tiger: The Innate Capacity to Transform Overwhelming Experiences.* Berkeley, CA: North Atlantic Books.

11

NASSA – NeuroAffective Structured Social Activity

Susan Hart, Knud Hellborn and Gitte Jørgensen

Case study 11.1

Benjamin, Melinda, Hassan, Marva and Nicklas, all aged around 9 years, have joined the NASSA group for a variety of reasons. Benjamin has begun to withdraw from shared play during the breaks and seems increasingly despondent. Melinda is perceived as a meddler by the other children. She rarely sits still for more than five minutes at a time, and she disturbs the other children with noisy behaviour. Hassan's emotional state fluctuates wildly. One moment he is extremely happy; the next he may be fuming with anger. The other children have difficulty reading him, and they are afraid of him when he threatens them. He and his family came to Denmark as refugees three years ago. Marva's closest girl-friend recently moved to another part of the country, far away from Marva. Since then, she has been virtually 'glued' to the girl she shares a desk with in class – who has now asked to be assigned a different seat. Marva seems to lack any perception of her own and other people's boundaries and therefore consistently oversteps them. Nicklas has always been bullied because others find him strange, geeky and introvert. The children come from very different backgrounds. Some of them live with their parents, brothers and sisters. Others live with one of their parents. One lives with a foster family. Some of the parents have faced particularly challenging life circumstances, which has led to depression, post-traumatic stress disorder (PTSD) and alcohol abuse. Others have become increasingly worried about their children over time, because they see them struggling with fitting into the school and after-school settings. The teachers have referred the children to the group on the common basis that they engage with the other children in a way that gives cause for concern.

Children primarily express themselves through play. By being invited into a group where adults frame the interactions and ensure that everyone has fun the children are gradually able to generate a shared sense of community and safety and enjoy being in the group. They meet regularly twice a week, and in the NASSA room, they share and co-create experiences that are special for everyone involved – children and adults alike.

What is the purpose of NASSA?

Children's social and emotional development depends on a safe and stable childhood environment with empathic and understanding adults. Sadly, some children grow up under very different conditions and therefore rely on supportive and preventive efforts in preschool and school. With NASSA we wish to offer knowledge about important aspects of the structure, organization and content of this effort.

NASSA is a developmental play-based group programme for 3–12-year-old children. The acronym stands for NeuroAffective Structured Social Activity.

The NASSA programme engages the children's capacity for self-regulation, mentalization and social relationships. The programme aims to prevent future problems by fostering and strengthening psychosocial resources, and it can be carried out by educators because it is designed to fit into preschool and school settings. This also means that some children require targeted treatment in addition to NASSA. In those cases, NASSA can be used as a screening instrument.

The NASSA programme aims to involve the parents and includes a home visit by a NASSA trainer both before and after the programme. The parents are also invited to attend and play an active role in the final session. The parents are deliberately not invited to attend the other sessions because one of the goals of NASSA is to offer the children their own free space.

The programme aims to bolster the children's emotional, personal and social resources through structured play. This enhances the children's self-awareness and relational resources and helps them develop greater resilience to psychological stressors. The programme focuses on helping the children to engage in interactions with others through synchronization, affect attunement and mentalization in social relationships. In relation to school and preschool teachers, the programme aims to promote awareness of the impact of early childhood conditions and of the steps that teachers can take to build an environment that provides optimum conditions for children's emotional and social development.

The development of NASSA

In 2010, the Municipality of Varde and the Department for Survivors of Trauma and Torture under the psychiatric services in the Region of Southern Denmark engaged in a partnership to develop a method to prevent traumatization in children in families with a history of trauma. The development project was concluded in autumn 2014 with a large conference and the release of the first NASSA manual (in Danish).

In early 2015 Susan Hart took over the programme and registered it under its Danish name, NUSSA (Neuroaffektiv Udviklingspsykologisk Struktureret Social Aktivitet; in English the programme is titled NASSA). In late 2015, NASSA was revised and reframed as a structured developmental programme, rather than a manual-based approach. This means that the progression of the programme is guided by the actual emotional and social development level of the children in the group, and selected sessions may be repeated if the group as a whole is not ready to proceed to the next level.

On a theoretical level, NASSA is framed by neuroaffective developmental psychology. Methodologically, the programme was initially inspired by so-called 'Joyful Playing', an approach developed in 1989 with the goal of strengthening the capacities of traumatized children. Joyful Playing was developed by the organization *Life is Good Playmakers* in Boston in cooperation with the trauma expert Bessel van der Kolk. He was aware that many traumatized children have difficulty engaging in play because they have experienced the world as a dangerous place, where the first priority is survival. The purpose of Joyful Playing, therefore, is to create a good play environment, where the children feel safe and are able to develop their mental and social capacities. The NASSA programme preserves this underlying premise but also draws inspiration from a wider range of games and play activities because play offers a space that enables shared experiences, which in turn enable children to build resources.

Who can benefit from NASSA?

Originally, the programme was aimed at children with traumas, but today the target group includes a wider range of children. Thus, the programme can be applied in preschool settings as a way of preparing children for school. It can also help children who have emotional, personality and/or social problems. It is important to notice both the children who act out and the more withdrawn and passive children. Children may show highly diverse emotional symptoms, including panic attacks, anxiety and phobias, hyperactivity, nightmares, avoidant behaviour, mood swings and impulsive outbursts, living in a fantasy world, regressive behaviour, etc.

The programme is also suitable for children living under particularly challenging circumstances: the children of parents who for some reason or another, for shorter or longer periods of time, lack the resources to engage in normal, attuned interactions with their children. This failure to engage may be due to psychological disorders, such as depression, PTSD, etc., or acute trauma, such as divorce, severe illness, etc.

Overview of the NASSA programme

In addition to the introduction and the closing session, NASSA consists of a play programme on four levels, with a total of 18 steps, and offers a series of games tailored to the child's zone of proximal development.

The programme can be used with groups of children aged 3–6 years, 6–9 years and 9–12 years. Thus, the games on the four levels exist in age-appropriate versions. Beginning with activities from Level 1 will be appropriate and beneficial for all children, regardless of age. The games at this level rely less on verbal content and aim primarily to promote attunement and synchronicity in the group.

The rationale behind the structure is that the content of each step at a given level should enable the children to develop the resources and competences they need to complete the next level. It is important to make sure that the children never feel that they are failing, and throughout the programme, the trainers need to ensure that the children are able to participate.

Step by step

The group meets approximately twice a week, and each step takes no more than 60 minutes. Each step begins and ends with a recurring group activity that serves as a recognizable element across the sessions. The NASSA trainers take charge and guide the process from the outset, creating a safe and secure atmosphere in the group. At the end of each session, the children take part in down-regulation activities, such as guided relaxation exercises, to round the session off with a calm, pleasant and relaxed feeling.

The NASSA trainers are always responsible for providing clear guidance along the way, in part to make sure that everyone is included. The activity of the day is a synchronizing, emotionally attuning activity, a role play, a collaborative activity or a combination of these types of activities. Each level has a specific theme that is always integrated into the activities. All the games and activities are aimed at encouraging the children to express a variety of emotions, which are activated in engaging interactions with the other children and the trainers. The activities are structured to make sure the children have positive experiences with engaging in social relationships and being part of a community. Because of the developmental structure of the programme, each level can be repeated several times until the group is ready to move on. Thus, the play catalogue contains several different games and activities, all adapted to match the theme of a particular level.

NASSA principles

Traumatized or at-risk children need to experience a fundamental sense of security when they are together with other children. A familiar setting and structure and recurring elements are key conditions for good and emotionally developing play. In addition, all activities have to be inclusive, which precludes competitive activities. The children should have a clear sense that they cannot possibly do anything wrong, and they should have the sense of being accepted and included in the group. The adults give the individual children positive acknowledgements during play to make sure each child has the experience of being seen and acknowledged as an important person in the group and to provide a structure that lets the children express themselves.

The programme promotes gradual development by preserving the structured framework and recognizable elements and then gradually integrating new elements within the theme for the given level. The recurring structural framework that makes each session reassuringly familiar is achieved, for example, with a ritual for the way the children enter the room and ending the session with a relaxation activity. Having recognizable routines and knowing what is going to happen in the NASSA room makes the children feel safe.

To promote this sense of security and familiarity, it is important to have the sessions in the same room every time. It has to be a well-defined room with space to unfold a parachute, for example, and engage in physically active games. It should also have a welcoming and cosy feel and pleasant colours.

NASSA ground rules

The ground rules for the group help define a framework for the children that helps them feel safe. The ground rules are simple. We go over them together the first time the group meets and repeat them every time. The adults are responsible for making sure the rules are respected. The purpose of the NASSA rules is to define a safe environment for everyone. Some of the children may have felt the need to create their own rules in games in order to maintain a sense of control. They may be used to having to be the strongest, the fastest, the cheekiest, etc. in order to be accepted into a group. Therefore, the adults need to be aware that for some of the children, NASSA presents a new pattern to learn. It is essential to acknowledge that a child may have powerful reasons for breaking the rules while still providing guidance to help the child stick to them. The rules are borrowed from Theraplay™ (see Chapter 5), a method that was originally developed in the United States in the late 1960s, and which is now increasingly used in Denmark:

- No hurts.
- Stick together and help each other.
- Have fun together.
- The adult is in charge (the NASSA trainer's implicit rule).

The frame around NASSA

From the outset, the adults have to provide a safe framework as a basis for building secure relationships in the group. There are two adults for each group – a NASSA leader and a NASSA assistant. The NASSA leader has the role of 'caravan leader', the person who manages every step, leads the way and provides instructions. The NASSA assistant assists the leader and helps the children follow the instructions. The NASSA assistant has the main responsibility for taking care of any children who are upset or have difficulty staying calm, so that the NASSA leader can focus on leading the session.

A key element of NASSA is to make sure that all the children find the NASSA experience fun and rewarding. It is the responsibility of the adults to create an appreciative atmosphere and to set clear guidelines. *Step 1 is focused on mutual introductions, explaining the framework of the programme and demonstrating some of the activities that are included in the NASSA process.* For example, Benjamin, Melinda, Hassan, Marva and Nicklas may be introduced to each other by standing in a circle, throwing a bean bag back and forth as their names are called out. Alternatively, the children could hold a blanket or a parachute stretched out as the NASSA leader places a ball in the centre. When the leader calls out a name, the children have to manoeuvre the ball over to the child who has been called. The two adults take part in the games along with the children, so that their names become familiar too.

Each NASSA step begins with a brief, fun activity that promotes a sense of bonding and cohesion in the group. Next follows the activity of the day – for example the parachute activity described above, and then the group moves on to the key activity of the day, which is related to the theme of the day. For Benjamin, Melinda, Hassan, Marva and Nicklas, the games and activities involve both an experiential dimension and an awareness dimension based on symbols and verbal statements.

The NASSA session is always concluded with a pleasant and relaxing activity, and the children have a small snack and some fruit juice. The first time the children meet, the NASSA trainers may ask the children about their likes and dislikes to make sure that all the children enjoy the snack. At every level, the session ends with a circle and farewell ceremony, and the relaxation activities are often repeated several times to ensure a familiar structure. The trainers should also be aware of the need for variation over time, however, and adapt the flow to match the children's age and maturity level.

For example, the NASSA leader might say, 'Today's session is just about over, but before we leave, let's give each other a weather forecast.' She instructs the children to sit down in pairs, one behind the other, and tells them which child sits in front. Both the NASSA leader and the assistant also pair up with a child. The NASSA leader instructs the massage: 'We begin by softly placing a hand, palm down, on our buddy's back, and then calmly move it in little circles up and down the back, up and down the arms and then up and down the back again. Like the rising sun that warms up the body. Then we gently tap our fingers all over our buddy's back, like lots of tiny snowflakes falling from the sky. Tap, tap, tap. And now, the rain is falling gently on our buddy's hair, we tap the hair softly. We end the weather forecast by gently laying our hands on our buddy's shoulders, saying "Thank you for letting me borrow your back".' The leader uses his or her voice in a way that matches the movements and varies the pace to match the different kinds of touch. Towards the end, the pace slows down, and the touch is firm and calm. Now, the children switch places, and the weather forecast is repeated.

The snack at the end of the session might be a little fruit and some nuts, which the adults give each of the children. To round off the day, everybody stands up at the same time while holding hands and waiting for the NASSA leader's count: '1, 2, 3, now!' The children are led out of the room as a group, the leader at the front and the assistant bringing up the rear, the same way they came in.

The four levels

As mentioned earlier, NASSA consists of a play programme on four levels with a total of 18 steps. The four levels are now described.

Level 1: Rhythm, synchronization and hullabaloo

Level 1 consists of *Steps 2–5*. It revolves around using rhythm and play to establish a relationship based on mutual trust, where the children can challenge each other, have fun together and cooperate. The level is centred around games and activities that give the children a sense of being together on a non-verbal level. The emphasis is on bodily regulation, rhythms, sensing and synchronization. Everything is securely managed by the adults, and the atmosphere is playful. The activities are mainly inspired by Theraplay™. The activities also include traditional games that many trainers will know from their own childhood, and which in a NASSA context is linked with theoretical insights into children's development. In this set-up, play is not only about having fun but deliberately targets the zone of development that is in focus at the given level. Adult regulation is crucial, as the children are not expected to be able to cooperate or self-regulate at this level on their own, without guidance.

The level consists of four steps aimed at helping the children regulate their arousal level, feel the difference between pleasant and unpleasant, and experience synchronization with the NASSA trainers and the other children. Children love familiar games, and therefore this level repeats some of the games on separate steps while others are varied. NASSA Level 1 differs from all the other levels by containing a number of brief, structured activities with a specific focus. At this level, the focus is not on cognitive understanding, symbols or words but on a fundamental sense of community based on rhythmic, synchronizing activities with an emphasis on bodily sensations and experiences. At this level, for example, Benjamin, Melinda, Hassan, Marva and Nicklas will play with balloons, blow feathers, make hand stacks, play with hula-hoop rings and take part in rhythmic activities with varying tempo. They are going to sing songs, dance in a circle and make rhythms with their hands. There will be fun and fast-paced activities such as throwing things to each other or playing cotton ball hockey. The specific games are selected based on the group's age and maturity level. The NASSA trainers have a wide variety of activities to choose from to make sure they cover the central elements in ways that are interesting for the specific group. For example, 10-year-olds have developed the necessary motor skills to handle more demanding activities than 3-year-olds.

Level 2: Bringing my feelings and your feelings into resonance

Level 2 consists of *Steps 6–9*. It is about helping the child feel positive emotions, such as joy and enthusiasm, as well as negative emotions, such as anger, sorrow and the fear of loss. Where and how are the emotions felt, and how can they be altered? At this level, the focus is on inner sensations of emotions and on registering others' emotions, including bodily expressions, facial expressions and the use of the voice. The children may engage in the activities as a big group or in pairs. At this level, there are no demands for a mature mentalization capacity. The adults seek to activate the children's capacity for synchronization and imitation, the precursors of a later capacity to express emotions independently. At one point, for example, the group plays with intonation, strength and tone of voice as well as the facial expression of emotions.

Hassan and Marva know different language sounds than the other children. They have a beautiful accent, which is included as an element in an activity where the NASSA leader says a word in several different ways, expressed with a variety of emotions, which the children then imitate. She also adds movements and mimics emotional expressions with her face, which the others imitate – resulting in much laughter. The NASSA assistant takes part in imitating the emotions along with the children. To them, this is just a fun and silly game.

The NASSA process also addresses the emotion of fear. One example of involving language is a shared talk about the feeling of being afraid; the talk includes symbolization in the form of a drawing. For example, the NASSA leader might say, 'I remember once, when I was little, and I was so afraid because I woke up in the middle of the night and I thought I heard a sound. I remember my heart was pounding really hard, and I hid under the blankets, until I realized it was just my Daddy getting himself a glass of water in the kitchen. Have any of you ever been so scared that your heart started pounding really hard?' Hassan raises his hand and says that he has had that when he wakes up from a nightmare. Nicklas says that he gets goose bumps when he is scared. Now, the leader asks the children to pick a colour and make a drawing that illustrates how it felt in their bodies when they were scared. The two NASSA trainers move around the room and talk quietly with the individual children about their drawings and experiences. Some children are eager to talk, while others may want to wait until they have finished their drawing.

The purpose of rehearsing the different elements of emotional communication is that they are part of any interaction, such as prosody, intonation, pace, volume, facial expressions and gestures. Some children may have trouble finding the right facial expression – for example, Nicklas often maintains the same expression regardless of the subject, but in this activity he plays with a wide variety of expressions, which to him is a new experience. The adults do not comment on this but make sure they support his ability to mimic their expressions.

Level 3: Stop, sense, feel, think

Level 3 consists of *Steps 10–13*. It is aimed at helping the children to pause and manage their own impulses and emotions, and their thoughts about themselves and others. Who am I? What makes me happy? What do I like, what don't I like? What needs might others have? What do I notice in others? What might make them happy?

At this level, the children should learn to engage in social interactions where common rules apply, even if they do not necessarily agree with them, and be able to show consideration for others, considering both their own and others' needs. How does one stop an impulse, and how can one handle frustrations over rules that seem unfair? This level builds on the preceding two by tying together sensations, the children's own emotions and their awareness of themselves and others.

One way of practising stopping impulses is so-called 'stop games'. The leader starts the music, and everybody dances and jumps around to the music. Without warning, the NASSA leader then pauses the music. Everybody freezes in whatever position they were in, like statues. When the music begins again, the children resume dancing. Another way to practise the skill of delaying an impulse is any kind of activity that includes a clear 'ready, steady, go' sequence.

For example, in one of the activities, all the children take turns acknowledging each other. First, Hassan, Melinda, Nicklas and Marva take turns saying appreciative things about Benjamin. The NASSA assistant writes these things down on a sticky note, which is posted on Benjamin himself. The NASSA leader helps the group get the group get started by saying, 'I think that Benjamin is nice to talk with,' and the NASSA assistant writes 'nice to talk with' on a sticky note that is attached to his sleeve. Another says, 'He is kind to others,' and the word 'kind' is attached to his shoulder.

The NASSA leader deliberately addresses personal qualities. What we often see with children at this level is that with a little help from the NASSA trainers, they gradually begin to come up with more statements of this nature, such as 'Benjamin helped me when I was new in class – he is a good buddy.' In NASSA, we are constantly aiming at the children's zone of proximal development as we gently guide their development.

In another activity at this level, everyone in the group helps each other draw the outline of their hands. Then they draw or write something about themselves in each of the fingers on one of the hands. In the drawing of the other hand, they draw or write something the others might say about them. For example, writing 'good at soccer' on one hand and 'fun to be with' on the other.

Level 4: Thinking and feeling clearly about myself, others and my surroundings

Level 4 consists of *Steps 14–17*. The goal at this level is to help the children mentalize in relation to themselves and their relationships with others outside the NASSA group as well as some of the big questions and considerations in life. At this level, the trainers support the children's capacity for mentalizing at a higher level. The activities are characterized by a greater emphasis on words and narratives than at the previous levels. Our wish for Hassan, Marva, Benjamin, Melinda and Nicklas is to help them see themselves from the outside and see others from the inside. At this level, sensations and emotions are connected with reflections on oneself and others. If the previous levels are not sufficiently developed, the children will not be able to mentalize.

One way of symbolizing the importance of others in one's life is to give the children a pre-printed drawing of concentric circles, like a dart board. The task is to position family and friends by writing their name or initials in the relevant rings. The ones closest to the child are placed in the centre. People that the child has a more distanced relationship with are placed farther away from the centre. The positioning is based on the child's felt perception, not on physical proximity in the child's life. The drawing may also include pets, as well as people who have passed away and who were important to the child. A person may also be placed outside the circle entirely. If the child symbolically places a person (or a pet) outside the circle, this makes it possible to talk about their emotional impact and role and to reflect on why they have been placed there. Does it feel nice like that? Is it conflicted? Is there someone the child would like to have closer to the centre? The drawings make it easy for the children to assess where various people should be positioned in relation to others. The subsequent talk is adapted to the children's development level and guided by concerns about what it is appropriate to bring up in the common forum.

With inspiration from Eia Asen, the trainers now introduce a round of 'speed-dating'. Benjamin, Hassan and Marva sit on chairs forming a small circle facing an outer circle of chairs where Melinda, Nicklas and the NASSA assistant are seated. These pairs now take turns to talk about a specific point for one minute each. The first point is: 'Talk about something that makes you happy.' The NASSA leader, meanwhile, keeps time with a stop watch. After exactly one minute, it is the other child's turn to talk. Then the children in the outer circle move one spot to the right, so that everyone gets a new partner. The NASSA leader reads out the next point: 'Talk about something that makes you angry.' The procedure continues:

a) Talk about something that makes you happy.

b) Talk about something that makes you angry.

c) Talk about something that made you sad.

d) Talk about a time when you made someone else happy/angry/ sad.

Alternative points may be used.

This activity creates a shared experience that is both fun and serious. This level relies more on language and symbolization than the previous levels.

The final session: Step 18

At the final step, *Step 18*, some of the familiar games are repeated. The children's parents are invited to be present and join in. In closing, the trainers guide a talk about what it was like to be part of the programme, and what the individual children noticed in particular. NASSA diplomas are handed out to everyone, and the adults and the children say a few words about each child, focusing on qualities they noticed in that particular child and how rewarding it has been to be with the child and get to know them. A final weather forecast (or one of the other down-regulating activities that the children have learned) is given – this time including the parents. It is time to say goodbye!

Before and after a NASSA process

A brief structured interview has been developed to assess the individual children's emotional and social competences before and after the NASSA programme. The interview is completed by adults who know the child well – for example parents and/or educators/teachers.

Prior to the programme, the interview aids group composition. Because the NASSA programme is developmentally based, it is helpful to make the groups as homogenous as possible with regard to the children's emotional and social development levels (not with regard to diagnosis or symptoms). Two aspects are relevant in considering the group composition: the biological age of the individual children as well as their emotional age and level of social competence.

After the programme, the interview examines functions as feedback to assess the development of the child during the NASSA programme.

Requirements to the NASSA trainer's ability to take part in engaged interactions

Through interactions with secure adults and other children with benevolent intentions, children develop a sense of self-worth and security and the ability to feel enthusiasm and focus in an activity. The NASSA trainers take charge of the games and other activities and need to convey a fundamental sense of optimism, trust and engagement. In order to do that, the NASSA trainers need to possess and express these feelings.

The trainers also need to be curious about who the children are as individuals, their resources and, not least, the causes underlying the children's behaviour and what the children are trying to convey with their behaviour. They have to be able to empathize with the children's situation, put themselves in their place and express this understanding in a way that is perceived as authentic by the children.

The NASSA trainers' ability to build good relations relies, to a high degree, on their curiosity about developing their own relational competences, which requires a high degree of self-agency. The adults may find the children's behaviour unexpected, surprising and provoking. They may be affected by a mood, feel powerless or regret that they failed to regulate a child in time. These feelings and experiences are all part of the process – and one of the reasons why one adult should not attempt to run the group alone.

Cooperation

The trainers do not learn the NASSA approach merely through a training course; they also need practice, personal involvement and adjustment to their own practical method and approach. This is best achieved in a supportive team, where the trainers all work with NASSA and feel confidence in each other's professional competence. We therefore recommend working with other professionals – for example, psychologists with experience of special needs – in the NASSA programme. That allows for ongoing support, feedback and supervision if situations arise where the trainer feels powerless or unsure about what to do. It also offers an opportunity for reflection where NASSA leaders and assistants can evaluate the progress of the children. In this set-up, NASSA offers development opportunities for both the children and adults involved.

12

Friendship, Empathy and Mindfulness in Children's Groups

Developing Children's Natural Capacities

Helle Jensen

For almost four decades, I have worked with children, families and professionals involved in working with children, either as teachers in schools and after-school programmes, as preschool teachers, as health visitors or as psychologists, counsellors and social workers involved in therapy and other forms of treatment for children and families. Whenever I have encountered children who were viewed as particularly challenging by their surroundings, a common denominator – regardless of age or diagnosis (if any) – has been deficient or inadequate self-contact. They have, to some extent, lost touch with themselves. Unfortunately, the adults who are supposed to care for the children and help them re-connect often similarly lose touch with themselves in this situation; their actions are guided more by frustration than by authentic and empathic mindfulness. That makes it difficult to build a relationship – when both children and adults are out of touch with themselves, neither side of the relationship is really present. And since developmental psychology has taught us that relationships are the essential forum for development, it therefore seems obvious that we need to help both children and adults re-connect with themselves as a condition for connecting with others and developing social and emotional skills and capacities (Hart, 2007, 2009).

In the early years of my career, I worked as a clinical psychologist at special needs centres in county and municipal settings. Later, I took additional training in family therapy and relational competencies with family therapist Jesper Juul at the Kempler Institute and began to teach relational competencies and family therapy to professionals. Initially, my teaching dealt exclusively with the relationship itself: interpersonal meetings, dialogue and the use of a personal language, with existential psychology as the overarching frame of reference.

In the mid-1990s, personal challenges in my own life led me to attempt to learn some of the meditation techniques that people have used for millennia to enhance their empathy, mindfulness and attention. I studied at Vaekstcenteret (Centre for Growth) in the Danish town of Nørre Snede, which was founded in the mid-1980s by doctor of philosophy Jes Bertelsen. He is known especially for his studies of various esoteric traditions aimed at promoting empathy, mindfulness and self-reliance through meditation training. Based on these studies, he has concluded that the basic training across these traditions has involved remembering the natural capacities that we are all born with: heart, mind, body, breathing and creativity (Bertelsen, 2010b, 2012, 2013; Jensen et al., 2012). I quickly sensed how helpful it was for me to use these techniques to work with my natural capacities, and how they helped me re-connect with myself, enabling me to stay balanced, even in challenging situations and encounters. This offered a different way of connecting with oneself and others than the dialogue, which had otherwise been my main instrument. But would the techniques also prove useful in my work with children and with the professionals supporting the children?

Based on these questions, I co-founded the Society for the Promotion of Life Wisdom in Children together with a group of people with a diverse range of professional backgrounds but held together by a shared interest in helping children connect with their own inner resources. Since then, we have engaged in a variety of activities – conferences, lectures, courses, books, articles and the initiation of and involvement in research projects – aimed at exploring whether these ancient meditation techniques can be used with children in combination with current educational and psychological insights. In this chapter, I describe what we have found so far, what it takes to apply the techniques, and how they can be applied. Throughout the chapter, I use 'we' to refer to Society for the Promotion of Life Wisdom in Children.

We have mainly worked with groups of children in mainstream school and preschool, including children with a typical development as well as children with various diagnoses (Rasmussen, 2012; Rasmussen and Kjems, 2011). Thus, we have tested our exercises in fairly large groups, as a standard class may include as many as 28 children (Nielsen and Kolmos, 2013), as well as in the smaller preschool groups with a maximum of ten children. In taking on this broad field, we have looked to studies concerning what provides a good environment for learning and development. These studies have found that empathy, group cohesion and mutual interest and respect are key factors in creating an optimum environment for learning and development (Nordenbo *et al.*, 2008). Thus, across school subjects, the development of social and emotional competencies is an essential condition for learning. Another focus in our work has been on the fact that so many children today have diagnoses that include attention deficit as a component. This also makes it interesting for us to discover ways to help individual children enhance their mindfulness and ability to focus their attention. Furthermore, we have found that the exercises that we introduce to the children and the professionals have a positive impact on their stress levels, helping them to rebalance their autonomous nervous system. This makes it easier for them to 'change gear' and thus avoid overloading the system by always running in the highest gear (Bech, Elbrønd and Stubberup, 2012).

Professional relational competencies

In order to lead and work with a group of children, professionals have to be in touch with the qualities that should characterize the relations among the children, the relations between children and adults and the overall atmosphere in the group. This includes qualities such as respect, empathy, mindfulness and focused attention, which are also the qualities that characterize good learning and development environments. This requires relational competencies, defined as the ability 'to "see" the individual on his or her own terms and adapt one's own behaviour accordingly without abandoning one's leadership role and responsibility for the relationship, as well as the ability to remain authentic in the contact' (Juul and Jensen, 2002, p.128). To do this, professionals need the courage to look at all three parties in the relationship: themselves, the relationship itself and the child or children. That is a tall order when facing a whole group of children, each with their own set of experiences and potential ways of learning and being. Perhaps the following example can help to illustrate this somewhat dry definition of relational competencies. The story takes place in a first-grade literacy lesson. The teacher brings in a bag full of objects beginning with the letter 'L'. There are five objects in the bag, and five children are allowed to take turns to reach in and feel inside the bag – without looking – describe the objects to the others and pick which volunteer gets to make a guess. Each time an object has been identified correctly, the teacher writes it on the blackboard with a big, clear 'L' as the initial letter. The entire activity may only take 15 minutes, but it contains a surprising number of elements that the teacher has to pay attention to in order to make the brief activity a meaningful learning experience for as many of the 25 children as possible.

The teacher–child relationship is asymmetrical in nature. The teacher has more power, knowledge and experience and thus also has responsibility for the quality of the relationship. This includes taking responsibility for the mood and atmosphere in the class and highlighting and maximizing mutual respect, empathy and interest. The presence of these qualities will enable the individual children to achieve the state of relaxed focus that is the optimal mental condition for learning (Terjestam, 2014, p.54). The teacher also needs to differentiate the activity to make sure that each individual child encounters appropriate learning and social challenges. This need to accommodate all the individual students requires good leadership competencies and the ability to maintain a firm grasp on the big picture as well as the details. In addition, the teacher's ability to be authentic in the engagement has a crucial impact on the learning environment in the class. Any relationship is an interpersonal meeting, and such a meeting is only possible if the person – in this case, the teacher – has the courage to be fully present in the relationship, aware of the impact of his or her actions and reactions on the child's or the children's development. That requires the professional to be able to 'see' the child: looking behind the child's actions to discover what it will take for the child to be seen and acknowledged in the meeting, on an existential level.

Case study 12.1

Benjamin and Claudia are first-grade students. They both grew up in families where they received extremely limited attention and acknowledgement; this has led to an inner sense of uncertainty that makes them insecure and unfocused in their everyday lives. They react to this in their individual ways: Benjamin by being restless and clingy most of the time, Claudia by being very quiet, slow and absent. Both rely on the teacher's ability to see their need for help to establish the sense of security that they need to learn. For the teacher, Benjamin's behaviour in particular presents a challenge. On this particular day, the teacher does not include Benjamin among the five children who are allowed to describe things inside the bag. Unlike many of his classmates, Benjamin has great difficulty dealing with his frustration over being passed over. The others might respond with a shrug or with a muted, 'Oh no, I never get to go,' but it does not take long before they are ready to return their attention to the activity. Benjamin, on the other hand, cries out in frustration and gets up abruptly, knocking over his chair. In addition to dealing with Benjamin's reaction, the teacher still has to teach the other children. Meanwhile, out of the corner of his eye, the teacher also sees that the light in Claudia's eyes, which had briefly lit up when she cautiously raised her hand in the hope of being picked, has now also been extinguished. It takes skill to find the right words to help the children refocus on the activity – for example, 'I can tell that you are upset, Claudia; you would have liked to go, and so would you, Benjamin. It's tough not to be picked when you really wanted to' – while resting a hand on the shoulder of the child who is standing ready, waiting to reach into the bag. The teacher's response gives all three children a chance to relax, because they are not blamed for their desire to learn. Also, they are not criticized or lectured about the need to wait their turn, which would only serve to increase their restlessness and thus diminish their chances of calming down enough to learn.

Although two decades have passed since Daniel Stern (Stern, 1995, 2004) and others changed the paradigm within developmental psychology, the old mindset still prevails in everyday situations. Children are born as social beings capable of entering into relationships with others, and throughout childhood, they remain profoundly dependent on being surrounded by adults who are able to include them in relationships based on equality. In this context, 'equality' means that both partners' points of view, emotions, experiences and self-concepts are treated as equally valuable for the establishment and development of the relationship, even if the relationship is asymmetrical in the sense that they differ in status and power (Jensen, 2009, 2010; Juul and

Jensen, 2002). To achieve this, the adult has to have the courage to enter into the relationship as one human being with another. The adult also needs to be aware how his or her own way of being helps shape the child's development. This brings the professional into play in a new way that not only engages his or her professional qualities but also his or her personal qualities. In this paradigm, the professional is put on the spot much more than in the paradigm that relied on reprimands or punishment as the means to promote children's development, and where the adult was always right. To work with children's groups, adults need to be willing to embrace the new paradigm and acquire the skills that are required to operationalize its inherent values.

A key skill in this context is to be authentic in one's contact with oneself and with the children. Therefore, part of the training for working with the children has involved learning to master a personal language that makes it possible to engage with respect for the other's personal integrity. To that end, we train professionals by examining the challenging situations they experience with the children. In an approach resembling collegial supervision, they learn to examine their own share and role in any conflicts that arise and to assume a leadership role and take responsibility for the relationship. The training is very direct in its approach to examining how key values – equality, respect and empathy – can be preserved in a tense situation in order to safeguard both the child's and the professional's integrity and self-esteem in a disagreement or conflict as much as possible; perhaps the experience may even lead to positive growth.

Part of the training thus consists in developing the professionals' relational competencies. We have found that the components involved in this training are largely the same as the components that are key in ensuring children's social and emotional growth and development. Thus, interactions based on equality, respect, empathy and mutual interest provide the optimum conditions for growth and development for both children and adults. These values form the basis for the basic meditation exercises that are described in this chapter. Another benefit of these exercises is that they are equally helpful for children and adults, providing a win–win scenario where children and adults can share a type of activity that is beneficial for both.

Natural competencies: the Pentagon

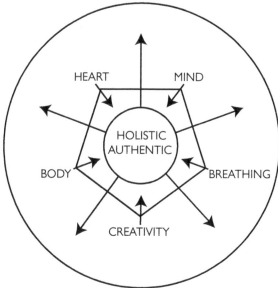

Figure 12.1: *The Pentagon: Heart, mind, body, breathing and creativity*
(Bertelsen, in Jensen, 2014)

One encouraging aspect of the exercises is that they are all based on something that we already know how to do. They build on competencies that we all possess from birth. Naturally, we are not born with these competencies fully unfolded, but we are born with the potential for unfolding them:

> The natural competencies are based on capacities that everyone already possesses: the heart's capacity for openness, the mind's capacity for alertness and for a more profound centring. The tools for discovering and stimulating these innate, natural possibilities are actually quite simple and essentially consist in making room for and being mindful of what is already there: the ability to sense the body, to feel from the heart, to breathe deeply and mindfully, to allow spontaneous creativity to flow unhindered and to be in the wakeful awareness of the moment... (Bertelsen, 2010b, pp.62–63)

Just think of a time when you watched a happy baby: full and content, simply being in the world. The infant's body is relaxed, perhaps in motion, the breath goes all the way into the belly with ease, the mind is alert, the heart is beating, and the child has an open emotional stance towards his or her surroundings, responding with natural creativity to whatever impulses arise in the environment or within the child, moving in response to the impulses from the body, maybe stretching after sleep or turning his or her head to attend to a noise. In this state, the infant is in touch with the five natural competencies that the exercises address.

Centuries of training by people who have worked with meditation exercises in the context of various cultural traditions have shown that working with these competencies can lead to a more holistic experience for the individual and a stronger sense of authenticity (Bertelsen, 2009, 2010b, 2012, 2013). Here, I offer a brief description of the individual competencies (for a more in-depth description, see Jensen *et al.*, 2012, and Jensen *et al.*, 2014).

Heart

On the emotional level, the heart is associated with qualities such as the capacity for giving and receiving kindness, love, acceptance, appreciation, compassion, empathy and trust. Since we are social beings from birth and develop in relationships (Juul and Jensen, 2002; Stern, 1995, 2004), it is essential that our need to feel valuable in close personal relationship is met. For children, this applies to both the family and school context and interactions with other children. Heart-centred exercises strengthen the sense of attachment and the awareness of the others in the group. These exercises may be based on games or massage, for example.

Mind

Very broadly speaking, this refers to the ability to simply be alert and aware that we have a waking mind, which may be either focused or openly observing, but which is always there. Paying attention to attention can help us strengthen our mindfulness. In the simple training I describe here, this is often pursued by being aware of breaks or pauses – the pause between thoughts or the pause between breaths.

When I have taught this to children (aged 7–14 years), they are often surprisingly quick to grasp the point. It can be done in simple steps. Step one might be to try to observe one's thoughts, monitoring the flow of images, emotions and content in the mind. Next, you could draw attention to the brief natural pauses that occur in this mind flow. Gaps between the thoughts. One image stops and disappears before the next appears. A thought pops up, it is present, and then it goes away again – pause – and another thought appears. (Bertelsen, 2010b)

Body

Unlike our thoughts, for example, the body is always in the moment, never in the past or the future. That is why good body awareness improves our capacity for being present in the moment and for relating to and connecting with others. As mentioned earlier, relaxed focus is the optimal mental state for learning, so for that reason too, it is important to stay in touch with one's body and to learn to be aware of it to avoid unnecessary tension that detracts attention and energy from the here and now.

Breathing

Breathing offers an effective anchor for turning our attention inward. Mindful breathing also helps us connect with the body's mid-line. Focusing attention on our breathing also often leads to deeper breathing and activates the parasympathetic nervous system, which is the part of the autonomous nervous system that helps us gear down. Shifting gears and introducing breaks are key factors in the effort to develop empathy and attention (Bech *et al.*, 2012).

Creativity

In this context, creativity should be understood as a broader concept than how it is typically applied. Here, it describes a sort of fundamental creativity that enables us to respond creatively to the impulses that reach us constantly – from our mind, from our senses and from our body. We react to and act on these impulses, and being aware of these impulses and our responses to them enhances our ability to be present in the moment. For example: where did my impulse to keep writing, just now, arise? Engaging in activities that we normally view as creative, such as drawing and painting, singing or dancing, also offers an opportunity for greater mindfulness by enhancing our attention of the creative capacity itself.

Training principles

As we grow up, most of us lose touch with these five innate capacities to some extent, because we devote so much energy to developing a functioning self (Jensen, 2014). Hence, we need to re-establish our connection with these natural capacities, a task that is often easier for children than for adults, because children are not as far removed from their original contactful state. Naturally, it is easier for some children than for others, but the training described above (Bertelsen, 2010b) has also been used with children with multiple and severe challenges. One group of 11–12-year-olds, for example, includes a child who has lost both parents and is now in foster care. Another child was adopted from Asia and has been diagnosed with early attachment disorder. A third child in the group lives alone with the father, while the mother is an alcoholic and lives on the street. These children take part in the exercises, but as with any form of learning, the teacher needs to consider and accommodate their developmental stage and their state on the given day. On some days, therefore, a given child may require extra support to be able to take part or may not take part at all, just as the child may sit out a maths lesson because he or she simply cannot focus and needs a break. As a general rule, however, everyone is included.

Once the connection with the individual capacities has been re-established, the child needs to practice staying in touch with several capacities at once. Eventually, the child practises being aware of the need to take a break and sensing the inherent value of breaks. Thus, the basic training principles are:

- Remember the natural, innate capacities.
- Gradually engage multiple capacities at once.
- Remember taking breaks and changing gears.

Learning to stay in touch with these capacities enhances our general capacity for staying in touch with ourselves, including our capacity for:

- balanced self-reliance without becoming self-sufficient

- mindfulness or focused awareness

- empathic engagements with others.

These are exactly the qualities that are strengthened in the work we do in children's groups based on the Pentagon and a focus on the role of pauses and breaks. Naturally, to teach the exercises to children, the teachers have to have first-hand practical experience with them. In addition to personal knowledge of the individual exercises, this also involves working the exercises into one's daily routine in order to have experience with them on an ongoing basis. Essentially, this is no different than any other form of teaching; teachers have to have a firm grasp of their subject, and they need to engage with it continuously to be able to build an optimal learning environment. In principle, this is quite simple, but that is not to say that it is easy! To build an environment where children feel at ease and are able to relax and be present in the moment, teachers must have good relational skills. This is not something that is acquired once and for all; it is a skill that requires lifelong training and development.

The role of exercises in the activities with children's groups

The exercises promote general human qualities that lay the foundation for working with individual school subjects and areas of development in preschool. The target group for this book is professionals who work with groups of children aged 4–12 years, which covers a wide and diverse range in terms of group sizes and subject matter. The exercises can be adapted to match the children's age and the size of the group. As mentioned above, the exercises promote self-reliance, mindfulness and empathy. Many factors in a child's life may cause the child to periodically lose touch with themselves and thus miss out on opportunities to develop the core qualities mentioned above. This may happen when the children face temporary challenges in their life, such as family issues due to bereavement, illness, unemployment, divorce, custody arrangements, etc. The child may also face challenges related to the school environment, well-being in the class, difficulties with school work, etc. In addition to these challenges, which are always present to some extent in a typical group of school or preschool children, there is the common challenge of a hectic and busy everyday life with many impulses and many quick changes and choices to be made throughout the day. Often, there is no time to pause or simply gear down instead of staying in the highest gear all day. This means that the exercises have their place in the contexts where the children spend time together on a daily basis with the common overall agenda of development and learning and, for preschoolers, the additional agenda of meeting the parents' need for childcare.

In the following, I present examples of exercises and suggest suitable settings and contexts for the individual activities.

At the beginning of the school day

It is helpful for teachers to begin the day by connecting – however briefly – with all the children that they are going to spend time with in the following lesson or lessons. Such an activity also helps mark the beginning of something new. One way to do it is to greet each other, perhaps simply by saying 'good morning' or by standing in a circle and holding hands while saying 'hello'. Next, you can guide the children to sense their own body and breathing. With younger children you can do this in the form of a game where everyone gets to move. For example, you can have the children pair up for a 'wheelbarrow race' or, if there are many children, play 'ambulance'. In the ambulance game, three or four children try to catch or 'tag' the others. When a child is tagged, he or she lies down on the spot and waits for some of the other children to come over, and carry him or her to hospital (a thick mat in the middle of the room). While the children are carrying a 'tag victim', they form an ambulance and are safe from being tagged. Once in the hospital, the 'tag victim' recovers by counting to ten and is now free to rejoin the game.

With both younger and older children, you can also use a grounding activity, where the children bend at the knee and 'bounce' in place without raising their feet from the floor; first on two legs, then on one leg, as they challenge themselves and their sense of balance by moving the body and the other leg. This invariably focuses attention on the feet and leads to better grounding. The group may complete the sequence by standing in a circle sensing their feet, their hands, their heads and, finally, their breathing, before rounding it all off by holding hands and saying 'hello', making eye contact, one by one, with everyone in the circle.

You can end the exercise here. If you would like to add some quiet time after the physical activity, you can ask the children to sit on the floor in a circle while you take them through a guided mental exercise, such as the following.

Someone you care for

The children sit down after sensing their feet, hands, head and breathing while standing.

When they are seated, they place their hands on their heart. They sit for a while, sensing the heartbeat and the whole area around the heart, sensing how it feels.

Then they are asked to think of someone they care for very much and to sense that feeling in their heart. They might think of a family member, a good friend or a cuddly toy.

Now, tell them to allow the sensation that this produces in their heart to spread to their entire body, taking some time to sense what that feels like.

For the younger children, the exercise might end here, while the older children might be instructed to get up and walk around the room quietly, silently greeting everyone else in the room by making eye contact.

When they are done, they return to their seats, sit down and wait quietly until everyone is seated.

When the children need a break or a change of gear

After working with a school subject for a while, the class may need a change of gear. This is the case both when there is a good and intense mood, and when it is harder to maintain the necessary focus and intensity. The following exercise, called 'chair jumping', is helpful both when the group is very restless and unfocused and when the energy level is running low:

Chair jumping – changing gears and attention

Stand facing a chair.

Within the span of one minute, climb up to stand on the seat of the chair and then back down to the floor as many times as possible.

Then do one single round, where you climb up to stand on the seat of the chair and then climb down. You can only do this once; it has to take a full minute, and you have to keep moving the entire time.

Now do one final round with your eyes closed.

End the exercise by sitting on the chair.

Sense your body.

Sense your hands, feet, face and the back of your neck.

Sense your breathing.

Sense your heart.

Sense your body, breathing and heart at the same time.

(Jensen, 2014, p.101)

The chair jumping activity involves a change of gear where the children go up in gear as well as down in gear within the same exercise. Children often need that, and this type of break is therefore a good alternative to the instruction to 'go outside, and run around the building to get a breath of fresh air!', which is widely practised in schools and other children's groups. The exercise does more than simply replace the run, because it also helps the children turn their attention inward – connecting with themselves – which is a condition both for maintaining one's focus and attention in individual activities and for remaining focused and empathic in engagements with others.

Another way of introducing a break or a change of gear is *massage*. Over the course of the school day, children often build up tension in the body as a result of the many academic, social and emotional challenges they face. This tension often causes them to lose touch with their body and breathing. Some children have learning difficulties, and find it very straining to meet the demands they face; others face challenges in interactions with the other children during recess or in less structured learning contexts; and others again have trouble dealing with large groups with all the noise and chaos they tend to involve. Some children find all these areas challenging. When using massage, of course, it is important to know how the individual children feel about touching and being touched and to allow for individual solutions – for example only giving and not receiving massage, or to opt out entirely. It is always important to take the child seriously, but it is similarly important to talk to the child to explore the source of the reluctance. Sometimes it may be possible to try something new and have a successful outcome, even if the child is initially reluctant.

The following exercise strengthens the children's attention, empathy and ability to be present in the moment.

Shoulder massage in pairs or in a circle –
empathy and changing gears

When instructing the massage, it is once again important to keep the basic principles of the exercises in mind: remembering the natural capacities, engaging multiple capacities at the same time, and remembering the importance of taking breaks.

Carefully guide the massage by instructing both the seated child, who receives the massage, and the child standing behind the chair, who gives the massage, to begin by first sensing the surface. This involves sensing the contact between the body and the chair and between their feet and the floor, before connecting with their breathing and sensing both the body and their breathing at once. Only then does the standing child place his or her hands on the shoulders of the seated child, and the actual massage begins.

During the massage, the children are silent and receive ongoing instructions reminding them to stay connected to their breathing, thus remaining connected, throughout, to themselves and to their partner.

When the massage is over, the standing child leaves his or her hands on the shoulders of the partner a little while before removing them, and then both children hold their positions a little while longer, without speaking.

Another way to use massage is after a physically active exercise that the children have done standing up. Here you can round off the activity by having the children stand in a circle, massaging the shoulders of the child in front of them and receiving a massage from the child behind them. This is often a little less intense than the paired massage, so the teacher will have to choose what seems most appropriate in the moment. For younger children, the instruction may take the form of storytelling.

Sensing the pause

In principle, virtually all exercises where the children work in pairs with massage and relaxation can be used to gear down and strengthen attachment and empathy. However, teachers should be aware that these situations often involve a tendency to direct most of the attention to the outside environment, which means losing touch with oneself and the well spring one draws from when assisting others by being empathic and present in the moment. Therefore, we pause during the exercises to ask the individual children to sense their own body (with more or less detailed guidance) and their own breathing. In connection with physically active exercises, where the children engage in various games, either in pairs or as a group, it is also important for the children to pause, stand still and sense their body and breathing and, sometimes, own heartbeat.

Contact and changing gears

For this exercise, the children may be either seated or lying down. Here I am going to describe a guided exercise where the children are seated on chairs. The guiding is very detailed and may be appropriate for older children. Younger children will need fewer words and thus also a briefer guiding.

Find a comfortable sitting position on your chair. Close your eyes, if you like. Sense your feet. Move them a little, sense them from the inside. Sense your toes. Sense the soles of your feet and the floor beneath them. Sense your legs. Sense the contact from the floor up through your feet and legs.

Now contact your hands. Move them a little, stretch and bend your fingers. Sense your hands from the inside. Sense your fingers. Sense your arms and the way they feel on your body.

Also sense the places where your body is resting against the chair. Sense your spine, sit up straight, and notice whether you are holding your head in a way that requires the smallest amount of energy to hold it. Relax the muscles in the back of your neck and in your face.

Now sense your entire body at once. And while you are doing that, allow your attention to be right here, right now. Allow it to rest on what is while it is there. Notice your body – how it is full of life, even when you are sitting still. Notice that when you breathe, it causes a little bit of movement in your body. Notice it, and let it be.

Notice that there are outside sounds. Simply register them, and let them be.

Notice how there may be thoughts coming and going. Simply notice them, and let them be. Allow them to come and go without interfering with them. Look at the thoughts the same way you do when you look into the sky and watch the clouds drift by. Maybe you can also notice that there is a small pause between the thoughts. Simply notice it, and allow it to be the way it is.

When you are sitting like this, you may also notice that your head and body calm down while you are sitting here, fully awake and calm, noticing what is going on inside your body and outside your body.

Then get ready to return to this room with your attention. Move a little, open your eyes, and be ready to continue your day here.

(Jensen, 2014, p.88)

However, a change of gear may also involve going up a gear, which implies physical activity and a faster pace. Here, you can find inspiration in all the familiar games that involve changing pace, for example dancing to music, 'freezing' when the music stops and remaining 'frozen' until the music begins again. When using these physically active exercises, you should include short breaks where the children are asked to focus on their breathing, their body, their heart or their mind.

Rounding off the lesson or the day

It is always a good idea to mark the end of a lesson or an activity, where we may have shared something meaningful and in any case have spent a small portion of our lives together. Especially in situations where the interactions may have been intense and perhaps emotionally charged – for example a lesson where the group discussed the well-being and atmosphere in the class or where they talked about ethical or existential questions based on a literary text – it sends a signal about the importance of children's and adults' time together that we take the time to round off the experience.

One way of doing this is to have the children stand in a circle for a moment, noticing their body and their feet against the floor, and then imagining breathing in through their heart and exhaling through their arms and hands. Although this is only make-believe, children often find this sort of thing really easy and also often sense a warm feeling and a good connection with their hands when they do it. Then have them hold each other's hands and give them a gentle squeeze as they look into each other's eyes as a way of saying 'goodbye' and thanks for now. Another way of rounding off is to have the children stand in a circle holding hands while everyone says a few words about what it was like to participate today. For many, that can be slightly more challenging, so you will need to use your judgment to determine what is most appropriate for your group.

Informing and involving the children's parents

It is always important to have the parents' support when working with children. The attachment and loyalty between parents and children has a positive effect when the parents support the experiences and challenges the children meet. Conversely, it is harder for children to acquire new learning or to enjoy an interaction if they sense that their parents do not approve of or have any faith in what the children are doing. Therefore, the task of informing and involving the parents is important. You can do this by organizing a brief orientation about the capacities that the exercises strengthen and develop in the children (as described in the introduction to this chapter), combined with a brief exercise programme to be carried out with the parents. In the schools that I have worked with, I have often given this orientation in connection with a parent–teacher meeting, similar to the orientation they receive about the other school subjects and scheduled activities for the school year. To help explain the work, I have shown clips from one of the three films that have been produced about the topic (Rasmussen, 2008, 2012; Rasmussen and Kjems, 2011).

If possible, you can also use the exercises with parents and children together – for example, in connection with events where children and parents are already doing activities together at the school. In connection with the courses we have held for school and preschool teachers and children over the years, we have heard that some parents and children use the exercises as part of the bedtime routine, as a way to begin homework sessions or as a way to relax when the family members meet up after work and school. In my work with schools, I have also taken part in parent–teacher meetings where I have found that the families also need inspiration for things that they can do together as a family in order to gear down and relax from the many challenges of work and family life rather than going to yoga, mindfulness or other individual activities to achieve relaxation. For example, several families have said that the exercise 'Someone you care for' is very rewarding for them to do together, or that listening to a guided relaxation or some relaxing music together can provide a good change of gear during the day or help them calm down when it is bedtime.

Conclusion

How can we work with mindfulness, empathy and attention to help ensure an environment that is as inclusive as possible for the individual children? The concept of inclusion is that it is the group environment that needs to adapt. Thus, inclusion does not depend on the personal qualities of the individual child but on qualities in the group environment, which places rather high demands on the group and especially on the adults in charge who are responsible for shaping the group environment. As mentioned earlier, the purpose of the exercises is:

- balanced self-reliance without becoming self-sufficient
- mindfulness or focused awareness
- empathic engagements with others.

These capacities play an important role in securing a quality group environment by creating a good learning and development environment in the group/class (Nordenbo *et al.*, 2008). Working with these aspects has never been an easy task, and never will be, and the challenges are many. For example, it will always require the professionals to continue developing their relational competencies and to be aware of their own role and responsibility, as the professional's ability to secure the key qualities of respect, interest, empathy and mindfulness in the group are crucial for inclusion.

On a theoretical level, the conditions for this work have never been better, since we now know how important relationships and thus the group community are for children's development. On a practical level, it is still going to take a considerable amount of work and training to translate this theoretical insight into everyday practices in schools and preschools.

The preliminary studies we are currently carrying out in cooperation with VIA University College in Aarhus and six of the schools that take trainee teachers are showing that school and preschool teachers see many benefits in including the exercises in their lessons. Several of the participating teachers have described that they enjoy teaching more, and that they find it easier to build an inclusive environment.

There are, however, remaining challenges that we hope to address together in this research and development project. The main challenge in primary and lower secondary school is for the teachers to find the time and courage to work on their own personal development as professionals. This involves not only doing the exercises on their own, which takes time and a regular routine, but also engaging in developing relationship in the collegial community. It is also challenging to convey the exercises and the mindset behind them to parents and to colleagues who are not involved in the project. Experience shows that the more frequently the teachers in the project practise this, the more they embed this mindset in their own work. In turn, this also enables them convey the mindset and the practices more effectively to others. Based on the preliminary findings, there are fewer challenges involved in using the practices in the classroom. Here, the general feedback is that the classes where the teachers have integrated the exercises into their classroom practice have a calmer working environment, the children are better able to concentrate and pay attention, and the class well-being is better. We also find that the teachers are showing a high degree of creativity in reaching and accommodating the children who have initial difficulties with the exercises.

The main point is to remember all the natural capacities, and that all children differ in how easily accessible the individual capacities are. Here too, teachers therefore need to offer differentiated instruction and cover every aspect of the Pentagon. Sometimes, this means offering a child individual support to take part in the exercises.

With regard to implementing mindfulness, attention and empathy exercises in our work with children, it is early days yet in Danish preschools and schools, and at this point, we only have the preliminary findings to guide us. Fortunately, however, our work is followed closely by researchers from the Danish School of Education, Aarhus University and VIA University Colleges, which means that we can expect to see research findings in the coming years. We hope that these findings will align with our preliminary experiences to support the inclusion of these important exercises in the daily work in schools and preschools.[1]

---

1   For training and courses, see https://trainingempathy.com.

References

Bech, G., Elbrønd, M. and Stubberup, M. (2012) *Next Practice – Best Practice: Familierettet Psykoedukation for Traumatiserede Flygtninge.* Aarhus: SYNerGAIA.

Bertelsen, J. (2009) 'Kan man lære børn selvberoenhed og empati?' *Kognition og pædagogik* 71(9), 24–30.

Bertelsen, J. (2010b) *Et Essay om Indre Frihed.* København: Rosinante.

Bertelsen, J. (2012) *Hvordan er muligheden for at bevare og udvikle børns eksistentielle og spirituelle intelligens?* (lecture). Available at www.rosinante-co.dk/et-essay-om-indre-frihed-id34414, accessed on 27 May 2016.

Bertelsen, J. (2013) *Det Drejer sig om Kærlighed: Undervisning med Jes Bertelsen.* Copenhagen: Rosinante.

Hart, S. (2007) Spejlneuroner, kontakt og omsorg. Psykolog Nyt, 61(11): 14–20.

Hart, S. (2009) *Den følsomme hjerne: Hjernens udvikling gennem tilknytning og samhørighedsbånd.* Copenhagen: Hans Reitzels Forlag.

Jensen, H. (2010) 'Den nærværende lærer og pædagog: Hjertet i pædagogisk arbejde.' In: L. Svinth, (ed.) *Nærvær i pædagogisk praksis: Mindfulness i skole og daginstitution.* Copenhagen: Akademisk Forlag.

Jensen, H. (2014) *Nærvær og Empati i Skolen.* Copenhagen: Akademisk Forlag.

Jensen, H., Bertelsen, J., Juul, J., Hildebrandt, S., Høeg, P. and Stubberup, M. (2012) *Empati: Det der Holder Verden Sammen.* Copenhagen: Rosinante.

Juul, J. and Jensen, H. (2002) *Pædagogisk Relationskompetence: Fra Lydighed til Ansvarlighed.* Copenhagen: Apostrof.

Nordenbo, S. E., Søgaard Larsen, S. M., Wendt, R., Østergaard, S. and Tiftikci, N. (2008) *Lærerkompetencer og Elevers Læring i Førskole og Skole: Et Systematisk review Udført for Kunnskapsdepartementet.* Oslo: Aarhus; Danmarks Pædagogiske Universitetsforlag.

Rasmussen, M. (2008) *The Ninth Intelligence – Intelligence of the Heart. As Practiced in a Danish School.* Available at www.filmkompagniet.dk/english-subtitles/, accessed on 11 July 2016.

Rasmussen, M. (2012) *Ro og Nærvær i Skolen: To Film fra Risskov Skole og Langå Skole.* Available with English subtitles at www.filmkompagniet.dk/english-subtitles/, accessed on 11 July 2016.

Rasmussen, M. and Kjems, J. (2011) *Mindfulness og Empati i Skolen – Seks Øvelser i Praksis: Den Nødvendige Empati.* Available online at www.filmkompagniet.dk/english-subtitles/ (see 'Empathy needed.' and 'What to do? – A training model.' by Jes Bertelsen).

Stern, D. (1995) *Motherhood Constellation: A Unified View of Parent-Infant Psychotherapy.* New York, NY: Basic Books.

Stern, D. (2004) *Present Moment in Psychotherapy and Everyday Life.* New York, NY: W. W. Norton.

Terjestam, Y. (2014) *Mindfulness i skolen: mental sundhed og læring hos børn og unge (Mindfulness in School: Mental Health and Learning in Children and Adolescents).* Frydenlund: Denmark.

13

Multi-Family Therapy with Groups of Children and Their Parents/Carers

Serena Potter

This chapter describes the application of a multi-family therapy model to families with children presenting with emotional and behavioural difficulties in schools in inner-city London. It was developed at the Marlborough Family Service, a systemically oriented child and family consultation service (Asen, Dawson and McHugh, 2001). Multi-family work is carried out with groups of children aged 5–14 years and their parents/carers. Some of the work is based in mainstream primary and secondary schools and it takes place in 'Family Classes' which run once a week. In addition, there is a specialist 'Family Education Centre' (FEC), which delivers intensive multi-family therapy four mornings a week, and children return to their respective mainstream schools in the afternoons. The aim in both settings is to provide a workshop context for children and parents together, under the guidance of family therapists/teachers, in order to increase resilience, improve affect regulation and foster better attachment relationships. Although specifically designed to meet the needs of children with complex emotional, psychological and behavioural difficulties, the approach can also be used with whole classes of children and their parents/ carers as part of programmes aimed at strengthening home/school relationships, reinforcing the possibilities of working with parents in schools as an integral part of teaching, and generally improving social skills in mainstream classrooms. Using multi-family activities as the context for change allows for different people's preferred ways of learning, and avoids an over-emphasis on the academic and linguistic capacities of parents and children. Although the reflection aspect of the model may in part rely on verbal skills, the use of an action-based approach offers an opportunity for all involved to use their relative strengths in learning, whether these are more visual, auditory, kinaesthetic or tactile.

Learning by experiencing

Most people learn well by 'doing' – by experiencing rather than simply being 'told'. For example, when children are learning about a historical period, they are likely to remember and understand it better if they have a multi-sensory experience. Being told about the period and reading from a variety of sources is one aspect, but dressing up in clothes of that period, preparing and eating a meal with food from that time, linking it with stories, poetry and performing arts, and generally bringing it alive, making it fun, interesting and capturing the imagination, hugely enriches the learning process. In the same way, participating in a multi-family activity, actually doing exercises or games rather than just talking, provides a more lived experience. Non-verbal and para-verbal modes of interaction are particularly relevant for parents and children who have a different first language, or who present with learning difficulties or speech and language problems. A multi-sensory approach links with the philosophy of Friedrich Froebel (1782–1852), who coined the term 'Kindergarten' and who is one of the most influential pioneers of early childhood teaching practice (Bruce 2005). Along with Maria Montessori and Rudolf Steiner, Froebel's influence on mainstream education has been significant. It could be said that his approach was 'systemic' as he saw the family as the most important first educator in a child's life. This was somewhat revolutionary in the 18th century as it implied working *with* rather than separately *from* the family when teaching children. Froebel saw the school as a community, where family and school could work together. He believed that the holistic development of the child was key, with the curriculum including the development of the physical, spiritual, feeling and intellectual aspects (Bruce 2005), and that learning through play and first-hand experience with all subjects being linked and integrated, as in life itself, was vital. An emphasis on self-discipline and of managing the 'disciplining' of a child through discussion, interaction and the development of a child's reflective capacity are illustrative of Froebel's philosophy. Froebel also thought that parents, the family, other children and the wider community teach and guide children and are influential in developing their emotional wellbeing and socialization skills.

Personal learning

I trained as a primary school teacher in the 1980s in London. My Bachelor of Education degree in Education and Contemporary Dance was completed at the Froebel Institute, part of Roehampton University. The philosophy of Friedrich Froebel was key during those four years of study as I learnt about child development and the ideology and philosophy of education, as well as about teaching, learning and the delivery of the curriculum. Froebel's philosophy of education instilled in me the importance of:

- considering the development of the 'whole child'

- learning through play

- the parent/carer as the child's 'first teacher'

- the importance of first-hand experience and learning by 'doing' with all subjects being connected, as in real life.

I subsequently worked as a teacher for many years in a 'Froebel School' where this philosophy formed the basis of the school ethos and was integral to the approach to learning. There was an emphasis on developing 'social skills', on being active in one's learning, on learning *how* to learn and on developing children's empathy and emotional intelligence. My main area of interest became Personal, Social and Health Education (PSHE), a subject in the English curriculum. The next stage of my professional career was to develop my interest in working with families. I learnt about systemic family therapy, and more specifically, multi-family therapy, at the Marlborough Family Service in London. I started first as a teacher in the Family Education Centre, working with and learning from my colleagues Brenda McHugh and Neil Dawson, themselves originally teachers who later trained as family therapists, and who had been developing a school-based multi-family therapy model for children with emotional and behavioural difficulties since the 1980s (Asen *et al.*, 2001). Alongside this work, I completed my systemic and family psychotherapy training at the Institute of Family Therapy in London. The multi-family model fitted well with my beliefs about education, namely that children thrive best when the two systems they inhabit, home and school, combine and work together. This was at a time when, in England, there was a strong emphasis on a content-driven curriculum, on achievement in an assessment- and exam-focused system, and at the same time a reduction of a broad-based creative curriculum for children.

Problem pupils – problem families?

We are a team of colleagues who are all dual-qualified as teachers and family therapists. Parents attend with their children and we work closely with each child's school and teachers, enabling the strengthening of lines of communication between the home and school systems. The children that are referred to the FEC are aged 5–14 years and come from schools in central London. They tend to be at high risk of permanent exclusion from their mainstream schools, and are thus likely to lose life chances via education and are vulnerable to entering or being maintained in a downward spiral of failure, social isolation, exclusion and criminality. Behaviours that teachers find difficult to manage in the classroom include:

- persistently disruptive behaviour

- hyperactivity and inattention, poor impulse control

- verbal and physical aggression

- anger

- refusal to follow instructions

- anxiety

- poor school attendance/refusal.

A common feature for many of the children is that they are described as having 'poor social skills', with difficulties in their interactions with other children, finding the classroom and playground places of hardship, becoming quickly distressed or angry and being isolated with few 'good friendships'. These children tend to have adults assigned to them (for example teaching assistants) – often for lessons and those trickier, less structured times such as playtimes. Schools find themselves in a bind, feeling the need to supervise the child at all times in order to keep them and others safe, but the very act of providing such intense support can isolate the child further from their peers, making them even more 'different' and removing the opportunity to develop the skills necessary for independence and autonomy. Many children referred to the FEC have also been described as having 'speech and language difficulties', often due to problems with receptive or expressive language, and may have been given extra support individually or in a small group.

A systemic framework, paying attention to context, takes into account the situations in which the children find themselves. Most obviously this is why the family situation of the child is always considered. Children may be living as 'young carers', preoccupied with concerns about their parent(s), they may be or have been in the past living in situations where they are continually on 'high alert' and vigilant, and they may have complex attachment difficulties. Within many of the families, the following can be found:

- parental depression and other mental health difficulties.
- disrupted family relationships
- bereavement
- substance misuse
- family violence
- migration and refugee issues
- social isolation/housing difficulties.

The family class work in schools was designed to work with children and families at an earlier stage of distress, and admission to the FEC was only considered for highly complex and 'chronic' cases. However, in practice, many of the cases we see in mainstream schools are as complex as those attending the FEC. A benefit of the family class work in mainstream schools is that it reaches a far larger number of families and, being school-based, mitigates the stigma that is often attached to a child and adolescent mental health clinic in our society.

Multi-family therapy – history and concepts

Multi-family therapy (MFT) derives its theory and practice from a combination of systemic family therapy and group therapy. It is widely acknowledged that Peter Laqueur, a psychiatrist working in

New York in the early 1950s with people with schizophrenia, is the founder of multiple family group therapy. Over the years MFT has been developed in a number of different settings and for a variety of needs. In 1980s England, the Marlborough Family Service, under the leadership of Alan Cooklin and then Eia Asen, developed a multi-family approach for highly complex 'multi-problem' families. These are usually involved with a considerable number of professionals and agencies and they experience long-term entrenched difficulties and little change (Asen, 2002). An intensive version of the model, with families attending several times per week and being immersed in multi-family therapy seemed a possible way forward and the 'Family Day Unit' – a setting in which up to eight whole families would attend daily for months – was thus born. The teachers working with the children of families attending the Family Day Unit realized that the emotional and behavioural needs of these children in an educational context were vital to consider. Consequently, the FEC was created (Asen et al., 2001).

Central to the model is the idea of 'families helping families'. Often, families attending the multi-family groups or the FEC are isolated in their lives; they may be exhausted from the difficulties they are facing and have run out of resources. Repetitive problematic patterns of behaviour and interactions which lead to problems can be challenged in the multi-family setting, with new ideas and perspectives offered. McFarlane (1982, p.17) described this beautifully when he stated: 'Families have an accurate eye for problems as therapists do and are remarkably attuned to the structural and interactional problems of other families'. The technique of 'cross-family linkage,' where children may 'partner' with another's parent during an activity, immediately offers the likelihood of new and different interactions, leading to the opportunity to experience themselves differently in relation to others. Parents are often more empathic and curious when working with someone else's child. Group cohesion is also likely to develop, encouraging inter-family connections to be made, giving hope for change and introducing new perspectives on old patterns. The teacher/ therapist's task, as an MFT coach, is to create contexts for change – for example via inventing or co-constructing with families activities and exercises which thematize typical problematic family issues and allow for these to be experienced and re-viewed differently, allowing the possibility of change.

Why *multi-family* therapeutic work?

- to overcome isolation and stigmatization
- to compare experiences and learn from each other
- to find oneself mirrored in others
- to stimulate multiple new perspectives
- to intensify interactions and experiences
- to observe and challenge stuck patterns
- to move from a helpless to helpful stance
- to share strategies
- to benefit from positive group pressure and to offer hope
- to provide mutual support and feedback
- to experience oneself in different relationship contexts (e.g. surrogate parenting and cross-family linkage)
- to establish social/community connections
- to strengthen mentalizing and attachments.

Mentalizing (Fonagy *et al.*, 1991, pp.200–217) is a term describing the ability to 'perceive and interpret human behaviour in terms of intentional mental states e.g. needs, desires, feelings, beliefs, goals, purposes, and reasons.' This refers to, amongst other processes, the human capacity to see oneself through another's eyes and to imagine, but not definitely 'know', what someone else might be thinking or feeling. This dual ability to make a reasonable guess about others' internal states *and* also to recognize and reflect upon one's own internal state is linked to the quality of attachment relationships (Asen and Fonagy, 2012). Past experiences and specific situations, such as being under intense stress, can temporarily compromise the capacity for mentalizing, and often 'fight, flight or freeze' responses take over. For children in the classroom who may be in a heightened state of arousal for much of the time, hyper-vigilant and hyper-reactive, their mentalizing skills become easily lost or poorly developed. Working with these children and their parents together offers the opportunity to address and repair attachment difficulties and enhance mentalizing capacity in both child and parent. Enhanced mentalizing leads to improved attachment relationships – and better attachment enhances mentalizing. Therapists aim to enhance family members' understanding of each other's – and their own – thinking and feeling states.

Multi-family activities

Multi-family activities and games aim to improve mentalizing abilities in pupils, parents and teachers, and they can also address a wide range of family issues and themes in playful and creative ways. They connect to both home and school as the skills, thinking and behaviour needed to participate successfully are clearly relevant to both contexts. For example, the ability to *take the perspective of others* and be able to predict and understand the *impact* of oneself on other people – and vice versa – can reduce the difficulties that impulsivity can cause for children and enables them to form more harmonious relationships with peers and adults. Games which require turn-taking, patience, managing winning and losing, following instructions and so on, are likely to be difficult for children and adults who may have poor mentalizing capacities. When life's difficulties are dominant and relationships are suffering, *playfulness, curiosity, flexibility in thinking, turn-taking, reflective contemplation* – all important ingredients of effective mentalizing – can disappear, and problem-saturated, rigid narratives can come to the fore, closing down the possibility of change. Children are likely to be more familiar with some of the activities used in multi-family therapy than their parents, who may have had difficult or very different experiences of school than their children. Parents may not have had the time or opportunity to have 'played' recently, for a number of reasons, and can become nervous and feel out of their comfort zone. It is important to keep in mind that the multi-family activities are a vehicle for producing relational events and are not an end in itself (Dawson and McHugh, 2012). Although the content of an activity is important, the processes elicited and set in motion through the activities are the real catalysts for change.

Planning, action, reflection (PAR)

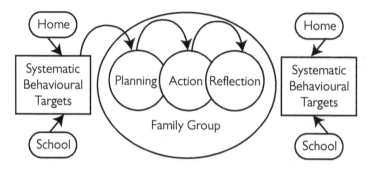

Figure 13.1: *Family group processes*
(Dawson and McHugh, 2012)

Whatever the multi-family activity, the important organizing framework contains the components of *planning, action* and *reflection* (PAR). It creates the structure by which skills, including mentalizing skills, can be developed, and relationships and communication improved. *Planning* consists of naming an aim for a session and identifying the skills needed for the subsequent activity. This gets the discussion and thinking started within the group and enhances group cohesion. *Action* describes the carrying out of the activity, providing the context in which family patterns can be demonstrated and observed by the group, as 'live' examples of problematic communications or 'enactments' (Minuchin, 1974), thus offering the opportunity for change to occur in the 'here and now'. *Reflection* takes part both during and after an activity and provides the space for observations to be named and discussed in the group setting. Without reflection, the focus tends to be only on the behaviours observed and can miss out on the thinking and meaning behind an action. Improving an individual's reflective capacity is the key to change in attachment patterns across the generations (Asen and Fonagy, 2012). Reflection can take place during an activity – when parents and children are asked to 'pause' for a couple of minutes and offer 'ad hoc' observations and thoughts. Curious questioning is the role of the MFT coach at this point, and feedback and ideas can be written down on a flipchart. Advice for doing the activity differently and more successfully can be invited from individual members of the multi-family group. The more questions and suggestions come from group members, the better, and the role of the MFT coach is to ask questions which stimulate this kind of curiosity about others. This process encourages the emergence of multiple perspectives and develops the capacity for observation and reflection across all the members of the multi-family group. 'Ad hoc' reflection should be brief, so as not to interrupt the flow of the activity too much or risk boredom, but sufficient to stimulate the expansion of active observation and disruption of habitual unhelpful patterns of behaviour. Following the activity, the group members can subsequently review and reflect together further upon the processes observed. The MFT coach leads the reflection, again asking for feedback and ideas from the group; the identified themes and skills can be revisited and observations deconstructed and reflected upon. The emerging discussion often moves into other relevant areas, such as the exploration of belief systems, culture and gender issues.

Film (re)-view

Recording multi-family group work with a camcorder and (re-)viewing it straightaway as a group on a television or interactive whiteboard is a highly effective way of reflecting on what happened from a meta-perspective. Watching oneself on film in a group setting, whilst perhaps embarrassing at first, is something that children and parents alike not only become quickly used to, but also enjoy. As curiosity takes over, group members frequently become 'mini experts' in analyzing family communications and interactions – if not their own, then certainly those of others! Film re-view offers ways of looking at interactions from different perspectives and it is also an effective way of drawing attention to behaviour patterns that can easily go unnoticed. The filming can be carried out by a child, a parent, by the MFT coach – or simply by a fixed camera.

Case study 13.1: Multi-family activities in the FEC

Eight families with children aged 6–10 years old start the last day of the programme this week with a *speed interviewing* session. Parents are invited to find out from each child what has and hasn't gone well this week, with the aim of finding out what the common themes are for working on in the rest of the session. One MFT coach rings the bell and the talk starts. Beginning quietly, the energy and noise in the room quickly rises. Ali (aged 6) doesn't want to move from his mother. His adjacent father pulls his chair closer, encouraging him whilst starting the conversation, with his mother still involved. Her new 'partner' hovers, waiting to sit; the group rebalances and in the next two minutes the activity has started. When the children are back with their parents, chairs are rearranged and the two therapists gather feedback, with one writing key points on the flipchart. The following themes are identified:

- being 'wound up' by other children at the end of break-times
- following adults' instructions the first time
- sharing and taking turns
- peer pressure impacting relationships at home and school
- developing independence and autonomy safely.

A parent points out that there is a strong theme of difficulty with managing the transition from playtime to the classroom, when excitement needs to calm and children need to be ready for lessons. Jake, aged 8 years, had an argument with another child when the class lined up in the playground. Mohammed's teacher spoke to his mother yesterday as he had been angry in a lesson and refused to wait his turn. The group agree that they will focus on these skills during the morning, and a game is suggested by one of the MFT coaches.

Parents are 'on duty' during break time and decide together to ring the bell and ask the children to line up at the end of playtime, as in school. One takes the lead, another records with the camcorder, and the therapists encourage others to notice what is happening and describe what they are seeing. Curious questioning and reflection are the aims.

Following a quick description of the available games, the group chooses a giant block stacking game. (Blocks of wood are stacked as a tower and, taking it in turns, the players remove a block at a time, putting it at the top of the tower. The game ends when someone topples the tower.) Because the weather is good the group decides to play outside.

The parents settle their children and the multi-family process of PAR (planning, action, reflection) commences. Identifying the skills needed for 'success' comes first. These include taking turns, patience and dealing with frustration. We suggest 'cross-family linkage' – parents and children are allocated to each other and the game begins.

Under the MFT coaches' guidance, Toni, Jake's mum, leads the parents. When Mohammed grabs an armful of bricks and ignores instructions, the parent team helps him slow down and listen. Nora, another child, explains to Islam why she thinks he must wait, and the others practise patience. Understanding how to play and interact safely with peers is crucial for Mohammed, who is currently excluded from school playtime. After ten minutes a therapist pauses the action and asks for observations and reflection from children and parents, referring to the skills the group identified earlier. Ian, a dad, observes how well most of the children listened. Mohammed is praised for 'turning it around'. The game continues until Jake takes a block and the tower collapses! There is more reflection at the end, and congratulations for specific achievements are given. Yvonne, Nora's mother, is particularly impressed by how kind and thoughtful Nora was towards Islam and gives her a 'well done' certificate.

The pragmatics of MFT

When running MFT groups, it is helpful to have two facilitators or 'coaches': one 'active' and one in an observing role. The active MFT coach creates the context, such as giving instructions for an activity and involving all members of the different families. The other coach observes not only the interactions in and between families, but also the interactions of the active coach with the various families and their individual members – for example, ensuring that the active coach does not stick to just one family or gets drawn into specifics without seeing the whole picture. Planning and practical organization are also enriched by a partnership. The following are essential considerations and ingredients for successful MFT work:

- a quiet room with enough space to accommodate up to ten children and at least one parent/carer each

- enough chairs and space for them to be put in a circle

- classroom tables for seated activities and games

- some tea/coffee-making equipment for either the beginning or end of the group, as families make connections over a cup of tea or coffee, facilitating group cohesion

- access to paper, pens, paint, balls and other props

- equipment for activities

- camcorder and replay facilities (TV screen, laptop or interactive whiteboard/projector screen)

- flipchart and pens.

Children cannot participate in MFT work on their own. Sometimes two parents/carers might attend and this is always welcome. If, however, neither is available, another important family member (e.g. an aunt or uncle, adult sibling or grandparent) can attend instead. If there is a group member who does not want to join in an activity, it can be suggested that they watch and join in later if they change their mind.

Warm-up games

These activities are important for the formation of group cohesion, engagement and the development of the 'Families Team'. They tend to be led predominantly by the MFT coaches, but opportunities to hand over the leading of the activity to parents and children offer excellent contexts for change. Much important relational information can be gleaned during these activities and this can be discussed in the subsequent reflection phase. However, warm-up games can also be used simply as an introductory activity to create an energetic group atmosphere and to generate enthusiasm.

Warm-up 1: Introductions

SETTING

Everyone sits on chairs in a circle, including the MFT coaches.

EQUIPMENT

A shell, small ball or other tactile object (this is passed around the circle to indicate whose turn it is).

ACTION

- The person with the shell introduces himself and the person either side – for example: 'I am [says name], this is [gestures at person at one side and says name] and this is [gestures to the person on the other side and says name].'
- The shell is passed to the next person in the circle and the pattern is repeated until the shell has been all round the circle.

DEVELOPMENT

- Instead of being passed to a neighbour, the shell can be passed to anyone in the circle, while saying their name.

Discussion

- This is good for new groups where not everyone knows the names of the other people. Individuals might have to ask for a name before being able to make an introduction, necessitating further interaction.

- People generally choose to sit next to their own family members and people they know. If desired, seating can be mixed up in many ways – for example, assigning people a number from 1 to 4 and then asked everyone with a particular number to stand up and swap places etc.

Reflection

- The use of eye contact and other non-verbal communication may be discussed.

- How to introduce people sensitively can be raised and thought about.

Warm-up 2: Finish the sentence

Setting

Everyone sits on chairs in a circle, including the MFT coaches.

Equipment

A small, soft ball.

Action

- A sentence is started and completed by the MFT coach.

- The ball is then thrown to another member of the circle, who completes the sentence according to their own choice and then throws the ball. This can be repeated until everyone has had a go. It can start off with simple and factual sentences as these tend to be non-threatening, particularly for a new group, but over time more abstract and relational subjects can be introduced.[1] Examples include:

  ○ 'My favourite…[e.g. food, colour, TV programme, hobby, possession, holiday] is…'

---

1   Further sentence starters can be found in *Developing Circle Time* (Bliss, Robinson and Maines, 1995).

- 'My favourite place at home is…'
- 'I'm good at…'
- 'I find…difficult.'
- 'If I was an animal I would like to be a…'
- 'One thing I like about being at home is…'
- 'One thing I like about being at school is…'
- 'One thing I like about my family is…'
- 'If I could be anywhere in the world right now I'd be in… (because…)'
- 'A good friend is someone who…'

DEVELOPMENT

- The ball can be thrown to someone at the same time as saying one fact about them that they have mentioned during the game.
- Other members of the group can think up sentences and take the lead.

DISCUSSION

- This kind of activity is good for engendering curiosity, and spotting similarities and differences.

REFLECTION

Here are some suggestions for reflection questions:

- 'What skills did you use to do this activity?' (For example: listening, focusing, memory, thinking.)
- 'Were there any surprises?'
- 'What was it like when you heard your child/parent say…?'

Warm-up 3: Speed-interviewing (based on the speed-dating principle)

SETTING

Parents and children sit opposite and facing each other, in two concentric circles.

EQUIPMENT

Chairs for all.

A timer (sand timer, watch or mobile phone timer).

A bell or object to signal the end the time period.

ACTION

- Families are asked to discuss a topic for two minutes – for example: 'How are things going at school this week?' 'What is going well and what is going not so well?' Ideas, thoughts and advice can be offered.

- After two minutes, the bell is rung and one group (either parents or children) are asked to move to the next chair (clockwise or anti-clockwise) and repeat the interview.

- This continues until each family is back with their own members.

DEVELOPMENT

- Almost any theme can be given as a discussion topic, or this format can be used as a 'getting-to-know-each-other' activity.

- Children can be asked to interview parents about a subject.

DISCUSSION

- This activity usually generates energy, curiosity and empowerment. People who may be shy in a large group can find this 1:1 setting, when everyone is talking at the same time, liberating, and a sense of agency develops.

- Parents can be accompanied by an interpreter if necessary.

- Feedback can be given at the end of the round, although the MFT coach should take care not to become too central to the discussion.

REFLECTION

Asking about the process can be as rewarding as asking about the content discussed. For example:

- 'How did you find that activity?'

- 'What was it like?'

- 'What did you notice about the atmosphere?'

Warm-up 4: Sit down

SETTING

Everyone stands in a circle, including the MFT coaches. Everyone needs a chair.

ACTION

- The aim is to get everyone sitting down using three clear rules. If any of these rules are broken the whole game must start all over again. The rules are as follows:
  - No one may talk.
  - People can't sit down at the same time.
  - If the person on either side of you sits down, then you can't be the next person to sit.

DISCUSSION

- As no talking is allowed, non-verbal cues are vital, for example eye contact. Everyone wonders who is going to make the first move to sit and will look around. Somebody has to be 'brave' enough to sit first, and if two do so at the same time, it starts again!

- For people who find tolerance or patience difficult this can trigger frustration at the game or annoyance with those who 'mess it up'.

- Some groups complete the challenge very quickly and successfully. A curious discussion about how this happened can be started and generalized into a debate about how non-verbal communication happens between people.

REFLECTION

Here are some suggestions for questions:

- 'What skills were used?' (For example: working as a team, focusing, managing frustration, patience, etc.)

- 'How can you tell if someone is frustrated etc.?'

- 'How did people manage feelings of frustration etc.?'

- 'How can we, as a team, do it better/quicker?'

- 'How did we finish so quickly?'

Warm-up 5: Zoom and Eek

SETTING

Everyone sits on chairs in a circle, including the MFT coaches.

ACTION

A 'car' (made from putting palms of the hand together and pointing them in the direction of movement) is sent around the circle, as follows:

- The MFT coach starts by saying 'zoom' and pointing his hands at one of his neighbours. This is sent on round the circle by each person saying 'zoom' and passing it on.

- A change of direction is made by someone saying 'eek' and pointing hands in the opposite direction. The 'car' continues for as long as desired, with the direction being changed by anyone who wishes.

DEVELOPMENT

- Two 'cars' can be sent round at the same time.

- A third action, 'boing', can be made by 'throwing' the car to someone across the circle.

DISCUSSION

- This is a good activity for skills such as concentration and managing when things don't go right.

- There is potential for some members of the group to become overexcited. This can be seen as an opportunity for reflection and change.

Skills-based activities

These could be games, art or curriculum activities. The giant block stacking game described above is one example. Attention can be paid in these kinds of activities to the skills needed to make such an activity 'successful'. During the *planning phase* everyone in the group can offer ideas about what skills are needed. Typical skills identified by children and parents often include:

- listening to and following instructions

- turn-taking and patience

- focusing and concentration
- managing conflict between peers and siblings
- agreeing
- managing disappointment/losing
- team work.

Examples of *curious questions* during reflection are:

- 'What was it like, doing that activity?'
- 'Can you say a bit more?'
- 'What do other people think about that idea?'
- 'What makes you think that?'
- 'What do you think your child/parent was thinking when...?' (For example, when you were giving instructions.)
- 'If you could step into his shoes at this moment, how do you think he is feeling right now?' (Ask parent/other parents/other children for their views.)
- 'What made it easier/harder?'
- 'What do you think might be happening now?' (For example, a child getting frustrated, upset about losing, parent getting impatient, child looking particularly happy or excited – draw attention to the positive as well as to the negative.)

When asking these types of questions, the MFT coach is modelling them, and parents and children who have more developed mentalizing skills can pick up on them and practise them with each other. This moves the reflective discussion into the multi-family arena and stimulates further curiosity and the discovery of resources previously unbeknown to family members. It allows the MFT coach to step back from being central and lets other members of the multi-family group take on the energy and be the drivers for change. It is important to be attuned to the atmosphere and the dynamic in the room, keeping it light and playful, spiced with respectful curiosity, and not intrusive, whilst keeping the flow of the activity going.

Skills 1: Following Lego® instruction

SETTING

Each child and parent sits opposite each other with a table between them. The tables can be set out as shown in Figure 13.2.

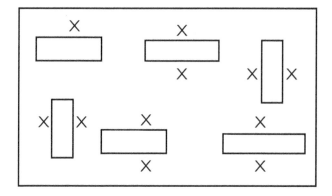

Figure 13.2: *Example of table/seating plan*

EQUIPMENT PER PAIR

A table (a typical rectangular classroom table is ideal).

A pack of four to six pairs of pieces of Lego (eight to twelve pieces in total) containing a selection of different colours, sizes and shapes.

A large book (or similar object) standing on the table to create a barrier between the two people.

ACTION

- Each pair divides the pieces of Lego so they have an identical selection.

- The adults make a shape using their Lego pieces and then give their children verbal instructions on how to make the same shape – without the children being able to see it (the large book is used as a barrier). The pair relies on words and body language – no looking at the actual model is allowed!

- When the shape has been completed, the roles are swapped and the children make a shape and instruct their parents on how to build it.

DEVELOPMENT

- Either the children or the parents are invited to move round to the next table and the process is repeated. Cross-family linkage is therefore introduced. Working with different, unfamiliar people offers the opportunity to experience different communication styles.

- The children can be invited to start first rather than the adults.

DISCUSSION

This activity can offer the opportunity to develop the following skills and abilities:

- giving and receiving instructions
- adapting language according to the need of the receiver
- sensitivity and attunement
- interacting
- listening
- language development
- patience
- dealing with frustration
- curiosity
- impact awareness.

REFLECTION

Reflection can take place at any point during the activity as well as at the end. (Group members are likely to finish at different times. Sometimes the MFT coach might suggest they swap roles within their pair straightaway, or the coach may ask everyone to wait until the last pair has finished.)

Below is a selection of questions and answers from a group of parents and children during the reflection phase of this activity. The children were aged 8–9 years and were from a mainstream class in London. Several parents had English as a second language. The answers to the questions led into further discussions within the group, particularly about managing relationships and communication with peers and teachers:

'What was it like?'

- 'Interesting, hard, fun, easy, interesting, and tricky.'
- 'Easier with someone not in your family!'

- 'Less frustrating with other children. I have less patience with my own child. You ignore your own parent! Your own children expect you to help them more.'

- 'Words can be difficult. The meaning can be different for different people.'

- 'I used maths language.'

- 'I changed my language.'

- 'I tried to trick my Mum.'

'What skills or techniques did you use?'

- 'Listening, thinking, concentration.'

- 'Repeating.'

- 'Eye contact.'

- 'Tone of voice.'

- 'Body language.'

'What did it make you think?'

- 'What questions can I ask?' (This led to discussion about how to ask questions, what words to use, how to adapt language and how to know when to adapt.)

- 'It's about interpretation.'

- 'Facial expression is important and can help (or not).'

- 'You learn from each other because we all do it differently.'

- 'We can have different opinions.'

- 'The speed matters – I asked him to slow down.'

- 'Check-in – you can ask more questions, it's ok to ask!'

Skills 2: Snakes and ladders

SETTING/EQUIPMENT

A giant set of the children's game 'snakes and ladders', where a person (child or adult) is the 'counter' and moves around the board.

ACTION

- Parents and children together discuss and agree the rules.

- Parents are encouraged to take the lead in managing the game, helping each other and their children.

Development

- 'Cross-family linkage' – when parents pair up with a different child.

Discussion

Skills commonly identified during the planning phase include:

- negotiation
- team work/helping each other
- taking part
- following instructions
- turn-taking
- managing disappointment/losing/frustration
- patience
- listening
- not cheating.

Skills 3: Composite portrait painting

Setting

Each child and parent sits next to each other at a table. Tables are placed in a circle. This activity can also take place with people sitting on the floor in a circle, depending on the space and mobility of the participants.

Equipment

Selection of different colour paints, palettes for mixing, paintbrushes of different thicknesses, water containers.

Large (A3 or A2) paper for painting.

Painting overalls and newspaper for covering tables (if necessary).

Washing-up facilities.

Action

- Each person writes their name in pencil on a large piece of paper.
- They pass it to their neighbour, who paints the outline of the owner's face.

- The paper is then passed to the next person and the second part of the face is painted.

- This process is repeated, covering the following parts of the portrait: outline/eyes/nose/mouth/ears/hair/neck and shoulders/skin colour.

- By the end of the exercise, each portrait has had a part painted by a different member of the group.

Figure 13.3: *Examples of composite portraits*

DISCUSSION

The following themes and skills are often identified:

- getting to know each other

- parents often painting for the first time in a long time

- 'having a go' – not worrying about getting it 'wrong'

- enjoyment

- sharing

- observation skills

- eye contact and interactions.

A rich discussion on similarities and differences can develop. Families can add the flag from their country of origin and they are encouraged to look at these places on a map, leading to discussions about cultural issues, parental migration and creating a deeper understanding within and between families.

Family/relationship activities

These are activities and exercises designed to explore and amplify specific family dynamics and relationships and to encourage families to experiment with new and different ways of interacting and communicating with one another.

Family 1: 'A moment in our life'

SETTING

Each child and parent sits together.

EQUIPMENT

Play-dough (or plasticine) in different colours.

Trays or boards to use as a base.

ACTION

- Parent and child are invited to make a 2D or 3D picture/construction of the statement 'A moment in our life' together.

DISCUSSION

The following themes often emerge with this activity:

- parent/child attunement[2]

- enjoyment of each other

- shared memories

- reflection on a moment in the past

- sharing of own culture/home/life

- speaking and listening and presentation skills

- development of respectful curiosity.

Many families from other countries produce pictures of their place of origin, offering them the opportunity to describe, construct, reflect and make connections through similarities and differences with others. During the feedback, questions are asked and other members of the different

---

2   During the reflection phase each family is offered the opportunity to describe their model. Children very often like to 'take the stage' and usually encourage their parents, who may initially be less confident.

families are also invited to do so. Their questions are more likely to be factual but this creates an appropriate and curious, non-threatening atmosphere. The MFT coaches can offer more mentalizing questions amongst the others. Quite often, one or more members of the group will pick up on questions and develop them, going along similar lines. Suggested questions include:

- 'What was it like doing this together?'
- 'How did you decide which moment to choose?'
- 'Why do you think your son/daughter/parent suggested that memory?'
- 'What is special about it?'
- 'In that (snapshot) moment, what do you think X and Y were thinking or feeling?'
- 'What makes you think that?'
- [To other members of the group] 'What do you notice about/ between X and Y [child and parent]?'

Family 2: Footsteps
SETTING
Children and parents sit at tables.

EQUIPMENT

Plain or sugar paper, pencils, coloured pens, scissors.

A skipping rope or length of string.

ACTION
This activity is best done where there is strong and safe group cohesion and people are familiar with each other as the subjects raised can be quite personal.

- Families are asked to draw around their feet/shoes on paper and cut them out to create four or five 'footsteps'.
- They are asked to choose together four or five significant events in their lives and write these on the paper feet, along with the year when these things happened.
- Paper feet are placed in chronological order along the skipping rope.

- Each family is invited to present their footsteps to the rest of the group.

Discussion

- This allows an opportunity for families to talk together about the past and identify important times in their lives.
- Marginalized discourses are enabled to come to the fore – for example, when there are current difficulties and remembering a positive time can interrupt habitual negative patterns of interaction.
- Families often mention the time when a child was born.

Family 3: Talk to the hand

Setting

Each child and parent sits together.

Equipment

Paper/card, pens, pencils, scissors.

Action

- Children and parents are asked to think about a relational question which may be connected to a current theme. For example:
  - What do parents and children need from each other?
  - What do children need from their parents to feel safe/less worried?
  - What do parents need from their children to know that they are safe?
  - What do they appreciate/value/love about each other?
- Parents draw around their child's hand, then the child draws around their parent's hand, and they cut out the hand shapes.
- Each person writes a word, sentence or picture in response to the question in each finger and in the palm of the paper hand.
- Feedback can take place in small groups or in one larger one.

DEVELOPMENT

- Cross-family linkage can be introduced by swapping parents and children.

DISCUSSION

- This offers the opportunity to explore the parent/child dyad attunement, develop mentalization skills such as perspective-taking and impact awareness and allow different voices to be heard.

- The feedback creates a menu of ideas and choices for families to take on and trial as they wish.

Outlook

Multi-family work in educational settings was started at the Marlborough Family Service in the 1980s. It has gone through different developmental phases since and been adapted to different educational settings. The Marlborough model has been exported to different parts of the United Kingdom and further afield; 'Family classes' and 'Family Schools' now exist in Scandinavia, Germany, Switzerland, The Netherlands and China. In England there has recently been substantial investment in this approach by the Department for Education, which has directly funded the establishment of The Family School, London – this opened in 2014. The School's co-founders, Brenda McHugh and Neil Dawson of the Anna Freud Centre (which is at the forefront of research, clinical practice and training in child and adolescent mental health), formerly ran the Marlborough Family Service Education Centre. But the most satisfying endorsement of the approach comes from parents, pupils and teachers – and they will have the last word, at least for the time being.

Feedback on MFT

Feedback from parents/carers

'It's a good way to learn/adapt from/to children's language.'

'It builds confidence. I saw them increase in confidence.'

'It's nice to work with other children from your child's class.'

'Seeing him speak out was great.'

'It was nice to know other things about other backgrounds and countries.'

'It was good to see your child amongst others.'

'It's interesting seeing us communicate in different ways.'

'It's a special time with my daughter.'

'Finding out about issues (e.g. winning or losing).'

'I saw my child be more motivated.'

'It was our own time of learning.'

'It's a good chance to do something with my son because at home I've got no time.'

'I enjoyed activities. I didn't want to miss them.'

'I've seen a change in my wife since she came to this – now she gets out of the house, she takes our son to school more and chats to him more.'

'She improved and is not getting so upset when things go wrong.'

'Fun being with children/parents in school and getting to know them.'

'Getting to know what's wrong (difficulties), watching each other, understand how to do things.'

'Nice to see them listening.'

'Not getting upset and not getting frustrated were good to practise – he got better!'

'I've got great memories of here.'

'It's been nice getting to know others. Now I look forward to Fridays.'

'Now I say "hello" in the playground to other parents.'

'When I was in hospital and couldn't come, I really missed it.'

'Educational and fun.'

'You don't know other children and you listen to them better [working with others].'

'I liked spending time with my son on his own, without my other children.'

'To be honest I was dreading it, because I'm not very confident with other people, but I've had a really great time.'

'It was fun to follow children's instructions, especially when it isn't your child.'

'More difficult to explain instructions to other children than my own.'

'It's really nice to be with your child in school.'

'It's a good way of getting to know other parents and children because in the morning it's such a rush, just dropping your child off.'

'You can spend time with your child in a different way from at home.'

'My child was calmer with another parent than with me.'

'It was good to see how my son interacts with other children and adults in school.'

'It's challenging but fun.'

Feedback from children

'The Lego® helped your brain to listen. You have to think of questions.'

'I liked doing the Lego. When you listen you have fun, and I listened to my Mum.'

'It's good seeing other parents and how they work and I liked working with them.'

'Giant snakes and ladders are more exciting because you get to use your whole body.'

'Portrait painting was hilarious.'

'You get to practise being an artist.'

'Spending time with Mum is good and fun.'

'It was fun to play this game with parents.'

'Fun – all the activities were exciting.'

'Getting to know each other was really good.'

'We all get to work and play with each other.'

'Exciting, amazing, beautiful.'

'It was relaxing.'

'You show your skills.'

'You learn from each other.'

'Fun and fantastic and funny.'

'I liked having fun with my Mum.'

'It doesn't matter if you win or lose – we don't get angry.'

'I was excited because I wanted to know who will be the winner.'

'We have to listen to each other when we play a game.'

'Sometimes we had to use our own language or body language to give instructions.'

'We agreed with parents by using signs, body moves and eye contact.'

'When I worked with different parent, I feel shy. It's a little bit difficult, sometimes difficult to understand the language.'

'We had to follow the instructions, play as a team and listen.'

'Sometimes it was frustrating when it didn't go our way.'

Feedback from teachers

'It's great to support the family and open up communication lines. Welcoming them in their children's environment can only be a positive and give them a better idea of how to interact with educationalists, their children and not be put off by the unknown.'

'The children have absolutely loved the experience and the chance to work with their parents. The children were taken out in small groups which I feel made them feel special and gave the group an exclusive feel! Our parents can be tricky to get involved initially but when they had been once, they came every week, meaning that they felt welcomed and important. The learning the children and parents did was invaluable for this very reason. Our parents are more likely now to have a go at 'school things' after having had such a positive experience with the Family Activities Project. The children told me they had been creative and had "so much fun"; they were gutted when it was other children's turn. As a teacher I feel the group was very worthwhile; in fact, I hope to re-create something similar in my new school.'

'The children and their families were offered the time and space to have some focused togetherness without any outside interruptions or distractions, and it benefited them greatly. Parents and children alike used and learned some good techniques to enjoy the moment and deepen relationships and communication.'

References

Asen, E., Dawson, N. and McHugh, B. (2001) *Multiple Family Therapy: The Marlborough Model and its Wider Applications*. London: Karnac.

Asen, E. (2002) 'Multiple family therapy: An overview.' *Journal of Family Therapy 24*, 3–16.

Asen, E. and Fonagy, P. (2012) 'Mentalisation-based therapeutic interventions for families.' *Journal of Family Therapy*. doi: 10.1111/j.1467-6427.2011.00552.x

Bliss, T., Robinson, G. and Maines, B. (1995) *Developing Circle Time*. London: Lucky Duck Publishing Ltd.

Bruce, T. (2005) *Early Childhood Education* (3rd edn). London: Hodder Arnold.

Dawson, N. and McHugh, B. (2012) 'The history and development of Marlborough multi-family groups in education.' *Context 123*, 8–12.

Fonagy, P., Steele, H., Moran, G. S., Steele, M. and Higgit, A. (1991) 'The capacity for understanding mental states: the reflective self in parent and child and its significance for security of attachment.' *Infant Mental Health 13*, 200–217.

McFarlane, W. R. (1982) 'Multiple-Family Therapy in the Psychiatric Hospital.' In H. T. Harbin (ed.) *The Psychiatric Hospital and the Family*. New York, NY: Spectrum.

Minuchin, S. (1974) *Families and Family Therapy*. London: Tavistock.

Jenny Mosley Consultancies www.circle-time.co.uk.

Epilogue

Susan Hart

We are living in an increasingly individualized world, a development that began in the Renaissance and which has accelerated throughout the 20th century. In our democratic societies, the individual citizens are required to find their own path in life and make their own choices. It is taken for granted that everyone possesses or is able to acquire these abilities, although we generally know little about how they develop. Therefore, our educational policies typically focus on individual learning styles, intelligence profiles and the call for students to take responsibility for their own learning. There appears to be a widespread lack of knowledge about how good communities develop and about the importance of communities for our personality development.

Empathy and compassion do not emerge automatically but are founded in early parent–child contact and later develop through children's mutual interactions in play. Play provides the context where children refine and expand their capacity for negotiation and their ability to vary between self-focus and other-focus. This is the context where children learn to accept constraints on their own freedom to act, and where they learn to compromise and resolve conflicts in a way that does not result in exclusion for anyone. A good school community is not just bliss and harmony; it also involves managing the conflicts that will inevitably occur. That is a challenge for everyone – not only for children with 'special needs'.

The motivation to establish emotional bonds is an innate capacity. In the infant's early life, the parents provide psychological cohesion, and both arousal and affect regulation develop from one second to the next. Good emotional and social development springs from an optimal caregiver–infant relationship and is subsequently transferred to other relationships later in life. The development of self-regulation competences begins in the child's asymmetrical relationships with close caregivers and continues later in relationships with other authority figures besides the parents. The child mainly practises these competences, however, in later symmetrical peer relationships. Virtually all interview studies with children who have thrived despite adversity have found that the children have benefited from the help of supportive adults or good friends. By offering structure, care and concern, these supportive adults and peers have helped the children develop adaptive life strategies. The child's capacity for self-regulation promotes confidence and self-esteem, which progress from trust in the caregiver to trust in oneself with the caregiver and, eventually, self-confidence. Children's social and cognitive statuses are closely linked. For example, children with limited social skills are more likely to drop out of school than children with good emotional and personal resources.

Successful inclusion in school depends essentially on whether the individual preschool and school teachers are given opportunities to develop not only their relationship skills and their ability to handle group processes but also their own personal self-agency. Emotional and personal competences should be respected and valued as being at least as important as cognitive competences. To build good relations and communities, teachers need to be curious about how to explore and enable other possible ways of acting. As Boel *et al.* (2013) point out, we cannot change others, but each of us can change the way we act towards others. This lets us change the situation, the interaction, the communication and thus also the relationship. Teachers face the dual challenge of needing to meet the individual child at his or her given developmental stage while simultaneously meeting a group of children, with their individual developmental potentials and challenges. In this diverse context, the teacher needs to facilitate a functioning community that helps all the children to develop and grow. That requires a high degree of self-agency, a theory for understanding the children's personal potentials and a method that facilitates a successful outcome of this complicated process.

Creating inclusive school is a big challenge, and the only way we can rise to this challenge is if the individual teachers begin to focus more on supporting the children's self-regulation and self-organization competences with due consideration for individual competences and the many possibilities found in play. A high mentalization capacity is one of the most highly evolved and sophisticated capacities in a late-modern society that aims to live up to calls for efficiency while also promoting democracy, solidarity, compassion, mutual understanding, support and care for the weaker members. Thus, it might be worth considering including 'relational skills' in the school curriculum. This book was written with the hope of inspiring and helping individual teachers promote and facilitate a development process that lets us teach children to engage in prosocial communities early in life – hopefully to the benefit of future generations.

References

Boel, K., Clasen, S., Jørgensen, J. K. and Westenholz, P. (2013) *Inklusion i Folkeskolen.* Copenhagen: Dansk Psykologisk Forlag.

About the Authors

Marianne Bentzen, psychotherapist MPF (member of the Danish Psychotherapist Assossiation), has been a somatic psychotherapist and trainer since 1980 and has taught training courses for psychotherapists, psychologists and psychiatric treatment groups around the world since 1982. She is currently involved in developing the neuroaffective theory on personality development and neuroaffective intervention methods in close cooperation with psychologist Susan Hart.

Phyllis Booth, MA, is Clinical Director Emeritus of the Theraplay™ Institute in Chicago. She trained at the University of Chicago, at the Tavistock Centre in London under John Bowlby and D. W. Winnicott, at the Anna Freud Centre in London and at the Family Institute at Northwestern University in Evanston, Illinois. Phyllis developed the Theraplay method together with Ann Jernberg and has conducted workshops and training in the method in the United States, Canada, England, Denmark, Finland, Norway, Sweden and South Korea.

Alé Duarte is trained in Somatic Experiencing and Rolfing therapy. He has had his own private practice since 1995 and developed the body therapy method Somatic Centering. Alé trains professionals working with psychology, education and body-oriented therapy and has worked closely with crisis teams that support the victims of natural disaster, war and other crisis situations around the world.

Susan Hart, MA, is a psychologist, specialist and supervisor in child psychology and psychotherapy. With a background in child, family and adult therapy, Susan is now self-employed. In her extensive lecture and workshop activity she develops and teaches neuroaffective theory developed from recent brain research.

Knud Hellborn is a psychologist who works at the Educational-Psychological Advisory Service in Halsnæs Municipality, Denmark, where he provides training and supervision, plans therapy courses and implements neuroaffective developmental psychology. Knud also provides training courses and theme days about neuroaffective developmental psychology.

Ulla Holck, MA, PhD, is a music therapist and Associate Professor at the Music Therapy Programme at Aalborg University, Denmark, and is Head of the Center for Documentation and Research in Music Therapy (CEDOMUS). She is trained as a bio-existential body psychotherapist and teaches and studies music therapy, primarily with children and young people with severe developmental disorders.

Stine Lindahl Jacobsen holds an MA and PhD in music therapy. She is Associate Professor and Head of the Music Therapy Programme at Aalborg University, Denmark. Stine developed the assessment instrument, Assessment of Parenting Competencies (APC), and certifies international music therapists in this method. Her teaching and her research publications mainly deal with music therapy with families and with music therapy assessment.

Helle Jensen, MA, is a specialist and supervisor in psychotherapy. She has worked since 1979 with children and families and with professionals in the education and treatment sectors. Helle teaches at Deutsch Dänisches Institut für Familientherapie (DDIF), in Berlin, Germany, and at Internationale Gesellschäft für Beziehungskompetenz (IgfB), in Innsbruck, Austria. She also teaches training courses in relational skills and focused presence, awareness and empathy in several European countries.

Gitte Jørgensen is a psychologist and works at the training and treatment centre Skole- og Behandlingshjemmet Skovgården, in Denmark, where she has many years of experience with child therapy, supervision, training and planning therapy courses.

Christine Lakoseljac-Andreasen is a paediatric occupational therapist and works at the motor skills house in Lyngby-Taarbæk Municipality, Denmark. She has special knowledge and experience in sensory integration and related areas, and she puts her extensive professional knowledge and practical experience to use in both individual and group-based treatment courses.

Bonnie Goldstein, PhD, specializes in helping children and young people manage life's challenges and transitions. She is the founder and director of Lifespan Psychological Center in Los Angeles, California, which offers individual and group therapy that integrates Sensorimotor Psychotherapy and aspects of interpersonal neurobiology and attachment. She has edited books on therapy for children and young people.

Pat Ogden, PhD, is the founder and educational director of the Sensorimotor Psychotherapy Institute in Colorado, an internationally recognized school specializing in somatic-cognitive approaches to the treatment of trauma and attachment issues. She is a pioneer in somatic psychology and active as a clinician, consultant, international speaker, trainer and author. Currently, Pat is involved in developing Sensorimotor Psychotherapy approaches aimed at children, families, couples and offenders, and at dealing with dissociative disorders.

Jaak Panksepp, PhD, is the Bailey Endowed Chair of Animal Well-Being Science and Professor of Integrative Physiology and Neuroscience at Washington State University, DC. He is a distinguished research professor of psychobiology at Bowling Green State University, Ohio, and Head of Affective Neuroscientific Research at Falk Center for Molecular Therapeutics, Northwestern University, Illinois. Jaak has written hundreds of scientific articles on emotional and motivation processes in the mammalian brain. His recent work has focused on social attachment and play mechanisms in the neural circuits and in their relationship with psychiatric disorders in children, including attention deficit hyperactivity disorder.

Serena Potter graduated as a teacher from the Froebel Institute in London in 1988. After working for many years as a teacher and head teacher, she has since specialized in family therapy, initially at the Marlborough Family Service at the Family Education Centre in London, where she worked with multi-family therapy concurrent with earning her master's degree in systemic and family psychotherapy at the Institute of Family Therapy in London. Since September 2014, Serena has been Deputy Headteacher at 'The Family School London', a specialist alternative provision for children aged 5–14 years.

Dorothea Rahm, PhD, is a psychologist, therapist and supervisor who is trained in a wide scope of therapeutic methods such as behavioural therapy, psychodynamic therapy, gestalt therapy, somatic experiencing and neuroaffective therapy. Dorothea has developed and conducted group therapy courses with severely traumatized children. She has taught in several European countries and is the author of several trade books.

Phyllis Rubin is a clinical psychologist, speech and language pathologist and a certified Theraplay™ therapist and trainer with a private practice outside Chicago, Illinois. She developed and teaches the Group Theraplay model and has co-authored a book and book chapters on this engaging technique.

Colwyn Trevarthen is Emeritus Professor of Child Psychology and Psychobiology at the University of Edinburgh and is also a Fellow of the Royal Society of Edinburgh and a Vice President of the British Association for Early Childhood Education. He has authored many books and over 200 scientific articles on vision and movement, brain development, infant communication, infant learning and emotional health and well-being and the psychological aspects of musicality in communication.

Eldbjørg Wedaa is a music/drama teacher, a certified psychotherapist and Director of Pinocchio Music and Drama in Norway. Eldbjorg offers group courses from preschool to about 12 years of age as well as individual courses and therapy.

Marlo Winstead trained as a social worker and is a certified Theraplay™ therapist, trainer and supervisor. She teachers and provides clinical supervision at the University of Kansas and at the Play Therapy programme at MidAmerica Nazarene University, Missouri. In addition, she is active as a therapist and supervisor for at-risk families, foster and adoptive families, persons with eating disorders, adults with mental illness and youth violence prevention.

Subject Index

Page numbers in *italics* refer to figures.

Author Index